MONOPSONY IN MOTION

MONOPSONY IN MOTION

IMPERFECT COMPETITION IN LABOR MARKETS

Alan Manning

PRINCETON UNIVERSITY PRESS
PRINCETON AND OXFORD

Library of Congress Cataloging-in-Publication Data applied for

ISBN 978-0-691-12328-8

British Library Cataloguing-in-Publication Data
A catalogue record for this book is available from the British Library.

This book has been composed in Sabon

Princeton University Press books are printed on acid-free paper, and
meet the guidelines for the permanence and durability of the
Committee on Production Guidelines for Book Longevity of the
Council on Library Resources

www.pupress.princeton.edu

10 9 8 7 6 5 4 3 2 1

To my family

Contents

Preface

I used to be like most other labor economists and think that the textbook model of monopsony was little more than a curiosum, perhaps relevant in a few times and places but not of much use for thinking about most labor markets. That view began to change after seeing a presentation of Burdett and Mortensen (1998) at the Centre for Economic Performance, LSE, in 1990. That made me realize that the assumption that employers have no market power over their workers is equivalent to the wildly implausible conclusion that a wage cut of a cent causes all existing workers to leave the firm immediately. I thought that the idea that frictions in the labor market give employers some power over their workers deserved more thought than was usually given to it. Those ideas then evolved into the belief that a perspective on labor markets based on the view that "monopsony" is important led to a much better understanding of a very wide range of labor market phenomena. And, eventually, this book is the result of the attempt to substantiate that belief.

Eventually, because this book took too much time to write. Along the way, I have been generously supported in time and money by many people. In particular David Card who arranged for me to spend time at the Industrial Relations Section, Princeton in 1994–1995 and the Center for Labor Economics, University of California Berkeley in 1998–1999, and who gave me so many valuable comments and so much support. When he asked me how it was going every time we met, my embarrassment at the lack of progress spurred me on. And, when he no longer enquired about the book, the guilty feeling that he had given up on me caused even greater embarrassment. He arranged a one-day conference on the bulk of the first draft in Berkeley in July 1999 that provided incredibly helpful comments: I would like to thank the other participants, Paul Beaudry, Marianne Bertrand, John diNardo (who also wrote, arranged and performed the song "Monopsony in Motion" that, in this multi-media age, goes with the book and can be found on my website), Steve Machin, Dale Mortensen, Sendhil Mullanaithan, Michael Ransom, and Craig Riddell.

Richard Layard of the Centre for Economic Performance at the LSE also generously provided a teaching buy-out that gave me a much-needed breathing space to work on the book.

Others who provided comments on the book are (in alphabetical order) Damon Clark, Richard Disney, Juan Dolado, Maarten Goos, Maia Guell, Marco Manacorda, Karl Ove Moene, Barbara Petrongolo, Jumana Saleheen, Steve Pischke, and Coen Teulings. Pat Nutt helped me avoid the tedious task of assembling the bibliography.

Part One ————————————————

BASICS

1

Introduction

WHAT happens if an employer cuts the wage it pays its workers by one cent? Much of labor economics is built on the assumption that all existing workers immediately leave the firm as that is the implication of the assumption of perfect competition in the labor market. In such a situation an employer faces a market wage for each type of labor determined by forces beyond its control at which any number of these workers can be hired but any attempt to pay a lower wage will result in the complete inability to hire any of them at all. The labor supply curve facing the firm is infinitely elastic.

In contrast, this book is based on two assumptions about the labor market. They can be stated very simply:

- there are important frictions in the labor market;
- employers set wages.

The implications of these assumptions can also be stated simply. The existence of frictions means that there are generally rents to jobs: if an employer and worker are forcibly separated one or, more commonly, both of the parties would be made worse off. This gives employers some market power over their workers as a small wage cut will no longer induce them to leave the firm. The assumption that employers set wages then tells us that employers exercise this market power. But, with these two assumptions, it is monopsony, not perfect competition, that is the best simple model to describe the decision problem facing an individual employer. Not monopsony in the sense of there being a single buyer of labor, but monopsony in the sense of the supply of labor to an individual firm not being infinitely elastic. The actions of other employers (notably their choice of wages) in the market will affect the supply of labor to an individual firm so, if one wants to model the market as a whole, models of oligopsony or monopsonistic competition are what is needed.[1] The usefulness of the monopsonistic approach rests on the two assumptions so they need some justification.

[1] The Oxford English Dictionary credits the word monopsony to Joan Robinson (1933) though she credits it to B. L. Hallward, a classical scholar at Cambridge, who though born in 1901 is still alive at the time of writing. The suffix is derived from OPSONEN which means "to make your purchases often of dried fish" and which is found in Aristophanes, the Wasps (twice), Plutarch and the New Testament. The natural ONEOMAI ("I buy") was rejected as it does not sound good with the MONO prefix (personal communication to David Card). The invention of the word oligopsony is credited to Walker (1943) who introduced it with the curious phrase "it is surely only a matter of time before market situation number 23 is christened oligopsony," the time referred to being the time necessary for him to finish writing the sentence.

That important frictions exist in the labor market seems undeniable: people go to the pub to celebrate when they get a job rather than greeting the news with the shrug of the shoulders that we might expect if labor markets were frictionless. And people go to the pub to drown their sorrows when they lose their job rather than picking up another one straight away. The importance of frictions has been recognized since at least the work of Stigler (1961, 1962).

What are the sources of these frictions in labor markets? In the *Economics of Imperfect Competition*, Joan Robinson argued that:

> there may be a certain number of workers in the immediate neighbourhood and to attract those from further afield it may be necessary to pay a wage equal to what they can earn near home plus their fares to and fro; or there may be workers attached to the firm by preference or custom and to attract others it may be necessary to pay a higher wage. Or ignorance may prevent workers from moving from one to another in response to differences in the wages offered by the different firms.
>
> (Robinson 1933: 296)

It is ignorance, heterogeneous preferences, and mobility costs that are the most plausible sources of frictions in the labor market. The consequence of these frictions is that employers who cut wages do not immediately lose all their workers. They may find that their workers quit at a faster rate than before or that recruitment is more difficult, but the extreme predictions of the competitive model do not hold. The labor supply curve facing the firm is, as a result, not infinitely elastic. The existence of frictions gives employers potential market power over their workers. The assumption that firms set wages means that they actually exercise this power. Let us now consider this assumption in more detail.

Given the existence of rents caused by frictions one needs to specify how they are divided between employer and worker. The existence of the rents makes the relationship between workers and employer one of bilateral monopoly (in part) so that we need a theory of how the rents are divided. The development of such a theory is an old problem in economics in general, and labor economics in particular, going back to the discussion of Edgeworth (1932) who argued that the terms of exchange in bilateral monopoly were indeterminate. This indeterminacy has never been resolved.[2]

[2] For example, in recent years, there has been considerable interest in models of bargaining in bilateral monopoly following on from the work of Rubinstein (1982) who, for a particular specification of the negotiation process between the two parties, showed that there was a unique equilibrium, that is, a determinate outcome. But this literature does not really solve the indeterminacy problem, it just pushes it back one more stage for the rules of the negotiation process generally determine the division of the rents and these rules are essentially arbitrary. So the indeterminacy problem re-emerges in the indeterminacy of the rules of the game.

Given this problem at the heart of economics, which this book is going to make no attempt to solve, there seems little alternative but to grasp the nettle and make some assumption about the way in which the rents are divided. One should choose an assumption that is a reasonable approximation to reality. This is made difficult by the fact that there is no universally right assumption for how rents are shared in the labor market: there are different mechanisms in different labor markets, perhaps even co-existing in the same labor market. In spite of this, we focus on one mechanism for most of this book.

In this book, it is assumed that employers set wages.[3] This is a more appropriate assumption in some labor markets than others. For example, it would not seem to be appropriate when workers are organized into a union (the consequences of this are discussed in chapter 12), or for senior management who often seem to have considerable ability to set their own wages, or for the self-employed, or (most importantly of course) for academic labor economists. But, for the average worker in a non-union setting, this does seem to be the appropriate assumption. Open the pages of a newspaper and one sees firms advertising jobs at given wages. One also sees advertisements saying "salary negotiable" though typically only for higher level jobs and the extent to which they are actually negotiable is often rather limited. But it is very rare to see advertisements placed by workers setting down the wage at which they are prepared to work.

This view that the relationship between the employer and worker is one-sided has a long tradition. In the *Wealth of Nations*, Adam Smith (1976: 84) wrote that "in the long run the workman may be as necessary to his master as his master is to him; but the necessity is not so immediate." And Alfred Marshall in his *Principles of Economics* (1920: 471) wrote that "labour is often sold under special disadvantages arising from the closely connected group of facts that labour power is 'perishable', that the sellers of it are commonly poor and have no reserve fund, and that they cannot easily withhold it from the market." To these arguments that a worker is typically more desperate for work than an employer is desperate for that particular worker, Sidney and Beatrice Webb (1897: 657–58) added the argument that

> the manual worker is, from his position and training, far less skilled than the employer ... in the art of bargaining itself. This art forms a large part of the daily life of the entrepreneur, whilst the foreman is specially selected for his skill in engaging and superintending workmen. The manual worker, on the

[3] Section 1.3 compares this assumption about wage setting with a prominent alternative, the ex post bargaining used in much of the matching literature (for a recent survey, see Mortensen and Pissarides 1999).

contrary, has the smallest experience of, and practically no training in, what is essentially one of the arts of the capitalist employer. He never engages in any but one sort of bargaining, and that only on occasions which may be infrequent, and which in any case make up only a tiny fraction of his life.

The view that the relationship between employer and worker is not one of equals was the origin of pro-labor legislation in many if not all countries. Section 1 of the US National Labor Relations Act of 1935 says "the inequality of bargaining power between employees who do not possess freedom of association or actual liberty of contract, and employers who are organized in the corporate and other forms of ownership association substantially burdens and affects the flow of commerce." Our assumption that employers set wages is in this tradition.

The claim that labor markets are, in the absence of outside intervention, pervasively monopsonistic probably comes as something of a surprise to readers of labor economics textbooks. Table 1.1 documents the number of pages devoted to a discussion of monopsony and the total length in a selection of popular textbooks. As can be seen, monopsony does not figure prominently and, where it is mentioned, the discussion is generally not favorable: the final column of table 1.1 contains a selection of quotes, some of which capture the idea that frictions give employers some market power but most of which do not.[4] There is a noticeable trend in the most recent textbooks towards less hostile views[5] and a recognition that it is the existence of labor market frictions that is the main argument for the relevance of monopsony. But, while the overall perspective on the plausibility of monopsony may be changing, the range of labor market issues that contain some discussion of the implications of monopsony remains very limited. The first two volumes of the *Handbook of Labor Economics* (Ashenfelter and Layard, 1986) contain only two references to monopsony out of a total of 1268 pages, one in the chapter on dynamic labor demand by Nickell and the other in the chapter on discrimination by Cain. The three subsequent volumes published in 1999 (Ashenfelter and Card, 1999) contain three references in 2362 pages, in the chapters on labor market institutions, minimum wages and matching.

---

[4] My personal favorite is taken from the first edition of Fleisher and Kniesner (1980, pp. 203–4) "we feel confident that monopsony is not a widespread phenomenon today. The primary reason is that fame and financial awards await the researcher who can demonstrate empirically that a significant number of workers are victims of monopoly power of employers. As yet, no one has claimed these prizes."

[5] A trend that can be confirmed by a fixed effect estimator, comparing the discussion of monopsony in different editions of the most popular textbooks.

TABLE 1.1
Monopsony in Labor Textbooks

Author	Pages on Monopsony	Total Pages	Selected Quotation
Borjas (2000)	7	470	"upward-sloping supply curves for particular firms can arise even when there are many firms competing for the same type of labour" (p. 191)
Ehrenberg and Smith (2000)	14	651	"while examples of a single buyer of labour services may be difficult to cite, the monopsony model still offers useful insights if the labour supply curves are upward-sloping for some other reason. Recently, economists have begun to explore a variety of labour market conditions that would yield upward-sloping labour supply curves to individual firms even when there are many employers competing for workers in the same labour market" (p. 71)
Filer, Hamermesh, and Rees (1996)	8	654	"it does not seem plausible given the vast number of firms employing teenagers in the US" (p. 174) "while the cost of commuting long distances leaves some residual monopsony power to isolated employers, this power is much less than when commuting was more difficult" (p. 189)
Sapsford and Tzannatos (1993)	15	420	
Elliott (1991)	6	536	"appealing as such an outcome is to the advocates of minimum wage legislation it has to be said that this theoretical possibility is seldom encountered in practice" (p. 306).
Kaufman (1991)	12	778	"the pure form of monopsony (the one-company town) is relatively rare, although conditions of oligopsony and monopsonistic competition may have a wider applicability" (pp. 422–23)
Reynolds, Masters, and Moser (1991)	2	610	"there is little evidence to suggest that monopsony is important to our economy. Most firms are located in urban areas where there are many firms in the labour market and relatively little collusion among employers" (p. 135)

TABLE 1.1 (*continued*)

Author	Pages on Monopsony	Total Pages	Selected Quotation
Fallon and Verry (1988)	3	311	"imperfect information may ... convey some monopsony power to the individual firm" (p. 103)
Gunderson and Riddell (1988)	19	600	"to a certain extent most firms may have an element of monopsony power in the short-run, in the sense that they could lower their wages somewhat without losing all their workforce. However, it is unlikely that they would exercise this power in the long run because it would lead to costly problems of recruitment, turnover and morale" (pp. 213–14) "Improved communications, labour market information, and labour mobility make the isolated labour market syndrome, necessary for monopsony, unlikely at least for large numbers of workers" (p. 224)
Hoffman (1986)	7	354	"A monopsonist is a firm that faces an upward-sloping supply curve for labor of a given quality. A university hiring economics instructors is most definitely *not* a monopsonist, because the relevant labor market is national and thus the number of other demanders is quite large" (p. 49)
McConnell and Brue (1986)	9	607	"monopsony outcomes are not widespread in the US economy" (p. 150)
Marshall, Briggs, and King (1984)	4	657	
Fleisher and Kniesner (1984)	16	536	"monopsony does not appear to be a widespread phenomenon in the United States, but rather specific to a few industries" (p. 219)
Hunter and Mulvey (1981)	4	403	
Fearn (1981)	8	272	"many modern American labor economists assume generally that labor markets are competitive. The presumption that labor markets are monopsonies, however, remains in the public consciousness, particularly in union circles and in the legislatures. The situation may represent a classic 'cultural lag'" (p. 117)

TABLE 1.1 (*continued*)

Author	Pages on Monopsony	Total Pages	Selected Quotation
Bloom and Northrup (1981)	4	836	
Kreps, Martin, Perlman, and Somers (1980)	9	477	"instances of monopsony are not that frequent as to make the chances that administered wages will not reduce employment" (p. 110)
Addison and Siebert (1979)	8	500	"we should qualify our discussion of monopsony by observing that imperfect worker information as to alternative wages will confer on each firm a margin of monopsony power. Thus, each firm will possess a degree of dynamic monopsony power arising from the imperfect information of its employees and can therefore administer wages" (p. 169)
Freeman (1979)	0	196	
Bellante and Jackson (1979)	4	351	"many economists argue that monopsony power by firms is likely to be greatly exaggerated given the occupational, industrial and geographical mobility that characterizes American labor markets" (p. 196)
Cartter and Marshall (1972)	11	570	
Lester (1964)	2	608	"the manipulation of wages by the purchase of labor according to monopsonistic calculations seems to be misguided academic speculation" (p. 281)
Phelps Brown (1962)	1	274	"the rate needed to attract labour in the first place is higher than that needed to retain it once it has settled in. Much of a firm's labour force is likely, for this reason, to be captive; the firm is a monopsonist in the short-run' (p. 137)

These statistics might be thought to be a little unfair as many of these textbooks interpret monopsony literally as being a situation of a single employer of labor rather than the interpretation of an upward-sloping supply curve of labor that is used here. But, mentions of oligopsony are even fewer than mentions of monopsony, and the general impression given by most textbooks is that employers have negligible market power over their workers or that this is, at best, a trivial side issue.

This situation contrasts strongly with the situation in another part of economics, industrial organization, where the standard assumption is that all firms have some product market power, although some are thought to have more market power than others. As a result, the bulk of the *Handbook of Industrial Organization* is about imperfect competition in product markets and virtually every chapter has some reference to monopoly or oligopoly. This contrast between labor economics and industrial organization is odd given that one might think frictions are more important in the labor market as it is more costly to change one's job than one's supermarket.[6] The premise of this book is that labor economics should adopt a similar attitude to that in industrial organization and start analysis from the position that all employers have some labor market power.

This book discusses most if not all of the issues in labor economics from the starting point that the labor market is monopsonistic. Given the evidence cited above on the paucity of references to monopsony in textbooks, one might expect a radical reworking of labor economics. Such an expectation will, more often than not, lead to disappointment. Often, we will be able to draw heavily on existing work and simply look at issues from a different angle. Many explanations of labor market phenomena implicitly assume that the labor market is monopsonistic without articulating that fact. Perhaps the best example of this is search theory, an approach used to analyze a wide range of issues. The early developments, following Stigler (1962), were one-sided, treating the distribution of wage offers in the market as exogenous. Stigler (1962) provides a careful and interesting discussion of why the "law of one wage" is likely to fail in the labor market but does not consider the process of wage setting from the perspective of employers. But, when the process of wage determination was considered, the early models often seemed to collapse, and were incapable of explaining the existence of a non-degenerate wage distribution, a point made forcefully by Diamond (1971) and Rothschild (1973). All of the models then developed to explain the existence of equilibrium wage dispersion (e.g., Butters 1977) essentially assume that firms have some market power. It would be an exaggeration to say

[6] For example, individuals in the British Household Panel Survey commonly report employment-related events as major life events but none report that one of the most important things that happened to them in the past year is that they stopped shopping at Sainsburys and started going to Tesco, two of the biggest British supermarkets.

that all coherent models of frictions imply firms have some market power but it is close to the truth.[7]

1.1 The Advantages of a Monopsonistic Perspective

The main advantage of the monopsonistic approach is that the way one thinks about labor markets is more "natural" and less forced. Currently, labor economics consists of the competitive model with bits bolted onto it when necessary to explain away anomalies. The result is often not a pretty sight. A good example is the analysis of the returns to specific human capital. If one is a strict believer in perfectly competitive markets, one should believe that workers get no return from firm-specific human capital: as Becker (1993: 41–42) puts it "one might plausibly argue that the wage paid by firms would be independent of training." But, Becker goes on to argue that employers need to give workers some share to "deter quits," an idea formalized by Hashimoto (1981) which is the standard reference for this conclusion. But (and this is discussed in more detail in chapter 5), Hashimoto simply assumes that the supply of labor to the firm is not perfectly elastic, that is, he assumes the labor market is monopsonistic, a rather helpless fudge that has sown only confusion ever since.

Assuming labor markets are monopsonistic also brings the thinking of labor economists in line with the way in which agents perceive the workings of labor markets. Workers do not perceive labor markets as frictionless and changing, getting, or losing a job are routinely reported as major life events: for example, in the UK British Household Panel Survey (BHPS), job-related events are the most common category of self-reported important life events after births, deaths, and weddings. And, employers perceive they have discretion over the wages paid. Human resource management textbooks routinely state that the choice

[7] It is instructive to consider the models of frictions that do not give employers some market power. In the "islands" model of Lucas and Prescott (1974), workers must make a decision about the island on which to work before the realization of island-specific demand shocks. There are frictions as there is no ex post mobility between islands after the realization of the shocks. But, even though there are frictions, workers get paid their marginal product as Lucas and Prescott use a "wildebeest" model of the labor market in which each island has huge herds of employers who bid the wage up to the marginal product. Somewhat similar are the models of Moen (1997), Acemoglu and Shimer (2000), and Burdett et al. (2001) where each "island" has only one firm, workers have an ex ante free choice of islands and the uncertainty about the demand shock is replaced by a matching friction in which it is hard to get employment once one is on an island. However, it is assumed that each firm commits in advance the wage it is going to pay so that the relevant labor supply curve is the perfectly elastic ex ante supply curve rather than the completely inelastic ex post one.

of the wage affects the ability of the employer to recruit and retain workers (see, e.g., Jackson and Schuler 2000, chapter 10) and the choice of a wage is a very real one.[8]

It is simple to give examples of how a monopsonistic perspective makes life more comfortable for labor economists. The existence of wage dispersion for identical workers can readily be explained as the natural outcome of a labor market in which the competitive forces are not so strong as to make it impossible for low-wage employers to remain in existence: no recourse is needed to "unobserved ability" to deny the existence of the phenomenon. When we find that workers paid (other things being equal) higher wages are less likely to be looking for another job or that they are less likely to leave their employers, this can be readily explained by the fact that these workers have been lucky enough to find themselves in one of the good jobs in their segment of the labor market. It does not have to be explained away in terms of higher-wage workers having more specific human capital (see, e.g., Neal 1998).

Similarly, the robust empirical correlation between employer characteristics and wages does not have to be explained away in terms of unobserved worker quality: it is exactly what one would expect to find in a monopsonistic labor market. When one observes that employers pay for general training for their workers, one does not have to claim that such training is really specific or that workers are paying for it indirectly. It is what one would expect in a monopsonistic labor market in which part of the returns to general training will accrue to employers.

When we find that equal pay legislation substantially raises the pay of women, and does not appear to harm their employment, this is readily explained by a monopsonistic perspective but a serious problem if one believes the labor market is perfectly competitive. Similarly, finding that the minimum wage does not harm employment prospects in some situations is no particular mystery if one believes in monopsony.

Other examples can be added and are discussed at various points in this book. But, many labor economists instinctively feel very uncomfortable with the idea that labor markets may be pervasively monopsonistic and the next section tries to allay some of these fears.

[8] Issues of labor quality muddy this as, in a competitive labor market, the choice of a wage is really the choice of quality of labor to employ on a job. But, if the competitive model of a labor market was correct, a firm that pays all its workers on a particular job the same wage (such firms are easy to find; see chapter 5) should have no variation in quality among these workers. There would be no such thing as a "most-valued" worker. However, employers are aware that there is heterogeneity in the quality of workers who are paid the same wage. So, it is probably best to think of the wage paid as affecting both the quantity and quality of workers; see Manning (1994b) for the working out of a model with this feature.

1.2 Objections to Monopsony and Oligopsony

Many labor economists find the claim that labor markets are pervasively monopsonistic inherently implausible. It is doubtful that anyone would claim literally that the labor supply curve facing a firm is, in the short run, infinitely elastic as the perfectly competitive model assumes. Almost certainly, most labor economists think of the elasticity as "high" and that the competitive model provides a tolerable approximation to reality. But, once one concedes that the competitive model is not literally true, it becomes an empirical matter just how good an approximation it is. The claim of this book is that, for many questions, the competitive model is not a tolerable approximation, and that our understanding of labor markets would be much improved by thinking in terms of a model where the labor supply curve facing the firm is not infinitely elastic.

The belief that the elasticity of the labor supply curve facing a firm is infinitely elastic is not based on any great weight of accumulated empirical evidence. The number of papers written about the elasticity of the labor supply curve at firm level can almost be counted on the fingers of one hand (see the discussion in chapter 4). Rather, it is introspection (or revelation) which is the source of the faith of many labor economists in the irrelevance of monopsony.

There are a number of sources of this faith. First, there is the belief that large employers are necessary for employers to have some market power and that the vast majority of employers are small in relation to their labor market; Bunting (1962) is the classic reference for US evidence on this. But the approach developed in this book does not require employers to be "large" in relation to their labor market. It only requires that a wage cut of a cent does not cause all workers to leave employment immediately.

Secondly, some labor economists argue that labor turnover rates are so high that workers cannot be thought of as "tied" to firms. But, the *level* of labor turnover is irrelevant: the issue is the *sensitivity* of labor turnover rates to the wage. Existing studies of this find that separations are related to the wage but that the elasticity is not enormous (again, this literature is discussed further in chapter 4).

Some other labor economists think that the supply of labor to a firm is irrelevant because they believe that the normal state of affairs is that employers are turning away workers who want a job at prevailing wages. Involuntary unemployment might be taken as one piece of evidence in this respect, low vacancy rates as another. But, we argue (in chapter 9) that the existence of monopsony and involuntary unemployment are essentially orthogonal issues. Employers have market power over their workers whenever the elasticity of the supply of workers that the employer might consider employing is less than infinite, while involuntary unemployment exists when the supply of the workers that the employer would want is less than the supply who would like to work at the going wage.

And, we argue (in chapter 10) that low vacancy rates and durations are perfectly consistent with the existence of labor supply being a constraint on employers. As job creation is costly, firms will not create jobs they do not expect to be able to fill. Hence, one should think of vacancies as "accidents" and a low vacancy rate is perfectly consistent with employers having some monopsony power.

Thus, the faith that so many labor economists have in the irrelevance of monopsony or oligopsony is not based on hard evidence, and the throw-away arguments sometimes heard are not as compelling as generations of labor economists have been led to believe. The idea deserves to be given more serious consideration and that is the aim of this book.

In much of the previous discussion, the idea of a monopsonistic labor market has been compared to the ideal of a frictionless labor market. But, there are other labor market models which acknowledge the existence of frictions yet would not commonly be thought of as monopsony models. Perhaps the most prominent example of these models is the Diamond–Pissarides matching model (see Diamond 1982; Pissarides 1985). How these models relate to the monopsony model is the subject of the next section.

1.3 Monopsony or Matching or Both?

Another tradition in labor economics, commonly called matching models (for a recent survey, see Mortensen and Pissarides 1999), also starts from the premise that there are important frictions in labor markets. But, these models differ from monopsony models in the assumptions made about wage determination. There are two main such differences (for an explicit formal comparison of the two approaches, see Mortensen 1998).

First, there is a difference in the assumption about the bargaining power of workers. In monopsony models, it is assumed that employers set wages unilaterally whereas the matching models typically assume some process of wage bargaining between employer and worker (although one could set up these models so that employers have all the bargaining power).[9]

---

[9] Adam Smith (1976, p. 84) had something to say about the practice of economists to see bargaining power of workers everywhere: "we rarely hear, it has been said, of the combinations of masters; though frequently of those of workmen. But whoever imagines, upon this account, that masters rarely combine, is as ignorant of the world as of the subject."

Secondly, there is a difference in the assumption made about the timing of wage determination. In the formal models of monopsony introduced in the next chapter, wages are modeled as being determined prior to an employer and a worker meeting each other: this is often called ex ante wage posting. In contrast, matching models typically assume that wages are determined after employer and worker have met (this is often called ex post wage bargaining).

If one judges theories by the realism of their assumptions, then I believe that the wage-posting monopsony model is to be preferred. This is not because it is the best description of the labor market in all circumstances (wage bargaining between employers and workers is observed), just that it is a better description most of the time. For example, chapter 5 documents the existence of a substantial number of firms (in labor markets without minimum wages or trade unions) that pay all their workers in a particular job the same wage. It is hard to see how this could be the outcome of individualized ex post wage bargaining between employers and workers given the heterogeneity of workers within the firms. Even in labor markets that one thinks of as being highly individualistic such as Wall Street, employers seem reluctant to engage in more than limited negotiation: Lewis (1989: 149) describes how Salomon Brothers lost their most profitable bond trader because of their refusal to break a company policy capping the salary they would pay. Models of wage posting seem to provide a better description of reality.

But, economists often also judge theories not by the realism of their assumptions but by the quality of their predictions. Comparing wage posting and wage bargaining models on this basis is difficult because so many of the predictions are the same and it may not matter greatly which assumption about wage determination is used in many circumstances.[10] There is a good reason for this: even though monopsony models appear to give all the bargaining power to the employer, both monopsony and matching models predict that the rents of the employment relationship get shared between workers and employers. In monopsony models, workers get some share of the surplus as long as employers are not perfectly discriminating monopsonists (and chap-

[10] However, there are some substantive differences. Ex post wage bargaining implies that all efficient matches will be consummated whereas ex ante wage posting may result in some efficient matches failing to be consummated (e.g., an unemployed worker with a particularly high reservation wage may not want the job at the offered wage even though there is a higher wage at which both employer and worker would gain from a match). However, ex post wage negotiation may not be effective in motivating ex ante investments by employers or workers as there is no guarantee that the rents from these investments will not be appropriated. On the other hand, the commitment implied by ex ante wage posting may be better able to motivate investments.

ter 5 argues that there are good reasons why they cannot be). Assuming that firms set wages and are monopsonists, at least in a formal sense, should not be taken to imply that their share of any rents is necessarily large.[11]

Another advantage of the monopsony over the matching approach is that it is much easier to forge links with other parts of labor economics. Although the underlying model of the labor market with frictions may be relatively complicated with a lot of dynamics and value functions, one can often represent and understand the decision problem of the individual employer in the monopsony model in terms of the textbook static model of monopsony. In contrast, the matching models do not have a simple static textbook counterpart model and the use of these models has led to unfortunate parallel literatures in which the same labor market phenomenon is "explained" by both a matching model and a conventional static model without the fundamental similarity between them being recognized. From those who specialize in the analysis of matching models, one often hears the claim that "dynamic models are different" to justify this state of affairs: while there is some truth in this statement, it is much less true than they commonly think. And empirical labor economists often feel that there is little benefit in terms of understanding and a considerable cost in terms of analytical complexity from using a dynamic model and fall back on the familiar textbook model of perfect competition.

Hence, although one should think in terms of monopsony and matching models as being fundamentally similar models of the labor market, the monopsony model is a better description of the way labor markets work and makes it much easier to forge links with the rest of labor economics.

1.4 Antecedents

As has already been pointed out, a number of distinguished economists have seen labor markets as operating in the way described in this book and bits and pieces of modern labor economics are, implicitly or explicitly, analyses of monopsonistic or oligopsonistic labor markets. But there are two particular traditions that need to be singled out as being important influences on this work.

The first is the labor economics of the so-called neorealist or neoclassical revisionist labor economists (Kaufman 1988) who thrived in the

[11] Some might object to the use of the word monopsony in a situation in which workers get some or even most of the rents. But, consumers are strictly better off with electricity than without although most people would be content with the description of the utility as a monopolist. The use of the word "monopsony" is simply meant to refer to the fact that employers set wages.

United States in the late 1940s and the 1950s before being supplanted by economists who drew their inspiration from Hicks' *Theory of Wages* and from the Chicago school of thought. These economists like John Dunlop, Clark Kerr, Richard Lester, and Lloyd Reynolds had been brought up on neoclassical economics but felt that the competitive model gave a seriously inaccurate picture of how labor markets operated.

There were two main reasons why they arrived at this conclusion. First, studies of labor mobility seemed to show that workers were extremely reluctant to change jobs and hence that the mechanism which was imagined to enforce the competitive law of one wage was, in reality, much weaker than most labor economists imagined. One consequence of this was that the "market" did not dictate the wage an employer had to pay or face ruin: employers had, in fact, considerable discretion in the wage that they chose to pay. Further evidence of this was the considerable dispersion in wages found in labor markets defined very tightly in terms of occupation and area (Lester 1946, 1948; Reynolds 1946a,b, 1951; Slichter 1950; Dunlop 1957, amongst others). They were well aware of the possibility that such wage dispersion might be driven by differences in the non-wage aspects of jobs or differences in worker quality, or be only short-term (see, e.g., the discussion in Lester 1952: 487–88) but they arrived at the conclusion (often more by the exercise of judgment than firm evidence) that the wage dispersion was real and permanent. The practical experience of several of these economists in the work of the War Labor Board which set out to find *the* market wage for particular classes of labor and found only wage dispersion was particularly important in convincing them that the competitive model suffered from serious deficiencies.

These economists were actively discussing the supply curve of labor to the firm, the issue that is at the heart of this book. Reynolds (1946a: 390) wrote in a paper entitled *The Supply of Labor to the Firm* that "the view that labor-market imperfections result in a forward-rising supply curve of labor to the firm appears to have been first elaborated by Mrs. Robinson. This conclusion has made its way rapidly into the textbooks and seems well on the way to being generally accepted as a substitute for the horizontal supply curve of earlier days." It is hard to imagine a paper with this title in the journals of today let alone a statement along these lines. Bronfenbrenner (1956: 578) wrote

> the typical employer in an unorganized labor market is by no means a pure competitor facing market wages which he cannot alter. The mobility of the labor force, even between firms located close together, is low by reason of the inability of workers to wait for employment or risk unemployment, plus the inadequacy of the information usually available to them regarding alternative

employment opportunities. This low mobility permits each employer to set his own rates and form his own labour market within limits which at some times may be quite wide. In the technical jargon of economic theory, the typical employer in an unorganized labor market has some degree of monopsony power and can set his own wage policy

a statement of the central themes of this book which would be hard to better.

So these economists were writing about the issues on which I write and thinking about explanations along the same sort of lines. Yet, I cannot help feeling that these labor economists would not necessarily welcome my embrace.[12] My bald assumption that employers set wages to maximize profits is the kind of crass generalization from which someone like Lester instinctively recoiled. He came to emphasize how the lack of cutthroat competition in the labor market gave leeway for employers to pursue many ends and this was, for example, one explanation of wage dispersion observed (see, e.g., Lester 1952). Perhaps this was because he saw any model based on a single objective (like profit maximization) predicting a determinate outcome, a prediction that was then obviously falsified by observation of the world. But, the general equilibrium models that are used (see, e.g., the model of section 2.4) have as an equilibrium a range of wages even when the objectives pursued by all firms are identical: in a sense they are models of determinate indeterminacy.[13]

While Reynolds wrote about the supply curve of labor to the firm, his final conclusion was that "in actuality, an employer can usually expand and contract employment at will without altering his terms of employment" (Reynolds 1951: 227) so that the competitive labor supply curve gave the right answer though for the wrong reasons. He arrived at this conclusion primarily because of the observation that it did not seem to cost much in terms of time or money to recruit extra workers: that is, vacancy durations were (and are) extremely low. This is a serious objection to the relevance of the monopsony model and one which is discussed at length in chapter 10. But my conclusion is different: I argue that what we know about vacancies is perfectly consistent with the existence of non-negligible monopsony power.

The other important inspiration for this book is a single paper: Burdett and Mortensen (1998).[14] This paper was presented at the

[12] If one looks at the representative quotes about monopsony in the textbooks authored by these economists, it would be hard to see any more favorable inclination to monopsony than is found in the others.

[13] Though Lester's position does receive some support if our basic model is tweaked to introduce mobility costs and preferences over non-wage job attributes when multiple equilibria tend to be rife.

[14] It may have been published in 1998 but was originally written at least 10 years earlier.

LSE in 1990 and it was a revelation to me. Here was a simple elegant analytical framework that could explain the existence of equilibrium wage dispersion (and other stylized facts about the labor market). If I had not been quite so ignorant I would have realized that proving the possibility of equilibrium price or wage dispersion was not as new or as difficult as I had imagined (one might cite Butters 1977; Salop and Stiglitz 1977; Reinganum 1979; Burdett and Judd 1983; Albrecht and Axell 1984; Lang 1991; Montgomery 1991a, among others which did more or less the same thing). But the advantage of the Burdett and Mortensen model to me was that, whereas many of the other models of price or wage dispersion were too stylized to be able to take to labor market data, their model was expressed in terms of quit and recruitment rates, and job offer arrival rates that had obvious empirical counterparts. So it is their model that forms the basis of much of what follows, though I imagine that one could have built much of it on some of the other papers.

1.5 Summary of Chapters and Main Results

This book is based on two assumptions:

- there are important frictions in the labor market;
- employers set wages.

The consequence of the first assumption is that the employers have market power in the labor market and the consequence of the second is that they exercise it. The labor supply curve facing employers is not infinitely elastic so that they have some monopsony power. The style of this book is to systematically apply these two assumptions to most areas of labor economics.

The book is divided into four parts. In the first part, chapters 2 through 4, some basic models and results are laid out. Each chapter presents both the relevant theory and empirical evidence based on US and UK data. Every attempt has been made to make the main body of each chapter as accessible as possible with the proofs of the propositions and more technical material confined to an appendix at the end of each chapter. And, because the same data sets are used throughout, there is also a Data Sets Appendix at the end of the book, providing details of how the data were constructed.

Chapter 2, *Simple Models of Monopsony and Oligopsony* starts by presenting some partial equilibrium models of static and dynamic monopsony. While these partial equilibrium models are adequate for analyzing many questions, there are others for which it is necessary to model inter-

actions between employers, that is, to model the labor market as oligopsonistic. The chapter then presents a model of oligopsony based on the
wage-posting model proposed by Burdett and Mortensen (1998).

The chapter derives the well-known result that the extent of employer
monopsony power is related to the wage elasticity in the labor supply curve
facing an individual employer: the less elastic the supply curve, the more
market power the employer possesses. It also argues that the greater the
ability of workers to move from employer to employer, the more wages
will be driven up towards their marginal product. It suggests that the
proportion of workers recruited directly from other jobs is a good simple
measure of the competitiveness of labor markets. For both US and UK data
sets, this proportion is shown to be in the region of 45–50%, a level that is
argued to suggest employers have substantial market power.

Chapter 3, *Efficiency in Oligopsonistic Labor Markets*, considers the
welfare implications of oligopsonistic labor markets in variations on the
model of Burdett and Mortensen (1998). Most of the book is about the
positive implications of assuming that employers have market power over
their workers. But while "monopsony" as used in this book should be
interpreted as a technical term to describe the situation where the labor
supply curve to the firm is not infinitely elastic, the term often has more
emotive connotations and is sometimes taken to imply that, in some
sense, wages are "too low." This is certainly true for the textbook analysis of a single monopsonist where, if the employer has market power, one
can always find a binding minimum wage that raises employment and
welfare. However, as chapter 3 shows, this simple conclusion breaks
down once one moves beyond the case of the single monopsonist. The
main conclusion of the chapter is that the free market equilibrium is
generally not efficient but that interventions like the minimum wage
may improve or worsen efficiency, depending on the particular model
being considered. Hence the chapter concludes that theory alone can be
of little use in evaluating policy.

The final section of chapter 3 presents a simple model of a "ghetto,"
emphasizing how, in labor markets with frictions, it is relatively simple to
generate multiple equilibria and agglomeration effects. For example, residents of a neighborhood may not invest in human capital if they think
there are no jobs in which to use them, while employers may not locate in
an area in which the residents have low levels of human capital. In a
market with frictions, there is no mechanism to ensure that an act of
investment in human capital by an individual will bring forward the
investment of physical capital to employ it.

Chapter 4, *The Elasticity of the Labor Supply Curve to an Individual
Firm*, presents evidence on the wage elasticity of the labor supply curve to
the individual employer. This is the natural place to start to make the case

that monopsony is empirically relevant as the assumption that the labor supply curve to individual employers is not perfectly elastic is the fundamental idea in monopsony. There are astonishingly few papers in the labor economics literature on the supply of labor to individual employers in contrast to the volumes written about labor demand and individual labor supply to the market as a whole.

In estimating the supply curve to an individual employer, the obvious place to start is to regress log wages on the log of employment (plus other relevant controls). One finds, consistent with monopsony, a very robust positive correlation between wages and employment. This employer size–wage effect is well known in labor economics though it is rarely interpreted as evidence of an upward-sloping labor supply curve to an individual employer. The chapter reviews the more common explanations for the employer size-wage effect, concluding that none of them can explain it all, and that part of the employer size-wage effect does seem to be the result of an upward-sloping supply curve of labor to the individual employer. However, once one has controlled for other relevant factors, the elasticity of wages with respect to employment is often low, in the region of 0.04, implying that the elasticity in the labor supply curve to the employer is high—about 25. But, these OLS estimates are likely to be biased downwards because shifts in the supply of labor to the employer will tend to induce a negative correlation between wages and employment. Reverse regressions in which employment is regressed on wages suggest a much lower wage elasticity of the labor supply curve—often in the range of 1.5–3.5. Finding a suitable instrumental variable is the obvious way to try to sharpen up these estimates but that is not an easy task as the instrument needs to be firm specific. The few studies that do take this approach suggest that labor supply to individual firms is relatively inelastic.

The second half of chapter 4 takes a different approach to estimating the labor supply elasticity, based more explicitly on a dynamic model of monopsony. As, in steady state, employment, N, is equal to the recruitment rate, R, divided by the separation rate, s ($N = R/s$), the wage elasticity of employment can be written as the wage elasticity of recruitment minus the wage elasticity of separations. There is a relatively large existing literature that estimates the sensitivity of separations to the wage but estimating the elasticity of recruits is more difficult. However, it is shown how in models of dynamic oligopsony there will be a tight relationship between the separation and recruitment elasticities. In the simplest model, they must be equal to each other and, in more complicated models, a weighted average must be equal. Using this approach the wage elasticity of the labor supply curve to an individual employer is estimated to be in the region of 0.75–1.5, that is, relatively low.

The second part of the book, chapters 5 through 8, is about how monopsony can help us towards a better understanding of the observed distribution of wages.

Chapter 5, *The Wage Policies of Employers*, discusses the incentives for an employer to pay different wages to identical workers, that is, to become a discriminating monopsonist, and the difficulties with doing so. For example, employers would like to be able to pay low wages to workers with low reservation wages but it may be very difficult to observe reservation wages. Employers are more likely to base wage discrimination on non-manipulable characteristics of the workers like job tenure and age. The chapter shows how there are incentives for employers to use seniority wage schedules in line with what is observed. However, it is argued that there are good theoretical reasons and empirical evidence to suggest that the ability to wage discriminate may be severely limited in practice.

Chapter 6, *Earnings and the Life Cycle*, examines the way in which earnings evolve over a working life. The human capital approach to this question emphasizes the way in which both general and specific human capital accumulate over a lifetime and empirical correlations of earnings with experience (or age) and job tenure are normally interpreted in the light of the human capital model. Section 6.1 starts by presenting evidence that there is something wrong with this way of interpreting earnings functions. For example, the earnings losses of displaced workers are increasing in the level of experience, something that should not happen if the returns to experience represent the returns to general human capital. Section 6.2 then shows that a substantial part of the observed cross-sectional returns to job tenure is the result of the bias caused by the fact that those in high-wage jobs are less likely to leave them.

Section 6.3 then introduces a job-shopping model as a way to explain correlations between wages, age, and job tenure even if the wage offer distribution does not depend on age and job tenure. For example, there may be a correlation of wages with age because older workers are more likely to have found the better-paying jobs (Burdett 1978). One can then explain why more experienced workers suffer larger wage losses after displacement as job loss causes a reduction in "search capital." And there may be a correlation of wages with job tenure as those who have been lucky enough to find a high-paying job are less likely to leave it. However, as section 6.3 makes clear, the correlations predicted by the search model are more complicated than this simple discussion suggests.

Section 6.4 then proposes a new framework for decomposing the life cycle profile of earnings into three components: the growth in earnings on the job, the costs of job loss, and the return to job mobility. It is shown how the returns to job tenure as conventionally measured are a weighted average of the change in the costs of job loss and the returns to job mobility but that this mixes up two very different processes as job mobility is mostly voluntary on the part of workers, leading to wage gains, while job loss is involuntary, leading to wages losses.

The final two sections then present two applications of this approach: estimating the returns to job mobility and the decline in average earnings among older men. It is shown how the decline in earnings among older men is primarily the result of substantial rates and costs of job loss.

Chapter 7, *Gender Discrimination in Labor Markets*, discusses how monopsony can help us understand the gender pay gap. It is argued that the weaker attachment of women to the labor market can go some way towards explaining the gender pay gap even if there is no gender productivity gap. The reason is that women will find it harder to work their way into the better-paying jobs. Furthermore, evidence is presented that women are less motivated than men by money in choosing jobs so that the female labor market is likely to be more monopsonistic than the male. Section 7.4 presents evidence for this from responses to questions on the motivation for changing jobs and section 7.5 presents evidence that the returns to job mobility are lower for women than for men. Human capital explanations of the gender pay gap also emphasize the weaker attachment of women to the labor market as a source of the gender pay gap but argue that this results in lower productivity. Two pieces of evidence inconsistent with this view are presented: in section 7.7, it is shown how the returns to job tenure are, if anything, larger for women than for men while section 7.8 analyzes the impact of the 1970 UK Equal Pay Act that resulted in a large increase in female relative wages but had no impact on relative employment contrary to the predictions of the human capital model.

Chapter 8, *Employers and Wages*, considers the well-known empirical "puzzle" that employer characteristics are correlated with wages. In a competitive market these correlations should not exist (abstracting from compensating wage differentials that do not seem to be empirically that important) as the wage should be determined solely by the characteristics of workers. However, as shown in section 8.1, we would expect wages to vary with employer characteristics like size, productivity, and profitability if employers have some market power. The "puzzle" is simply what we would expect.

Sections 8.2 and 8.3 discuss the implications of monopsony for the estimation of compensating wage differentials. It is argued that the conventional approach to estimating the value of non-pecuniary aspects of jobs that is based on estimating earnings functions is flawed if employers have market power as there is no reason to believe that utility is equalized across jobs in the labor market. In particular, there is good reason to think that utility will be lower in jobs with worse work conditions. An alternative approach to estimating the value of non-pecuniary benefits based on estimating separation functions is proposed and an application to estimating the disamenity associated with night work is presented. Section 8.4 discusses the likely effect of mandated benefits, intervention to regulate the non-wage conditions of work, for example, health and safety legislation, maximum hours legislation, etc. In a competitive labor market, it is often argued that such legislation is likely to be bad as it imposes an inefficient wage-benefit combination and may actually harm rather than help workers. However, it is shown that this is not necessarily the case if employers have some market power: regulation of non-wage aspects of jobs will make workers better off as long as the non-wage attribute is a "normal" good and the regulation is not too onerous.

Finally, section 8.5 applies the framework established earlier in the chapter to the analysis of hours of work. The determination of hours of work as considered in the labor supply literature is normally treated as a completely different subject from the analysis of other non-wage job attributes. But there is no good reason for this: given the level of earnings, higher hours increase output and reduce worker utility just like any other non-wage attribute. It is argued that, if employers have monopsony power, then workers are likely to be overworked in the sense of being forced to work more hours than they would like given their wage.

The third part of the book, chapters 9 through 11, is concerned with the "quantity" side of the labor market, the supply of and demand for labor, and the determinants of investment in human capital.

Chapter 9, *Unemployment Activity and Labor Supply*, considers the determinants of the level and structure of unemployment and inactivity from the perspective of the worker. The employment rate of individual workers is determined by the rate at which they get jobs when not in employment and lose them when in employment. The main way in which individuals can influence the rate at which they get jobs is by their choice of job search activity. Section 9.1 endogenizes the choice of search intensity both on and off the job. The relative effectiveness of these two types of job search is important and a new test is proposed based on the fact that the reservation wage should depend positively (negatively) on the productivity of workers as off-the-job search is more (less) effective than on-the-job search. This empirical evidence strongly suggests that off-the-job search is more effective. Section 9.2 then discusses the distinction between unemployment and inactivity as defined in labor market statistics. Competitive models of the labor market do not have a meaningful distinction between these two labor market states but because the unemployed are defined as those with job search intensity above a critical level, the framework of this chapter makes the distinction easy to understand. An application to the discouraged worker effect suggests that, when aggregate labor market conditions worsen, job search intensity falls resulting in a rise in measured inactivity rates.

Section 9.3 considers the job search intensity of the employed. Monopsony has a strong prediction, that job search activity should be declining in the wage as there are then fewer opportunities to find a better job. The empirical evidence reported is strongly in support of this prediction. Section 9.4 then considers the determinants of the rate at which workers will quit jobs for non-employment. Consistent with the empirical evidence, the model predicts that quit rates will be declining in the wage.

Sections 9.6 and 9.7 are concerned with conceptual issues about the nature of unemployment in labor markets where employers have market power. In the simplest models of monopsony, unemployment appears "voluntary" in the sense that all employers would like to hire more workers at the going wage. This seems hard to reconcile with the observation that jobs often seem to be hard to find and the feeling that many economists have that unemployment is "involuntary." However, as sections 9.6 and 9.7 show, it is a simple matter to reconcile models of monopsony with models of involuntary unemployment (represented by efficiency wage models).

Chapter 10, *Vacancies and Labor Demand*, considers the determinants of the level of employment from the perspective of employers. Sections 10.1 and 10.2 are concerned with the interpretation of vacancy statistics. It is argued that, to have a meaningful model of vacancies, one has to have a model in which the creation of jobs requires some ex ante investment and in which the supply of labor to the firm is stochastic. With these features, a model of the labor market in which employers have considerable market power is quite consistent with the observation that vacancy rates are low, and vacancies are typically of short duration and have relatively small numbers of applicants. Empirical evidence supports the conclusion that those firms that pay higher wages have fewer difficulties in filling vacancies.

Sections 10.3 and 10.4 are concerned with the technology by which workers and employers are matched. A crucial issue turns out to be whether large employers have an intrinsic advantage over small firms in recruiting workers, because this is important in determining the wage elasticity in the supply of labor to the firm. However, it is shown that large employers are not more likely than small firms to use recruitment methods in which they might be thought to have an advantage, like social contacts.

Finally, section 10.6 contains a brief discussion of the determination of lay offs, arguing that there are good reasons to think that they will occur while there is still some surplus in the relationship remaining for workers.

Chapter 11, *Human Capital and Training*, considers the incentives for the acquisition of human capital in monopsonistic labor markets. Section 11.1 considers the incentives for workers to engage in the acquisition of education before they enter the labor market. Because part of the returns to any such education is likely to accrue to future employers of the worker, there is a prima facie case for believing there will be underinvestment in human capital. However, there is some reason to believe that the labor market for more educated workers may be less monopsonistic in which case it may be that this conclusion is misleading. Section 11.2 then considers the provision of employer-provided general training. A key prediction of the monopsony model which contrasts very strongly with that of the competitive model is that employers will be prepared to pay for some investments in general training because they can expect to get some returns from it. However, because future potential employers of a worker might also expect to get a share of the returns from any investment in human capital, one would expect to see underinvestment. Section 11.3 then considers firm-specific training. A striking conclusion is that workers may capture a higher share of the returns to firm-specific investments than of general investments if employers have market power. Section 11.4 concludes with a discussion of the empirical evidence on training.

The final part of the book, chapters 12 and 13, considers the impact of institutions that interfere with the ability of employers to set wages and draws some conclusions.

Chapter 12, *Minimum Wages and Trade Unions*, is concerned with the impact of these wage-setting institutions on wages and employment. Although these institutions are often seen as essentially similar (they both raise wages above the market-clearing level), their effects in a monopsonistic labor market are likely to be rather different. For example, minimum wages have a direct impact on the lowest wages in a given labor market so are likely to "push" the wage distribution from below, while trade unions are likely to set the highest wages in a given market so will "pull" the wage distribution from above. Section 12.1 discusses the impact of the minimum wage on the wage distribution. Empirical evidence is presented that spillover effects from the minimum wage onto the US wage distribution are substantial. Section 12.2 then argues that much of the evolution of wage inequality in the bottom half of the US wage distribution from 1980 to 2000 can be explained by variation in the minimum wage. Section 12.3 then discusses the controversial issue of the impact of the minimum wage on employment. While a minimum wage does not necessarily cost jobs in an oligopsonistic labor market, it is shown that the simple result from the model of a single monopsonist, that a suitably chosen minimum wage must raise employment, does not carry over to a labor market in which one models interactions between firms and hetero- geneity among them. An open-minded empirical approach is appropriate for investigating the impact of minimum wages on employment.

Section 12.4 discusses how models of trade unions need to be modified to recognize the fact that employers have some market power. It also discusses the argument that "corporatist" systems of wage bargaining can do something to alleviate the problems caused by a "free market" system of wage determination. Section 12.5 discusses the impact of trade unions on wages. It focuses on the impact of unions on non-union wages, arguing that in a labor market where employers have some power over wages, the impact of unions on non-union wages is likely to depend on whether an on- or off-the-job search is more effective. The evidence presented in chapter 9 suggests that an off-the-job search is more effective in which case unions would be expected to raise non-union wages. Empirical evidence for this is presented and it is argued that the correla- tions cannot be explained by the "threat" effect.

Chapter 13, *Monopsony and the Big Picture*, offers some conclusions. Section 13.1 reviews the sources of monopsony power and the evidence that employers have it. Section 13.2 argues that recognizing the existence of monopsony power in the labor market does not mean supplanting all existing competitive analysis: in many cases, it simply adds to it. One might wonder about how important monopsony is in understanding the "big" issues of the day. Section 13.3 addresses this argument by arguing that a view that the labor market is monopsonistic is necessary for an adequate understanding of changes in the bottom half of the US labor market since 1980. Section 13.4 then discusses what monopsony has to say about the design of labor market policy. The main substantive conclusion is that labor economists should be more open-minded about the likely impact of labor market interventions: empirical evidence is more powerful than theory. Too often (e.g., in discussions of European unemployment), labor economists simply assume (often unthinkingly) that the alternative to a regulated labor market is a labor market that is well approximated by the perfectly competitive model.

In the book as a whole, virtually all of the main topics of labor economics are covered although not necessarily in a familiar order. Table 1.2 presents a simple key to where some topics may be found in this book.

TABLE 1.2
Topics in Labor Market Analysis

Traditional Subject	Location in this Book
Labor supply (hours)	Chapter 8
Labor supply (participation)	Chapter 9
Labor demand	Chapter 10
Compensating wage differentials	Chapter 8
Employers and wages	Chapter 8
Gender discrimination	Chapter 7
Earnings functions	Chapter 6
Employment contracts	Chapter 5
Efficiency wages	Chapter 9
Rent sharing	Chapter 8
Employer-size wage effect	Chapter 4
Human capital	Chapter 11
Minimum wages	Chapter 12
Trade unions	Chapter 12

2

Simple Models of Monopsony
and Oligopsony

THIS chapter introduces some simple models of monopsony and oligopsony which form the foundation for the analysis in the rest of the book. The first three sections present some partial equilibrium models: the textbook static model of monopsony, a simple model of dynamic monopsony, and what is called a generalized model of monopsony where the firm has instruments other than the wage to influence the flow of recruits. The fourth section then presents a general equilibrium model of dynamic oligopsony (based on a simplified version of Burdett and Mortensen, 1998) to show how the framework is a fully coherent vision of the labor market as a whole. Although this model is highly stylized, it does capture the most important features of a labor market with frictions. Workers are faced with a distribution of wages so that there are good jobs and bad jobs. They try to get themselves into the good jobs but their progress resembles a game of "snakes and ladders." Sometimes they meet a "snake" and suffer the misfortune of losing their job and sometimes they find a "ladder" and have the good fortune to move to a better job. From the perspective of employers, the frictions in labor markets give them some discretion in setting wages. If they lower wages, they find it more difficult to recruit and retain workers but the existing workers do not all leave immediately and they continue to be able to recruit some workers so that they retain some workers even in the long run. The wages that employers set are influenced by competition from other employers but this competition is neither so cutthroat as to enable workers to extract all the surplus from the employment relationship, nor so weak as to enable employers to extract all the rents.

The chapter concludes by arguing that the fraction of recruits from non-employment is a good "back-of-the-envelope" measure of the extent to which workers are able to freely move between employers and, hence, of competition among employers for workers and the extent of market power possessed by employers in the labor market. Empirical evidence from the United Kingdom and the United States suggests that 45–55% of recruits were previously non-employed, a level which is likely to give employers considerable market power.

2.1 Static Partial Equilibrium Models of Monopsony

Given the lack of attention paid to monopsony in much of labor economics it is perhaps helpful to start with a quick review of the static textbook
model of monopsony. In this model, the firm is assumed to face a labor
supply curve that relates the wage paid, w, to the level of employment, N.
Denote the supply of labor to the firm if it pays w by $N(w)$. Also, denote
the inverse of this relationship by $w(N)$. Both $N(w)$ and $w(N)$ will be
referred to as the labor supply curve to the individual firm. Total labor
costs are given by $w(N)N$. Assume that the firm is a simple monopsonist
who has to pay a single wage to all its workers (the incentives for wage
discrimination are discussed in chapter 5). Assume the firm has a revenue
function $Y(N)$. It wants to choose N to maximize profits which are given
by

$$\pi = Y(N) - w(N)N \tag{2.1}$$

This leads to the first-order condition

$$Y'(N) = w(N) + w'(N)N \tag{2.2}$$

The left-hand side of (2.2) is the marginal revenue product of labor. The
right-hand side is the marginal cost of labor, the increase in total labor
costs when an extra worker is hired. The marginal cost of labor has two
parts: the wage, w, that must be paid to the new worker hired and the
increase in wages that must be paid to all existing workers. The solution is
represented graphically in figure 2.1. Equilibrium is on the labor supply
curve with the wage paid to workers being less than their marginal
revenue product. Although the employer is making positive profit on
the marginal worker, there is no incentive to increase employment
because doing so would require increasing the wage (to attract the
extra worker) and this higher wage must be paid not just to the new
worker but also to all the existing workers. One particularly useful way
of representing the choice of the firm is that marginal cost of labor is a
mark-up on the wage, the mark-up being given by the elasticity of the
labor supply curve facing the firm. Let us write the elasticity of the labor
supply curve facing the firm as $\varepsilon_{Nw} = wN'(w)/N(w)$ and let ε be the
inverse of this elasticity. Then (2.2) can be written as

$$\frac{Y' - w}{w} = \frac{1}{\varepsilon_{Nw}} = \varepsilon \tag{2.3}$$

so that the proportional gap between the wage and the marginal revenue
product is a function of the elasticity of the labor supply curve facing the
firm. The gap between the wage and the marginal revenue product is what
Pigou (1924) and Hicks (1932) referred to as the rate of exploitation and

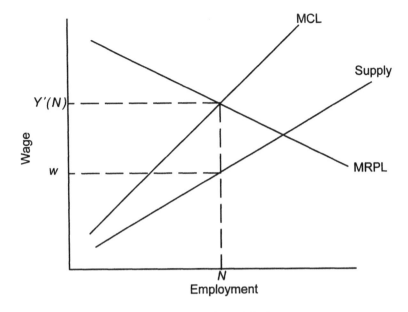

Figure 2.1 The textbook model of monopsony.

we will follow this tradition. Perfect competition corresponds to the case where $\varepsilon_{Nw} = \infty$ and $\varepsilon = 0$ in which case (2.3) says that the wage will be equal to the marginal revenue product.

Some of the comparative statics of the static monopsony model are the same as in the competitive model and some are different. For example, an increase in the marginal revenue product of labor will lead to an increase in employment and a rise in wages. The former would occur in a competitive model but the latter would not as a competitive firm would simply continue to pay the market wage. The impact of shifts in the labor supply curve to the firm are more complicated as the impact depends on how the change affects the marginal cost of labor and not just the average cost of labor. An increase in the supply of labor to the firm that keeps the elasticity the same will result in a rise in employment and a fall in wages just as in the competitive model. But, matters are more complicated if the elasticity of the labor supply curve changes as the average and marginal cost of labor can move in opposite directions; the most familiar example of this is the impact of a minimum wage. The minimum wage raises the average cost of labor but (if it is binding) reduces $w'(N)$ so its effect on the marginal cost of labor (see (2.2)) is ambiguous. In fact, one can show that a minimum wage that just binds must raise employment (a demonstration of this can be found in most labor economics textbooks).

2.2 A Simple Model of Dynamic Monopsony

One might wonder how this completely static model of the labor market corresponds to the description of the labor market in the first chapter that was based on dynamic arguments. The static and dynamic models can be linked in the following way. Assume that workers leave the firm at a rate s that depends negatively on the wage paid, and recruits arrive at the firm at a rate R that depends positively on the wage. If the firm had N_{t-1} workers last period and pays w_t this period, its labor supply will be

$$N_t = [1 - s(w_t)]N_{t-1} + R(w_t) \qquad (2.4)$$

where $s(w)$ is the separation rate and $R(w)$ the recruitment rate.

In a steady state, total separations sN must equal recruits R so that we have

$$N(w) = \frac{R(w)}{s(w)} \qquad (2.5)$$

giving us a positive long-run relationship between employment and the wage.[1] In this case the elasticity of the labor supply curve facing the firm can be written as

$$\varepsilon_{Nw} = \varepsilon_{Rw} - \varepsilon_{sw} \qquad (2.6)$$

where ε_{Rw} is the elasticity of recruits with respect to the wage and ε_{sw} is the elasticity of separations with respect to the wage.

In a dynamic model, there is an important distinction between the elasticity of the short-run labor supply curve facing the employer and the long-run elasticity. The elasticity of (2.6) is the long-run elasticity of the labor supply curve facing the firm. The short-run elasticity, denoted by ε^s_{Nw}, is the elasticity of N_t with respect to w_t holding N_{t-1} fixed. Differentiating (2.4), we have

$$\varepsilon^s_{Nw} = \frac{w_t}{N_t}\frac{\partial N_t}{\partial w_t} = -w_t s'(w_t)\frac{N_{t-1}}{N_t} + \frac{w_t R'(w_t)}{N_t}$$

$$= -\varepsilon_{sw}s(w_t)\frac{N_{t-1}}{N_t} + \varepsilon_{Rw}\frac{R(w_t)}{N_t}$$

$$= s(w_t)[\varepsilon_{Rw} - \varepsilon_{sw}]\frac{N_{t-1}}{N_t} + \varepsilon_{Rw}\frac{N_t - N_{t-1}}{N_t} \qquad (2.7)$$

In a steady state in which $N_t = N_{t-1}$, the elasticity of the short-run labor supply curve facing the firm, ε^s_{Nw}, can, using (2.6), be written as

---

[1] One can invert $N(w)$ to give $w(N)$, the wage the firm must pay if it wants to have N workers.

$$\varepsilon^s_{Nw} = s(w_t)\varepsilon_{Nw} \tag{2.8}$$

(2.8) shows that the short-run labor supply curve facing the firm is less elastic than the long-run one (as $s(w_t) < 1$), and the difference is greater the lower the separation rate.

In a dynamic monopsony model, it is not immediately clear whether the short- or long-run labor supply elasticity is most relevant for wage determination. If firms must commit to a particular wage and do not discount the future, they will be interested in maximizing steady-state profits and the formula in (2.3) will still hold where the relevant elasticity is the long-run one. But, suppose firms do discount the future at a rate D and cannot make long-term commitments on the wage. In particular, suppose the firm cannot commit itself to a particular wage for more than a single period in advance so that the promise of a particular wage this period carries no guarantee that it will be paid next period.[2] The following result (Boal and Ransom 1997) tells us about the steady-state relationship between the marginal revenue product of labor and the wage in this case.

Proposition 2.1. *In a steady state, the relationship between the marginal revenue product and the wage is given by*

$$\frac{Y'(N) - w}{w} = \varepsilon\left[1 + \frac{(1 - D)(1 - s)}{s}\right] = (1 - D)\varepsilon^s + D\varepsilon \tag{2.9}$$

where ε is the inverse of long-run elasticity of the labor supply curve and ε^s is the inverse of the short-run elasticity.

Proof. See Appendix 2.

(2.9) says that the rate of exploitation is a weighted average of the long-run and short-run elasticities with the weight on the long-run elasticity being the discount factor. The more employers discount the future, the greater the weight given to the short-run elasticity and the larger will be the rate of exploitation (as it will be the case that $\varepsilon^s > \varepsilon$). The intuition is that cutting wages is more attractive when employers discount the future more heavily as the costs of this strategy (lower future labor supply) do not weigh so heavily on their minds.

One variant of (2.9) is where the length of the "period" (of wage commitment) goes to zero. If the length of period is Δ, and d and ς are the instantaneous interest and separation rates, respectively, we will have

---

[2] It is convenient to work in discrete time although we will consider the limit as the length of time between periods goes to zero.

$D = e^{-d\Delta}$ and $s = 1 - e^{-\varsigma\Delta}$. Then taking the limit as $\Delta \to 0$, we have

$$\frac{Y'(N) - w}{w} = \varepsilon\left[1 + \frac{d}{s}\right] \tag{2.10}$$

The difference between the right-hand sides in (2.3) and (2.10) is probably rather small for plausible values of d and ς (perhaps an annual interest rate of 5% and 20% for the labor turnover rate) although (2.10) does suggest a larger rate of exploitation than (2.3).

In the interests of simplicity, most of the theoretical analysis in this book is based on the assumption that employers do not discount the future and choose wages once-for-all. In this case, it is the long-run labor supply elasticity that is important and, as this section has demonstrated, this is likely to understate the true extent of monopsony power.

2.3 A Generalized Model of Monopsony

In the models of monopsony considered so far, there is only one way for a firm to get employment of N and that is to pay the wage $w(N)$. In reality, firms can influence their employment through other means, for example, by varying the intensity of their recruitment activity. In this section we present a simple, yet general and flexible framework for thinking about monopsony in this situation.

Define the labor cost function, which we denote by $C(w, N)$, as the cost per worker, excluding direct wage costs, of keeping employment at N when the firm pays a wage w.[3] Some examples might make the idea clearer. For example, if recruiting and training a worker costs T (independent of the number of recruits) and the separation rate is $s(w)$, a flow of sN recruits is needed to maintain employment at N so that $C(w, N) = T/s(w)$. In this case, the labor cost function is independent of N. But, if it becomes increasingly hard to recruit and train workers

---

[3] One can think of both perfect competition and the static model of monopsony as being particular forms (albeit, non-differentiable) of the labor cost function. The traditional static monopsony model implicitly assumes that a firm that pays a wage w incurs no recruitment costs if it wants employment less than the labor supply forthcoming at that wage, but that there is no way at all for the firm to attract more workers. So, the form of the labor cost function in this model is $C(w, N) = 0$ if $N < N(w)$ and $C(w, N) = \infty$ if $N > N(w)$. The labor cost function for the competitive labor market model is the following. If there are no recruitment/training costs then, if w^c is the competitive wage, the labor cost function for the competitive model can be thought of as $C(w, N) = 0$ if $w \geq w^c$, and $C(w, N) = \infty$ if $w < w^c$. This says that any amount of labor can be recruited at zero cost as long as the wage paid is at or above the competitive level, but that no labor is available at any cost if a wage below the competitive wage is offered.

then the cost of recruiting and training workers $T(R)$ will be an increasing function of R and the labor cost function will take the form $C(w, N) = T(N/s(w))/s(w)$ in which case it will depend positively on employment. The issue of whether there are diseconomies of scale in recruitment and training turns out to be of some importance.

Now consider the optimal choice of the wage and employment. If we assume the firm has a revenue function $Y(N)$, steady-state profits can be written as

$$\pi = Y(N) - [w + C(w, N)]N \qquad (2.11)$$

A more sophisticated analysis would recognize that recruitment takes time and there is a need to pay attention to the date at which costs are incurred and revenues accrue but the decision problem at the end of the day can normally be written as something that looks like (2.11) (for an explicit justification of this claim, see Manning 2001a).

A difference from the basic monopsony model is that the firm has a choice of the wage it can pay if it wants to maintain employment at N so that both wages and employment are choice variables that can vary independently of each other. Given N, it is optimal for the firm to choose w to minimize direct and indirect labor costs so let us define the function $\omega(N)$ as

$$\omega(N) = \min_{w} w + C(w, N) \qquad (2.12)$$

Profits can then be written as

$$\pi = Y(N) - \omega(N)N \qquad (2.13)$$

A comparison of (2.1) and (2.13) should make apparent the relationship between the model presented here and the basic monopsony model: it is that the labor supply curve $w(N)$ needs to be replaced by the labor supply curve $\omega(N)$. As $\omega(N)$ is the relevant labor supply curve, let us call it the effective labor supply curve. We can represent the decision problem for the employer as in figure 2.1 with $w(N)$ replaced by $\omega(N)$, the effective supply of labor to the firm. Unsurprisingly, it is going to be of some interest whether $\omega(N)$ is increasing in N which would give us the equivalent of an upward-sloping labor supply curve.

By application of the envelope theorem to (2.12), we have

$$\omega'(N) = C_N(w(N), N) \qquad (2.14)$$

where $w(N)$ is the wage chosen if employment is N. Hence, the effective labor supply curve facing the firm is upward-sloping if the labor cost function is increasing in employment, that is, if there are diseconomies of scale in recruitment and training. If the level of employment has no impact on recruitment and training costs, then the effective labor supply curve facing the firm will be infinitely elastic and will resemble the labor supply curve in a perfectly competitive market. Given this discussion, it should be apparent that the form of the labor cost function $C(w, N)$ is of some importance.[4] The labor market is "monopsonistic" if $C_N > 0$ so that the non-wage costs are increasing in employment and "competitive" if $C_N = 0$.

There is a reasonable argument that the labor cost function $C(w, N)$ should be used in all the analysis that follows, and that analysis suggests we should focus on the effective labor supply function $\omega(N)$ rather than the labor supply function $w(N)$. However, this is hard to do as we rarely have the requisite data on non-wage labor costs like training and recruitment costs. However, in chapter 10 we present some evidence that $C_N > 0$ so that there are diseconomies of scale in recruitment activity.

All of the models considered so far in this chapter have been partial equilibrium models in which the influence of factors external to the individual firm have been buried in its labor supply curve, $N(w)$. One could introduce general equilibrium considerations by explicitly allowing the actions of other firms to affect the supply of labor to the firm (or the labor cost function). But, such an approach would inevitably be ad hoc and it is best to construct an explicit general equilibrium model of an oligopsonistic labor market to check that the model as a whole is internally consistent. This is the subject of the next section.

2.4 A General Equilibrium Model of Oligopsony

Any general equilibrium model of oligopsony must model interactions between employers in an internally consistent manner. There are a number of ways in which this has been done in the literature: for example, Bhaskar and To (1999) use a Hotelling-style location model. Here we outline another such model developed by Burdett and Mortensen (1998) which can be thought of as a general equilibrium version of the dynamic monopsony model described in section 2.2. The assumptions made about the labor market are the following.[5]

(A1) Workers: There are M_w workers all of whom are equally productive and attach equal value, b, to leisure.

(A2) Employers: There are M_f employers, each of which is assumed to

---

[4] More detailed analysis of the comparative statics of the generalized model of monopsony can be found in Manning (2001a).

[5] These assumptions have been chosen to be the simplest possible whilst retaining the essential features of an oligopsonistic labor market. Many of these assumptions are relaxed at various points in the book or in other papers in the literature.

be infinitesimally small in relation to the market as a whole.[6] All employers have constant returns to scale, the productivity of each worker being p. For future use, denote the ratio of firms to workers by $M = M_f/M_w$.

(A3) Wage-setting: Employers set wages once-for-all to maximize steady-state profits (which is equivalent to assuming there is no discounting). All workers within a firm must be paid the same wage. Denote the cumulative density function of wages across employers by $F(w)$ and the associated density function by $f(w)$.

(A4) Matching Technology: Both employed and non-employed workers receive job offers at a rate λ. Job offers are drawn at random from the set of firms, that is, from the distribution $F(w)$. Employed workers leave their jobs for non-employment at an exogenous job destruction rate δ_u. All workers, both employed and non-employed, leave the labor market at a rate δ_r, to be replaced by an equal number of workers who initially enter non-employment. For future use, define $S = S_u + S_r$.

These assumptions are simpler than those used in Burdett and Mortensen (1998) but capture the essence of their model. Now, consider the equilibrium in the basic model.

The Behavior of Workers

The behavior of workers in this labor market is very simple. An employed worker will move to another job whenever a wage offer above the current wage is received. A non-employed worker will accept a job whenever the wage offer received is above some reservation wage, r. As job offers arrive at the same rate whether employed or non-employed, the decision to accept a current job offer has no consequences for future job opportunities. So, the job will be taken if it makes a worker better off now than they would be if non-employed, that is, if the wage exceeds the value of leisure. Hence, the reservation wage, the lowest wage for which workers will be prepared to work will simply be equal to b, the value of leisure. Later, in chapter 9, we analyze the determinants of the reservation wage in a more complicated setup where on- and off-the-job searches differ in their effectiveness.

The Employer's Decision

The employer's decision in this model is to choose the wage to maximize profits $\pi = (p - w)N(w; F)$ where $N(w; F)$ is the steady-state level of employment in a firm that pays a wage w when the distribution of wages in the market as a whole is F. So, prior to considering the profit

[6] Note that this assumption implies that employers do not have to be "large" to possess market power.

maximization decision, we need to consider employment determination.

Employment Determination

An employer who pays a wage w will recruit workers from among the non-employed (as long as w is larger than the reservation wage b) and from workers in other firms that pay less than w. The employer will lose workers who exit to non-employment or leave the labor force or who quit to other firms that pay higher wages. In general terms, if $s(w; F)$ is the separation rate and $R(w; F)$ is the recruitment rate, we must have in a steady state that

$$s(w; F)N(w; F) = R(w; F) \tag{2.15}$$

so that $N(w; F)$ is the level of employment at which the flow of recruits equals the flow of separations. In deriving $N(w; F)$, a very useful result is the following.

Proposition 2.2. *If $\infty > \lambda/\delta > 0$, the equilibrium must be a distribution of wages without any spikes.*

Proof. See Appendix 2.

The result that the equilibrium of this model must have wage dispersion even though all agents (both workers and firms) are assumed identical is the most striking feature of Burdett and Mortensen (1998). The intuition for it is not that easy to understand but the result comes from the fact that if there is a wage paid by a non-negligible fraction of employers, then paying an infinitesimally higher wage means that the employer starts to recruit workers from these employers leading to a discontinuous jump in the number of workers but only an infinitesimal fall in profits per worker. Hence, profits must rise and the initial situation could not have been in equilibrium.

The proposition implies that the equilibrium outcome must be a wage distribution with a continuous cumulative density function, $F(w)$. As all firms are identical but, in equilibrium, choose different wages which yield the same level of profit, there is an indeterminacy in equilibrium in the sense that which firms choose which wages is not defined and one might think there is a potential problem in ensuring that the right distribution of wages results from the uncoordinated choices of firms. This is a common problem in much of economic theory where the equilibrium involves mixed strategies. But, it is not a real problem here. The smallest differences in firms will result in a fully determinate equilibrium (see chapter 8).

As it is reasonable to believe that firm heterogeneity exists, the model presented here should be thought of as the limiting equilibrium as firm heterogeneity disappears.

From the analytical point of view this proposition is extremely convenient as it means that we can restrict attention to wage distributions $F(w)$ that are continuous. From a more practical point of view, the result has both advantages and disadvantages. The advantage is that the model can explain the existence of equilibrium wage dispersion, the well-documented fact that equally productive workers receive different wages according to who they work for (see, e.g., Lester 1946, 1952; Slichter 1950; Reynolds 1951; Dunlop 1957; Krueger and Summers 1988; amongst others). The disadvantage is that we do observe concentrations of workers (or "spikes") at particular points in wage distributions, often at the minimum wage or at "round" numbers.[7]

Now, consider how we can derive the supply of labor to a firm who pays a wage w. From (2.15) it is helpful to derive the separation and recruitment rate separately. The separation rate in a firm that pays w is

$$s(w; F) = \delta + \lambda[1 - F(w)] \qquad (2.16)$$

as workers leave for non-employment at a rate δ, receive other job offers at a rate λ and a fraction $[1 - F(w)]$ of these offers are better than their current wage.

Deriving the flow of recruits to the firm, $R(w; F)$, is slightly more complicated. It is helpful to first derive the non-employment rate and the distribution of wages across workers.

The Non-Employment Rate

The non-employment rate, u, is simply given by

$$u = \frac{\delta}{\delta + \lambda} \qquad (2.17)$$

as workers leave employment for non-employment at a rate δ and obtain jobs at a rate λ.

The Distribution of Wages Across Workers

The distribution of wages across firms is denoted by $F(w)$. This is not the same as the distribution of wages across workers as the systematic search by workers for better-paying jobs means that they will be concentrated in

---

[7] Modifying the model to allow for the existence of spikes (e.g., because of mobility costs) is likely to increase the monopsonistic elements in the model so moves us even further away from the competitive model than the current framework.

higher-wage firms. Denote by $G(w; F)$ the fraction of employed workers receiving a wage w or less when the wage offer distribution is F. The following proposition shows that there is a simple relationship between G and F.

Proposition 2.3. *The fraction of workers in employment receiving a wage w or less is given by*

$$G(w; F) = \frac{\delta F(w)}{\delta + \lambda[1 - F(w)]} \tag{2.18}$$

Proof. See Appendix 2.

From inspection of (2.18) one can see that $G(w; F) < F$ for $0 < F < 1$ so that workers are concentrated in the better-paying jobs, implying that such firms must have a higher level of employment. This is easy to understand: higher-wage firms have lower separation rates and higher recruitment rates so that they have more workers in a steady state. Some special cases may help the understanding of (2.18): as $\lambda \to 0$ so that opportunities to move up the job ladder once in employment are reduced, then $G(w; F) \to F(w)$ so the distribution of wages across workers converges to the distribution of wages across firms. On the other hand, as $\lambda \to \infty$ so that opportunities to move up the job ladder once in employment come at a very fast rate then $G(w; F) \to 0$ if $F(w) < 1$ and $G(w; F) \to 1$ if $F(w) = 1$ so that all workers end up in the firm that pays the highest wage.

The Flow of Recruits to a Firm

Now let us go back to deriving the level of employment in a firm that pays w. Recruits to this firm will come from non-employment and those employed in lower-wage jobs. There are $\lambda u M_w$ non-employed workers who receive job offers which are shared equally over the M_f firms so that the flow of non-employed recruits to the firm will be $\lambda u M_w / M_f = \lambda u / M$. Similarly, there are $\lambda(1 - u)G(w; F)M_w$ workers currently earning less than w who get job offers which again are spread over the M_f firms. So, the total flow of recruits to a firm that pays w is given by

$$R(w; F) = \frac{\lambda}{M}[u + (1 - u)G(w; F)] = \frac{\delta\lambda}{M[\delta + \lambda(1 - F(w))]} \tag{2.19}$$

where the second equality follows from use of (2.17) and (2.18). Combining (2.15), (2.16), and (2.19), we finally have the following expression:

$$N(w; F) = \frac{\delta\lambda}{M[\delta + \lambda(1 - F(w))]^2} \qquad (2.20)$$

for the supply of labor to the firm. This captures the most important idea in the analysis of monopsonistic labor markets, namely that the labor supply to an individual firm is increasing in the wage paid so that the labor supply curve facing an individual firm is not infinitely elastic as is assumed in perfect competition. Employment is increasing in the wage because the separation rate is decreasing in the wage (a higher wage means workers are less likely to get a better job offer) and the flow of recruits is increasing in the wage (a higher wage means there are more workers in lower-wage firms).

The wages paid by other firms are also important in determining the supply of workers to a firm. In fact, in (2.20) the position of the firm in the wage offer distribution is a sufficient statistic for the supply of labor to the firm. This is not true in more general models but one should still think of the supply of labor to the firm as being determined by the wage offered relative to the alternatives of non-employment or employment in other firms.

The Employer's Decision Revisited

Given (2.20), profits can be written as

$$\pi(w; F) = \frac{\delta\lambda(p - w)}{M[\delta + \lambda(1 - F(w))]^2} \qquad (2.21)$$

Every firm will choose its wage to maximize profits.

Equilibrium

We need to find an equilibrium wage distribution $F(w)$. $F(w)$ will be an equilibrium if two conditions are satisfied:

- all wages that are offered yield the same level of profits;
- no other wage yields a higher level of profits than a wage that is offered.

For the special model considered here, one can (as Burdett and Mortensen 1998 showed) derive a closed-form expression for the equilibrium wage distribution w. The easiest way to derive this equilibrium is in stages.

Proposition 2.4. *The lowest wage offered in equilibrium is the reservation wage, b.*

Proof. See Appendix 2.

The intuition for this result is simple. There is no point in an employer paying a wage lower than b as no workers will accept such a low wage offer and employment and profits will be zero. And there is no point in the lowest-wage employer paying a wage strictly above b as, from (2.20), the supply of labor to the firm is a function of its position in the wage distribution (F) and not the actual wage paid. So, cutting the wage to b will lead to the same level of employment but higher profits per worker.

Given that the lowest wage offered is b (which is also the reservation wage), the equilibrium level of profits, π^*, can be found by using this fact in (2.21) to give

$$\pi^* = \frac{\delta\lambda(p - b)}{M[\delta + \lambda]^2} \tag{2.22}$$

The equilibrium wage distribution $F(w)$ can then be found by equating (2.21) to (2.22). After some re-arrangement this leads to the following.

Proposition 2.5. *The offered wages lie in the interval*

$$b \le w \le p - \left(\frac{\delta}{\delta + \lambda}\right)^2 (p - b) \tag{2.23}$$

and, within this interval, the equilibrium wage offer distribution is given by

$$F(w) = \frac{\delta + \lambda}{\lambda}\left[1 - \sqrt{\frac{p - w}{p - b}}\right] \tag{2.24}$$

The equilibrium wage distribution across workers, $G(w)$, is given by

$$G(w) = \frac{\delta}{\lambda}\left[\sqrt{\frac{p - b}{p - w}} - 1\right] \tag{2.25}$$

The expected wage, $E(w)$, is given by

$$E(w) = \frac{\delta}{\delta + \lambda}b + \frac{\lambda}{\delta + \lambda}p \tag{2.26}$$

Proof. See Appendix 2.

Let us now discuss some implications of these results.

2.5 Perfect Competition and Monopsony

The formulae for the equilibrium wage offer distribution and the wage distribution are not very intuitive.[8] But the formula for the expected wage is simple, saying that the expected wage is a weighted average of the marginal product of labor and the reservation wage (the value of leisure), the weight on the marginal product being an increasing function of (λ/δ), the ratio of the arrival rate of job offers to the job destruction rate.

In equilibrium, all workers get paid a wage below their marginal product (note that the upper bound for wages in (2.23) is below p). This contrasts with the perfectly competitive labor market in which workers receive a wage equal to their marginal product. One might wonder about the relationship between the equilibrium here and the perfectly competitive equilibrium. It turns out that perfect competition is a special case in which job offers arrive infinitely fast for employed workers.

Proposition 2.6. *As $(\lambda/\delta) \rightarrow \infty$, the distribution of wages across workers collapses to the perfectly competitive equilibrium in which all workers get paid their marginal product, p.*

Proof. Take the limit of (2.26) and note that $E(w) = p$ implies all workers get paid p as no workers ever get paid more than p.

This proposition corresponds well with our notion of perfect competition as a market in which there is fierce competition among employers for workers and the high arrival rate of job offers means that the threat of workers leaving if they are paid a low wage is a very real one. As the result implies that perfect competition is a special (but extreme) case of our labor market, conclusions reached using a competitive analysis are not inevitably wrong; they will be correct or nearly correct if labor market frictions are small. But it is important to correct the impression that those who believe that employers have some market power over workers are extremists—the reality is that those who believe in perfect competition are the fanatics as perfect competition is one point at the edge of the parameter space and every other point in the parameter space gives employers some monopsony power. But, although it is extreme to assume the labor market is frictionless, it may be that this is a good approximation to reality if the frictions are "low." It would be helpful to have some quick way of deciding the extent of monopsony power possessed by employers.

---

[8] Indeed, they should not be taken too literally as the wage distribution of (2.25) has an increasing density, a prediction that is at variance with empirical observation. There is a literature (see van den Berg and Ridder 1998; Mortensen 1998; Bontemps et al. 1999, 2000) which extends the basic model to make its predictions more consistent with the observation while preserving its qualitative features. This is discussed in more detail in section 4.8.

2.6 A Simple Measure of Monopsony Power

What limits the ability of employers to lower wages is the ability of workers to leave for another employer. So, one way to understand the result in Proposition 2.6 is that a high arrival rate of job offers makes the workers' quit threat more powerful and increases direct competition among employers for workers. The extent to which workers do freely move among employers is then likely to be a good way to measure the extent of competition in the labor market.[9] But the separation rate itself is not a good measure of labor market competition as it does not matter much to employers if workers quit freely if there is a high flow of workers recruited from non-employment to replace them. In terms of Proposition 2.6, one can see that it is (λ/δ) that is important and not just λ. A simple statistic that captures this idea is the proportion of recruits that come from other firms. The higher this proportion the more intense the competition among employers and the lower we would expect the extent of monopsony to be.

This is likely to be a good "back-of-the-envelope" measure of the extent of labor market competition in many models of the labor market but the following proposition verifies the intuition by showing that, in the simple Burdett–Mortensen model, the proportion of recruits from non-employment is a monotonic function of (λ/δ).

Proposition 2.7. *The higher the fraction of recruits from non-employment, the more monopsonistic is the labor market. The fraction of recruits from non-employment in the Burdett–Mortensen model is given by*

$$\frac{\lambda}{\delta + \lambda} \frac{1}{\ln\left(\frac{\delta + \lambda}{\delta}\right)} \tag{2.27}$$

and is monotonically decreasing in (λ/δ).

Proof. See Appendix 2.

(2.27) demonstrates that the fraction of recruits from non-employment is a function of the ratio of the job offer arrival rate to the job

[9] This implicitly assumes that threats to quit if paid low wages do, in equilibrium, turn into actual quits. Some economists are inclined to argue that threats can be important even if they are never actually carried out so may not like the statistic proposed here to measure the extent of competition in labor markets. But, Proposition 2.7 shows that, although the limiting competitive case of the Burdett–Mortensen model has no wage dispersion among workers, there is a very large amount of actual worker mobility that lies behind this.

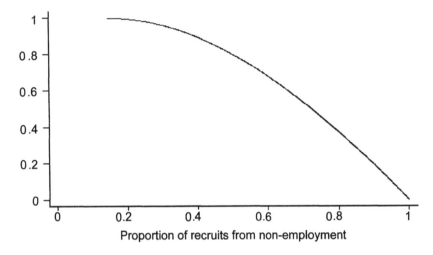

Figure 2.2 The relationship between the weight on marginal product and the proportion of recruits from non-employment.
Notes. The weight on the marginal product in the expected wage is derived from (2.26) so the left-hand axis is $\lambda/(\lambda + \delta)$. The relationship between this variable and the fraction of recruits from non-employment is given by (2.27).

offer destruction rate so is related to the indices of monopsony power described above. The relationship between the fraction of recruits from non-employment and $\lambda/(\lambda + \delta)$ is represented in figure 2.2. Remember that, from (2.26), $\lambda/(\lambda + \delta)$ is also the weight on the marginal product in the expression for the expected wage and the labeling of figure 2.2 reflects this. As one can see, the relationship is non-linear: if the proportion of recruits from non-employment is below 25% the weight on productivity in the expected wage will be above 98%. But if the proportion of recruits from non-employment is 50%, the weight will be only 80%. This discussion suggests that a simple but crude way of getting some a priori idea of the extent of monopsony is to examine the proportion of recruits that come from non-employment.

The main labor market surveys, the Current Population Survey (CPS) for the United States and the Labour Force Survey (LFS) for the United Kingdom, can be used for this purpose. Both the CPS and LFS are rolling panels: in the CPS, individuals are in the sample for four consecutive months, followed by four months out and then another four months in. In the LFS, individuals are in the sample for five successive quarters. Neither the CPS nor the LFS allow us to directly observe the fraction of recruits that were previously in non-employment as they do not contain continuous data on employment. Our approach is to approximate the proportion by considering new recruits and recording whether their labor market status at the previous wave was employment or non-employment. As the time interval between observations on labor market status in the CPS is only a month, this is likely to be a reasonably good estimate.[10] The quarterly time interval in the LFS is perhaps more problematic.

Both the CPS and the LFS are address-based surveys so that individuals who move address between surveys are dropped from the sample. This is not a problem if the fraction of recruits from non-employment is the same for those who change address and those who do not, but one would like to be reassured on this. Fortunately, the LFS does contain information that allows us to infer labor market transition rates for those who move address. We would expect that, for every individual who leaves a sample address (a "mover-out" in the jargon), there is someone who moves into a sample address (a "mover-in"). As all employed workers are asked about their job tenure in their current job, and those who report being in their current address less than 3 months are asked about their labor market status 3 months ago,[11] one can use this information to compute the fraction of recruits from non-employment for the movers-in. In practice, this makes very little difference (47% of new recruits who are movers-in having come from non-employment as compared to 44% for the residential stayers).

Table 2.1 presents some statistics on the fraction of recruits from non-employment using the data sets described above. In the CPS, the fraction of new recruits who were not employed a month ago is 55%. This proportion includes the 5% who reported being on temporary lay-off last month. Quite how those on temporary lay-offs should be treated is

---

[10] In fact, in a labor market in steady-state one can show that the observed proportion of hires from non-employment in a period of unit length is given by $\xi[1 - \exp(-(\delta/\xi)(\xi + (1 - \xi)\theta))]/[1 - \exp(-(\delta/\xi))][(\xi + (1 - \xi)\theta)]$ where ξ is the true proportion, θ is the ratio of the rate at which the non-employed find jobs to the rate at which the employed change jobs, and δ is the rate of entry into non-employment. There is a bias to the extent that θ differs from 1. As one would expect that $\theta > 1$, one can show that one is likely to understate the proportion coming from non-employment.

[11] There is some reason to believe that the responses to such retrospective questions understate labor market transition rates. For the LFS we can get some information on this as, each spring, individuals are asked about their labor market status one year ago. For those in the final wave, this answer can be compared to the one they gave a year ago in the first wave. Overall the accuracy is high: over 95% of individuals for whom we have panel information and retrospective information gave answers to the retrospective questions that were consistent with the panel information. But this overall figure hides an important difference in the consistency of response: for those whose labor market states were the same in the two years (assuming the panel information is correct) about 98% gave consistent answers. But, for those who had made a labor market transition, the proportion of consistent answers fell to about 78% (the nature of the transition does not matter). However, we are using information on quarterly transitions here so we might expect this problem to be less serious.

TABLE 2.1
The Proportion of Recruits from Non-employment

Country	Data Set	Sample	Period of Observation of Labor Market Status	Fraction of Recruits from Non-employment
US	CPS	1998–99, age 18–60	Monthly	0.551
US	CPS	1998–99 (ignoring temp lay-offs), age 18–60	Monthly	0.525
UK	LFS	1992–99, age 18–60	Quarterly	0.443
UK	BHPS	1990–98, age 18–60	Continuous	0.465

Notes.
1. The fraction of recruits from non-employment is computed by taking all those in new jobs and computing the fraction for whom the economic activity before starting the job was non-employment.

not clear and it is hard to work out whether those now in employment have returned to the job from which they were originally laid off. So, the second row simply excludes them: this slightly lowers the proportion previously non-employed to 52%. The third row reports UK estimates from the LFS: the fraction of recruits from non-employment is lower than in the United States, approximately 45%. One might be concerned that this is the result of the fact that observations on employment are only at quarterly intervals. However, the fourth row of table 2.1 reports estimates from the British Household Panel Survey (BHPS) which has a continuous record of employment. The estimate of the proportion of recruits from non-employment is reassuringly similar to that derived from the LFS. So, it does seem that a lower proportion of recruits come from non-employment in the United Kingdom as compared to the United States: this is perhaps the result of the lower flows from employment into non-employment in the United Kingdom.

The aggregate figures in table 2.1 hide a lot of variation across individuals and over time. This is investigated in table 2.2 where probit models for whether an individual has been recruited from non-employment are reported. We first estimate equations for men and women jointly and then separately as there are important differences.

For the United States, table 2.2 suggests that the fraction of recruits from non-employment is higher for women, for young and very old workers, for the less-qualified, for those in full-time education, and for blacks (although the difference is only significant for men). Table 2.2 also shows

TABLE 2.2
Disaggregated Analysis of the Proportion of Recruits from Non-employment

	(1) US: CPS All	(2) US: CPS Women	(3) US: CPS Men	(4) UK: LFS All	(5) UK: LFS Women	(6) UK: LFS Men
Female	0.099			0.037		
	(0.002)			(0.003)		
Experience	0.036	−0.007	0.080	−0.057	−0.091	−0.029
1–5 years	(0.004)	(0.009)	(0.010)	(0.005)	(0.007)	
Experience	−0.015	−0.024	−0.023	−0.062	−0.039	−0.087
6–10 years	(0.004)	(0.010)	(0.011)	(0.006)	(0.008)	
Experience	−0.003	0.025	−0.032	−0.045	0.012	−0.111
11–20 years	(0.004)	(0.008)	(0.010)	(0.005)	(0.007)	
Experience	0.024	0.010	0.046	−0.039	−0.038	−0.040
31–40 years	(0.004)	(0.010)	(0.012)	(0.006)	(0.009)	(0.009)
Experience	0.066	0.062	0.049	0.098	0.127	0.077
41+ years	(0.011)	(0.027)	(0.027)	(0.009)	(0.014)	(0.012)
High school drop- out (US), no qualifications (UK)	0.103 (0.004)	0.109 (0.009)	0.108 (0.009)	0.068 (0.005)	0.074 (0.007)	0.065
Some college (US), A levels (UK)	−0.046 (0.003)	−0.064 (0.008)	−0.035 (0.008)	−0.051 (0.005)	−0.026 (0.007)	−0.060 (0.006)
College degree	−0.115	−0.102	−0.108	−0.059	−0.059	−0.069
	(0.004)	(0.008)	(0.009)	(0.005)	(0.005)	(0.007)
Student	0.158	0.065	0.235	0.244	0.227	0.270
	(0.005)	(0.012)	(0.011)	(0.006)	(0.008)	(0.009)
Black	0.033	0.020	0.103	0.106	0.101	0.112
	(0.018)	(0.039)	(0.038)	(0.014)	(0.019)	(0.021)
Hispanic (US), Asian (UK)	−0.056 (0.018)	−0.031 (0.038)	−0.048 (0.038)	0.104 (0.011)	0.104 (0.016)	0.103 (0.015)
Male employment/ population ratio	−0.130 (0.082)	−0.132 (0.112)	−0.105 (0.118)	−0.093 (0.153)	−0.015 (0.215)	−0.233 (0.219)
Observations	172464	88797	83667	96086	48644	47442
Mean of dependent variable	0.545	0.587	0.501	0.443	0.463	0.422
Pseudo-R^2	0.032	0.021	0.041	0.040	0.035	0.057

Notes.
1. The sample is all those who have just started jobs. The dependent variable is a binary variable taking the value one if the individual was recruited from non-employment.
2. The sample period is 1994–2000 for the CPS and 1992–2000 for the LFS.
3. Reported coefficients are marginal effects. Standard errors in parentheses.
4. Regressors are, as far as possible, defined in the same way for the US and UK data. Where there are unavoidable differences (in education and race), the appropriate variables are defined in the first column.
5. Student is defined as anyone who has not completed full-time education. Qualifications are coded as zero for these individuals. The omitted education category for the United States is a high school graduate and for the United Kingdom someone with O levels.
6. The CPS regressions also include month, year and state dummies. The LFS regressions also include month, year and region dummies.

very similar results for the United Kingdom. Women also have a rather different experience profile in both countries, being more likely to have been recruited from non-employment when they have between 11 and 20 years of experience: this is likely to be associated with withdrawal from and return to the labor market connected with having children. What is worth noting is that those groups that do badly in the labor market in terms of wages also do badly in terms of more frequently being recruited from non-employment. This is in line with the basic prediction of the theory where competition among employers for workers is more intense (and wages end up higher) when a lower fraction of recruits are from non-employment.

The estimated models in table 2.2 also include the prime-age male employment/population ratio to see whether there is cyclical variation in the proportion of recruits from non-employment. For the United Kingdom, the results in Burgess (1993) suggest that the proportion of recruits from non-employment falls as the labor market tightens as job-to-job moves are very pro-cyclical (although Fallick and Fleischman 2001 conclude this is not true for the United States). The results in table 2.2 provide some weak support for this conclusion although the coefficient is never significantly different from zero.[12]

In this section we have proposed that the fraction of recruits from non-employment is a crude but simple measure of the extent of competition among employers for workers. Differences in this measure across different types of workers also mirror wage differences as the theory predicts (although others might also do so).

2.7 Positive and Normative Aspects of Monopsony and Oligopsony

In an oligopsonistic equilibrium, workers are "exploited" in the sense of that term used by Hicks and Pigou: that is, they receive a wage less than their marginal product. But, the word "exploitation" has emotive power that is unfortunate in the current context. In the static model of monopsony it makes sense to use the marginal product of labor as a point of comparison for the wage. The efficient outcome is to set the wage equal to the marginal product and a minimum wage set at that level leads to a first-

---

[12] Although one explanation for this is that most of the variation in the employment/population ratio is absorbed by the time and regional dummies. The United Kingdom does show a remarkable fall in the proportion of recruitments from non-employment from almost 50% in 1992 to just above 35% in 1999, consistent with the rise in employment in the same period. However, there is no noticeable trend in the fraction of recruits from non-employment in the United States over a similar period.

best outcome. However, that is not necessarily true in the models of oligopsony discussed here. Even though Proposition 2.7 says that, in a frictionless market, workers would get paid their marginal product, one cannot wish away the existence of frictions and, given their existence, it is not clear that efficiency would be best served by raising wages to the marginal product. The bulk of this book is positive: about how we can achieve a better understanding of a wide variety of labor market phenomena from the distribution of wages to the provision of training to the impact of minimum wages and trade unions by recognizing that employers have non-negligible market power over their workers. There is little normative content: no judgment is made about whether these things are "good" or "bad," although, as we shall see, the approach taken here does suggest approaching many issues with a more open mind than a fanatical believer in perfect competition might be inclined to do. This emphasis on the positive aspects of the subject is not because the normative issues are unimportant but because the normative concerns are sufficiently complex that it is simply not credible to be able to draw normative conclusions from theoretical introspection or from casual empirical analysis. Justifying this conclusion is the subject of the next chapter: this can be skipped for those who are only interested in the positive implications of oligopsony.

2.8 Implications and Conclusions

The models of this chapter have been highly stylized with assumptions chosen for analytical convenience more than for realism. Nonetheless, they do convey the essence of a labor market with frictions in which employers set wages influenced in part by competition from other employers but in which this competition is not so cutthroat as to enable workers to extract all the surplus from the employment relationship, nor so feeble as to enable employers to get all the surplus.

A lot of the analysis in this chapter has been very formal. But, one should not allow this to distract attention away from the basic insights into the workings of labor markets that the monopsonistic approach provides. The rest of this book is concerned with the determinants of prices and quantities in the labor market, a traditional pre-occupation of microeconomics. The study of prices is essentially the study of the distribution of wages while the study of quantities is the study of the level and distribution of unemployment, the level of employment in firms, and of the quality of labor (as influenced by the acquisition of human capital). The implications of monopsony or oligopsony are summarized briefly for these issues.

In perfect competition we normally think of the distribution of wages as being determined by the distribution of marginal products[13] and attempt to explain wage differentials in cross-section and over time in this way. In a monopsonistic labor market, marginal productivity continues to be an important explanation of wages but other factors are also important. Perhaps the simplest way to see this is to look at the expression for the expected wage in (2.26). Marginal product, p, appears but so does:

- the value of leisure (the reservation wage);
- job offer arrival rates;
- job destruction rates.

As monopsony gives the labor economist a wider menu of possible explanations of the distribution of wages, we might hope for a richer explanation than can be provided when constrained by the straitjacket of perfect competition. In chapters 5 through 8, we show how such an approach can improve our understanding of the distribution of wages. For example, chapter 7 attempts to explain part of the gender wage gap in terms of the different labor market transition rates of men and women. There is also one final factor that is important in influencing wages: luck. The existence of wage dispersion among identical workers means that there is likely to be some part of the distribution of wages that can never be explained by economic factors: some workers will simply have been in the right place at the right time.

The differences in the determinants of quantities in the labor market might appear to be less dramatic, largely because search models are already commonly used to understand both theoretical and empirical aspects of unemployment. For example, in the model presented in this chapter, the level of non-employment is influenced by the job offer arrival rate when non-employed, the job destruction rate, and the level of wages relative to the reservation wage. This is not very different from the usual list of suspects although a strict perfect competition approach would suggest that only a comparison of the marginal product with the value of leisure is relevant.

The rest of the book aims to demonstrate how we can gain a better understanding of labor markets by this less dogmatic approach based on the perspective that employers have some market power.

Before we move on to these positive and empirical issues, the next chapter is concerned with more normative concerns, for example, is the oligopsonistic labor market efficient? and, if not, is the inefficiency of any

[13] Abstracting from compensating wage differentials (discussed in chapter 8) and the fact that marginal products may themselves be endogenous, varying with the level of employment.

particular type? and are there any policy interventions that might be expected to improve the operation of the labor market? This discussion is entirely theoretical: for those uninterested in it, one can summarize the conclusions now:

- the oligopsonistic labor market is not generally efficient;
- it is hard a priori to say anything about the direction of the inefficiency;
- it is hard to make a strong theoretical case for any particular policy intervention.

These conclusions then justify the approach in the rest of the book which is to use the perspective of employer market power to understand a wide variety of labor market phenomena, without making any value judgment as to whether the world could be improved by an appropriate policy intervention.

Appendix 2

Proof of Proposition 2.1

At any date t the state variable for the firm will be the labor force that it had last period, N_{t-1}. Define a value function $\Pi(N_{t-1})$ to be the maximized discounted value of future profits from date t onwards. So, using dynamic programming arguments, we have

$$\Pi(N_{t-1}) = \max_{(w_t, N_t)} Y(N_t) - w_t N_t + D\Pi(N_t) \qquad (2.28)$$

This needs to be maximized subject to a dynamic labor supply curve of (2.4). Note that this dynamic labor supply curve depends only on the current wage: this implicitly assumes workers are myopic. An alternative would assume it depends on the value of the job.

Taking the first-order condition of (2.28) with respect to w_t and taking account of the dependence of N_t on w_t leads to the following first-order condition:

$$[Y'(N_t) - w_t + D\Pi'(N_t)]\frac{\partial N_t}{\partial w_t} - N_t = 0 \qquad (2.29)$$

We also have the envelope condition which allows us to derive the derivative of the value function. Differentiating (2.35) we have that

$$\Pi'(N_{t-1}) = [Y'(N_t) - w_t + D\Pi'(N_t)]\frac{\partial N_t}{\partial N_{t-1}} \qquad (2.30)$$

If the firm is in a steady state (and it is an interesting question whether there is a steady state) where wages and employment are constant, then we can solve (2.30) for $\Pi'(N)$ which leads to

$$\Pi'(N) = \frac{\dfrac{\partial N_t}{\partial N_{t-1}}[Y'(N) - w]}{1 - D\dfrac{\partial N_t}{\partial N_{t-1}}} \tag{2.31}$$

Substituting this into (2.29) and re-arranging, one can derive

$$\frac{Y'(N) - w}{w} = \left[1 - D\frac{\partial N_t}{\partial N_{t-1}}\right]\frac{N_t}{w(\partial N_t/\partial w_t)}$$

$$= \left[1 - D + D\left(1 - \frac{\partial N_t}{\partial N_{t-1}}\right)\right]\frac{N_t}{w(\partial N_t/\partial w_t)}$$

$$= (1 - D)\varepsilon^s + D\varepsilon \tag{2.32}$$

where the last equality follows from the fact that differentiation of (2.4) implies that

$$1 - \frac{\partial N_t}{\partial N_{t-1}} = s$$

and the relationship between the short- and long-run elasticities implied by (2.8).

Proof of Proposition 2.2

Suppose there is a mass of firms offering the wage w. If $w = p$, then all these firms must be making zero profits. A firm that lowers its wage can make higher profits as long as it can retain some workers in steady state, that is, as long as its separation rate is finite and its recruitment rate positive. A non-zero, finite value of (λ/δ) guarantees this.

If there is a mass of firms paying $w < p$ then consider what happens if a firm deviates by paying an infinitesimally higher wage. Profit per worker is only infinitesimally reduced but the number of workers is measurably higher (as long as $\lambda > 0$) as recruits now come from workers in all the firms who continue to pay w. Hence, profits must rise and the initial situation could not have been in equilibrium.

Proof of Proposition 2.3

The simplest way to prove Proposition 2.4 is by equating inflows and outflows from the group of workers earning w or less. The outflow rate from this group will be $[\delta + \lambda(1 - F(w))]$ as workers leave the group either to non-employment or to better-paying jobs. Recruits to this group must come from non-employment as no workers who earn more than w will ever accept a wage offer less than w. There are $M_w u$ non-employed workers who receive offers less than w at a rate $\lambda F(w)$. So the flow of recruits to jobs paying less than w will be $\lambda F(w) M_w u$. Equating inflows and outflows, we then have

$$[\delta + \lambda(1 - F(w))](1 - u)G(w; F)M_w = \lambda F(w)uM_w \qquad (2.33)$$

as total employment of those earning w or less will be $(1 - u)G(w; F)M_w$. Using (2.17) leads, after some re-arrangement, to (2.18).

Proof of Proposition 2.4

Suppose a firm pays below b. This firm will have no workers so will make zero profits which cannot be an equilibrium.

Suppose the lowest wage offered is strictly above b. The lowest-wage firm will only recruit workers from non-employment at a rate $(\lambda u/M)$ and will lose workers whenever they get another job offer, that is, at a rate $(\delta + \lambda)$. So, employment in the lowest-wage firm will be given by

$$\frac{\lambda u}{M[\delta + \lambda]} = \frac{\delta \lambda}{M[\delta + \lambda]^2} \qquad (2.34)$$

that is, independent of the wage offered. If the lowest-wage firm cuts its wage (but not below b) the recruitment and separation rate will be unchanged and hence so will employment. But, profit-per-worker will rise so profits will increase. This means the original situation could not have been in equilibrium.

Proof of Proposition 2.5

Equating (2.21) and (2.22) leads to (2.24) after some re-arrangement. The right-hand side of (2.23) is then just the value of the wage that makes $F = 1$. (2.25) comes from (2.18) and (2.24).

Now the expected wage can be written as

$$E(w) = \frac{M_f \int wN(w; F)f(w)dw}{M_f \int N(w; F)f(w)dw} = p - \frac{M_f \int (p - w)N(w; F)f(w)dw}{M_w(1 - u)}$$

$$= p - \frac{M \int \pi^* f(w)dw}{(1 - u)} = p - \frac{M\pi^*}{(1 - u)} = p - \frac{\delta(p - b)}{\delta + \lambda} \qquad (2.35)$$

where the second equality follows from the fact that the two denominators in the first line are both expressions for total employment; the third equality follows from the fact that, in equilibrium, $(p - w)N$ must be the same for all firms; and the final equality follows from (2.22) and (2.17).

Proof of Proposition 2.6

The recruits to position F in the wage distribution, $R(F)$, can be written as

$$R(F) = \lambda u M_{\text{w}} + \lambda M_{\text{w}}(1 - u)G(F) = \frac{\lambda \delta M_{\text{w}}}{\delta + \lambda(1 - F)} \qquad (2.36)$$

where $G(F)$ is the fraction of workers employed at position F or below and is given by (2.18). Note that the position in the wage distribution is a sufficient statistic for the number of recruits so we do not have to worry about the actual wage paid. Using the fact that F must be distributed uniformly over the unit interval, we have that the total flow of recruits in the economy is given by

$$R = \int_0^1 R(f)df = M_{\text{w}} \int_0^1 \frac{\lambda \delta df}{\delta + \lambda(1 - f)} = M_{\text{w}} \delta \ln\left(\frac{\delta + \lambda}{\delta}\right) \qquad (2.37)$$

As the flow of recruits from non-employment is $\lambda M_{\text{w}} u$, this gives (2.27) for the fraction of recruits from non-employment.

3

Efficiency in Oligopsonistic Labor Markets

Discussions of the partial equilibrium static model of monopsony often emphasize that the free market equilibrium is inefficient in a very particular way. Both the wage and employment are too low and full efficiency can be restored by ensuring that the wage is equal to what it would be in a perfectly competitive labor market. One way of achieving this outcome is by means of an artfully chosen minimum wage. This chapter considers whether general equilibrium models of oligopsony allow such clear-cut policy prescriptions: the conclusion is that they do not, although there is no presumption that the "free market" equilibrium is efficient.

This chapter discusses the efficiency issue using the Burdett and Mortensen (1998) model introduced in chapter 2. The simple version of the model presented in the previous chapter cannot provide an adequate analysis of efficiency because the equilibrium is fully efficient as all matches between unemployed workers and firms are consummated. Any distribution of the surplus between employer and workers is consistent with this equilibrium outcome. For example, any minimum wage up to the level of p, the marginal product of workers, results in the same outcome in terms of employment and only affects the division of the surplus between wages and profits.

But, this conclusion is the result of simplifying assumptions made for expositional reasons. Efficiency is not an interesting issue in this version of the model because very few decisions of employers and workers are free to respond to incentives. However, there are a number of ways in which one might modify the model to endogenize decisions of both firms and workers so that they can be affected by incentives.

First, the model of the previous chapter assumed that the supply of both workers and firms to the market is inelastic, that is, the number of workers and firms in the market are fixed at M_w and M_f, respectively. A natural way to introduce incentives is to assume that the supply of both firms and workers is not inelastic. For firms, the simplest way to do this is to assume that there is free entry (i.e., to go to the opposite extreme and to assume that the supply of firms to the market is perfectly elastic). For workers, one could make an analogous assumption that a fixed cost (perhaps the cost of acquiring skills necessary for employment) must be paid to enter the labor market but there are alternative ways to make the overall labor supply have some elasticity. For example, section 3.4 discusses the case where there is heterogeneity in the value of leisure (hence the reservation wage) so that not all workers will be interested in every job.

But, even once agents have decided to participate in the market there are other decisions that might be influenced by incentives. For example, firms can decide how much effort to spend in looking for recruits and workers can decide how hard to look for work. Jointly, these decisions about search intensity can be expected to determine the arrival rate of job offers, λ.

Agents may make some investments in match quality before a match is realized. For example, workers may make decisions about how much human capital to acquire before they start looking for a job. And firms may have to commit capital to jobs before they start looking for workers for those jobs. Both of these decisions will be affected by expected future returns to the agents.

All of these "margins" of decision are likely to be present in reality. But, to include all of them simultaneously in a model of the labor market is a recipe for indigestion. Consequently, this chapter presents only the simplest possible models to make the relevant points. The models examined in sections 3.1–3.5, their main conclusions, and their implications for one particular policy intervention (the minimum wage) are summarized in table 3.1.

TABLE 3.1
The Structure of the Chapter

Section	Model	Efficiency of Free Market	Optimal Minimum Wage
3.1	Free entry of firms (perfectly elastic supply of firms to the market)	Too many firms, employment too high	Minimum wage to ensure appropriate division of surplus
3.2	Endogenous recruitment activity of firms	Too much recruitment, employment too high	Minimum wage to ensure appropriate division of surplus
3.3	Free entry of workers (perfectly elastic supply of workers to the market)	Too few workers in labor force, employment too low	Minimum wage to ensure appropriate division of surplus
3.4	Heterogeneity in reservation wages	Employment too low	Minimum wage equal to marginal product
3.5	Heterogeneity in reservation wages + free entry of firms	Employment may be too high or too low	Minimum wage may not be desirable

58   CHAPTER 3

The main conclusions of sections 3.1–3.5 are as follows:

- there are good reasons to believe the free market equilibrium is inefficient;
- it is hard to say anything a priori about the direction of the inefficiency;
- it is hard to make unambiguous predictions about policy from theoretical
  models alone.

Thus, issues of efficiency are more complicated and subtle in general
equilibrium dynamic models of oligopsony than the static partial equilibrium textbook model of monopsony might suggest. The conclusion that
theory provides little in the way of a guiding principle is, in many ways,
an unsatisfying one as it suggests a failure to find the most general result.
One might wonder whether one can find better guidance elsewhere in the
literature.

Other "search" models of the labor market have discussed whether the
free market equilibrium is likely to be efficient. This debate probably
started with Friedman's (1968) celebrated article on the natural rate of
unemployment. Commentators like Tobin (1972) argued that the free
market equilibrium was likely to be inefficient and there have been papers
on the subject ever since (e.g., Albrecht and Jovanovic 1986; Hosios
1990; Moen 1997; Acemoglu and Shimer 2000; among others). Many
(though not all) of the papers appear to arrive at sweeping conclusions
but readers must recognize that they are based on very specific models and
are not robust to reasonable changes in the assumptions.[1] Perhaps there is
a result to be derived about the efficiency or otherwise of the free market
in a class of reasonably general models. Armed with such a result, there
might also be general prescriptions about policies to get to the first-best
(the Coase Theorem and the prescription to define property rights springs
to mind as an example from another part of economics). But, a combination of lack of intellect and laziness on the part of this author means this
book does not provide such a general result and it certainly does not exist
in the current literature. My conjecture is that, whenever a model of the
labor market is proposed that has strong conclusions, one will be able to
provide another, observationally equivalent, model with different conclusions. If this conjecture is correct, theory alone is not going to help us very
much. This conclusion is similar in spirit to that of Lucas and Prescott
(1974, p. 206) who criticized Tobin's (1972) conclusion that the free
market *must* be inefficient while recognizing that "the question of

---

[1] For example, Albrecht and Jovanovic (1986, p. 1256), conclude that "in contrast to the
competitive equilibrium, the monopsonistic equilibrium is shown to be inefficient involving
too much search and too little employment." This is, of course, a correct conclusion in their
model but the model is not a general one and the conclusion would be relatively simple to
overturn.

whether there exist important external effects in *actual* labour markets, remains, of course to be settled."

The plan of the chapter is as follows. Section 3.1 considers the welfare properties of the equilibrium when there is free entry of firms, section 3.2 when employers can choose their level of recruitment activity. Section 3.3 then considers the case where there is free entry of workers and section 3.4 assumes some heterogeneity in the reservation wages of workers. Section 3.5 puts together the model of the sections 3.1 and 3.4, illustrating how the whole is rather different from the sum of the parts. Section 3.6 shows how easy it is to generate multiple equilibria in models of oligopsony, a feature that is potentially useful in explaining a range of phenomena from agglomeration to ghettoes.

3.1 Free Entry of Firms

In this section the basic Burdett–Mortensen model of section 2.4 is extended to the case where there is a perfectly elastic supply of firms to the market so that the number of firms is M_f is endogenous. To produce an equilibrium with a finite number of firms one needs to assume that there is a fixed cost of entry which we will denote by C_f. Firms enter until profits are equal to C_f. Using results derived in the previous chapter, equilibrium profits are given by (2.22). The number of firms affects profits as it affects $M (= M_f/M_m)$. But it also plausibly affects λ, the arrival rate of job offers for workers. Suppose that the number of matches between workers and firms is given by $m(M_w, M_f)$. It is conventional and convenient (for a recent survey, see Petrongolo and Pissarides 2001) to assume that the matching function has constant returns to scale so that the arrival rate of job offers for workers can be written as

$$\lambda = \frac{m(M_w, M_f)}{M_w} = m(1, M) \equiv \lambda(M) \tag{3.1}$$

where $\lambda(M)$ is an increasing concave function of its argument so that a fall in the number of firms reduces the arrival rate of job offers for workers. M will be given by the level at which profits are equal to C_f. Taking account of (3.1) and (2.22), one can write this free entry condition as

$$\frac{\delta\lambda(M)(p - b)}{M[\delta + \lambda(M)]^2} = C_f \tag{3.2}$$

By differentiating the left-hand side of (3.2) one can readily verify that profits are a strictly decreasing function of M if $\lambda(M)$ is an increasing concave function of M so that (3.2) defines a unique equilibrium.

Now, let us consider the efficient level of M. If the non-employment rate is u, then a fraction $(1 - u)$ of workers are in employment producing p, while a fraction u are not in work which has a value b. In addition, the total fixed costs paid in the economy are $M_f C_f$. Hence, the total social surplus can be written as

$$\Omega(M) = M_w[(1 - u)p + ub] - M_f C_f = M_w\left[p - \frac{\delta(p - b)}{[\delta + \lambda(M)]} - MC_f\right]$$
(3.3)

where the second equality follows from the non-employment rate of (2.17).[2]

The following proposition summarizes the efficiency of the free market equilibrium.

Proposition 3.1

1. *The free market has too many firms if $\lambda(M)$ is a strictly concave function of M.*

2. *The first-best can be attained by setting a minimum wage, w_m, which satisfies*

$$\frac{p - w_m}{p - b} = \varepsilon_{\lambda M} \equiv \frac{M\lambda'(M)}{\lambda(M)}$$
(3.4)

where M is the efficient number of firms relative to workers.

Proof.   See Appendix 3.

The intuition as to why the free market equilibrium has too many firms is that some of the employment of new entrants comes not just from workers who would otherwise be unemployed but also from those employed in other firms. While this source of employment is a private gain, it has no social purpose. The second part of the proposition shows that a well-chosen minimum wage can attain the first-best, although the case for a minimum wage is that the minimum wage causes exit of firms from the market and reduces employment but these are "good" things. This argument for minimum wages is slightly curious as proponents of minimum wages do not often argue for it on the grounds that it destroys

---

[2] Note that this specification of the welfare function assumes risk neutrality on the part of workers. If workers are risk averse, then the wage dispersion that is characteristic of the free market equilibrium has a welfare cost and there would be a case for policies to reduce this dispersion.

jobs. One should note that policies other than the minimum wage could be used to attain the first-best. For example, one could pay unemployment benefits to ensure that the reservation wage of workers is w_m or one could use a profits tax.

One interpretation of (3.4) is that the share of the total surplus going to the employer in the lowest-wage firm should be equal to the elasticity of the matching function with respect to the number of firms. This is outwardly very similar to the efficiency rule derived by Hosios (1990) in the context of a Diamond–Pissarides matching model in which wages are determined by an ex post sharing rule. There is one important difference, namely that (3.4) refers only to the sharing of the surplus in the lowest-wage firm. The employer's share of the surplus in all the other firms will be lower than that given in (3.4) as they all pay wages higher than w_m. This is important, because knowledge of the Hosios rule might have led one to conclude that, because workers do get a share of the surplus in the basic Burdett–Mortensen model, it is not obvious a priori whether wages are too high or too low. As the above discussion has made clear, wages are unambiguously too low.

3.2 Endogenous Recruitment Activity

In this section, firms are allowed to influence the flow of recruits by expenditure on recruitment activity. For the moment, assume that the number of firms, M_f, is exogenously given. Denote by z the intensity of the recruitment activity of the firm. Define z so that, other things being equal, the arrival rate of workers to the firm is proportional to z. Assume that the cost of z is given by a function $c(z)$. One could interpret this cost function narrowly as the cost of advertisement but it is probably better to think of it more widely as the cost of recruitment and training new employees as the administrative costs of handling applications and the induction of new workers are typically much larger than the direct costs of job advertisements.

In equilibrium there will be some function $z(w)$ which relates recruitment activity to the wage paid. Denote by Z the average level of recruitment activity in the economy as a whole, that is, assume Z is given by

$$Z = \int z(w)dF(w) \qquad (3.5)$$

Make the simplifying assumption that the rate at which job offers arrive to workers depends on Z as well as M so can be written as $\lambda(Z, M)$. Assume that an individual employer's share of these matches is given by (z/Z). The equilibrium can be described by the pair of functions

$\{z(w), F(w)\}$ which give the distribution of wages across firms and the recruitment intensity associated with each wage.

The following proposition summarizes the nature of equilibrium and its efficiency.

Proposition 3.2

1. *In equilibrium, all firms recruit at the same intensity, z, which is given by*

$$\frac{\delta\lambda(z, M)(p - b)}{M[\delta + \lambda(z, M)]^2} = zc'(z) \tag{3.6}$$

2. *The free market has too much recruitment activity, if $\lambda(z, M)$ is a strictly concave function of z.*

3. *The first-best can be attained by setting a minimum wage, w_m, which satisfies*

$$\frac{p - w_m}{p - b} = \varepsilon_{\lambda z} \equiv \frac{z\lambda_z(z, M)}{\lambda(z, M)} \tag{3.7}$$

Proof. See Appendix 3.

The first part of this proposition says that (whatever their chosen wage) all firms spend the same amount on recruitment activity in equilibrium. Paying a higher wage encourages recruitment expenditure as a higher fraction of workers contacted will be interested in the job and the expected job duration of a recruit is longer. But, the profit to be made from each recruit per period is less. So, there are off-setting effects of the wage on the incentives to recruit and the proposition simply says that the equilibrium wage distribution for the case analyzed here is such that these different effects cancel out and the incentives to recruit are independent of the wage.[3]

As in the free entry case of the previous section, the intuition for the excess recruitment activity of the second part of the proposition is that the employment of an extra firm comes not just from workers who would otherwise be unemployed but also at the expense of other firms. And, as in the case of free entry, there are a number of policies that might be used to correct this inefficiency. The final part of the proposition says that a minimum wage that ensures a particular division of the surplus in the lowest-wage firm can attain full efficiency. As long as $\lambda(Z, M)$ is a strictly

---

[3] This intuition also suggests that the independence result will fail if there are decreasing returns to labor or if there is firm heterogeneity. See Mortensen (1998) for an analysis of this case.

concave function of z, it is optimal to have $w_m > b$. But, as in the free entry case, a binding minimum wage will reduce employment as it reduces the recruitment activities of firms. (3.7) has an obvious similarity to the Hosios rule derived for the free entry case in (3.4) except that it is now the elasticity of the arrival rate of job offers with respect to the recruitment intensity that is important. This might make us wonder what happens if we combine free entry and endogenous recruitment activity. It is fairly simple to show that a simple minimum wage now can only attain the first-best if $\varepsilon_{\lambda M} = \varepsilon_{\lambda z}$ (i.e., if the matching function can be written as $\lambda(zM)$). In this case, the two Hosios conditions (3.4) and (3.7) are identical.

So far, we have only considered decisions of firms that respond to incentives. Even then, there is reason to believe that wages are "too low" although the other side of this coin is that employment is "too high." But, as discussed in the introduction, some decisions of workers are also likely to respond to incentives. The following sections introduce this topic.

3.3 Elasticity in Labor Supply: Free Entry of Workers

The basic Burdett–Mortensen model of section 2.4 assumed that the supply of workers to the labor market is inelastic. This section introduces some elasticity into labor supply in a very simple way: by assuming that, to participate in the labor market, individuals must pay an up-front cost of C_w. This is a crude way of introducing some elasticity in labor supply (an alternative is discussed in the next section), but it does have the virtue of being a natural analogy to the way some elasticity in the supply of firms to the market was introduced in section 3.1. If pushed, one could interpret the fixed cost as the cost of acquiring the human capital necessary to get employment or as an investment in the skills necessary for job search.

Let us distinguish between the value of being unemployed V^u, the value of non-participation V^n, and the value of being employed at wage w, $V(w)$. The value functions are given by

$$\delta_r V^u = b + \lambda \int_{w_m} [V(x) - V^u] dF(x) \qquad (3.8)$$

$$\delta_r V^n = b + C_w \qquad (3.9)$$

$$\delta_r V(w) = w - \delta_u [V(w) - V^u] + \lambda \int_w [V(x) - V(w)] dF(x) \qquad (3.10)$$

where w_m is the lowest wage. (3.9) captures the fact that those who choose non-participation also save the fixed cost C_w. Free entry of workers means that, in equilibrium, we must have $V^u = V^n$. The following proposition summarizes the important results.

Proposition 3.3

1. *The free market equilibrium has too few workers in the market.*

2. *The first-best can be attained by setting a minimum wage such that:*

$$\frac{p - w_m}{p - b} = \varepsilon_{\lambda M} \qquad (3.11)$$

Proof. See Appendix 3.

(3.11) should, by now, be a familiar formula. The share of the surplus in the lowest-wage firm should, for efficiency, be equal to the elasticity of the arrival rate of job offers with respect to M. Because the share of workers in the surplus in the lowest-wage firm is zero in the free market equilibrium, wages are in some sense "too low" and too few individuals choose to participate in the labor market.

The effect of a minimum wage on this labor market differs from that in the labor market with free entry of firms. A binding minimum wage causes more individuals to participate in the labor market and total employment rises so that the employment/population ratio rises. But, the unemployment rate also rises as the increase in the number of agents in the labor market causes some crowding-out of job opportunities.

This section has made the supply of workers to the market perfectly elastic. Without further modification, one could not combine this model with free entry of firms as the scale of activity in the economy would then be indeterminate (for versions of this model in which there is an arbitrary degree of elasticity in the supply of both firms and workers to the market, see Manning 2001b). The next section takes a different approach to introducing some elasticity into the supply of labor to the market.

3.4 Elasticity in Labor Supply: Heterogeneity in Reservation Wages

In the models discussed so far, all workers have been assumed to have the same value of leisure, b, which, given our other assumptions, is also the reservation wage. This section modifies the model and assumes that there is some heterogeneity in b. Denote the cumulative density function of b by $H(b)$ and the associated density function by $h(b)$. It is helpful (although not essential) to assume that $H(b)$ is log-concave. For convenience, assume that $H(p) = 1$ so that all workers have $b \leq p$.[4] Furthermore, assume that b is not observed by employers so that wage offers cannot be conditional on it. As a result, not all wages that are offered in equilibrium will be attractive to all workers. If a worker has value of leisure b (which will also be their reservation wage), then only a fraction $[1 - F(b)]$ of jobs will be desired.

The following proposition analyzes this case.

Proposition 3.4

1. *The free market equilibrium is inefficient with employment too low.*

2. *A minimum wage equal to p can restore full efficiency.*

Proof. See Appendix 3.

In this model, employment is, in general, too low. It is efficient to consummate all matches with $p \geq b$ yet matches are only consummated when $w \geq b$. Because $w < p$, some efficient matches are not consummated. If the number of firms (and their recruitment activities) are fixed, then attaining the first-best is simple: set a minimum wage equal to p and the inefficiency disappears. As in the other models discussed in this chapter, there is an efficiency case for a minimum wage but, now, a binding minimum wage is associated with increases in employment. This model is the closest oligopsony model to the static monopsony model as both employment and wages are too low in the free market equilibrium and full efficiency can be restored by ensuring wages are equal to marginal products.

However, this discussion has assumed that the supply of firms is completely inelastic: the next section considers what happens when we introduce an elastic supply of firms as in the model of section 3.1.

3.5 Heterogeneity in Reservation Wages and Free Entry of Firms

In this section we combine the model of the previous section with the model of section 3.1 in which there is a completely elastic supply of firms to the market.

One might have thought that because a minimum wage can improve efficiency in the two constituent models (the free entry model of section 3.1

---

[4] If $b > p$ there is no point in a worker being in the labor market as they will never be able to find employment at a wage acceptable to them.

and the heterogeneous reservation model of section 3.4), it must be of potential benefit in the current model. But, the following proposition shows that this is not necessarily the case.

Proposition 3.5

1. *Social surplus may be increasing or decreasing in the number of firms.*

2. *A just-binding minimum wage may increase or reduce efficiency.*

Proof.   See Appendix 3.

This result is an example of the general principle of the second-best, that moving towards the first-best in one dimension may worsen welfare. In this case, a binding minimum wage, because it reduces the number of firms, tends to reduce the social surplus if there are too few firms in equilibrium, and may reduce the social surplus. The intuition for the ambiguity about the optimal number of firms is that, on top of the congestion effect which tends to lead to too many firms in the free market equilibrium, the entry of a new firm now improves the wage offer distribution which results in more workers being in employment thus increasing efficiency.

What policies can attain efficiency in this case? It should be readily apparent that a simple minimum wage can no longer lead to the first-best outcome. To consummate all efficient matches, the minimum wage would need to be equal to p but this results in no firms entering the market. So, a minimum wage of p would need to be combined with a subsidy to the entry of firms.

It should be apparent that we have quickly arrived at a point where theory provides little guidance about the nature of inefficiency in the free market equilibrium and the types of policies that might help. One could proceed further to consider more complicated models combining all the decisions we have endogenized here and even adding new ones. But, the payoff from this strategy is likely to be small as the qualitative conclusions we have drawn are unlikely to be altered.

3.6 Multiple Equilibria in Models of Oligopsony: An Application to Ghettoes

All the oligopsony models presented so far in this chapter have a single equilibrium. But, it is important to realize that it is relatively simple to produce oligopsony models with multiple equilibria that may further complicate welfare analysis. This is because of the way in which supply and demand factors interact in markets with frictions: it is possible that, in a sense to be made clearer below, "supply can create its own demand" (and vice versa).

In a frictionless competitive market, there is a sense in which it is good to be unique (because of diminishing marginal productivity). If one acquires some specialized skill that requires some specialized capital with which to work, there is no problem in meeting the person with that capital or in inducing someone to make that specific capital investment. However, in a market with frictions, uniqueness is not necessarily an advantage. If employers have to make some ex ante investment in creating jobs, they may not choose to make that investment if the chance of finding a suitable person to fill those jobs is very low. In that case, an increase in the supply of workers of a particular type may encourage employers to create jobs tailored for that type of worker and hence create its own demand. The problem is that there is no mechanism to ensure that an individual act of investment by either worker or employer will be matched by the equivalent investment on the other side of the market that is necessary for the investment to have its full effect. This problem is a potent source of multiple equilibria.

There are numerous examples of this type of model in the economics literature, probably beginning with Diamond (1982) but including Acemoglu (1998) and Machin and Manning (1997), among others. They can be used to explain a number of potentially important facts: why some countries are industrialized and others are not, and the phenomenon of agglomeration.

Here, we illustrate these ideas by presenting a simple model of how ghettoes may arise. The stylized picture of the ghetto is that of an area where both wages and employment are lower than in neighboring areas. This does seem to have something to do with the disadvantage experienced by certain ethnic groups as, in the United States, inclusion of family background variables plus good measures of educational attainment (e.g., the AFQT in the NLSY) seems to be able to eliminate much, if not all, of the observed black–white wage differential (see Neal and Johnson 1996; Altonji and Blank, 1999).[5] This suggests paying attention to pre-market factors more than labor market outcomes in looking for the origins of the black–white wage differential. Some of these pre-market factors (e.g., family background) may be the product of more explicit racial discrimination that undoubtedly existed in the past, while others may be the result of the poorer quality of education typically received by blacks. But, it is also possible that some of it represents decisions not to acquire human capital that are rational given the economic situation faced.

[5] Although there is a debate about whether the AFQT test scores themselves contain a racial bias.

As a simple example of this type of mechanism, consider the Burdett–Mortensen general equilibrium model of an oligopsonistic labor market discussed in section 2.4. But modify it, so that workers, before they enter the labor market, are assumed to have a choice about the level of human capital they acquire. This will determine their productivity p. We assume that acquiring productivity of p requires a cost of $c(p)$. We also assume that the distribution of wages facing a working of productivity p is $F(w; p)$ as given by (2.24). This implies that firms offer a different wage to workers of each quality level.

Given this, p will be chosen to maximize $V^u - c(p)$. In a frictionless market, workers with quality p would earn p with probability 1 for their entire life of expected length $(1/\delta_r)$. Hence, workers would invest to the point where $\delta_r c'(p) = 1$.

In a labor market with frictions we can prove the following proposition.

Proposition 3.6

1. *The optimal choice of p is given by*

$$\delta_r c'(p) = \left(\frac{\lambda}{\delta + \lambda} \right)^2 \tag{3.12}$$

    assuming an interior solution.

2. *The optimal p is increasing in λ tending to the competitive level as $\lambda \to \infty$.*

Proof. See Appendix 3.

Unsurprisingly, Proposition 3.6 says that the faster the rate of job offers arrive, the greater the incentive to invest in human capital and that human capital investment will approach the competitive level as the labor market becomes frictionless. So we would expect p as a function of λ to be something like the line marked "investment decision of workers" in figure 3.1.

Now consider the investment level by firms. Let us model this investment decision as a simple entry decision. Assume, as in section 3.1, that entry requires a fixed investment of cost C_f, and that M_f firms enter the market. We will assume that the rate at which job offers present themselves to workers depends on M_f so that we have $\lambda(M_f)$. Invert this function to write $M_f(\lambda)$. In equilibrium, the number of firms is determined by the free entry condition so that

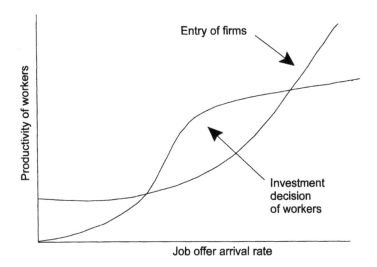

Figure 3.1 Multiple equilibria in the model of a ghetto.

$$\frac{\delta\lambda(p - b)}{M_f(\lambda)[\delta + \lambda]^2} = C_f \tag{3.13}$$

This gives λ as an increasing function of p with $\lambda \to \infty$ as $p \to \infty$. A possible outcome is given by the line marked "entry of firms" in figure 3.1. Inspection of figure 3.1 shows the possibility of multiple equilibria. As drawn, one can argue that only the high-level equilibrium is stable but one could always draw pictures with more than two stable equilibria. If this is the case then high-level equilibria will have high levels of human capital investment, high wages, high employment rates, and many firms. The differences in labor market outcomes can all be "explained" by differences in productivity but these differences in productivity are themselves the result of the poor expected labor market outcomes.

In this model, firms do not invest in the ghetto because of the poor "quality" of workers who live there. The residents do not invest in improving their skills because there are no jobs. A vicious circle is at work.

3.7 Conclusions

This chapter has considered the issue of efficiency in a number of theoretical models of oligopsonistic labor markets. It has one positive message: the free market must not be presumed efficient. But, beyond this, theory has been shown to provide little guidance about the direction of the efficiency or policies that might be expected to improve matters. Employment may be too "high," or too "low." A minimum wage may raise employment or reduce it. If a theoretical paper claims a strong conclusion about the direction of inefficiency in the free market equilibrium, then this is almost certainly because they have not considered a rich enough model in the sense that there are not enough "marginal" decisions to be influenced by incentives. This chapter has introduced three such margins: elasticity in the supply of firms to the market, elasticity in the supply of workers, and endogenous recruitment intensity, and has shown how the nature of the inefficiency induced by each of them is rather different. As discussed in the introduction, there are other margins and these may be as important. We have introduced only enough to make the point that theory alone is going to be an unreliable guide to policy-making.

The rest of the book concentrates on positive rather than normative implications of employer market power. Even though the word "monopsony" conjures up emotive images of workers being exploited (in the sense of the word used by Hicks and Pigou) by employers, one should resist such temptations. Monopsony should simply be taken to mean that the supply of labor to the firm is not perfectly elastic. Although a recurrent theme is that the perspective of monopsony encourages one to be more open-minded about the likely impact of a range of policies than a strict believer in perfect competition would be inclined to be, the book is primarily concerned with what labor market phenomena can be better understood from the perspective of monopsony.

Appendix 3

Proof of Proposition 3.1

The derivative of the social surplus with respect to M is

$$\Omega'(M) = \frac{\delta\lambda'(M)(p - b)}{[\delta + \lambda(M)]^2} - C_f \tag{3.14}$$

At the free market level of M we have, using (3.2), that

$$\Omega'(M) = C_f\left[\frac{M\lambda'(M)}{\lambda(M)} - 1\right] < 0 \tag{3.15}$$

where the final inequality follows from the fact that $\lambda(M)$ is a strictly concave function of M. (3.15) implies that there are too many firms in the free market equilibrium and that the social surplus would be maximized by having fewer firms.

A binding minimum wage of w_m becomes the lowest wage offered in equilibrium. Hence, the profits made by the lowest-wage firm (and hence the equilibrium level of profits) is given by the left-hand side of

$$\frac{\delta\lambda(M)(p - w_m)}{M[\delta + \lambda(M)]^2} = C_f \tag{3.16}$$

and the equilibrium number of firms will solve (3.16). If this is to be equal to the socially efficient level of M (the level that solves $\Omega'(M) = 0$), it must be the case that

$$\frac{p - w_m}{p - b} = \frac{M\lambda'(M)}{\lambda(M)} \tag{3.17}$$

where the right-hand side should be evaluated at the efficient level of M: this is (3.4).

Proof of Proposition 3.2

Denote by $M_w(1 - u)G(w)$ the number of workers in equilibrium who are employed at a wage w or less:[6] this is the notation used previously in chapter 2.

Consider the flow of recruits to a firm that spends z on recruitment and offers a wage w. The fraction of total matches of workers to firms is given by the share of this firm in total recruitment activity, that is, by (z/Z). Of these matches only those involving employed workers in a job currently paying less than w or who are unemployed result in recruitment so that the flow of recruits to the firm is given by

$$R(w, z) = \frac{z}{Z}\left[\frac{\lambda(Z, M)}{M}(1 - u)G(w) + \frac{\lambda(Z, M)}{M}u\right] \tag{3.18}$$

Steady-state employment will be given by $N(w) = R/s(w)$ where $s(w)$ is the separation rate so that profits can be written as

$$\pi(w, z) = (p - w)\frac{(z/Z)[\lambda(Z, M)(1 - u)G(w) + \lambda(Z, M)u]}{M[\delta + \lambda(1 - F(w))]} - c(z)$$

$$\equiv \frac{z}{Z}\pi(w) - c(z) \tag{3.19}$$

where $\pi(w)$ is the term in (3.19) that does not involve z. (w, z) will be chosen by firms to maximize (3.19). For this profit maximization to be well defined, we obviously require that $c(\cdot)$ be convex, otherwise profits can be increased without bound. All combinations of (w, z) that are offered in equilibrium must yield the same level of profit. Maximizing

---

[6] These functions will also depend on $\{z(w), F(w)\}$ but this is suppressed to keep the notation simple.

(3.19) with respect to z while holding w constant leads to the conclusion that the optimal z will be a positive function of π and, by the envelope theorem, total profits must then be an increasing function of π. As all firms must make the same level of profits in equilibrium, $\pi(w)$ and, hence z, must be constant across firms. Given this fact, a comparison of (3.19) and (2.21) shows that, conditional on the chosen z, the distribution of wages must be the same as in the basic model derived in section 2.4.

Is the level of recruitment activity efficient? The social surplus can be written as

$$\Omega(z, M) = M_w[(1 - u)p + ub] - M_f c(z) - M_f C_f$$

$$= M_w\left[p - \frac{\delta(p - b)}{[\delta + \lambda(z, M)]} - MC_f - Mc(z)\right] \qquad (3.20)$$

The first-order condition for the derivative of Ω with respect to z is

$$\Omega_z(z, M) = \frac{\delta\lambda_z(z, M)(p - b)}{[\delta + \lambda(z, M)]^2} - Mc'(z) \qquad (3.21)$$

where a subscript denotes a derivative with respect to that variable. At the free market level of z we have, using (3.6), that

$$\Omega_z(z, M) = Mc'(z)\left(\frac{z\lambda_z(z, M)}{\lambda(z, M)} - 1\right) < 0 \qquad (3.22)$$

where the final inequality follows from the fact that $\lambda(z, M)$ is assumed to be a concave function of z. (3.22) implies that there is excessive recruitment activity in the free market equilibrium and that the social surplus would be increased by reducing recruitment activity.

A binding minimum wage of w_m becomes the lowest wage offered in equilibrium. Hence, the level of z chosen by firms in the free-market equilibrium will be given by

$$\frac{\delta\lambda(z, M)(p - w_m)}{M[\delta + \lambda(z, M)]^2} = zc'(z) \qquad (3.23)$$

If this is to be equal to the socially efficient level of z, from (3.21) it must be the case that

$$\frac{p - w_m}{p - b} = \frac{z\lambda_z(z, M)}{\lambda(z, M)} \qquad (3.24)$$

where the right-hand side should be evaluated at the efficient level of z.

Proof of Proposition 3.3

Differentiate (3.10) to yield

$$\frac{\partial V(w)}{\partial w} = \frac{1}{\delta + \lambda(1 - F(w))} \tag{3.25}$$

Now integrating the integral term in (3.8) by parts and using (3.25), we can obtain

$$\int_{w_m} [V(x) - V^u]dF(x) = [V(w_m) - V^u] + \int_{w_m} \frac{\partial V(x)}{\partial x}[1 - F(x)]dx \tag{3.26}$$

Now, using (3.10), we have that

$$[V(w_m) - V^u] = \frac{w_m - b}{\delta + \lambda} \tag{3.27}$$

Using (3.25), (3.26) and (3.27) in (3.8) then leads to the following expression for V^u:

$$\delta_r V^u = b + \frac{\lambda}{\delta + \lambda}(w_m - b) + \int_{w_m} \frac{\lambda[1 - F(x)]dx}{\delta + \lambda(1 - F(x))} \tag{3.28}$$

Integrating the final integral term in (3.28) by parts yields

$$\delta_r V^u = b + \frac{\lambda}{\delta + \lambda}(w_m - b) + \int_{w_m} (x - w_m)\frac{\delta\lambda f(x)dx}{[\delta + \lambda(1 - F(x))]^2} \tag{3.29}$$

Using (2.20), this can be written as

$$\delta_r V^u = b + \frac{\lambda}{\delta + \lambda}(w_m - b) + M\int_{w_m} (x - w_m)N(x)f(x)dx \tag{3.30}$$

Using the expression for the aggregate non-employment rate in (2.17), this can be written as

$$\delta_r V^u = b + \frac{\lambda}{\delta + \lambda}(w_m - b) + \frac{\lambda}{\delta + \lambda}[E(w) - w_m]$$

$$= b + \frac{\lambda}{\delta + \lambda}(E(w) - b) \tag{3.31}$$

Now, in equilibrium, it must be the case that

$$(p - w)N(w) = (p - w_m)N(w_m) \tag{3.32}$$

for all offered wages. Taking expectations, using (2.17) and (2.20) for the lowest-wage firm and rearranging, yields

$$E(w) = p - \frac{\delta}{\delta + \lambda}(p - w_m) \tag{3.33}$$

Substituting this into (3.31) leads to

$$\delta_r V^u = b + \frac{\lambda}{\delta + \lambda}(w_m - b) + \frac{\lambda^2}{(\delta + \lambda)^2}(p - w_m) \qquad (3.34)$$

In the free market equilibrium we must have $V^u = V^n$ and $w_m = b$. Using (3.9) and (3.34), the free market entry condition can be written as

$$\frac{\lambda(M)^2}{(\delta + \lambda(M))^2}(p - b) = C_w \qquad (3.35)$$

To derive the social surplus, assume that wages are always equal to p so all the social surplus goes to workers. Then, the value functions, (3.8) and (3.10), become

$$\delta_r V^u = b + \lambda[V(p) - V^u] \qquad (3.36)$$

$$\delta_r V(p) = p + \delta_u[V^u - V(p)] \qquad (3.37)$$

which implies that

$$\delta_r V^u = b + \frac{\lambda(p - b)}{\delta + \lambda} \qquad (3.38)$$

Now the total social surplus is $(V^u - V^n)M_w$ as V^u is the lifetime expected utility of a worker entering the labor market. This, using the fact that $M = M_f/M_w$, yields

$$\Omega(M) = \left[\frac{\lambda(M)}{\delta + \lambda(M)}(p - b) - C_w \right] \frac{M_f}{M} \qquad (3.39)$$

Differentiating (3.42), we obtain

$$\Omega'(M) = -\left[\frac{\lambda(M)}{\delta + \lambda(M)}(p - b) - C_w \right] \frac{M_f}{M^2} + \frac{\delta\lambda_M(M)}{[\delta + \lambda(M)]^2}(p - b)\frac{M_f}{M} \qquad (3.40)$$

which, using (3.35) to eliminate $(p - b)$ in (3.40) yields, after some rearrangement,

$$\Omega'(M) = \frac{\delta M_f C_w}{\lambda M^2}[\varepsilon_{\lambda M} - 1] < 0 \qquad (3.41)$$

so that there are too few workers entering the labor market. This proves part 1 of Proposition 3.3.

Now consider part 2. If we set $\Omega'(M) = 0$, then (3.40) can be written as

$$\frac{\lambda(M)}{\delta + \lambda(M)}(p - b) - C_w = \frac{\delta M\lambda_M(M)}{[\delta + \lambda(M)]^2}(p - b) \qquad (3.42)$$

If $V^u = V^n$, then from (3.34) and substituting the expression for C_w, the equilibrium condition for efficiency can be written as

$$\frac{\lambda(M)}{\delta + \lambda(M)}(p - w_m) - \frac{\lambda(M)^2}{[\delta + \lambda(M)]^2}(p - w_m) = \frac{\delta M \lambda_M(M)}{[\delta + \lambda(M)]^2}(p - b) = C_w$$

$$(3.43)$$

which, on rearrangement, leads to (3.11).

Proof of Proposition 3.4

In proving this proposition, it is helpful to first prove the following lemma on the equilibrium of the model.

Lemma 3.1

1. *If a firm pays a wage w, the supply of labor to it, N(w) will be given by*

$$N(w; F) = \frac{\delta \lambda H(w)}{M[\delta + \lambda(1 - F(w))]^2} \qquad (3.44)$$

2. *The lowest wage offered in the free market equilibrium, w_0, is the solution to*

$$w_0 = \text{argmax}(p - w)H(w) \qquad (3.45)$$

3. *The equilibrium level of profits, π^*, is given by*

$$\pi^* = \frac{\delta \lambda(p - w_0)H(w_0)}{M[\delta + \lambda]^2} \qquad (3.46)$$

4. *The equilibrium wage offer distribution is found by solving*[7]

$$\frac{(p - w)H(w)}{[\delta + \lambda(1 - F(w))]^2} = \frac{(p - w_0)H(w_0)}{[\delta + \lambda]^2} \qquad (3.47)$$

Proof. For workers with a reservation wage b, the non-employment rate will be

$$u(b) = \frac{\delta}{\delta + \lambda[1 - F(b)]} \qquad (3.48)$$

as only a fraction $[1 - F(b)]$ of job offers are acceptable.

---

[7] One might be concerned that the solution $F(w)$ to (3.47) need not be a legitimate distribution function as it is possible that it decreases for some w. If this occurs, the equilibrium wage distribution is the upper envelope of the solution to (3.47). But log-concavity of $H(w)$ is sufficient to ensure the solution to (3.47) is a legitimate distribution function.

Define $M(w)$ to be the number of workers with a wage less than w. By analogy to the argument used in deriving Proposition 2.3, we must have

$$[\delta + \lambda(1 - F(w))]M(w) = \lambda M_w \int^w [F(w) - F(b)]u(b)h(b)db \quad (3.49)$$

as unemployed workers with reservation wage b accept jobs paying w or less at a rate $\lambda[F(w) - F(b)]$. The supply of labor to an individual firm can then be written as

$$[\delta + \lambda(1 - F(w))]N(w; F) = \frac{\lambda}{M_f}\left[M(w) + M_w \int^w u(b)h(b)db\right] \quad (3.50)$$

Substituting (3.48) and (3.49) into (3.50) leads, after some rearrangement to (3.44) which proves part 1.

Using (3.44), profits can be written as

$$\pi(w; F) = \frac{\delta\lambda(p - w)H(w)}{M[\delta + \lambda(1 - F(w))]^2} \quad (3.51)$$

Suppose the lowest wage is above w_0 as defined by (3.45). Then profits in the lowest-wage firm can be increased by cutting wages to w_0 as $F(w)$ will still be equal to zero. Similarly if the lowest wage is below w_0 then profits can be increased by increasing the wage paid as $(p - w)H(w)$ must rise and $F(w)$ cannot fall.

In equilibrium, all offered wages must yield the same level of profit. Using (3.51) and (3.46) leads to (3.47). This completes the proof of the lemma.

The proof of Proposition 3.4 is now very simple. As long as some offered wage is below the highest value of b, some efficient matches will not be consummated. A minimum wage of p guarantees that this does not happen.

Proof of Proposition 3.5

Suppose the social planner is choosing the number of firms. They obviously want to maximize employment for all those with $p > b$ so that the social surplus can be written as

$$\Omega(M) = \left[\frac{\lambda(M)}{\delta + \lambda(M)} \int(p - b)h(b)db - MC_f\right]M_w \quad (3.52)$$

and the first-order condition for the efficient level of M can be written as

$$\Omega'(M) = \left[\frac{\delta\lambda'(M)}{[\delta + \lambda(M)]^2} \int(p - b)h(b)db - C_f\right]M_w = 0 \quad (3.53)$$

Using (3.46), we have that at the free market equilibrium, C_f is equal to the level of profits given by (3.47). Hence, the derivative of the social surplus with respect to M is

$$\Omega'(M) = \frac{\delta\lambda(M)}{M[\delta + \lambda(M)]^2}\left[\varepsilon_{\lambda M}\int(p - b)h(b)db - (p - w_0)H(w_0)\right]M_w$$

(3.54)

The sign of this is ambiguous. One the one hand, $\varepsilon_{\lambda M} < 1$ which tends to make (3.54) negative implying there are too many firms. On the other hand,

$$(p - w_0)H(w_0) = \int^{w_0}(p - w_0)h(b)db < \int^{w_0}(p - b)h(b)db$$

$$< \int(p - b)h(b)db$$

(3.55)

which tends to make (3.54) positive. This proves the first part of the proposition.

If the unemployment rate of workers with reservation wage b is $u(b)$, then total surplus per worker can be written as

$$\Omega = \int(p - b)h(b)db - \int(p - b)u(b)h(b)db - MC_f$$ (3.56)

Now, if the lowest wage paid is w_m (that might be determined by a binding minimum wage), then using (3.48), this can be written as

$$\Omega = [p - E(b)] - \frac{\delta}{\delta + \lambda}\int^{w_m}(p - b)h(b)db - \int_{w_m}^{\hat{w}}\frac{\delta(p - b)h(b)db}{\delta + \lambda[1 - F(b)]}$$

$$- \int_{\hat{w}}(p - b)h(b)db - MC_f$$

(3.57)

where $\hat{w}$ is the highest wage.

Now, from (3.47) we can eliminate $F(b)$ from the third term on the right-hand side of (3.57) and write Ω as

$$\Omega = [p - E(b)] - \frac{\delta}{\delta + \lambda}\int^{w_m}(p - b)h(b)db$$

$$- \frac{\delta\sqrt{(p - w_m)H(w_m)}}{\delta + \lambda}\int_{w_m}^{\hat{w}}\frac{(p - b)h(b)db}{\sqrt{(p - b)H(b)}}$$

$$- \int_{\hat{w}}(p - b)h(b)db - MC_f$$

(3.58)

and the free entry condition can be written as

$$\frac{\delta\lambda(M)(p - w_{\mathrm{m}})H(w_{\mathrm{m}})}{M[\delta + \lambda(M)]^2} = C_{\mathrm{f}} \tag{3.59}$$

From the free entry condition, we have that the effect of the minimum wage on the number of firms is given by

$$\left[\frac{\lambda'(M)}{\lambda(M)} - \frac{1}{M} - \frac{2\lambda'(M)}{\delta + \lambda}\right]\frac{\partial M}{\partial w_{\mathrm{m}}} = -\frac{\Psi'(w_{\mathrm{m}})}{\Psi(w_{\mathrm{m}})} \tag{3.60}$$

where $\Psi(w) \equiv (p - w)H(w)$. Note that a minimum wage set at w_0 (i.e., just binds) will have no effect on the number of firms as $\Psi'(w_0) = 0$. But a minimum wage above w_0 will have $\Psi'(w_m) < 0$.

Now, differentiating (3.58), we have that

$$\frac{\partial\Omega}{\partial w_{\mathrm{m}}} = \left[\frac{\delta}{[\delta + \lambda]^2}\int^{w_{\mathrm{m}}} (p - b)h(b)db\right.$$

$$+ \frac{\delta\sqrt{(p - w_{\mathrm{m}})H(w_{\mathrm{m}})}}{[\delta + \lambda]^2}\int_{w_{\mathrm{m}}}^{\hat{w}} \frac{(p - b)h(b)db}{\sqrt{(p - b)H(b)}}\left.\right]\lambda'(M)\frac{\partial M}{\partial w_{\mathrm{m}}}$$

$$- \frac{\delta\Psi'(w_{\mathrm{m}})}{2\sqrt{\Psi(w_{\mathrm{m}})}[\delta + \lambda]}\int_{w_{\mathrm{m}}}^{\hat{w}} \frac{(p - b)h(b)db}{\sqrt{(p - b)H(b)}} - C_{\mathrm{f}}\frac{\partial M}{\partial w_{\mathrm{m}}} \tag{3.61}$$

Using (3.60) to eliminate the term in $\Psi'(w_{\mathrm{m}})$, one can write this as

$$\frac{\partial\Omega}{\partial w_{\mathrm{m}}} = \frac{\partial M}{\partial w_{\mathrm{m}}}\left[\frac{\delta\lambda'(M)}{[\delta + \lambda]^2}\int^{w_{\mathrm{m}}} (p - b)h(b)db\right.$$

$$+ \frac{\delta\sqrt{\Psi(w_{\mathrm{m}})}[\varepsilon_{\lambda M} - 1]}{2M[\delta + \lambda]}\int_{w_{\mathrm{m}}}^{\hat{w}} \frac{(p - b)h(b)db}{\sqrt{(p - b)H(b)}} - C_{\mathrm{f}}\left.\right] \tag{3.62}$$

If the minimum wage just binds, all these terms are zero as they all involve $\partial M/\partial w_{\mathrm{m}}$ which is zero at that point. But, for strictly binding minimum wages we have that $(\partial M/\partial w_{\mathrm{m}}) < 0$ so that the sign of (3.62) is determined by the sign of the terms in the square brackets on the right-hand side. The first term is positive and the others negative, making the overall sign ambiguous.

Proof of Proposition 3.6

From Proposition 3.4 and (3.34) we know that, for the case where the lowest wage is equal to b, the value of being non-employed can be written as

$$\delta_r V^u = b + \left(\frac{\lambda}{\delta + \lambda} \right)^2 (p - b) \qquad (3.63)$$

Maximizing $\delta_r V^u - c(p)$ then leads to (3.12).

4

The Elasticity of the Labor Supply Curve to an Individual Firm

THE single most important idea in this book is that the wage elasticity of the labor supply curve (ε_{Nw} in the notation of previous chapters) is not infinite or close to it. Hence, the most direct way to establish the existence of employer market power over its workers is to estimate the wage elasticity of the labor supply curve facing the firm. Studies of this elasticity are few and far between: one might cite Reynolds (1946a), Nelson (1973), Sullivan (1989), Machin et al. (1993), Boal (1995), Beck et al. (1998), Staiger et al. (1999), and Falch (2001) as an almost complete list. This lack of literature contrasts with entire books written about the demand for labor or the supply of labor by individuals and with the literature on industrial organization on estimating the extent of product market power (for a survey, see Bresnahan 1989). It is testament to the faith that most labor economists have that $\varepsilon_{Nw} = \infty$. But, given the paucity of the literature, this is nothing but faith and some of us might want some evidence that ε_{Nw} is "high" if not infinite.

The plan of this chapter is as follows. The first section discusses the problems of using correlations between wages and employment to estimate the wage elasticity of the labor supply curve facing the firm. We review the literature on the employer size–wage effect, arguing (in the third section) that the evidence suggests that part (though not all) of the employer–size wage effect is the result of an upward-sloping labor supply curve to the individual firm. We argue that, in the absence of good instruments in the form of firm-level demand shocks, it is hard to get a good estimate in this way of the wage elasticity of the labor supply curve facing an individual employer. The fourth section then discusses an alternative method based on using a dynamic monopsony model and estimating the elasticity of separations and recruits with respect to the wage. Finally, the chapter discusses estimates derived from more structural estimation of equilibrium search models.

The main conclusion is that the elasticity of the labor supply curve facing the firm does not seem to be close to infinite but that it is hard to get a very precise estimate of it. An estimate in the region of 2–5 seems to be reasonable. These estimates imply that employers have sizeable amounts of monopsony power: even an elasticity of 5 implies that wages will (using (2.3)) be 17% below the marginal revenue product.

4.1 The Employer Size–Wage Effect

A simple-minded approach to estimating the elasticity of the labor supply curve facing the firm would be to simply regress the log of the wage that the firm pays on the log of employment plus any other variables that might be thought to be important controls. If the market is perfectly competitive we should find a coefficient of zero on employment whereas monopsony would predict it to be positive and the size of the coefficient would give an estimate of the extent of the monopsony power possessed by the firm (as it estimates $\varepsilon = (1/\varepsilon_{Nw})$). There is a large empirical literature that estimates this type of regression and finds a significant positive relationship between wages and employment—what is commonly known as the employer size–wage effect (ESWE). However, an upward-sloping labor supply curve is not the only explanation proposed for the ESWE (for surveys, see Brown and Medoff 1989; Brown et al. 1990; or Oi and Idson 1999) and plausible alternatives need to be considered. Indeed, much of the literature on the ESWE does not even consider an upward-sloping labor supply curve to an individual employer as a possible explanation.[1] This is in spite of the fact that an innocent might think that the first hypothesis an economist would investigate when observing a positive relationship between a price (the wage) and a quantity (employment) is that it is a supply curve. However, Brown and Medoff (1989: 1056) do not manage to identify the cause of the employer size–wage effect and conclude that "our analysis leaves us uncomfortably unable to explain it." Here, we argue that monopsony can fill that void.

Consider a very simple stripped-down model. Assume that firm i has a revenue function which is given by

$$Y_i = \frac{1}{1 - \eta} A_i N_i^{1-\eta} \qquad (4.1)$$

where A_i is a shock to the marginal revenue product of labor (MPRL) curve. On the supply side of the labor market, assume that the wage that the firm pays is given by

$$w_i = B_i N_i^{\varepsilon} \qquad (4.2)$$

---

[1] For example, the otherwise very thorough and even-handed survey of the relationship between employer size and wages of Brown and Medoff (1989) does not mention monopsony at all with the possible exception that there is some discussion of the rather involved and convoluted "labor pools" model of Weiss and Landau (1984) which could be seen as a sort of monopsony model.

where B_i is a shock to the supply curve. These supply shocks could represent differences in local labor market conditions (because of skill or regional differences) or differences in the attractiveness of non-wage attributes in different firms. We are interested in obtaining a consistent estimate of ε, the inverse elasticity of the labor supply curve facing the firm.

The firm will choose a level of employment where the MPRL equals the marginal cost of labor so that the chosen employment level will satisfy

$$A_i N_i^{-\eta} = (1 + \varepsilon) B_i N_i^{\varepsilon} \tag{4.3}$$

or, in log-linear form

$$\log(N_i) = \frac{1}{\varepsilon + \eta} [a_i - b_i - \ln(1 + \varepsilon)] \tag{4.4}$$

where $a = \log(A)$ and $b = \log(B)$. The chosen wage will be given by

$$\log(w_i) = \frac{1}{\varepsilon + \eta} [\varepsilon a_i + \eta b_i - \varepsilon \ln(1 + \varepsilon)] \tag{4.5}$$

(4.4) and (4.5) are easy to understand. Positive shocks to the MRPL cause employment and wages to rise, although there is only an effect on wages to the extent that the employers do have some labor market power ($\varepsilon > 0$). Positive shocks to the labor supply curve cause employment to fall and wages to rise.[2]

Now make the following assumptions about the observability of the shocks (a,b):

$$a_i = \beta_a x_i + \nu_{ai}$$

$$b_i = \beta_b x_i + \nu_{bi} \tag{4.6}$$

where x is a set of explanatory variables observable to the researcher. In the interests of notational simplicity assume that the same variables affect both a and b. Of course, a particular variable can be constrained to affect only demand or supply shocks by imposing the restriction that its coefficient in the other equation is zero. Assume that the shocks ν are independent of x and jointly normally distributed with mean zero and covariance matrix Σ. Denote by σ_a^2 the variance of ν_a, σ_b^2 the variance of ν_b and σ_{ab} the covariance between ν_a and ν_b.

Now consider how one might set about estimating ε. First, one might think about estimating by OLS the relationship between the log wage and

---

[2] The model used here is simple in the sense that it uses a static labor supply curve and assumes the employer can only use the wage to influence the supply of labor to the firm: Appendix 4B presents analyses of dynamic labor supply curves and what happens if the generalized model of monopsony of section 2.3 is used.

log employment controlling for other factors thought to be relevant (the x variables in our notation). If one thought of the aim of this as being to estimate a supply curve facing the firm, then one might think of including only those x variables which affect supply (i.e., exclude those affecting only demand). However, many researchers have not thought of their purpose as estimating the supply curve facing a firm so have not used this argument for excluding some variables. For example, when estimating earnings functions, it is common practice to include employment as simply another regressor and the researcher does not think of their aim as being to estimate a supply curve to the individual firm. So, again, we would like to have some idea of the consequences of using this "kitchen sink" approach or using the regressions of others to estimate ε.

A regression of $\log(w_i)$ on $(\log(N_i), x_i)$ estimates $E(\log(w_i) \mid \log(N_i), x_i)$. The following proposition tells us what we would expect to find.

Proposition 4.1. *Running a regression of* $\log(w_i)$ *on* $(\log(N_i), x_i)$ *estimates*

$$E(\log(w_i) \mid \log(N_i), x_i) = (\varepsilon + \rho(\varepsilon + \eta)) \log(N_i)$$

$$+ \rho \ln(1 + \varepsilon) + (\beta_b - \rho(\beta_a - \beta_b))x_i \quad (4.7)$$

where

$$\rho \equiv \frac{\sigma_{ab} - \sigma_b^2}{\sigma_a^2 + \sigma_b^2 - 2\sigma_{ab}} \quad (4.8)$$

Proof. See Appendix 4A.

(4.7) says that the kitchen sink approach will only give an unbiased estimate of ε if $\rho = 0$ which implies that v_a can be written as v_b plus some uncorrelated noise. A special case of this is when there are no unobserved supply shocks. In this case, all firms have the same labor supply curve (conditional on x) and variation in N caused by unobserved demand shocks will trace out the labor supply curve. In any other situation one will end up with a biased estimate of ε. If v_a and v_b are uncorrelated, the estimate of ε has a downward bias as (4.8) then implies that $\rho < 0$. Intuitively unobserved shifts in the labor supply curve cause wages and employment to move in opposite directions making the slope of the supply curve seem less positive than it really is.

(4.7) can also be used to understand the arguments that the estimated employer size–wage effect overstates the true value of ε (which must be the case if one believes that labor markets are competitive and $\varepsilon = 0$). The two main arguments are unobserved labor quality and compensating wage differentials. One would expect high-quality workers to have a high level of a (as their productivity is high) and a high level of b as b will partly reflect the wages paid by other firms. So, one would expect unobserved labor quality to result in $\sigma_{ab} > 0$. But, from (4.7) and (4.8) this is not sufficient to imply an upward bias: for that we require $\sigma_{ab} > \sigma_b^2$ (or, equivalently that the expectation of $(a - b)$ is increasing in b). If, for example proportional differences in a are reflected in proportional differences in b, then this is exactly the situation in which we obtain an unbiased estimate of ε. However, the fact that workers with high levels of observable skills are more likely to work in large firms does suggest that the condition $\sigma_{ab} > \sigma_b^2$ might be satisfied if the same is true of unobserved skills.[3] One can also understand compensating differentials as a positive correlation between a and b (as the disamenity must have some positive effect on productivity) so that the previous discussion is also relevant for this case. Let us consider the evidence that all of the ESWE can be explained through these effects.

4.2 Competing Explanations for the Employer Size–Wage Effect

Among the strongest contenders for an explanation of the size–wage effect (apart from an upward-sloping labor supply curve) are

- unobserved worker quality;
- compensating wage differentials;
- rent sharing.

All of these possibilities are discussed by Brown and Medoff (1989) in their survey and much of the discussion here is similar.

Table 4.1 presents some basic information on the size–wage effect for the United States (from the April 1993 Contingent Worker Survey (CWS) supplement to the CPS) and the United Kingdom (from the LFS). In both countries, information on employer size is banded, the bands used differing slightly in the two countries. The measure of employer size used is workplace size although the CPS also has information on firm size (which also seems to have a positive impact on wages independent of workplace size). The distribution of workers by establishment size reported in the column headed "sample percentages" is remarkably similar in both countries, the median worker being in a workplace with slightly more than 50 workers.

The column marked (1) for both countries presents estimates of the size–wage effect when there are no other controls in a wage equation. The

---

[3] In the United States, 12.6% of college graduates work in plants with less than 10 employees and 34% in plants with more than 250. For those who are not college graduates, the figures are 26% in plants with less than 10 workers and 24% in those with more than 250. The United Kingdom is similar.

TABLE 4.1
The Employer Size–Wage Effect in the United States and the United Kingdom

Number of Employees	United States (April 1993 CPS)			United Kingdom (LFS)		
	Sample Percentage	(1)	(2)	Sample Percentage	(1)	(2)
1–10	19.9	−0.226 (0.022)	−0.118 (0.019)	18.4	−0.268 (0.004)	−0.151 (0.004)
11–19	} 13.5	−0.044 (0.024)	−0.015 (0.020)	9.5	−0.097 (0.005)	−0.040 (0.004)
20–24				4.4	−0.048 (0.007)	−0.018 (0.005)
25–49	14.9	0	0	12.5	0	0
50–99	13	0.098 (0.024)	0.067 (0.020)	} 55.2	0.157 (0.006)	0.073 (0.006)
100–249	13.1	0.163 (0.024)	0.098 (0.020)			
250+	27.6	0.289 (0.020)	0.182 (0.018)			
Other controls	n.a.	No	Yes	n.a.	No	Yes
Number of observations	7854	7854	7854	220868	220868	220868
R^2	n.a.	0.1	0.36	n.a.	0.07	0.42

Notes.
1. The dependent variable is the log of the hourly wage. The other controls included are marital status, children, experience, tenure (all interacted with gender), region, race, and (for the LFS) month dummies. Standard errors are reported in parentheses.

reference category is a workplace with 25–49 workers. The gap in average log wages between the smallest (1–10 employees in both the CPS and the LFS) and the largest workplaces (250+ employees in the United States, 50+ in the United Kingdom) is 0.515 log points in the United States and 0.425 in the United Kingdom. Introducing controls (the columns marked (2)), reduces the magnitude of the effect to approximately half. In both countries it is the introduction of controls for education, experience, and tenure that has the biggest effect in reducing the size–wage effect.

The reduction in the size–wage effect when controls are introduced suggests that part of the raw size–wage differential can be explained by differences in worker quality. But, are estimates that control for worker quality inevitably better than those that do not? To answer this question, let us return to (4.7).

Controlling for labor quality is likely to reduce the unobserved parts of the labor supply and MRPL equations (v_a and v_b in (4.6)) so that σ_a^2 and σ_b^2 are reduced in magnitude as, presumably, is σ_{ab}. For a single equation, the standard formula for the extent of omitted variable bias might lead one to believe that the bias is reduced and the resulting estimates are "better." But, matters are more subtle in a simultaneous equations model as the unexplained part of the regressor (here, employer size) is also reduced by the introduction of controls. In fact, (4.7) and (4.8) show that it is (σ_a^2/σ_b^2) and the correlation coefficient between v_a and v_b that determines the bias so it is relative, not absolute, variances that are important in determining whether the introduction of controls reduces or increases the bias.

Why does the coefficient on employer size tend to fall when other controls are included? If one thinks that it is mostly "labor quality" and regional variables that induce the correlation between v_a and v_b, then we might expect that the correlation between these residuals falls when we improve our controls for these variables. If (for want of a better reason) we assume the relative variances are constant then, using (4.8), it is simple to check that a fall in the correlation between v_a and v_b reduces the coefficient on employer size. But, is this reduced coefficient a better estimate of the true value of ε? Not necessarily: as the previous discussion has made clear, reducing the correlation between v_a and v_b to zero will lead to an underestimate of the true labor supply elasticity (set $\sigma_{ab} = 0$ in (4.8)). Hence, one should not leap to the conclusion that controlling for labor quality inevitably leads to a better estimate of ε.

However, in spite of this, the reduction in the size–wage effect when controls are introduced does suggest that part of the raw size–wage differential might be explained by differences in worker quality. As a large part of worker quality is unobserved, this has led some to argue that all of the size–wage effect might be explained by differences in worker quality. A common way of controlling for unobserved worker quality is to use panel data to estimate a fixed-effects model: that is, regress changes in wages on changes in employer size. Neither the CPS nor the LFS used above are panel data sets so we use the BHPS for the United Kingdom to investigate this. The results are reported in table 4.2. To make the presentation of the results simple, estimates of a simple elasticity of wages with respect to employer size are presented. Log employer size is computed using the mid-points of the reported bands: more sophisticated attempts to predict employer size conditional on characteristics made little difference to the results.

The first four rows present estimates of the elasticity from the CPS and LFS both with and without controls. Without controls the elasticity of wages with respect to employer size is 0.11 in the United States and 0.14

TABLE 4.2
The Elasticity of Wages with Respect to Employer Size

	Country (Data)	Sample	Other Controls	Elasticity (SE)	Number of Observations	R^2
(1)	US (CPS)	Cross-section	No	0.108 (0.004)	7854	0.10
(2)	US (CPS)	Cross-section	Yes	0.064 (0.003)	7854	0.36
(3)	UK (LFS)	Cross-section	No	0.145 (0.002)	220868	0.07
(4)	UK (LFS)	Cross-section	Yes	0.074 (0.001)	220868	0.42
(5)	UK (BHPS)	Cross-section	No	0.086 (0.002)	13365	0.09
(6)	UK (BHPS)	Cross-section	Yes	0.047 (0.002)	13365	0.49
(7)	UK (BHPS)	Panel	Yes	0.013 (0.002)	13813	0.02
(8)	UK (BHPS)	Panel movers	Yes	0.035 (0.007)	1340	0.11
(9)	UK (LFS)	Dual job holders	No	0.037 (0.007)	5342	0.01

Notes.
1. The dependent variable is the log of the hourly wage. Employer size is coded as the mid-points of the relevant bands with the open-ended top category being coded as twice the lower bound. The elasticity is the coefficient on the log of the employer size variable.
2. The other controls included are marital status, children, experience, tenure (all interacted with gender), region, race, and (for the LFS) month dummies. Standard errors are reported in parentheses.

in the United Kingdom. Introducing controls reduces the estimates by 40–50% to 0.064 in the United States and 0.074 in the United Kingdom. The fifth and sixth rows estimate the elasticity using the BHPS: the elasticity here is smaller than that found in the LFS. The seventh row estimates an equation for wage growth including change in employer size as a regressor. The estimated elasticity drops to 0.013 although it remains significantly different from zero. This might suggest that controlling for unobserved worker quality makes most of the size–wage effect disappear. However, there is good reason to think that this is an understatement of the true elasticity as the employer size variable is likely to have a lot of measurement error (think of the diffi-culty in answering a question about the size of your workplace)[4] and this measurement error will be compounded when we estimate a model in first-differences. To get some idea of the extent of the problem, we compared worker responses to the employer size question in the BHPS to management responses to a similar question in the 1998 UK Work-place Employee Relations Survey (WERS).[5] In the BHPS only 63% of workers who did not change jobs reported their employer being in the same size class as one year ago: for WERS the (employee-weighted) figure is 88%. For the largest workplaces (those with 1000+ workers) 97% of the WERS sample reported being in the same category the previous year and the remaining 3% were in the next category (500–999 workers). In the BHPS, only 72% reported having 1000+ employ-ees previously and 10% reported their employer previously having less than 200 employees. It is clear that there is a lot of measurement error in reported changes in employer size from employee data. This measure-ment error in the change in employer size is likely to be less important for workers who change jobs as the signal to noise ratio is likely to be higher. The eighth row of table 4.2 estimates a wage growth model on a sample of movers—the estimated elasticity rises to 0.037. Similar results are reported on US data sets by Brown and Medoff (1989).

[4] Measurement error is another reason why estimates that include controls may be worse than those that do not as was originally pointed out by Griliches (1977). Intuitively, the fraction of the variation in the employer size variable that is measurement error after intro-ducing controls is likely to be higher. In the present context, measurement error should be interpreted broadly to mean any transitory shocks to employment. For example, it may be that wages are related to a long-run measure of employer size because there are pressures which limit the extent of variation in wages (see chapter 5 for a discussion of this) but that there are year-to-year variations in employment that do not get reflected in wages. This will have the same effect as measurement error on the estimated ESWE.

[5] WERS reports the actual level of employment now and a year ago, so we converted this to the size classes used in the BHPS. As WERS only reports weights which can be used to gross to the population of workplaces with 10+ employees, we also restricted this analysis to workers who report 10+ employees in the BHPS.

TABLE 4.3
Job Mobility and Employer Size

	(1)	(2)	(3)
Log employer size	−0.054 (0.008)	−0.038 (0.009)	−0.023 (0.009)
Log wage			−0.269 (0.042)
Other controls	No	Yes	Yes
Number of observations	13928	13886	13886
Pseudo-R^2	0.005	0.1	0.11

Notes.
1. The data set used is the BHPS. The sample is all of those in continuous employment between one interview and the next. The dependent variable takes the value 1 if the individual changed jobs and 0 if they did not: a probit model is estimated.
2. The other controls are sex, race, education, experience, tenure, region, marital status, children, and year dummies.

The LFS offers another way to control for individual fixed effects as, for those who have more than two jobs, it asks questions about earnings and employer size for both jobs.[6] The ninth row of table 4.2 regresses the difference in log wages on the difference in log workplace size; the estimated elasticity is 0.037, identical to that obtained from the BHPS movers. These estimates suggest that controlling for worker quality does reduce the size–wage effect but it remains significantly different from zero, implying a gap of about 10% in wages between the 75th and 25th percentile of workplace size: this is similar to the magnitudes reported by Brown and Medoff (1989).

One other hypothesis to explain the size–wage effect is that it is the result of a compensating wage differential. It may be that people dislike working in large firms per se or that other working conditions tend to be worse in large firms. Observed indicators of working conditions do not suggest that large firms tend to be worse places to work but these indicators are far from perfect. Perhaps the simplest way to test the compensating wage differentials hypothesis is to examine quit rates. If the size–wage effect is simply a compensating wage differential, utility would be equalized across firms of different sizes so there is no reason to believe that quit rates would differ by firm size. In fact, workers are much less likely to leave large employers. Table 4.3 presents some evidence from the BHPS on this point. The sample is those in continuous employment where the dependent variable takes the value 1 if the individual changed jobs and 0 if they did not. In column (1) we simply estimate a probit model with the log of employer size as a regressor. It

[6] Lemieux (1998) was the first to use this approach as a way to estimate the union wage mark-up.

is significantly negative. The second column then introduces some extra controls. The impact of employer size is reduced but still significant. Finally, the third column also introduces the log wage. It is not clear whether the wage should be included or not as the impact of employer size on quits should be through the wage. Again, the coefficient on employer size is reduced but remains significantly different from zero. This evidence suggests that workers are better off in large firms, which suggests that the size–wage correlation cannot be explained solely by compensating wage differentials.

The evidence discussed so far suggests that the size–wage effect cannot be readily explained by a competitive model of the labor market. However, this does not prove that an upward-sloping supply of labor to the individual employer is the correct explanation: there are other potential non-competitive explanations, for example, efficiency wage or rent sharing theories. While efficiency wage theories are often too vague to test, rent sharing is a tighter idea. The hypothesis is that workers manage to get a share of the rents and successful firms with large rents tend to have high levels of employment. If this is the case, we would expect that workers are better at extracting a share of the rents when they are unionized than when they are not so we would expect to see a larger employer size–wage effect in the union sector. In fact, the opposite is the case. Table 4.4 shows that in the CPS, the LFS and the BHPS the size–wage effect is 3–4 times larger in the non-union sector than the union sector (for similar findings, see Brown and Medoff 1989,

TABLE 4.4
The ESWE in Union and Non-union Sectors

	Country (Data)	Sample	Other Controls	Elasticity (SE)	Number of Observations	R^2
(1)	US (CPS)	Union cross-section	Yes	0.019 (0.008)	1231	0.30
(2)	US (CPS)	Non-union cross-section	Yes	0.067 (0.004)	6623	0.37
(3)	UK (LFS)	Union cross-section	Yes	0.017 (0.003)	22737	0.42
(4)	UK (LFS)	Non-union cross-section	Yes	0.086 (0.003)	24135	0.4
(5)	UK (BHPS)	Union cross-section	Yes	0.018 (0.002)	6619	0.47
(6)	UK (BHPS)	Non-union cross-section	Yes	0.077 (0.003)	6746	0.49

Notes.
1. As for table 4.2.

Mellow 1982).[7] This seems strong evidence against the rent sharing hypothesis; Green et al. (1996) provide a more extensive discussion of this for UK data.

This section has discussed competitive and rent sharing arguments for the employer size–wage effect. The employer size–wage effect survives all of these attempts to explain it away. The following section returns to the question of how we might try to estimate the true value of ε.

4.3 Reverse Regressions

The estimates so far suggest that, while an upward-sloping labor supply curve is a plausible explanation for part of the employer size–wage effect, the elasticity of wages with respect to employment is small (perhaps about 0.04) after we have controlled for observed and unobserved worker quality. Using the formula for the Hicks–Pigou rate of exploitation in (2.3) this elasticity is also the proportionate amount by which wages fall short of marginal product so an elasticity of 0.04 suggests only small deviations from perfect competition. But, there is no reason why one might not run a regression of log employment on the log wage (and the x variables), hope to estimate ε_{Nw} from the coefficient on wages in this regression, and then invert the elasticity to give ε. We will term this the reverse regression after the discussion in Goldberger (1984).

This regression provides an estimate of $E(\log(N_i) \mid \log(w_i), x_i)$. The following proposition tells us what we would expect to find in this case.

Proposition 4.2. *Running a regression of* $\log(N_i)$ *on* $(\log(w_i), x_i)$ *estimates*

$$E(\log(N_i) \mid \log(w_i), x_i) = \frac{1 - \rho'(\varepsilon + \eta)}{\varepsilon} \log(w_i) + \rho' \ln(1 + \varepsilon)$$

$$- \frac{\beta_b - \rho'(\varepsilon\beta_a + \eta\beta_b)}{\varepsilon} x_i \qquad (4.9)$$

where

$$\rho' \equiv \frac{\varepsilon\sigma_{ab} + \eta\sigma_b^2}{\varepsilon^2\sigma_a^2 + \eta^2\sigma_b^2 + 2\varepsilon\eta\sigma_{ab}} \qquad (4.10)$$

Proof. See Appendix 4A.

---

[7] It is also worth noting that Teulings and Hartog (1998) find that the ESWE is smaller in "corporatist" countries where the level of wage bargaining is above that of the individual employer.

In the reverse regression, OLS only gives unbiased estimates of $(1/\varepsilon)$ if $\varepsilon\sigma_{ab} = -\eta\sigma_b^2$. But, of course, the bias will generally be different from that in the wage equation; compare (4.9) and (4.7). If $\sigma_{ab} = 0$, then the true estimate of ε must lie between that estimated by a regression of $\log(w)$ on $\log(N)$, and one obtained from a regression of $\log(N)$ on $\log(w)$.

Now compare the direct and reverse regressions. Table 4.5 presents some further estimates of (4.7) and (4.9) using data from the US CPS and the UK LFS that have already been used in table 4.2. In each row we report the coefficient on employer size when (4.7) is estimated in the column headed "coefficient on log employer size" while the inverse of the coefficient on the log wage when (4.9) is estimated is reported in the column headed "inverse of coefficient on log wage." As these are both estimates of ε, one would hope that these coefficients are similar.

In fact, they are very different. Consider the US results first. The first row reports the results when no other controls are included and subsequent rows add personal controls, education controls, regional controls, industry controls, and occupation controls, finishing with a model with all variables included. There are several general conclusions. First, for both the United States and the United Kingdom, there is always a large gap between the coefficient on log employer size and the inverse of the coefficient on the log wage. For example, in the first row of table 4.5, the second column suggests an elasticity of the wage with respect to employment of 0.116 while the third suggests an elasticity of 1.000. Secondly, the inclusion of controls always reduces the coefficient in the second column and raises the coefficient in the third column.

What is the explanation for this pattern of results? The gap in the two estimates of ε suggests the presence of the biases identified in (4.7) and (4.9) or of measurement errors in wages or employment, or both. But, why should this gap widen when controls are introduced?

As discussed earlier, the biases in (4.7) and (4.9) depend on relative variances and the correlation coefficient of the errors in the labor supply and MRPL equations, and in a complicated way. It is possible that the biases move in different directions when the introduction of controls changes the relative variances and the correlation coefficient but it is hard for intuition to deliver any firm expectation.

The measurement error argument of Griliches (1977) is perhaps more plausible so some consideration of the likely sources of measurement error in both employer size and wages is likely to be worthwhile. For employer size, individuals have no reason to know the size of their workplace and seem to often make big mistakes as the earlier discussion has made clear. If this is the case, one would expect the coefficient on a better measure of employer size in the direct regression to be larger. It is plausible to believe that managers in workplaces have better information than

TABLE 4.5
Direct and Reverse Regressions

Sample	Coefficient on Log Employer Size	Inverse of Coefficient on Log Wage	Personal Controls	Education Controls	Regional Controls	Industry Controls	Occupation Controls
US	0.116 (0.004)	1.000 (0.033)	No	No	No	No	No
US	0.099 (0.004)	1.070 (0.041)	Yes	No	No	No	No
US	0.071 (0.004)	1.273 (0.065)	Yes	Yes	No	No	No
US	0.095 (0.004)	1.110 (0.044)	Yes	No	Yes	No	No
US	0.085 (0.004)	1.392 (0.067)	Yes	No	No	Yes	No
US	0.078 (0.004)	1.181 (0.055)	Yes	No	No	No	Yes
US	0.060 (0.004)	1.608 (0.101)	Yes	Yes	Yes	Yes	Yes
UK	0.144 (0.003)	1.908 (0.037)	No	No	No	No	No
UK	0.115 (0.003)	1.988 (0.045)	Yes	No	No	No	No
UK	0.092 (0.002)	2.070 (0.054)	Yes	Yes	No	No	No
UK	0.110 (0.002)	1.964 (0.045)	Yes	No	Yes	No	No
UK	0.085 (0.003)	2.671 (0.088)	Yes	No	No	Yes	No
UK	0.075 (0.002)	2.368 (0.073)	Yes	No	No	No	Yes
UK	0.062 (0.002)	2.737 (0.109)	Yes	Yes	Yes	Yes	Yes

Notes.
1. US data are from the Contingent Worker Survey to the April 1993 CPS. The sample is restricted to the non-union sector. UK data are from the LFS.
2. The dependent variable is the log of the hourly wage.
3. Personal controls are sex, race, a quartic in experience, marital status, and the presence of children.
4. The column headed "coefficient on log employer size" gives the results from estimating a regression of log wages on log employer size and other controls. The column headed "inverse of coefficient on log wage" gives the results from estimating a regression of log employer size on log wages and other controls.

TABLE 4.6
The ESWE: Evidence from WERS

	Coefficient on Log Employer Size	Inverse of Coefficient on Log Wage	Controls	Method of Estimation (Instrument)
(1)	0.120 (0.010)	–	No	OLS
(2)	0.051 (0.007)	–	Yes	OLS
(3)	0.050 (0.007)	–	Yes	IV (first lag)
(4)	0.056 (0.007)	–	Yes	IV (fifth lag)
(5)	–	3.383 (0.365)	Yes	OLS
(6)	–	1.408 (0.188)	Yes	Between-firm

Notes.
1. Data are from the 1998 UK WERS. The number of observations is approximately 25,000. The dependent variable is the log of the hourly wage for rows (1)–(4) and the log of employers size in rows (5) and (6).
2. The controls included are sex, race, education, age, occupation, and industry. Observations are weighted to be representative of all workers in plants with more than 10 employees (smaller plants are excluded). Standard errors are computed assuming clustering on the workplace.

their workers about employer size, although it might be better to have administrative data like that used by Bayard and Troske (1999). The 1998 UK WERS can be used to investigate this. Some results are reported in table 4.6. The first row reports the result of a simple regression of log wages on log employer size. Log wages are reported by the individual workers concerned and employer size by the manager so these regressions are very similar to those reported earlier except that employer size is manager-reported. However, the coefficient on log employer size is similar to what we have seen before. The second row introduces controls: the drop in the coefficient on log employer size is very similar to what we have seen before. There is little evidence here to suggest substantial worker misreporting of employer size although the earlier results on the excessive apparent changes in employer size in the BHPS did suggest the existence of large measurement errors.[8]

An additional reason for why the coefficient on log employer size may be underestimated is the existence of transitory shocks to employment that are not reflected in wages. WERS also allows us a way to investigate this as employers are asked to report workplace employment one and five years previously. A simple regression of the log of employment this year on the log of employment last year has a coefficient of 0.97 on the lagged dependent variable suggesting a lot of permanence in the level of employment. The

---

[8] It is possible that the comparison of BHPS and WERS results is made difficult by the different nature of the two data sets.

third row of table 4.6 shows the coefficient on log(N) when it is instrumented by lagged employment to try to pick up the permanent component in employment. The instrumental variable coefficient is very similar to the ordinary least squares. The fourth row uses the fifth lag of employment as an instrument with very similar results. These results suggest that transitory shocks to employment that are not reflected in wages are not particularly important in explaining the estimated size of the ESWE.

The discussion so far has focused on measurement errors and transitory shocks to employment. But, there are reasons to think there might be similar problems surrounding wages. Perhaps the most important is that the wage used in the regressions in table 4.2 refers to the wage of a single worker in the plant. This is an unbiased estimate of the average log wage in the plant but obviously contains some measurement error. As a result, the coefficient on log wages in the reverse regression is likely to be biased towards zero. Evidence for this effect can be seen in the fifth and sixth rows of table 4.6. The fifth row reports the result of a reverse regression on the WERS data. The implied value of ε is very high. The sixth row reports the result of a between-plant regression on the same data, exploiting the fact that the data set contains observations on multiple workers within plants. This effectively runs a regression of the log of employment on the average log wage. The coefficient on the wage variable rises implying a lower value of ε, as one would expect.

None of the discussion so far gives us much confidence that OLS, either a direct or reverse regression, gives us a good estimate of ε. On the basis of the results reported, one could argue either that labor supply to the firm is very inelastic or that it is quite elastic. It is perhaps better to conclude that these regressions are just not very informative. But, while it might have been nice for OLS to deliver reliable results, perhaps it was expecting too much and a simpler potential solution presents itself.

To identify the labor supply curve (which is all we want here), a variable that shifts the MRPL curve without shifting the supply curve is needed. One can then use this as an instrument for the wage or employment in estimating the supply curve (depending on which way round we are estimating the supply curve). This procedure will yield consistent estimates of ε. But, of course, it requires us to be able to provide such an instrument.

If one is interested in estimating the elasticity of labor supply to an individual firm, then the instrument needs to be something that affects the demand curve for that firm but has negligible impact on the labor market as a whole. The reason is that a pervasive labor market demand shock will raise the general level of wages so is likely to be correlated with B in (4.2). So, for example, the approach of using demand shocks caused by exchange rate fluctuations (as in Abowd and Lemieux 1993) does not seem viable here.

There are a number of studies that attempt to use firm-level instruments. For example, Sullivan (1989) uses the population in the area surrounding the hospital as an instrument affecting the demand for nurses, and Beck et al. (1998) use the number of children in a school district as an instrument for the demand for teachers. These represent serious attempts to deal with a difficult problem but their instruments are not beyond criticism. If the main variation in the number of children or the number of patients comes from variation in population, it is also likely that the supply of nurses and teachers in an area is proportional to population as well. Perhaps the best studies are Staiger et al. (1999) and Falch (2001). Staiger et al. (1999) examine the impact of a legislated rise in the wages paid at Veteran Affairs hospitals. This combined with a plausible argument that these hospitals were allowed to hire as many staff as they wanted (which is required to make sure we are estimating the supply curve) seems as close to an exogenous increase in wages as anything else in the literature. They estimate the short-run elasticity in the labor supply to the firm to be very low—around 0.1 implying an enormous amount of monopsony power possessed by hospitals over their nurses. Falch (2001) investigates the impact on the supply of teachers to individual schools in Norway in response to a policy experiment that selectively raised wages in some schools. Again, he finds that the elasticity in the supply of labor to individual schools is very low. How plausible are these estimates and whether they can be generalized to the rest of the labor market are open questions as the markets for nurses and teachers are ones that might conventionally be thought of as having some monopsonistic elements.

This is all rather depressing: a good estimate of the elasticity of the labor supply curve facing the firm seems very elusive so perhaps there is a very good reason for the lack of research into this area. Progress seems to be dependent on finding a good firm-level instrument.

4.4 Estimating Models of Dynamic Monopsony

The previous part of this chapter has used the static model of monopsony as a way to think about the issue of estimating the elasticity of the labor supply curve facing an individual firm. The rest of this chapter uses a more explicitly dynamic, theoretical approach to estimate this elasticity. In a steady state, we know that the supply of labor to the firm $N(w)$ must be given by $N(w) = R(w)/s(w)$ where $R(w)$ is the flow of recruits to the firm and $s(w)$ is the separation rate. As pointed out by Card and Krueger (1995) and discussed earlier in section 2.2, this implies that

$$\varepsilon_{Nw} = \varepsilon_{Rw} - \varepsilon_{sw} \tag{4.11}$$

so that knowledge of the elasticities of recruitment and quits with respect to the wage can be used to estimate the elasticity of labor supply facing the firm. This section discusses how we can estimate ε_{Rw} and ε_{sw}.

One of the advantages of this approach is that there is a well-established literature that discusses the elasticity of the separation rate with respect to the wage (e.g., Pencavel 1972; Parsons 1972, 1973; Viscusi 1980; Light and Ureta 1992). However, an apparent disadvantage is that it might be unclear how the elasticity of the recruits with respect to the wage should be estimated. Card and Krueger (1995) use estimates of the elasticity of job applicants with respect to the wage from Holzer et al. (1991) and Krueger (1988) but the justification for this is not obvious. One of the contributions here is to show that there is a close connection between ε_{Rw} and ε_{sw} so that estimates of the separation elasticity are informative about the recruitment elasticity.

Consider the basic Burdett and Mortensen (1998) model of dynamic monopsony introduced in section 2.4. In this model, we have

$$s(w) = \delta + \lambda[1 - F(w)] \tag{4.12}$$

$$R(w) = R^u + \lambda \int^w f(x)N(x)dx \tag{4.13}$$

where $s(w)$ is the separation rate in a firm that pays wage w, $R(w)$ is the flow of recruits, δ is the rate (assumed exogenous) at which workers leave employment for non-employment, λ is the arrival rate of job offers, $F(w)$ is the distribution of wage offers, R^u are the recruits from unemployment (which does not depend on the wage offered) and $N(w)$ is the employment level in a firm that pays w. By differentiating (4.12) and (4.13), we have

$$\varepsilon_{sw} = \frac{ws'(w)}{s(w)} = -\frac{\lambda wf(w)}{s(w)} = -\frac{\lambda wf(w)N(w)}{R(w)} = -\frac{wR'(w)}{R(w)} = -\varepsilon_{Rw} \tag{4.14}$$

where the third equality sign follows from the fact that, in steady state, $s(w)N(w) = R(w)$. (4.14) says that, in a steady state, the recruitment elasticity is simply minus the separation elasticity so that (using (4.11)) one can simply double the separation elasticity to get an estimate of the labor supply elasticity. The explanation for the connection between the two elasticities is that separations from one firm for a wage-related reason must be the recruit of some other firm so that quits and recruits are two sides of the same coin.

Although this result is neat, one might wonder about its robustness. So, let us consider some generalizations. First, relax the assumption that workers always quit for a better-paying job and never quit for a job with lower pay. Suppose that a worker currently being paid w accepts a job offer of x with probability $\phi(x/w)$. We assume that it is the ratio of the wages that matters which seems a reasonable restriction as there is no reason to think that a general increase in wages would have any effect on job-to-job mobility rates. Note that the model of (4.12) and (4.13) corresponds to the case where $\phi(x/w) = 0$ if $x < w$ and $\phi(x/w) = 1$ if $x > w$. The separation rate and recruitment functions will now be given by

$$s(w) = \delta + \lambda \int \phi\left(\frac{x}{w}\right) f(x) dx \qquad (4.15)$$

$$R(w) = R^{u} + \lambda \int \phi\left(\frac{w}{x}\right) f(x) N(x) dx \qquad (4.16)$$

The following proposition tells us that a suitably weighted separation elasticity must be equal to a suitably weighted recruitment elasticity.

Proposition 4.3. *If the separation and recruitment functions are given by (4.15) and (4.16), then the recruit-weighted separation and recruitment elasticities must be equal, that is,*

$$\int \varepsilon_{sw}(w) R(w) f(w) dw = -\int \varepsilon_{Rw}(w) R(w) f(w) dw \qquad (4.17)$$

Proof.   See Appendix 4A.

If the separation and recruitment elasticities are both constant, (4.17) says that they must be equal. If they vary with the wage then they can differ but probably not by much. For example, if the separation elasticity is finite everywhere, the recruitment elasticity cannot be infinite for any positive measure of employees.

However, the separation and recruitment functions of (4.15) and (4.16) are still quite restrictive in that they assume that separations to and recruitment from non-employment are not sensitive to the wage.

Write total separations as $s(w) = s^{n}(w) + s^{e}(w)$ where $s^{n}(w)$ is the separation rate to non-employment and $s^{e}(w)$ is the separation rate to employment. Denote by θ_s the share of separations which are a direct move to another job. Similarly write total recruits as $R(w) = R^{n}(w) + R^{e}(w)$ where $R^{n}(w)$ is the flow of recruits from non-employment and $R^{e}(w)$ is the flow of recruits from employment. Denote by θ_R the share of recruits from employment. The overall elasticity of labor supply with respect to the wage can be written as

$$\varepsilon_{Nw} = \theta_R \varepsilon_{Rw}^{e} + (1 - \theta_R)\varepsilon_{Rw}^{n} - \theta_s \varepsilon_{sw}^{e} - (1 - \theta_s)\varepsilon_{sw}^{n} \qquad (4.18)$$

so that knowledge of the four elasticities can be used to compute the elasticity of the labor supply curve facing the firm. The two separation elasticities can be estimated straightforwardly (see below) so the only problem is how to estimate the recruitment elasticities. The following proposition shows that a suitably weighted recruitment elasticity from employment is equal to a weighted separation elasticity to employment.

Proposition 4.4. *If the separation and recruitment functions to and from employment are given by*

$$s^e(w) = \lambda \int \phi\left(\frac{x}{w}\right) f(x) dx \qquad (4.19)$$

$$R^e(w) = \lambda \int \phi\left(\frac{w}{x}\right) f(x) N(x) dx \qquad (4.20)$$

then a suitably weighted average of the separations elasticity must be equal to a weighted average of the recruitment elasticities. In particular,

$$\frac{\int \varepsilon^e_{sw}(w) s^e(w) N(w) f(w) dw}{\int s^e(w) N(w) f(w) dw} = - \frac{\int \varepsilon^e_{Rw}(w) R^e(w) f(w) dw}{\int R^e(w) f(w) dw} \qquad (4.21)$$

Proof. See Appendix 4A.

(4.21) says that a weighted average of the separation elasticity and the recruitment elasticity must be equal but that the weights are not equal, as in (4.17).[9] However, this still means that if both the separation and recruitment elasticities are constant, they must be equal.

Unfortunately, there is no equivalent result relating the separation and recruitment elasticities for transitions to and from non-employment. For example, if there is heterogeneity in the reservation wages of workers but the reservation wage for an individual worker never changes, recruits from non-employment are increasing in the wage but separations to non-employment are not. However, if there is a stochastic component to the reservation wage, separations to non-employment are also sensitive to the wage. The basic problem is that, whereas a move from one job to another is a quit for one firm and immediately a recruit for another firm, this is not true of flows between employment and non-employment.

So, we cannot use the wage elasticity of separations to non-employment to estimate the wage elasticity of recruits from non-employment: we need a different method. The share of recruits from employment is given by

[9] The separation elasticity is weighted by separations to other jobs while the recruitment elasticity is weighted by recruits from other jobs. We would expect the weight on the elasticity in high-wage firms to be larger for the recruitment than the separation elasticity.

$$\theta_R(w) = \frac{R^e(w)}{R^e(w) + R^n(w)} \tag{4.22}$$

This enables us to prove the following relationship between $\varepsilon_R^e(w)$ and $\varepsilon_R^n(w)$.

Proposition 4.5. *If the share of recruits from employment is given by (4.22), then the relationship between the wage elasticity of recruits from non-employment, $\varepsilon_{Rw}^n(w)$, and the wage elasticity of recruits from employment, $\varepsilon_{Rw}^e(w)$, is given by*

$$\varepsilon_{Rw}^n(w) = \varepsilon_{Rw}^e(w) - \frac{w\theta_R'(w)}{\theta_R(w)[1 - \theta_R(w)]} \tag{4.23}$$

Proof. See Appendix 4A.

If, for example, we model $\theta_R(w)$ as a logistic function $e^{\beta x}/(1 + e^{\beta x})$ where x includes the log wage, then $(w\theta_R'/\theta_R(1 - \theta_R)) = \beta_w$ where β_w is the coefficient on the log wage.

Summarizing all this information, our strategy for estimating the elasticity of the labor supply curve facing the firm is

- estimate separations equations for separations to employment and non-employment, and obtain the wage elasticities;
- use the wage elasticity of separations to employment to estimate the wage elasticity of recruits from employment (based on Proposition 4.4);
- estimate a logit model for the probability that a recruit comes from employment and then use (4.23) to estimate the elasticity of recruits from non-employment;
- use these elasticities and information of the share of separations to and recruits from employment in (4.14) to estimate the elasticity of the labor supply curve facing the firm.

Let us now put this into practice.

4.5 Estimating the Wage Elasticity of Separations

We model the instantaneous separation rate as $s = e^{\beta x}$. One of the x variables will be the log of the wage so that the elasticity of the separation rate with respect to the wage will simply be the coefficient on the wage. From the previous discussion, we also need to model the separations to employment and non-employment separately. Write the separation rate to other jobs as $s^{ee}(x) = \exp(\beta^{ee}x)$ and the separation rate to non-employment as $s^{en}(x) = \exp(\beta^{en}x)$. We assume that, conditional on x, the two sorts of separation are independent.

Define an indicator variable y^{en} which takes the value 1 if the individual has a spell of non-employment in a period of time τ and 0 otherwise and an another indicator variable y^{ee} which, if the individual does not have a spell of non-employment, takes the value 1 if the individual changes jobs and 0 if they do not. The probabilities of the different outcomes are given by

$$\Pr(y^{en} = 1 \mid x) = 1 - \exp(-s^{en}(x)\tau)$$

$$\Pr(y^{en} = 0, y^{ee} = 1 \mid x) = \exp(-s^{en}(x)\tau)(1 - \exp(-s^{ee}(x)\tau)) \quad (4.24)$$

$$\Pr(y^{en} = 0, y^{ee} = 0 \mid x) = \exp(-s^{en}(x)\tau)\exp(-s^{ee}(x)\tau)$$

so that the individual contribution to the log-likelihood function can be written as

$$\log L = y^{en} \ln[1 - \exp(-s^{en}(x)\tau)] + (1 - y^{en}) \ln[\exp(-s^{en}(x)\tau)]$$

$$+(1 - y^{en})[y^{ee} \ln[1 - \exp(-s^{ee}(x)\tau)] + (1 - y^{ee}) \ln[\exp(-s^{ee}(x)\tau)]](4.25)$$

The important feature of (4.25) is that one can estimate the separations elasticity to non-employment and other jobs separately. To estimate the elasticity of separations to non-employment, the whole sample is used and we have as a dependent variable whether the individual had a period of non-employment in the year. To estimate the elasticity of separations to other jobs the sample of those who have been in continuous employment is used and we have as a dependent variable whether the individual remains in the same job. Note that the overall elasticity will be a weighted average of these two elasticities, the weight being the fraction of separations that are to non-employment.

The most serious problem in estimating the wage elasticities is, as always, going to be the result of a failure to control adequately for other relevant factors. One potential source of problems in estimating the separation elasticity is a failure to control adequately for the average level of wages in the individual's labor market. Separations are likely to depend on the wage relative to this alternative wage so that a failure to control for the alternative wage is likely to lead to a downward bias in the wage elasticities. On the other hand, we would expect separations to be more sensitive to the permanent component of wages than to the part of wages that is a transitory shock or measurement error. In this case, the inclusion of controls correlated with the permanent wage is likely to reduce the estimated wage elasticity. Table 4.7 estimates some separations equations with and without controls for the PSID, NLSY, BHPS and

TABLE 4.7
The Sensitivity of the Separation Elasticity to Specification

	PSID (US)	NLSY (US)	BHPS (UK)	LFS (UK)
All separations				
Mean separation rate	0.21	0.55	0.19	0.058
No controls	−0.944 (0.030)	−0.515 (0.019)	−0.798 (0.032)	−0.646 (0.021)
With controls	−0.973 (0.041)	−0.536 (0.032)	−0.720 (0.041)	−0.500 (0.028)
Tenure controls	−0.575 (0.037)	−0.340 (0.026)	−0.503 (0.064)	−0.343 (0.032)
Separations to employment				
Mean separation rate	0.12	0.43	0.12	0.032
No controls	−0.759 (0.050)	−0.307 (0.018)	−0.631 (0.038)	−0.529 (0.030)
With controls	−0.867 (0.038)	−0.359 (0.032)	−0.688 (0.049)	−0.425 (0.039)
Tenure controls	−0.450 (0.042)	−0.156 (0.027)	−0.429 (0.050)	−0.207 (0.044)
Separations to non-employment				
Mean separation rate	0.08	0.12	0.07	0.025
No controls	−1.010 (0.067)	−0.750 (0.028)	−0.916 (0.048)	−0.748 (0.029)
With controls	−0.892 (0.087)	−0.850 (0.055)	−0.632 (0.066)	−0.578 (0.041)
Tenure controls	−0.569 (0.068)	−0.713 (0.056)	−0.493 (0.071)	−0.477 (0.045)

Notes.
1. This table reports the elasticities of separations with respect to the wage. The PSID, NLSY, and BHPS samples are those described in the Data Sets Appendix. The LFS sample is from September 1997 to November 1999. The LFS also differs from the other data sets in modeling labor market transitions from one quarter to another instead of one year to another. This is why the means of the dependent variables are so much lower. The row headed "no controls" simply includes the wage. The rows marked "with controls" include gender, education, race, marital status, children, region, a quartic in experience, and year dummies. The row headed "tenure controls" includes a quartic in tenure in addition to the usual controls.

LFS. First consider the wage elasticity for all separations (the top panel of table 4.7). All the estimated wage elasticities are negative and significantly different from zero. They range from -0.5 for the NLSY to -0.9 for the PSID. The bottom two panels estimate separate wage elasticities for separations to employment and non-employment. There is evidence that the elasticities for both separations to employment and non-employment are both sensitive to the wage with the latter being larger than the former.

Inclusion of standard human capital controls does not make much difference to the estimated wage elasticities. However, one variable whose inclusion or exclusion makes a lot of difference to the apparent estimated wage elasticity is job tenure.[10] The inclusion of job tenure always drastically reduces the estimated wage elasticity as high-tenure workers are less likely to leave the firm and are more likely to have high wages. There are arguments both for and against the inclusion of job tenure. One of the benefits of paying high wages is that tenure will be higher so that one needs to take account of this indirect effect if one wants the overall wage elasticity when including tenure controls: in this situation, excluding tenure may give better estimates. On the other hand, if there are seniority wage scales, the apparent relationship between separations and wages may be spurious.

Unobserved heterogeneity that is correlated with the wage causes familiar problems but the wage elasticity is likely to be biased even if there is heterogeneity uncorrelated with the wage. To see this, suppose that the separation rate is $\xi w^{-\beta}$ where ξ is unobserved and independent of the wage. To keep things tractable we will assume that ξ has a gamma distribution with mean μ and variance σ^2. The following proposition summarizes the effect of unobserved heterogeneity on the estimated wage elasticity.

Proposition 4.6.   *The elasticity of the separations rate with respect to the wage is biased towards zero with gamma-distributed unobserved heterogeneity that is uncorrelated with the wage. The shorter the time period over which the data are observed, the smaller is the bias.*

Proof.   See Appendix 4A.

The result on the existence of a bias is unsurprising: we are using survivor functions to estimate the wage elasticity and it is well known that unobserved heterogeneity has an effect on the estimated coefficients in duration models (see Lancaster 1990). Table 4.8 investigates whether the time horizon makes any difference to the estimated wage elasticity

[10] The word "apparent" is appropriate here because the dependence of job tenure on the wage needs to be taken into account when estimating the full wage elasticity.

TABLE 4.8
The Effect of the Time Horizon on the Separation Elasticity: UK LFS

Controls	No	Yes
1 quarter	−0.646 (0.021)	−0.500 (0.028)
2 quarters	−0.640 (0.018)	−0.497 (0.024)
3 quarters	−0.586 (0.017)	−0.471 (0.023)
4 quarters	−0.547 (0.017)	−0.429 (0.023)

Notes.
1. The reported coefficients are the coefficients on the log wage from the estimated separations model as described in section 4.5. The controls included are gender, race, education, experience, martial status and dependent children, region, and month.
2. The dependent variable in the row marked 1 quarter is whether the individual left the initial job over the first quarter, that for 2 quarters whether the individual left over the first two quarters, etc.

using data from the UK LFS. Results are reported for the wage elasticity estimated over a period of one to four quarters. The results are consistent with the predictions of Proposition 4.6. Both with and without other controls, the estimated wage elasticity is higher over short periods than long. As all the other data sets used in table 4.3 use a time horizon of a year, this suggests the estimates may be understating the true wage elasticity. However, the results in table 4.8 do not suggest the size of the bias is large. The estimated elasticity of separations with respect to the wage rises (in absolute terms) from −0.43 to −0.5 as the time horizon is narrowed from one year to one quarter and hardly narrows at all as the time horizon falls from two quarters to one quarter.

4.6 The Proportion of Recruits from Employment

Proposition 4.5 says that we need to know how the fraction of recruits from employment varies with the wage. Table 4.9 reports the results of estimating a logit model for a recruit coming from employment for our four data sets. In all data sets, the higher the wage, the higher the probability that a recruit comes from employment: this is as the theory predicts. This implies that the wage elasticity of recruits from employment is higher than the wage elasticity of recruits from non-employment.

4.7 The Elasticity of the Labor Supply Curve Facing the Firm

We are now in a position to provide an estimate of the labor supply curve facing the firm using the results of the previous two sections and (4.18).

TABLE 4.9
The Probability of a Recruit Coming from Employment

Data Set	Mean of Dependent Variable	Coefficient (SE) on Log Wage Without Controls	Coefficient (SE) on Log Wage with Controls	Number of Observations
PSID	0.29	1.011 (0.036)	0.948 (0.054)	14277
NLSY	0.32	0.533 (0.037)	0.674 (0.042)	13653
BHPS	0.36	1.129 (0.065)	1.384 (0.080)	4649
LFS	0.51	0.824 (0.035)	0.746 (0.042)	12071

Notes.
1. The dependent variable is a dummy variable taking the value 1 if a worker was recruited from employment and 0 otherwise. The sample is all recruits. The estimation method is logit. The other controls are gender, race, experience, education, region, and year dummies.

The results of this are reported in table 4.10 where no attempt has been made to correct the wage elasticities for the problems caused by measurement error and the time horizon. These labor supply elasticities are low—in the region of 1. There are a number of reasons why one might argue that these elasticities are underestimates but it is clear that extremely large adjustments to these estimates are necessary to make perfect competition an acceptable approximation. For example, the evidence on the size of the bias caused by the interaction of the time horizon and unobserved heterogeneity would not dramatically increase these elasticities. One can only conclude that the elasticity of separations with respect to the wage is low and that this results in a low elasticity in the supply of labor to individual employers.

TABLE 4.10
The Elasticity of the Labor Supply Curve Facing the Firm

Data	PSID	NLSY	BHPS	LFS
Elasticity of separations to employment	0.867	0.359	0.631	0.529
Elasticity of separations to non-employment	0.892	0.850	0.632	0.578
Share of separations to employment	0.62	0.78	0.63	0.56
β_w	0.948	0.674	1.384	0.746
Elasticity of labor supply curve	1.38	0.68	0.75	0.75

Notes.
1. These computations used table 4.7 for the separation elasticities and the share of separations to employment, table 4.9 for the estimate of β_w, and (4.18) for the elasticity of the labor supply curve. The share of recruits from employment is assumed to be equal to the share of separations to employment as must be the case in steady state.

4.8 The Estimation of Structural Equilibrium Search Models of the Labor Market

This is the best place in this book to discuss a small but relevant literature on the structural estimation of equilibrium search models. The earliest empirical model, Eckstein and Wolpin (1990), used the Albrecht and Axell (1984) model but most later contributions have based their empirical analysis on some variant of the Burdett and Mortensen (1998) model described in section 2.4 (for surveys, see van den Berg 1999; Mortensen 2002). Because the parameters of that model contain all the necessary information (assuming, of course, that the model is correctly specified) for working out the supply of labor facing the firm, these estimates contain within them an estimate of the wage elasticity of the labor supply to an individual firm. Sometimes this elasticity is made explicit, although more often it is not.

Whether this general equilibrium approach to empirical modeling is a superior methodology depends on the purpose to which one is going to put the estimates. If one wants to model the general equilibrium effects of a change in an economy-wide policy, then such an approach may be essential. But if one simply wants an estimate of the extent of employer market power there are reasons to think that the structural approach offers few advantages and many disadvantages. The earliest estimates of equilibrium search models (e.g., Kiefer and Neumann 1993; van den Berg and Ridder 1998) emphasized how the general equilibrium model provided a tight link between the wage distribution and labor market transition rates that was exploited in the structural estimation. But, this link was more of a problem than a help and the models did not explain the distribution of wages well. More sophisticated models were introduced that added employer and worker heterogeneity (see Bontemps et al. 1999, 2000) and generalizing the wage policy used by employers (see Postel-Vinay and Robin 2002). The effect of these reasonable generalizations is effectively to allow the distribution of wages to vary independently of the labor market frictions. In this case, joint estimation of transition rates and the wage distribution offers no real advantages, and the complication of the models hides the simple economics at work. For all their sophistication one ends up with estimates of the extent of frictions that are not much more advanced than the back-of-the-envelope calculations in section 2.6. And, the partial equilibrium approach described in this chapter dominates that approach as it makes less in the way of stringent assumptions about the economy. So, it is probably the case that these equilibrium search models have told us little about the extent of frictions in the labor market that we could not have learned in their absence.

The discussion here mirrors a wider debate in econometrics about the merits of structural modeling. Structural models provide excellent estimates if the model is correct but may not be robust to small deviations from the maintained model, and tractability may restrict attention to implausibly simplistic models. A more pragmatic approach is likely to provide more robust estimates that may not be fully efficient if one pretends to know the true model. As Wolpin (1992: 558) put it 10 years ago "methods for estimating dynamic stochastic models of this kind are still in a relatively undeveloped stage, and knowledge about the effects of model and solution misspecification is very limited. ... exactly, how seriously one should take these particular estimates as reflecting real phenomena is open to debate." Unfortunately, 10 years on, the debate remains just as open and little progress has been made. For example, a state-of-the-art paper in the area (Postel-Vinay and Robin 2002) apparently shows that a model based on the totally implausible assumption of universal offer-matching (with the implication, among others, that unemployed workers are indifferent about getting a job or not) to maximize profits (in an economy, France, where union coverage approaches 100%) is consistent with the observed data, it is time to start worrying about identification as at least one other model of the labor market (the correct one) must also be consistent with the data. My gut feeling is that, for the purpose of estimating the wage elasticity in the supply of labor to an individual employer, a pragmatic approach is more likely to deliver credible results.

4.9 Conclusions

The fundamental difference between monopsony or oligopsony and perfect competition is the size of the elasticity of the labor supply curve facing a firm. Perfect competition assumes it is infinite, imperfect competition that it is finite. There is remarkably little literature on estimating the elasticity of this labor supply curve and this chapter has tried to fill that gap. It has investigated two main methods: one based on the correlation between wages and employment (the employer size–wage effect) and the other based on the estimation of separations functions. The two approaches give rather different results. OLS estimates of the ESWE suggest that the wage elasticity of the labor supply curve to individual employers is in the region of 10–15 leading to a wage that is 6–10% below marginal revenue product. However, there are reasons to think that OLS overstates the wage elasticity and IV estimates are a lot lower. The approach based on estimating the wage elasticity of separations suggests a wage elasticity of the labor supply curve to individual employers that is around one. While there are reasons to think these may be underestimates, it would certainly be hard to argue on the basis of these estimates that the labor supply elasticity is anywhere near 10. However, neither approach is entirely satisfactory: progress really needs good firm-level instruments although these are likely to be hard to find. Given this, it would probably be unwise to base one's belief in the market power of employers too much on these estimates if there were no other evidence. But, as the rest of the book sets out to show, there are very good reasons for believing that employers do have non-negligible market power.

Appendix 4A

Proof of Proposition 4.1

Taking logs of (4.2), we have

$$E(\log(w_i) \mid \log(N_i), x_i) = E(b_i \mid \log(N_i), x_i) + \varepsilon \log(N_i)$$

$$= \beta_b x_i + E(v_{bi} \mid \log(N_i), x_i) + \varepsilon \log(N_i) \quad (4.26)$$

Now, from (4.4) and (4.6) we can derive

$$E(v_{bi} \mid \log(N_i), x_i)$$

$$= E(v_{bi} \mid v_{ai} - v_{bi} = (\varepsilon + \eta) \log(N_i) - (\beta_a - \beta_b)x_i + \ln(1 + \varepsilon))$$

$$= \frac{\sigma_{ab} - \sigma_b^2}{\sigma_a^2 + \sigma_b^2 - 2\sigma_{ab}} [(\varepsilon + \eta) \log(N_i) - (\beta_a - \beta_b)x_i + \ln(1 + \varepsilon)] \quad (4.27)$$

where the second equality follows from standard results on bivariate normal distributions. This can be written as (4.7) and (4.8).

Proof of Proposition 4.2

Taking the log of (4.2), leads to

$$E(\log(N_i) \mid \log(w_i), x_i) = \frac{1}{\varepsilon} \log(w_i) - \frac{1}{\varepsilon} E(b_i \mid \log(w_i), x_i)$$

$$= \frac{1}{\varepsilon} \log(w_i) - \frac{\beta_b}{\varepsilon} x_i - \frac{1}{\varepsilon} E(v_{bi} \mid \log(w_i), x_i) \quad (4.28)$$

Now, from (4.5) and (4.6) and standard results on the bivariate normal distribution, we can derive

$$E(\nu_{bi} \mid \log(w_i), x_i)$$

$$= E(\nu_{bi} \mid \varepsilon\nu_{ai} + \eta\nu_{bi} = (\varepsilon + \eta)\log(w_i) - (\varepsilon\beta_a + \eta\beta_b)x_i + \varepsilon\ln(1 + \varepsilon))$$

$$= \frac{\varepsilon\sigma_{ab} + \eta\sigma_b^2}{\varepsilon^2\sigma_a^2 + \eta^2\sigma_b^2 + 2\varepsilon\eta\sigma_{ab}}[(\varepsilon + \eta)\log(w_i) - (\varepsilon\beta_a + \eta\beta_b)x_i + \varepsilon\ln(1 + \varepsilon)]$$

$$(4.29)$$

which, substituting into (4.28) leads to (4.9) and (4.10).

Proof of Proposition 4.3

Differentiating (4.15), we have

$$s'(w) = -\lambda \int \frac{x}{w^2} \phi'\left(\frac{x}{w}\right) f(x)dx \qquad (4.30)$$

so that

$$\int \varepsilon_{sw}(w)R(w)f(w)dw = \int \frac{ws'(w)}{s(w)} R(w)f(w)$$

$$= -\lambda \int\int \frac{x}{w} \phi'\left(\frac{x}{w}\right) f(x)N(w)f(w)dxdw \qquad (4.31)$$

where we have used the steady-state relation $sN = R$. Now, exchanging the roles of x and w in (4.16) and differentiating with respect to x we have

$$R'(x) = \lambda \int \frac{1}{w} \phi'\left(\frac{x}{w}\right) f(w)N(w)dw \qquad (4.32)$$

so that (4.31) can be written as

$$\int \varepsilon_{sw}(w)R(w)f(w)dw = -\int xR'(x)f(x)dx = -\int \varepsilon_{Rw}(x)R(x)f(x)dx$$

$$(4.33)$$

which is (4.17).

Proof of Proposition 4.4

Differentiating (4.19) with respect to w, we have

$$s^{e'}(w) = -\lambda \int \frac{x}{w^2} \phi'\left(\frac{x}{w}\right) f(x)dx \qquad (4.34)$$

so that

$$\int \varepsilon^e_{sw}(w)s^e(w)N(w)f(w)dw = -\lambda \int \int \frac{x}{w}\phi'\left(\frac{x}{w}\right)f(x)N(w)f(w)dxdw$$

$$(4.35)$$

Exchanging the roles of x and w in (4.20) and differentiating with respect to x, we have

$$R^{e'}(x) = \lambda \int \frac{1}{w}\phi'\left(\frac{x}{w}\right)f(w)N(w)dw \qquad (4.36)$$

so that (4.35) can be written as

$$\int \varepsilon^e_{sw}(w)s^e(w)N(w)f(w)dw = -\int xR^{e'}(x)f(x)dx = -\int \varepsilon^e_{Rw}(x)R^e(x)f(x)dx$$

$$(4.37)$$

Now, in the economy as a whole (but not firm by firm), total recruits from employment must equal total separations to employment which means that $\int s^e(w)N(w)f(w)dw = \int R^e(w)f(w)dw$. Dividing both sides of (4.37) by this leads to (4.21).

Proof of Proposition 4.5

Rearranging (4.22), we have

$$R^n = \frac{1 - \theta_R}{\theta_R}R^e \qquad (4.38)$$

which can be written as

$$\log(R^n) = \log(R^e) + \log\left(\frac{1 - \theta_R}{\theta_R}\right) \qquad (4.39)$$

Differentiation leads to (4.23).

Proof of Proposition 4.6

Denote the density function of ξ by $\varphi(\xi)$. The survivor function over a length of time τ will now by given by

$$S(w, \tau) = \int \exp(-\xi_w - \beta_\tau)\varphi(\xi)d\xi \qquad (4.40)$$

and the estimate of the wage elasticity will be given by the elasticity of $-\log(S(w, \tau))$ with respect to the wage.

If ξ has a gamma distribution, then (4.40) can be written as

$$S(w, \tau) = \frac{\mu/\sigma^2}{\Gamma(\theta)} \int \exp(-\xi_w - \beta_\tau)\exp\left(-\xi\frac{\mu}{\sigma^2}\right)\left(\frac{\mu\xi}{\sigma^2}\right)^{(\mu/\sigma)^2} d\xi \qquad (4.41)$$

After some rearrangement, this can be written as

$$S(w, \tau) = \left(\frac{(\mu/\sigma^2)}{w^{-\beta}\tau + (\mu/\sigma^2)} \right)^{\xi} \frac{1}{\Gamma(\xi)} \int \exp\left(-\xi_w - \beta_\tau + \frac{\mu}{\sigma^2} \right)$$

$$\times \left(w^{-\beta_\tau} + \left(\frac{\mu}{\sigma^2} \right) \right)^{(\mu/\sigma)^2} \xi^{(\mu/\sigma)^2 - 1} d\xi$$

$$= \left(\frac{(\mu/\sigma^2)}{w^{-\beta_\tau} + (\mu/\sigma^2)} \right)^{(\mu/\sigma)^2} \tag{4.42}$$

Taking logs, we have

$$(w, \tau) = \left(\frac{\mu}{\sigma} \right)^2 \left(\log(\mu) - \log(\mu + \sigma^2 w^{-\beta_\tau}) \right) \tag{4.43}$$

Taking the elasticity of $-\log(S)$ with respect to the wage leads to

$$\frac{\partial \log(-(w, \tau))}{\partial \log(w)} = -\beta \frac{(\sigma^2/\mu)w^{-\beta_\tau}}{1 + (\sigma^2/\mu)w^{-\beta_\tau}} \frac{1}{\log(1 + (\sigma^2/\mu)w^{-\beta_\tau})} > -\beta$$

$$\tag{4.44}$$

(4.44) shows that the estimated wage elasticity is biased towards zero by the presence of unobserved heterogeneity. The size of the bias is increasing in τ so the bias will be lower when a shorter period is used for estimation.

Appendix 4B

This appendix considers two generalizations of the static model of section 4.1.

The Employer Size–Wage Effect and Dynamic Labor Supply Curves

For the most part, our regressions have been of the current wage on current employment. As there is likely to be a difference between the short-run and long-run elasticity of the labor supply curve (see the discussion in section 2.2), one might wonder which elasticity is estimated using cross-sectional data when the true labor supply curve is dynamic.

Suppose the dynamic labor supply curve can be written in the following log-linear isoelastic form:[11]

[11] This might come from the equation $N_t - N_{t-1} = R(w_t) - s(w_t)N_{t-1}$ which says that the change in employment is the difference between recruits and quits.

$$w_t = \varepsilon^s(n_t - n_{t-1}) + \varepsilon n_{t-1} + \nu_{wt} \qquad (4.45)$$

where ε^s is the short-run elasticity and ε the long-run elasticity. When one estimates a static regression of w_t on n_t one will estimate

$$E(w_t \mid n_t) = \varepsilon^s n_t + E((\varepsilon - \varepsilon^s)n_{t-1} + \nu_{wt} \mid n_t) \qquad (4.46)$$

To work out the last term one needs to know the correlation between n_t and n_{t-1}. A simple model is the following:

$$n_t = \beta n_{t-1} + \nu_{nt} \qquad (4.47)$$

where β is a measure of the persistence in employment. One should think of this as being a reduced-form equation for employment. We will assume that $\nu_t = (\nu_{wt}, \nu_{nt})$ is independent of n_{t-1} and jointly normally distributed with mean zero and covariance matrix Σ. Denote by σ_w^2 the variance of ν_w, σ_n^2 the variance of ν_n and σ_{wn} the covariance between ν_w and ν_n. Given these assumptions, the unconditional distribution of n_t (and n_{t-1}) will be normal with variance $\sigma_n^2/(1 - \beta^2)$ and $\mathrm{Cov}(n_t, \nu_{nt}) = \sigma_n^2$. Hence, we will have

$$E(\nu_{wt} \mid \nu_{nt}) = \frac{\sigma_{wn}}{\sigma_n^2} \nu_{nt}$$

$$E(\nu_{nt} \mid n_t) = (1 - \beta^2)n_t \qquad (4.48)$$

Putting these into (4.48) leads to

$$E(w_t \mid n_t) = \left(\beta\varepsilon + (1 - \beta)\varepsilon^s + \frac{\sigma_{wn}(1 - \beta^2)}{\sigma_n^2} \right) n_t \qquad (4.49)$$

The last term is the simultaneous equations bias caused by the potential correlation between the errors in wage and employment equation: this term could be eliminated by the use of suitable instruments. The other term shows that the estimated elasticity will be a weighted average of the short- and long-run elasticities with the weight being determined by the persistence in employment. So, if employment has no persistence, we will estimate the short-run supply curve and if it has full hysteresis, then we will estimate the long-run elasticity. As the evolution of employment within plants seems quite close to a random walk, it is likely that the cross-sectional correlation between wages and employment estimates the long-run elasticity.

The Employer Size–Wage Effect and the Labor Cost Function

Section 2.3 introduced the generalized model of monopsony and recommended the use of the labor cost function to think about the extent of monopsony in the labor market. Yet, section 4.1 has reverted to a simple monopsony model in which the wage is the only instrument available to the employer for influencing its supply of labor. In this section, we show that the conclusions of the previous section are robust to using the labor cost function approach. Recall that the labor cost function $C(w, N)$ gave the per worker costs of recruitment and training if the firm pays a wage w and wants to have employment of N. To capture this idea assume that, if the firm spends C per worker on recruitment/training activities, its labor supply curve, (4.2), is modified to become

$$w = BC^{-\gamma}N^{\varepsilon} \tag{4.50}$$

where the isoelastic functional form is chosen for convenience. The formula for the rate of exploitation needs to be modified for the presence of C: the natural measure to use is $[Y' - w - C]/[w + C]$ as workers should not expect to receive their costs of training and recruitment.

As C is likely to be unobserved by the econometrician, one might think that the presence of C makes it very difficult to estimate the rate of exploitation. However, the following proposition shows that, once one has appropriately modified the formula for the rate of exploitation, the unobservability of C causes no problems and an estimate of the ESWE gives us the correct parameter estimate.

Proposition 4.8. *The rate of exploitation is given by*

$$\frac{Y'(N) - (w + C)}{w + C} = \frac{\varepsilon}{1 + \gamma} \tag{4.51}$$

and the "reduced-form" labor supply curve after concentrating out the optimal choice of C is given by

$$w = \gamma^{-\gamma/(1+\gamma)}B^{1/(1+\gamma)}N^{\varepsilon/(1+\gamma)} \tag{4.52}$$

Proof. Given N, C will be chosen to minimize $(w + C)$ which, using (4.50), leads to the first-order condition

$$1 = \gamma BC^{-(\gamma+1)}N^{\varepsilon} \quad \Rightarrow \quad C = \gamma w \tag{4.53}$$

Substituting this expression for C into (4.50) and rearranging leads to

$$w = \gamma^{-\gamma/(1+\gamma)}B^{1/(1+\gamma)}N^{\varepsilon/(1+\gamma)} \tag{4.54}$$

which is (4.52). N will then be chosen to maximize $Y(N) - (1 + \gamma)wN$ where w is given in (4.54). Using the fact that (4.53) implies that $(w + C) = (1 + \gamma)w$, leads to the first-order condition of (4.51).

(4.51) says that we want to be able to estimate $\varepsilon/(1 + \gamma)$ to estimate the rate of exploitation while (4.52) says that it is exactly the parameter we would expect to estimate if we run a regression of $\log(w)$ on $\log(N)$. Of course, all the problems we have discussed earlier surrounding the estimation of (4.52) still apply: it is just that acknowledging the labor cost function causes no additional problem.

Part Two

THE STRUCTURE OF WAGES

5

The Wage Policies of Employers

To maximize profits employers would like to obtain workers at the lowest possible cost. In the models used in previous chapters, employers were constrained to set a single wage for all their workers. The choice of this wage forces the employer to trade off the number of workers (the higher the wage the easier is recruitment and retention of workers) against the profit per worker (the higher the wage the higher are labor costs). The employer ends up paying some workers more than it needs to recruit them and misses out on the recruitment and retention of other workers it could have profitably retained at a different wage. There is an incentive for employers to find alternative wage strategies to increase profits. In the jargon of economists, employers have been assumed to be a simple monopsonist, but there are incentives for them to become a discriminating monopsonist.

The ways in which employers might try to do this are the subject of this chapter. It has two main conclusions. First, that employers with market power are predicted to use wage policies similar to those observed, for example, the use of seniority wage schedules. This is confirmation of the usefulness of our approach to labor markets but it also raises the possibility that conclusions based on the simple models of previous chapters could be misleading. In the static theory of monopsony, it is well known that inefficiency is eliminated if employers can practice perfect wage discrimination although all surplus would then all go to the employer. In dynamic models of monopsony and oligopsony, matters are more complicated: chapter 3 came to the conclusion that there are situations in which increasing the employer share of the surplus may reduce efficiency; in this case wage discrimination may worsen performance. For example, if employers do manage to extract all surplus from matches with workers, then there are no incentives for workers to search or invest in human capital. The important distinction is between ex ante and ex post efficiency, a distinction that does not arise in a static model.

The chapter then argues that, in practice, evidence strongly suggests that employers are severely limited in their ability to be discriminating monopsonists. In particular, wage variation is very low among workers who do the same job: the reasons for this are not entirely clear but may well have something to do with worker demands for fairness. Although these forces that limit wage variation are somewhat mysterious they do seem to act as a powerful constraint on the ability of employers to be discriminating monopsonists.

5.1 The Discriminating Monopsonist

In the simple Burdett–Mortensen model of section 2.4, a firm that pays all workers a single wage w is missing out on two potential sources of extra profits:

- employed workers who leave the firm when they get a better offer from elsewhere but who could be induced to stay if their current wage was raised sufficiently;
- workers employed in other firms at higher wages who could be profitably induced to move to this firm by the offer of a higher wage.

In addition, if there is heterogeneity in the reservation wages of workers (as in the modified Burdett–Mortensen model of section 3.5), then paying a single wage also misses out on profits from:

- new workers hired from non-employment whose reservation wage is below w so could have been hired more cheaply;
- non-employed workers whose reservation wage is above w but who could be profitably employed at a higher wage.

There are incentives for firms to design strategies to capture some of these untapped profits. As this means paying different wages to different workers according to their circumstances (but not their productivity which, in this chapter, is assumed identical), this is a form of wage discrimination.

Extra profits from the last two groups of workers can be captured if the reservation wage can be observed. There are obvious difficulties in doing this as it is not clear how the employer can obtain the requisite information on the reservation wage. For example, in the simple model of sections 2.4 and 3.5, the reservation wage is simply the value of leisure.[1] It is plausible to assume that the value of leisure is the private information of the worker in which case the only incentive compatible contract would be to offer the same contract to all workers.[2] To the extent that the reservation wage is correlated with some observable characteristics, we

---

[1] In the more complicated model of the reservation wage introduced in section 9.1, the value of leisure continues to be important.

[2] This is because employment is a 0–1 decision in the current model: if there was a continuous employment decision, for example, the choice of hours, then it is possible that, by using a wage–hours package, the employer may be able to successfully wage discriminate although this discrimination will generally be less than perfect.

would expect to see employers making different wage offers to these groups, an idea that we pursue further in chapter 7 when we discuss discrimination. But, unless the reservation wage can be perfectly predicted, the employer will be unable to capture all the surplus in this way and some workers who could be profitably employed will remain unemployed.

Now consider the strategy for dealing with workers who are already in employment. If all other firms are following single wage strategies, then it is optimal for this firm to pursue a strategy of offer-matching. When an existing worker receives a better offer from elsewhere, the employer should match that offer (as long as it does not exceed the marginal product of the worker). And, when matched with a worker currently employed elsewhere, this employer should match their wage (or pay them slightly above it) to induce them to move, again subject to the proviso that this wage offer does not exceed their marginal product.

Of course, we would expect other firms to pursue a similar strategy so let us consider briefly what would happen in general equilibrium if all firms pursued offer-matching strategies (a question analyzed by Postel-Vinay and Robin 2002). In modeling such a labor market, the most important decision is how to model what happens when an employed worker manages to match with another employer. One assumption is that the two potential employers make offers to the worker who then accepts the higher of the two. The firm that values the worker most will hire the worker at a wage equal to the productivity of the worker in the other firm. In the present model where the productivity of the worker is the same in all firms, this means that the wage will immediately get bid up to p as soon as the first external wage offer when in employment is received.[3] This may seem to be very destructive of the firm's profits as no employer then makes any further profit from the worker but the initial wage paid to workers recruited from unemployment can be adjusted downwards as workers will be very enthusiastic to get into employment. Because there is no competition among employers for workers entering jobs from non-employment, workers may do worse in a labor market with offer-matching than in the labor market with the single wage policy even though one might have thought that offer-matching would be good for workers. Workers will certainly be worse off when there is no variation in reservation wages across workers as the employers can then set the initial wage to extract all the surplus from workers.[4]

---

[3] Matters are much more complicated if there is heterogeneity in the productivity of firms; see Postel-Vinay and Robin (2002) for an analysis of this case. But, the conclusion that offer-matching is to the disadvantage of workers remains.

[4] We will not present a formal analysis of this labor market as it is isomorphic to the model of seniority wages that we consider later.

Although offer-matching is seen in some labor markets (perhaps most familiarly the American academic labor market), it is relatively rare. Even in labor markets that one thinks of as being highly individualistic, such as Wall Street, employers seem reluctant to engage in offer-matching: Lewis (1989: 149) describes how Salomon Brothers lost their most profitable bond trader because of their refusal to break a company policy capping the salary they would pay. Weiss (1990: 46) cites a *Wall Street Journal* article on the subject of offer-matching and suggests a number of possible reasons for its rarity.

First, he suggests that if an offer-matching strategy is pursued, workers will have an incentive to search for outside offers with the result that they leave jobs more quickly. Offer-matching is then to the disadvantage of employers. But, if the outside wage offers are treated as exogenous (so there is no bidding game for the worker among potential employers) workers end up with a wage that they would have received in the absence of offer-matching (the only difference being which employer they work for) so the incentives to search are the same both with and without offer-matching. With offer-matching, as the firm gets to keep the worker and continue to make profits from them in some situations where they would have quit in the absence of offer-matching, this argument alone cannot explain the rarity of offer-matching. But it is plausible to assume that workers also receive some non-pecuniary benefit from the job that is their private information. Then, a worker who particularly likes the job and who has no intention of moving unless they get a much better wage offer may not search much if there is no offer-matching but may search harder when there is offer-matching.

The second argument that Weiss presents is that it may be very difficult for the employer to verify outside wage offers. If, at the extreme, the employer has no ability whatsoever to observe outside offers, then any employer that instigated an offer-matching strategy would find that its workers immediately generated outside wage offers that just happened to be equal to their marginal product within the firm.[5] The appeal of this approach is that it can explain why offer-matching seems more frequent in some labor markets than others. For example, in the US academic labor market, there is an enormous amount of information about both workers and employers: a professor who wanted a raise because he/she claimed he/she had a fantastic job offer from the East Kansas Bible School of Business would lack credibility. But, offer-matching is much rarer in labor markets for unskilled workers because they are much more anonymous: a worker in Kentucky Fried Chicken who claimed they had a good outside offer from East Kansas Fried Chicken just

---

[5] It might be recognized that even this is not a problem if entry fees can be charged for workers to the firm: this insight is discussed in the next section.

might be telling the truth.[6] So, we might expect offer-matching to be more frequent in less anonymous labor markets where there is good information about alternative employers and workers.

Finally, Weiss suggests that offer-matching is bad for morale. The distribution of wages among the workers in the firm will reflect, not just productivity, but who has been lucky enough in exciting the interest of outside employers: it is commonly argued that such wage variation is disliked intensely by workers and is avoided by employers. We will present evidence later in this chapter that there is surprisingly little wage variation within firms which suggests that there may be some truth in this. Many economists are unhappy with assuming that workers have preferences of this sort but these economists often make the mistake of imagining that the conventional way in which the utility function is modeled with the individual caring only about what happens to themselves is anything more than an arbitrary (although convenient) assumption (for the confession of a largely neoclassical economist in this regard, see Rees 1993).

So, there are a number of powerful reasons why there may be serious limits to the offer-matching strategies that can be pursued by employers and this puts limits on their ability to act as discriminating monopsonists.

5.2 Non-Manipulable Wage Discrimination

The basic problem with the wage discrimination strategies described above is that they are extremely vulnerable to exploitation by workers when the employer's information is less than perfect. For example, paying different wages according to the worker's reservation wage or matching outside offers is unlikely to be a sensible strategy when reservation wages are unobservable, when the worker obtains an unobservable non-pecuniary benefit from the job, or when outside offers are unverifiable. The point that feasible labor contracts are severely limited by the information available to employers is one also made by Hall and Lazear (1984) who use similar arguments to the ones presented here. But, these arguments do not mean that the firm cannot practice any wage discrimination: it just means that any wage discrimination that is practiced must be based on characteristics of the worker that are non-manipulable. Chapter 7 considers discrimination on the grounds of sex. Here we consider two other characteristics of the worker that are observable: age and job tenure.

[6] In fact, to the best of my knowledge, there is no East Kansas Fried Chicken but there is a Kansas Fried Chicken along with Tennessee, Miami, Tex-Ann, Dixy, Kennedy, KCFC among others.

5.2.1 Seniority Wages

This section considers the optimal contract when the firm is allowed to pay different wages to workers according to their seniority on the job. In particular, we assume that a wage $w(t)$ is paid to a worker with job tenure t. For reasons that will become apparent, we also assume that a worker joining the firm makes a lump-sum payment of B to the employer. We assume that the employer can commit to the contract $\{w(t), B\}$ so a worker offered a contract believes it will be honored.

The important consequences of this contract structure can be conveyed in a partial equilibrium model. So, at the risk of some abuse of the notation used in previous chapters, assume that the distribution of the *value* of outside jobs is $F(V)$ and assume that this does not vary with job tenure in this firm on the grounds that workers are forced to start anew in any new job. Assume that the flow of recruits to the firm also depends on the value of the job: denote this function by $R(V)$.

The value of a job in this firm obviously depends on the tenure of the worker. Denote by $V(t)$ the value of the job to a worker with tenure t.[7] $V(t)$ must satisfy

$$\delta_r V(t) = w(t) - \delta_u[V(t) - V^u] + \lambda \int_{V(t)} [V - V(t)]dF(V) + V'(t) \quad (5.1)$$

where we have assumed from the outset that the value function is differentiable (as will turn out to be the case).

The separation rate for workers of tenure t will be $\delta + \lambda[1 - F(V(t))]$ so that the employment of workers of tenure t, $N(t)$ must satisfy the following differential equation:

$$N'(t) = -[\delta + \lambda[1 - F(V(t))]]N(t) \quad (5.2)$$

Employment of new workers, $N(0)$ must be given by the new recruits so that

$$N(0) = R(V(0) - B) \quad (5.3)$$

which reflects the fact that the entrance fee has not been included in the specification of the value function in (5.1). In a steady state, profits, Π, will be given by

$$\Pi = \int_0^\infty [p - w(t)]N(t)dt + BN(0) \quad (5.4)$$

The employer wants to choose $\{w(t), B\}$ to maximize (5.4) subject to (5.1)–(5.3). The solution to this problem is contained in the following proposition.

---

[7] Note that the argument of the value function used here is job tenure, not wages as in most other parts of the book.

Proposition 5.1. *An optimal wage strategy for the firm is to set the wage equal to marginal product, p, at all tenures and choose the "entry fee" B to maximize*

$$\Pi = BR(V^* - B) \qquad (5.5)$$

where V^* is the value of the job to the workers when the wage is always equal to the marginal product.

Proof. See Appendix 5.

There is a very simple intuition behind this result. In the situation where the employer is a simple monopsonist setting a single wage for all workers with no entry fee, the level of the wage is determined by two conflicting pressures. On the one hand, high wages reduce the profit per worker but, on the other hand, high wages reduce quits. As soon as seniority wage schedules and entrance fees are allowed, high wages can be used to deter quits without necessarily reducing profits because the benefit to the worker of higher future wages can be captured by the firm in the form of higher entrance fees.

It should be noted that the optimal contract is not unique. For example, if a wage below p is high enough to prevent all quitting to other employment, then that wage can also be optimal together with a reduced value of B.[8] Stevens (1998) provides a more thorough analysis of the set of optimal wage policies and shows that all optimal policies must have the same turnover outcomes and the same value of a job for workers joining the firm.

The idea that the wage structure can be used to deter quits is not new. Ioannides and Pissarides (1985) present a two-period model of a monopsonistic labor market, where it is optimal for older workers to be paid their marginal product and younger workers to be paid less. They argue that their result shows that it is optimal for wages to increase with job tenure. However, Proposition 5.1 shows that the optimal wage structure in a model with more than two periods does not really resemble a smooth relationship between wages and job tenure. It is optimal to pay all workers a wage equal to their marginal product but to make new workers "buy" their jobs: this point is obscured in a two-period model.

Proposition 5.1 shows that the employer can increase profits by moving from a contract in which the only payment between employers and workers is a constant wage to one in which this constant wage is supplemented by an entry fee. But, one might also wonder if the firm cannot do even

---

[8] The optimal contract in this case can also be thought of as the optimal contract in the presence of offer-matching where B is interpreted as the value of the low initial wage paid to workers recruited from unemployment.

better by introducing a richer form of labor contract. For example, one might wonder whether an improvement could be made if lump-sum payments were made between worker and firm not only when the worker joins the firm but also when the worker leaves the firm, that is, to consider severance payments and/or bonding arrangements. To investigate this, let us assume that the wage contract can be represented by $\{w(t), S(t), B\}$ where $S(t)$ is a payment made by the worker to the firm whenever they leave it (which could be negative). One might want to allow for these severance payments to differ by the reason why the worker leaves the firm. But it seems reasonable to assume that this is not feasible as a worker could always artificially induce a period of unemployment before starting a new job if it was beneficial to do so. The following proposition shows that allowing for severance payments introduces no new freedom for the employer.

Proposition 5.2. *An employment contract with severance payments is equivalent to one without. In particular, the contract* $\{w(t), S(t), B\}$ *with severance payments is exactly equivalent to the following employment contract without severance payments:*

$$\tilde{w}(t) = w(t) - S'(t) \tag{5.6}$$

$$\tilde{B} = B + S(0) \tag{5.7}$$

Proof.   See Appendix 5.

The intuition for this result (which can also be found in Stevens 1998) is very simple. First consider the case where the severance payment is constant. A worker joining the firm knows that he/she will leave it at some point, thus incurring the severance payment, so that the real effective entrance fee is the actual entrance fee plus the severance payment.[9] If the severance payment is not constant, then one can think of the reward to staying with the firm for an extra period as being the wage payment minus the change in the severance payment which is (5.6). The effective entrance fee is now the actual entrance fee plus the initial severance payment.

The optimal contract derived here is not really close to anything that is observed in most of the labor market. Seniority wage schedules do exist, but they do not have the extreme form suggested by the model derived

---

[9] This uses the assumption that agents do not discount the future. One might reasonably wonder if this is important: it is not if both workers and employers have the same discount rate although the equations need modification. But, equivalence will fail if the discount rates of worker and employer differ.

above. In particular, entrance fees are extremely rare. To understand the reasons for this, we can draw here on discussion of another labor market model, the shirking version of the efficiency wage model (Shapiro and Stiglitz 1984) which attempts to explain the existence of involuntary unemployment. This debate is about whether firms can get workers to post bonds that are forfeited in the case of bad performance (Carmichael 1985).

One argument about the limit to entrance fees is that the access of workers to capital and insurance markets is often limited and workers want to smooth consumption both over time and across states of nature (although we have implicitly assumed they only care about the expected discounted income stream). So, workers might simply not be able to afford the entrance fee demanded by the first-best contract.[10] In addition, some of these workers might lose their jobs very quickly so will not have had time to recoup any of the gains. To some extent one can avoid these problems by judicious use of severance payments. For example, one could implement the first-best contract without any entrance fee by setting a severance payment equal to the optimal entrance fee and then paying workers their marginal product. Workers are not then required to put any money up front into the firm. But, they are still exposed to substantial risk as a worker who is unlucky enough to be forced to leave the job very quickly has a large liability to the employer and their ability to pay will again be limited by capital market imperfections.[11] However, large severance payments are problematic in many countries where anti-slavery laws make courts reluctant to enforce any labor contract that looks like it gives the worker no choice but to remain with their employer.

Another problem with the use of entrance fees is the potential for abuse of the system by employers. There are obvious incentives for the employer to take the entrance fee from the worker and then fire them. This potential problem has been addressed in the context of the shirking model by Macleod and Malcomson (1989) who argue that this is not a serious problem. Put in the context of the current model, their argument is essentially that employers do not have a positive incentive to fire workers after they have paid their entrance fee as workers are being paid less than their marginal product and reputation effects will prevent employers from behaving in this way. But, their model is too optimistic in one important way. It is implicitly assumed that firms have sunk some investment in the

---

[10] Burdett and Coles (2001) analyze a model of the type considered here with risk-averse workers.

[11] Better insurance could be achieved if the severance payment could differ according to whether the worker leaves for unemployment or another job as the move to the new job, being voluntary, must make the worker better off whereas the involuntary move to unemployment does not.

creation of the job so that all employers have something to lose if they get a reputation for cheating workers. The assumption that creating a job is costly is a reasonable assumption when the employment contract is a constant wage as workers know that any employer offering this presumably has some productive job behind it or else they would not make any profit. But, imagine what would happen if the form of employment contracts was such that workers were asked to put money up front into a job. There is then an incentive for rogue employers to try to recruit workers even if they have no real job. As the set-up costs for a fake job are likely to be very low, the market would become swamped with fraudulent employers who promise workers jobs, take their entrance fees, and run. So, it does seem a reasonable argument that any employer that tried to offer an employment contract with large entrance fees would be treated with the utmost suspicion by workers. In fact, many newspapers, London lamp posts (and increasingly e-mails) contain advertisements for jobs which promise very large rewards—so large, that I would be well advised to apply for them. On investigation (something I would recommend just for the curiosity value) these "jobs" typically require the purchase of materials or training information (which are equivalent to entrance fees as I suspect they are substantially above the marginal cost of these materials) and, if one is unwise enough to pursue this further, one often finds it is very hard to get any money at all out of the "employer" as one's work is often deemed unsatisfactory. I suspect that I and most other workers are wise in their avoidance of these tempting job offers.

One simple way of modeling the constraints imposed by capital market constraints and employer opportunism is to impose a restriction on the optimal contract that the worker can never be in debt to the firm, that is,

$$-B + \int_0^t w(s)ds \geq 0 \qquad \text{for all } t \tag{5.8}$$

(5.8) requires the total cumulative payment from firm to worker at any tenure t to be non-negative. This requires that $B \leq 0$ and that $w(t)$ must start off positive. One optimal contract with this restriction is given by the following proposition.

Proposition 5.3. *If workers can never be in debt to employers (i.e., the constraint (5.8) is imposed on the set of feasible contracts), then it is optimal for the employer to offer a zero wage for a certain period of time and then to raise the wage to the marginal product.*

Proof.   See Appendix 5.

This type of contract (which Stevens calls a step contract) begins to bear some resemblance to what is commonly observed where workers are offered a low starting wage for a probationary period and the wage is then raised to their marginal product.[12] Again, Stevens (1998) has shown that the optimal contract is not unique but that employers can never do better than using a step contract.

A final problem with the use of entrance fees is that a lot of information is needed to set them. In particular, one needs to know the value of the job to workers when they are paid their marginal product which needs knowledge of their quit rates. There is a certain amount of empirical evidence (Weiss 1984; Farber 1994) that there is important individual heterogeneity in quit propensities. An employer's information about individual quit propensities is likely to be very imperfect so that it is reasonable to think of the quit rate of workers as being their private information in which case the entrance fee cannot be made contingent on it. A contract with a high entrance fee now has the rather undesirable feature that it is unattractive to workers with high quit propensities.[13] Analyzing the optimal contract in this case is rather difficult. So we will proceed by considering a simple example.

Suppose that, once in employment, workers only leave the job to exit the labor force and there is no potential for job-to-job mobility. A worker with quit rate δ in employment then has an expected revenue of (p/δ). If the supply of workers with quit rate δ is given by $R(V, \delta)$ then profits from δ workers will be given by

$$\Pi = \left(\frac{p}{\delta} - V\right)R(V, \delta) \qquad (5.9)$$

Suppose that δ is observable. Then V will be chosen to maximize (5.9): denote the choice by $V^*(\delta)$. The optimal contract is not uniquely determined: any $\{w(t), B\}$ which satisfies

$$\int_0^\infty w(t)\exp(-\delta t)dt - B = V^*(\delta) \qquad (5.10)$$

will do the job. In our previous model, this indeterminacy was partially resolved by the fact that the employer also wants to deter quits.

Now suppose that δ is not observable and that only a single contract $\{w(t), B\}$ can be offered by the employer.[14] The employer can obtain the

---

[12] One could also impose a subsistence requirement that workers wages cannot fall below a strictly positive amount. This would have straightforward consequences for the optimal contract.

[13] This disadvantage may be a blessing in disguise if there are training costs. Salop and Salop (1976) present such a model in which entrance fees are used to discourage workers with high quit propensities.

[14] We are ignoring here the possibility of self-selecting contracts being offered by the firm.

first-best if it can find a contract that satisfies (5.10) for all δ. This is possible in some cases. For example, suppose that $R(V, \delta) = r(\delta)V^{\alpha}$ so that the supply is isoelastic with the same elasticity for all δ. Then it is simple to show that $V^*(\delta) = [\alpha/(1 + \alpha)](p/\delta)$. This is attainable even if δ is not observable if a constant wage is offered with $w = [\alpha p/(1 + \alpha)]$ and no entrance fee. Of course, with other specifications of the supply curve a different result would be obtained, but the isoelastic specification is the most natural place to start. So, in the absence of competition for workers from other employers, it is likely that the employer will offer a rather flat wage–tenure schedule. With competition from other employers, it is likely that the employer will try to choose the wage structure to hit two conflicting targets: a steep wage–tenure profile to deter quits but a flat one so that workers with a high quit propensity are still attracted to the firm.

The optimal contract in this case is likely to be a mess but that is probably the right conclusion. The important point is that the degrees of freedom available to the employer in designing its wage policy are unlikely to be sufficient to meet all its conflicting objectives. Different employers are likely to find different wage policies optimal and that accounts for the very considerable diversity that is observed.

It is also worth mentioning the ingenious discussion of Stevens (1998) about the general equilibrium features of a monopsonistic labor market in which employers can use these policies. She shows that the Burdett–Mortensen conclusion that there must be wage heterogeneity across firms disappears and all firms offer equivalent wage–tenure contracts. However, wage dispersion remains as identical workers receive different wages within the firm according to their seniority. However, Burdett and Coles (2001) show that employer heterogeneity in equilibrium contracts is re-established if workers are risk averse.

5.2.2 Wage Discrimination by Age

There are also incentives in the Burdett–Mortensen model for employers to pay different wages to workers of different ages. The reason for this is that the non-employment rate of workers is declining with age so that an older worker is more likely to be recruited from other firms and to be in higher-wage jobs. Both factors encourage the employer to pay higher wages to older workers. But, as long as some workers of every age are recruited from non-employment it will never be optimal for the employer to pay a worker of any age their marginal product.

In practice, the non-employment rate by age is fairly flat after the age of 25 so that this effect might not be expected to be very important for adults. But for younger workers, it is potentially important and could account for the widespread practice of paying distinct (and lower) youth wages.

5.3 Empirical Evidence

In this section, we present empirical evidence in support of two of the main claims made above. First, that employers do have wage structures that are broadly consistent with the model, notably that they do tend to pay higher wages to older and more senior workers. Secondly, that the wage policies pursued by employers show evidence that they are not flexible enough to attain all objectives so that they fall some way short of attaining their ideal of being perfectly discriminating monopsonists.

5.3.1 Wages, Age and Tenure Within the Firm

It is well known that there are generally positive correlations between wages, age, and tenure in the labor market as a whole. The next chapter examines the hypothesis that part of the cross-sectional returns can be explained by the fact that, in a labor market with frictions, it takes time to find a good job and, once one has found it, one tends to keep it. But, that is not what interests us here. We are interested in whether, *within firms*, employers pay higher wages to older or more senior workers.

There are obviously other theories as to why older and more senior workers get paid more. The most popular explanation is based on human capital theory: that older workers are paid more because they are more productive, and that more senior workers have accumulated more firm-specific human capital and it is optimal for the employer to give workers a share of these rents.

Although human capital theory is the accepted way of thinking about the returns to tenure, the reasoning behind it is not as sound as one is often led to believe. Strictly speaking, an employer has no need to pay a worker in a competitive labor market a wage any higher than what they could obtain in the open labor market, that is, "if all training were completely specific, the wage that an employee could get elsewhere would be independent of the amount of training received. One might plausibly argue, then that the wage paid by firms would also be independent of training" (Becker 1993: 41–42). But Becker (1993) argues that if the worker was only paid his/her outside option then, if he/she quits, the rents lost by the employer would not be taken into account. But, in the perfectly competitive world of full information where outside options are perfectly known and costlessly available, this argument is unpersuasive. If the worker's outside option rises and he/she threatens to quit, then the simple thing to do is to match the outside option. This is not only simple, but efficient. There is no reason why the wage paid should be determined

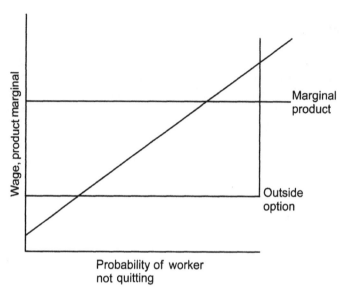

Figure 5.1 The Hashimoto model.

by anything other than the outside option, that is, we would not expect it to be related to the extent of job-specific human capital. It is simple to understand this in terms of figure 5.1. The quit probability of the worker is 1 for a wage below the outside option and zero for a wage above it leading to the "backward-L" shaped labor supply curve of figure 5.1. The profit-maximizing thing to do is then to pay the outside option and this is independent of the productivity of the worker in this particular firm. One way to understand this is to think of the retention function as being the labor supply curve facing the firm and to recognize that this labor supply curve is the competitive one as it is perfectly elastic at the outside wage.

Becker's informal argument about the sharing of the returns to specific human capital is normally argued to be supported by the more formal model of Hashimoto (1981). The optimal contract in his model is derived by assuming that the outside option is either unobserved by the firm or that it is simply too costly to write a contract contingent on it. The retention probability of the worker is no longer the right angle of figure 5.1 but a smooth increasing function of the wage as also drawn in figure 5.1. Hashimoto then shows that the optimal wage to pay is increasing in the productivity of the worker.[15]

But, it is important to realize that this result is only obtained by effec-

---

[15] His model is actually more complicated as he has uncertainty about the returns to specific human capital within the firm so that he can also focus on the possibility of firing.

tively assuming that the labor market is monopsonistic, that is, that the supply curve of labor facing the firm is not perfectly elastic as the higher the wage paid, the higher the probability of retaining the worker, and, hence, the higher the level of expected employment. Becker (1993: 44) admits as much: "the likelihood of a quit is not fixed but depends on wages." But, once one allows this, all other sorts of problems emerge. For example, one could argue that the labor market remains competitive because, at the moment the worker is hired, there is a well-defined outside option which is the market price for the worker. But, if one wants to assume that the outside option of the worker is uncertain ex post, then it seems natural to argue that it is also uncertain at the point of hiring and then labor markets are truly monopsonistic with all that that implies. For example, there seems no good reason why the outside option available to the worker in the Hashimoto model should be his /her marginal product in other firms, yet that is the assumption made. Not for the first time, we find monopsony arguments being used when convenient but a failure to fully think through the implications of the assumption being made. It is much better to think of the Hashimoto model as showing why, in a monopsonistic market, firms in which workers (for whatever reason) have higher productivity will pay higher wages; we return to this subject in chapter 8.[16]

However, there is some evidence that we should be skeptical of the statement that more experienced, senior workers are indeed more productive. To test this hypothesis one obviously needs data on the productivity of workers independent of the wage and that is hard to come by. For example, Medoff and Abraham (1980, 1981) found that in two US corporations the correlation between the pay of professional and managerial workers and their experience was much stronger than the correlation between performance and experience.

There are other non-competitive explanations of why wages may vary with age and tenure independent of productivity. For example, shirking versions of efficiency wage models have suggested that an upward-sloping wage profile is a cost-effective way of providing incentives for workers (Lazear 1979; Akerlof and Katz 1989). There is no way that the available data can sort out this hypothesis from ours as they are extremely similar. In both cases the wage policy of the firm is determined by the struggle between two competing problems: the desire to lower labor costs and the desire to ease recruitment and retention in our case, and the desire to provide incentives not to shirk in the incentive models. In fact, we freely

---

[16] One implication of this discussion is that even if one did show, as Brown (1989) claims, that firm-specific wage growth occurs almost exclusively during periods of on-the-job training, this could legitimately be taken as evidence of the existence of monopsony rather than the validity of a competitive human capital story as one would expect employers to raise wages when productivity is raised by training.

used ideas from this efficiency wage literature in our discussion of the constraints on the wage policy of the firm.

5.3.2 Constraints on Wage Policies

The evidence of the previous section suggests that the variation in wages within firms cannot all be explained by variations in productivity as the traditional human capital approach would suggest. This leaves open the possibility that employers do practice some wage discrimination and are not simple monopsonists. The natural next question is whether employers manage to get sufficient flexibility in their wage structures to be usefully seen as perfectly discriminating monopsonists. To address this question directly would require information on the productivity of workers and their alternative sources of employment in the labor market and this is simply not available. So, this section takes another approach to the question.

There is considerable evidence that wage policies within firms are not individualized to any great degree: there seem to be powerful forces making the terms and conditions offered to workers in a given job within a firm very similar. Given that it is plausible that there is considerable heterogeneity among the workers within a firm, this evidence implies that the firm is not able to take account of the specific circumstances of an individual worker in determining his/her contract of employment and, hence, is not able to get close to being a discriminating monopsonist. This view of the lack of individuality in employment contracts is not new: Webb and Webb (1897: 281) wrote that "the most autocratic and unfettered employer spontaneously adopts Standard Rates for classes of workmen, just as the large shopkeeper fixes his prices, not according to the higgling capacity of particular customers, but by a definite percentage on cost."

We present two pieces of evidence on the lack of individuality in employment contracts. First, we have data from a survey of wages in vacancies posted in UK job centers conducted by the Manchester Low Pay Unit in the spring of 1994. On 1 September 1993 the Wages Councils that had previously set minimum wages in a number of low-paying sectors were abolished and (except in agriculture) the United Kingdom had no minimum wage. Because of the standard provisions of employment law, employers were unable to cut wages for existing workers. But, there were no such restrictions placed on the wages that could be offered to new recruits. So, when the Manchester Low Pay Unit conducted a survey of wages offered to new recruits in sectors that had been covered by the Wages Councils there was no reason why the minimum wage that had previously been in force would have any particular salience. Yet, what they found was a spike of wage offers at or very close to the minimum wage. The data are shown in table 5.1. On average, 18% of vacan-

TABLE 5.1
Starting Wages in Old Wages Council Industries

Wages Council	Hotels/ Restaurants	Cafes	Pubs/ Clubs	Food Retail	Non-food Retail	Clothing	Hair- dressing	All
Minimum wage at abolition	2.92	2.99	5.01	5.17	5.15	2.71	2.88	n.a.
Number of vacancies	702	182	469	293	471	270	127	2514
Average wage	5.16	5.07	5.10	5.19	5.32	5.01	5.16	5.16
Percent at old minimum	15	5	45	15	10	3	12	18
Percent at closest "focal" wage	1	27	12	4	10	6	2	8
Percent within 1% of old minimum	16	35	59	33	19	8	16	27
Percent within 5% of old minimum	56	59	81	55	53	23	42	56

Notes.
1. Source is data collected in spring 1994 by Manchester Low Pay Unit (Cox 1995). The data are the wages at which vacancies are advertised in Manchester job centers.

cies were at exactly the old minimum wage although the percentage varies considerably from 3% in clothing manufacturing to 45% in pubs and clubs. It should be noted that the minimum wages were set at hourly wages which were not round numbers at which one typically sees spikes in wage distributions. For example, the minimum wage was set at £2.99 in cafes and 5% of vacancies offered exactly this, but one never normally sees hourly wages reported that end in "99" (e.g., in the US CPS only one in a thousand workers report an hourly wage ending in a "99"). But unsurprisingly there was a larger spike at £3.00 per hour so the next row reports the size of the spike at the nearest "focal" wage, that is, an hourly wage ending in a zero or a five. The last two rows report the fraction of wage offers within 1% and 5% of the old minimum: these are large numbers. Even in the industries where there is a small spike close to the old minimum, this is because there is a very large spike at some other wage (25% at £3 per hour in cafes). All this suggests a picture in which initial wages are not very sensitive to the characteristics of the individual job applicant.

But, this is about the wages posted by employers at job centers: it says nothing about wages actually paid. But we do see a similar picture among wages actually paid. Machin and Manning (2002) report the results of a survey of workers in residential homes for the elderly on the south coast of England in 1992 and 1993. There was no minimum wage in this sector, nor any unions or prospect of unions, so the wage structures we observe are the "free" choices of the employers. Yet, we still see a lack of individuality in the wages paid. 26% of workers work in the 31% of firms that have only a single hourly wage paid to all their care assistants (the main occupation). And the fraction of the total variation in wages that is within-firm is, as table 5.2 reports, much lower than the fraction of any other variable on which we have data (age, hours, and job tenure).[17] This remains true even if we have very detailed geographical controls and if we restrict attention to the larger firms in the sample.

All this adds up to a picture of a labor market in which there are serious constraints on the ability of firms to individualize wages and that these constraints will act as a limitation on the ability of firms to act as discriminating monopsonists. The obvious next question is "why don't firms individualize wages?" There are a number of possible explanations for this. Webb and Webb (1897) saw "practical convenience and the growth of large establishments" as the reason, while a number of authors (e.g., Akerlof and Yellen 1990; Solow 1990; Bewley 1999) have suggested that morale of workers suffers if the wage policy is felt to be unjust.

---

[17] It is important to remember that we are looking at wage dispersion in a very tightly defined occupation. The wage gap between managers and cleaners is almost certainly largely within-firm.

TABLE 5.2
Wage Dispersion Within Firms: Evidence from UK Residential Nursing Homes

		Log Wage	Log Age	Log Tenure	Log Hours
All workers					
No controls	1992	0.74	0.25	0.32	0.36
	1993	0.80	0.20	0.30	0.36
Area controls	1992	0.68	0.24	0.33	0.35
	1993	0.76	0.21	0.29	0.35
Town controls	1992	0.57	0.18	0.26	0.24
	1993	0.65	0.15	0.21	0.23
Workers in firms with more than five workers					
No controls	1992	0.72	0.20	0.28	0.31
	1993	0.80	0.16	0.27	0.29
Area controls	1992	0.65	0.19	0.30	0.30
	1993	0.75	0.17	0.25	0.28
Town controls	1992	0.48	0.11	0.20	0.16
	1993	0.59	0.10	0.15	0.12

Notes.
1. The data in this table come from a survey of workers in residential care homes for the elderly on the south coast of England conducted in 1992 and 1995. The results presented here refer only to those workers classified as "day care assistant." See Machin et al. (1993) and Machin and Manning (2002) for more details of this data set.
2. The number in each column represents the fraction of total dispersion in the relevant variable (log wage, age, tenure, or hours) that is between-firm.

Although the recent literature has primarily emphasized concerns for fairness among workers, concerns for fairness among employers may also be important. Some older work (e.g., Reynolds 1951) argued that employers see other employers who actively poach workers as being engaged in unfair competition to some extent and this could also act to preserve company wage policies.[18] This requires at least some implicit collusion among employers, and we lack any study of the extent of such collusion in modern labor markets, although most economists probably think it rather limited. And, the evidence of Freeman and Medoff (1984) that intra-firm wage dispersion is reduced by the activities of unions suggests that the preferences of workers is important.

Another possible problem is that once wages become individualistic, workers may also realize they have some bargaining power because of

---

[18] Consider the following quotes from Reynolds (1951): "each personnel manager knows that, if he steals a worker today, someone else will steal from him tomorrow, and all have an interest in playing by the game" (p. 51), and "the more significant meaning of competition is impersonal rivalry in which each employer establishes terms of employment designed to attract the number and types of workers he wants" (p. 216).

labor market frictions and use this to obtain higher wages for themselves. This is the assumption usually made in the matching literature (e.g., Diamond 1981, 1982; Pissarides 1985). Peters (1991) has shown that firms may be better off if they could post wages in advance; the problem being whether this is credible. Non-individualistic wage policies could be one way of sustaining credibility. Firms want to get a reputation for not responding to worker attempts to use their bargaining power to get higher wages. Because an employer typically has more than one worker, there is an incentive to build such a reputation while in many labor markets where workers are essentially anonymous, there is little incentive for workers to build a reputation for not accepting employer-dictated wage policies. According to this line of argument, non-individualistic wage policies should be seen as a way for employers to ensure that they retain control over wage-setting.[19]

The non-individualistic nature of employment contracts has other important implications that are not pursued here. For, if the wages of new recruits are tied to those of existing workers and the wages of existing workers cannot be reduced, this could be a powerful source of nominal and cyclical wage rigidity forcing the burden of adjustment to variations in demand onto employment rather than wages. Given this evidence one might think of constructing models of the labor market in which the wage offers of employers are not altered with the productivity of workers. Manning (1994b) pursues this idea further but we will not follow that line here.

5.4 Conclusions

In this chapter we have argued that employers do have incentives to choose wage policies in an attempt to become discriminating monopsonists. We see evidence of these pressures in the observed wage policies of firms, notably increased wages for senior and older workers. But, we also see evidence of severe limitations to the ability of the employer to be a perfectly discriminating monopsonist. Private information of workers (about reservation wages, non-pecuniary benefits from jobs, and outside offers) makes it difficult for employers to design wage contracts that extract all the surplus from workers. In addition, there seem to be powerful forces limiting wage variation across workers within jobs. Ironically it may be these forces that make the model of the simple monopsonist setting a single wage not such a bad approximation for thinking about

[19] Ellingsen and Rosen (2002) analyze a model in which some firms decide to post wages and others to negotiate wages with their workers, both forms co-existing in equilibrium.

the behavior of labor markets. So it is the simple model that we use in later chapters.

Appendix 5

Proof of Proposition 5.1

Suppose that $w(t)$ is not equal to p. We show that moving $w(t)$ to p with an appropriate off-setting adjustment to B can never reduce profits and will increase them as long as there is some effect on the separation rate. Suppose that the initial contract is $\{w(t), B\}$. Now consider replacing it by a contract in which $w(t) = p$ for all t and B is given by B_1 where B_1 satisfies

$$B_1 = B + \frac{\int_0^\infty [p - w(t)]N(t)dt}{R} \qquad (5.11)$$

where R is the level of recruits in the old contract, and $N(t)$ is the level of employment of workers with tenure t. As the new contract only makes profits from the entrance fee, profits from the new contract will be $R_1 B_1$ where R_1 is the level of recruits in the new contract so that, using (5.11), we have

$$\Pi_1 = R_1 B_1 = \frac{R_1}{R}\left[RB + \int_0^\infty [p - w(t)]N(t)dt \right] = \frac{R_1}{R}\Pi \qquad (5.12)$$

where Π is the level of profits on the old contract. So, profits cannot fall with the new contract if $R_1 \geq R$ and will rise if this is a strict inequality. Whether recruits rise depends on whether $V_1(0) - B_1$ is larger than $V(0) - B$.

To show that recruits cannot fall, consider the following argument. By integrating (5.1). we can write the value of the job under the old contract as

$$V(t) = \int_t^\infty \left[w(\tau) + \delta_u V^u + \lambda \int_{V(\tau)} VdF(V) \right]$$

$$\times \exp\left(-\int_t^\tau [\delta + \lambda[1 - F(V(\tau'))]]d\tau' \right)d\tau \qquad (5.13)$$

Now suppose that the quit decision of workers remains the same in the old contract as in the new contract (it will actually be lower as wages are raised to p but we will return to that). Then the value of the job under the new contract will be given by

$$V_1(t) = \int_t^\infty \left[p + \delta_u V^u + \lambda \int_{V(\tau)} V dF(V) \right]$$

$$\times \exp\left[-\int_t^\tau \delta + \lambda[1 - F(V(\tau'))] d\tau' \right] d\tau \qquad (5.14)$$

Hence the difference in the value of the two contracts to a new recruit can be written as

$$[V_1(0) - B_1] - [V(0) - B]$$

$$= \int_0^\infty [p - w(\tau)] \exp\left[-\int_0^\tau [\delta + \lambda[1 - F(V(\tau'))]] d\tau' \right] d\tau - B_1 + B \,(5.15)$$

Now, from (5.2) we can write $N(t)$ as

$$N(\tau) = R \exp\left[-\int_0^\tau [\delta + \lambda[1 - F(V(\tau'))]] d\tau' \right] \qquad (5.16)$$

so that (5.15) can be written as

$$[V_1(0) - B_1] - [V(0) - B] = \frac{\int_0^\infty [p - w(\tau)]N(\tau) d\tau}{R} - B_1 + B = 0 \,(5.17)$$

where the zero follows from (5.11). This shows that if the separation rate remains the same under the new contract as it was under the old contract, then the value of a job to a new recruit will be unchanged and hence, from (5.12), profits will be the same. But, the mobility rule will not remain the same as wages are raised (assuming there are firms paying higher wages) and, as the mobility rule is determined by the worker to maximize the value of the job, it must be that the value of the job rises with the new contract leading to more recruits and higher profits.

Proof of Proposition 5.2

Continue to denote by $V(t)$ the value of the job at tenure t excluding any severance payments. Then, in the presence of severance payments, (5.1) is modified to

$$\delta_r V(t) = w(t) - \delta_u[V^u - V(t) - S(t)]$$

$$+ \lambda \int_{V(t) + S(t)} [V - V(t) - S(t)] dF(V) + V'(t) - \delta_r S(t) \qquad (5.18)$$

where we have used the fact that workers will only now move to other firms when the offer V exceeds $[V(t) + S(t)]$. Profits (5.4) will now be

$$\Pi = \int_0^\infty [[p - w(t)]N(t) - S(t)N'(t)]dt + BN(0) \qquad (5.19)$$

which takes account of the fact that $-N'(t)$ workers of tenure t leave, each of which must make the payment $S(t)$ to the employer. Integrating the term $-S(t)N'(t)$ by parts, we can write (5.19) as

$$\Pi = \int_0^\infty [p - w(t) + S'(t)]N(t)dt + [B + S(0)]N(0)$$

$$= \int_0^\infty [p - \tilde{w}(t)]N(t)dt + \tilde{B}N(0) \qquad (5.20)$$

where we have used the transversality condition that $\lim_{t\to\infty} S(t)N(t) = 0$. (5.20) shows that replacing the contract with severance payments by the one without leads to the same level of profits as long as employment is exactly the same. Showing this requires showing that initial recruits and separation rates will be the same under the two contracts. Define $V(t)$ to be the value of the job with the contract $\{\tilde{w}(t), \tilde{B}(t)\}$ so that

$$\delta_r \tilde{V}(t) = \tilde{w}(t) - \delta_u[\tilde{V}(t) - V^u] + \lambda \int_{\tilde{V}(t)} [V - \tilde{V}(t)]dF(V) + \tilde{V}'(t)$$

implies

$$\delta_r \tilde{V}(t) = w(t) - \delta_u[\tilde{V}(t) - V^u] + \lambda \int_{\tilde{V}(t)} [V - \tilde{V}(t)]dF(V) + \tilde{V}'(t) - S'(t)$$

$$(5.21)$$

Comparing (5.21) and (5.18), one can see that we must have $\tilde{V}(t) = V(t) + S(t)$ which implies that separation rates must be the same and recruits must be the same. Hence, expected profits must be the same.

Proof of Proposition 5.3

We use a technique of proof similar to that used in Proposition 5.1 to show that replacing an arbitrary contract by one in which wages are initially at zero level and then, after some period, jump to p can only increase profits. Consider an initial contract $\{w(t)\}$. Consider replacing it by a contract which pays zero in the period $[0, t_0]$ and p thereafter where t_0 is chosen to satisfy

$$\int_{t_0}^\infty pN(t)dt = \int_0^\infty w(t)N(t)dt \qquad (5.22)$$

where $N(t)$ is employment on the initial contract. t_0 must exist and be strictly positive as long as the employer is making positive profits on the original contract. Using (5.22) we can write the difference between profits on the new contract, Π_1, and on the old contract, Π, as being

$$\Pi_1 - \Pi = \int_0^{t_0} pN_1(t)dt - \Pi$$

$$= \int_0^{t_0} p[N_1(t) - N(t)]dt + \int_0^{\infty} pN(t)dt - \int_{t_0}^{\infty} pN(t)dt - \Pi$$

$$= \int_0^{t_0} p[N_1(t) - N(t)]dt + \int_0^{\infty} [p - w(t)]N(t)dt - \Pi$$

$$= \int_0^{t_0} p[N_1(t) - N(t)]dt \qquad (5.23)$$

where $N_1(t)$ is employment on the new contract. So, if it can be shown that employment never falls with the new contract, then profits cannot fall either, and if there is a strict increase in employment, then profits must also rise. Whether employment rises or not depends on whether the value of the job rises or not.

We use the same technique as in Proposition 5.1 and start by assuming that the worker mobility decision remains the same under the new contract as it was under the old contract. Then, using (5.1), (5.13), (5.14), and (5.22), we have

$$V_1(t) - V(t) = \int_t^{\infty} [I(\tau, t_0)p - w(\tau)]N(\tau)d\tau \qquad (5.24)$$

where $I(\tau, t_0)$ is an indicator function taking the value 1 if $\tau \geq t_0$ and zero otherwise. For $t = 0$, we must have $V_1(t) = V(t)$. For $\geq t > 0$, we must have $V_1(t) \geq V(t)$. But, again the mobility rule will change with the new contract so as to increase $V_1(t)$ which means that employment can never decrease. Hence, profits can never decrease with the new contract and, if there is any effect on the value of the job, the new contract will actually increase it.

6

Earnings and the Life Cycle

SINCE at least the work of Mincer (1962, 1974) earnings functions have
been an essential part of the toolbox of labor economists. These earnings
functions are typically cross-section regressions of some measure of the
wage or earnings on worker characteristics such as experience, job
tenure, education and training, sex, race (even beauty and sexual orienta-
tion), and employer characteristics (for a survey, see Polachek and Siebert
1992). Estimating the returns to education, the extent of discrimination
and diagnoses of the causes of rises in wage inequality are just some of the
uses to which earnings functions have been put. The relationship between
wages and gender is considered in chapter 7 and the relationship between
wages and employer characteristics in chapter 8. The aim of this chapter
is to understand the role of job search in the observed returns to experience and job tenure, or, put more broadly, the life-cycle profile of earnings.

This chapter differs from previous ones in that it is concerned with the
behavior of workers rather than that of employers and treats the behavior
of employers as given. From the perspective of workers, an oligopsonistic
labor market presents itself as one in which there is wage dispersion, that
is, there are good jobs and bad jobs and the worker wants to try to get
him/herself into one of the good jobs, a process that might be described as
job shopping. The analysis that follows then applies to any labor market
in which there is wage dispersion although virtually all models of wage
dispersion have, at their heart, a mechanism that gives employers some
market power.

The cross-sectional relationship between earnings and experience for
American and British men is presented in figure 6.1 (using data from the
CPS and the LFS, respectively). In this chapter we focus exclusively on
men because the observed cross-sectional profile for women is also heavily influenced by cohort effects resulting from the increase in the labor
market participation of women. The basic facts about the profile are well
known. Hourly earnings are a concave function of experience reaching a
maximum at 25–30 years of experience for men with a modest decline
towards the end of the working life. The experience profile is steeper in
the United Kingdom than the United States with maximum gains of 120
log points for British men and 70 log points for the Americans. This is

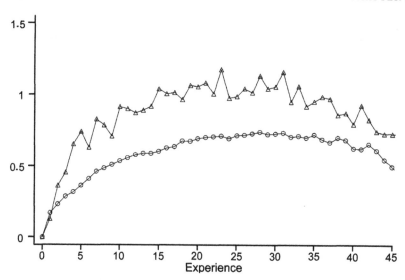

Figure 6.1 The returns to experience for American (O) and British (△) men.
Notes. The vertical axis is the gain in log hourly wages relative to workers with zero experience. Data sources are the CPS, January 1998 to December 1999, for the United States and the LFS, December 1992 to November 1999, for the United Kingdom. See Data Set Appendix for details of construction of experience. Data points are cell means. The US profile is smoother than the UK profile because of the larger size of the cells.

largely the result of faster wage growth in the first five years in the labor market in the United Kingdom than in the United States. In empirical work, the profile is often represented by a quadratic, but as Murphy and Welch (1990) emphasize, this is not really a good approximation (they suggest the use of a quartic).

The conventional way to understand the shape of the life-cycle profile of earnings is based on human capital theory and derives from the work of Mincer (1962) and Becker (1993). The profile observed in figure 6.1 is made up partly of true returns to experience and partly the returns to job tenure (average job tenure is, unsurprisingly, higher for more experienced workers). The returns to experience are interpreted as returns to general human capital (net of any current investment in this capital; see Mincer 1974; Ben-Porath 1967) while returns to job tenure are interpreted as a share in the returns to firm-specific human capital (although we criticized the foundation of this argument in the previous chapter). This chapter shows that the empirical evidence is not all supportive of the conventional interpretation of the observed returns to job tenure and experience (there is an empirical literature on the returns to tenure, discussed further below, that also reaches this conclusion; see Altonji and Williams 1997). Restricting oneself to the human capital perspective misses out on important aspects of the way earnings evolve over the life-cycle.

This chapter argues for a more general way of thinking about the returns to experience and job tenure based on the returns to job mobility and the cost of job loss. It shows that traditional measures of the returns to tenure are weighted averages of the changes in returns to job mobility and costs of job loss. This way of thinking about the life-cycle profile of earnings is consistent with the way in which people perceive their lives; job changes and job loss are often perceived as "big" changes. Job-shopping models predict there will be cross-sectional correlations between wages, experience, and job tenure even if the evolution of wages within jobs is unrelated to these variables. Burdett (1978) pointed out that the more time one has spent searching for a job, the more likely it is that one has found a good one: hence average wages are likely to rise with experience. And, once a worker has found that dream job, they are less likely to leave it so their job tenure is likely to be long. As we shall see, the actual relationships predicted by the job-shopping model are more subtle than this discussion might suggest but we should not be surprised that there is a relationship at all.

The plan of this chapter is as follows. In the next two sections, we present two pieces of evidence that there is something wrong with the conventional human capital interpretation and specification of cross-sectional earnings functions. Section 6.1 examines the earnings losses of displaced workers, those individuals who have lost jobs through no fault of their own. It shows that earnings losses are related not just to previous tenure on the job but also to the level of experience, something we should not see if the returns to experience are the returns to general human capital. Also, the earnings of displaced workers are positively related to tenure on their previous job, something that is inconsistent with the view that the returns to job tenure are the returns to firm-specific human capital.

Section 6.2 shows that a considerable part of the returns to experience and tenure observed in a cross-section is the result of the fact that those who remain in a job are not randomly selected. The implication is that cross-sectional returns to tenure cannot be used as an estimate of the earnings growth that an individual can expect if they remain in their job.

Section 6.3 considers whether a job-shopping model can do better than the human capital model in explaining these empirical findings. We show that the job-shopping model can readily explain many of them but others are not entirely consistent with the pure search model. A more general framework for thinking about the life-cycle profile of earnings is necessary.

Section 6.4 proposes a new way of decomposing the life-cycle profile of earnings into earnings growth on-the-job, a cost of job loss, and a return to job mobility. The conventional measure of the return to job tenure is shown to be a function of the cost of job loss and the return to job mobility. We argue that this definition makes sense if all the returns to experience are returns to general human capital, and returns to tenure are returns to specific human capital, but we have already presented evidence that they are not. In this case, our decomposition is preferable.

In the final two sections, we present two applications of this approach. In section 6.5 we present some estimates of the returns to job mobility and, in section 6.6, we use the approach to try to understand the decline in earnings among older workers seen in figure 6.1.

6.1 The Earnings Losses of Displaced Workers

There are many studies (e.g., for surveys, see Jacobson et al. 1993a,b; Kletzer 1998) of the earnings of displaced workers, those workers who have lost their jobs through plant closures (which is taken to be involuntary on their part). As Jacobson et al. (1993a: 26) write "much academic research on displacement has examined whether human capital theory can account for the observed earnings reduction following dislocation." Human capital theory predicts that a worker experiencing job loss suffers some loss in his/her specific human capital but does not lose any general human capital. As specific human capital is presumed to be embodied in the observed returns to job tenure and general human capital in the returns to experience, the theory predicts that earnings losses should be associated with tenure on the previous job but not with experience. A large part of the literature on displaced workers has focused on showing that earnings losses are positively related to previous job tenure (e.g., Topel 1991; Farber 1997). But virtually all studies of displacement also find that, contrary to the standard interpretation of earnings functions, losses are also related to experience. This casts doubt on the human capital interpretation of the returns to experience. In addition, Kletzer (1989) and Neal (1995) find that earnings of displaced workers are related to tenure on the previous job, casting doubt on the hypothesis that all these are returns to firm-specific human capital.[1]

Let us look at some evidence on the magnitude of the earnings losses suffered by workers after displacement. In the United States we are fortu-

[1] Neal (1995) also finds that the impact of pre-displacement experience and tenure on the change in earnings are greater for those who change industries.

nate to have an occasional supplement to the CPS which is explicitly designed to focus on the fortunes of displaced workers: the Displaced Worker Survey (DWS). We use two of these surveys which were conducted in 1996 and 1998 although the results in Farber (1997) and other papers would indicate that the results presented also hold for the earlier surveys.

In this survey, workers are asked whether, in the previous three calendar years, they have lost or left a job "because a plant or company closed or moved, your position or shift was abolished, insufficient work or another similar reason," that is, the intention is to identify job loss that occurs for reasons beyond the control of the worker. Those workers who have experienced job loss are then asked about the job they lost, about how long it took them to find work again, and about their current job (if they are in employment). The structure of the survey and the fact that it is based on respondents' recall mean that it is difficult to use the survey to make calculations of the incidence of job loss (Evans and Leighton 1995) so that one cannot really use estimates of earnings loss from this survey to make inferences about the loss that would be suffered if the "average" worker lost their job. However, we have a more modest aim: to look at the way in which earnings losses are associated with job tenure and experience. Approximately 5% of the sample report being displaced in the previous three years. The average earnings loss is of the order of 10%. Properly measured, it should be larger than this as an average of 18 months had elapsed since job loss and earnings would have normally grown in that period, partly due to inflation and partly due to the normal life-cycle evolution of earnings.

Table 6.1 presents some earnings loss equations that are essentially the same as other papers in this area. We experimented with the inclusion of higher order terms in tenure and experience but they were never significant. One should note that the earnings on the current and displaced job are at two different points in time so that one would not expect the earnings to be the same even if there was no cost of job loss: for this reason we also include the time elapsed since job loss. Earnings losses are greater if the worker had more seniority on the previous job with each year of tenure leading to a loss of 1.2% in weekly earnings. It should be noted that this is much less than the return to tenure observed in the cross-section, the implication being that earnings on the new job are positively related to tenure on the previous job (Kletzer (1989) and Neal (1995) document this for earlier DWS) suggesting that not all returns to tenure are returns to firm-specific human capital.

It is also true that older workers suffer a greater earnings loss: a worker with 20 years of experience loses 14% more than a worker with no years of experience. Note also that the constant in these regressions can be interpreted as an estimate of the earnings loss for a worker for whom

TABLE 6.1
Estimates of Earnings Loss from Displacement: United States

	(1) All	(2) All	(3) Men	(4) Women
Previous tenure	−0.012	−0.014	−0.012	−0.014
	(0.0017)	(0.0025)	(0.0021)	(0.0030)
Previous experience	−0.007	−0.008	−0.008	−0.006
	(0.001)	(0.001)	(0.001)	(0.002)
Female	−0.041	−0.071		
	(0.021)	(0.031)		
White	−0.007	−0.070	−0.043	0.033
	(0.032)	(0.050)	(0.043)	(0.049)
<High school	0.015	−0.102	0.004	0.031
	(0.038)	(0.058)	(0.045)	(0.069)
High school graduate	−0.026	−0.067	−0.058	0.018
	(0.025)	(0.038)	(0.033)	(0.039)
College graduate	−0.017	−0.116	−0.042	0.027
	(0.028)	(0.040)	(0.035)	(0.046)
Dummy for 1996	0.025		0.025	0.024
	(0.010)		(0.013)	(0.016)
Years since displacement	0.183	0.184	0.172	0.187
	(0.073)	(0.112)	(0.093)	(0.116)
Years since displacement	−0.046	−0.050	−0.041	−0.050
squared	(0.022)	(0.033)	(0.028)	(0.035)
Previously union	−0.121	−0.150	−0.104	−0.163
	(0.032)	(0.048)	(0.038)	(0.059)
Change of industry		−0.122		
		(0.037)		
Current tenure		0.017		
		(0.005)		
Constant	−0.031	0.228	0.027	−0.146
	(0.494)	(0.098)	(0.080)	(0.097)
Number of observations	4293	1688	2478	1815
R^2	0.05	0.08	0.05	0.04

Notes.
1. The data used in these regressions come from the 1996 and 1998 displaced worker supplements to the CPS. The dependent variable is the log of the ratio of the post- to the pre-displacement hourly wage.
2. Standard errors are in parentheses.

all the regressors are zero, that is, the earnings loss for a worker in the reference category (male, black, some college in 1994) with zero years of experience and tenure who gets a job immediately after displacement from a non-union job. The constant is small and insignificantly different from zero suggesting that such a worker does not suffer large earnings losses after displacement: it is the older, more senior, previously union workers who do. As the estimated impact of many individual characteristics on the earnings loss is small, this conclusion can be taken to apply to workers of all genders, race, and education. The second column also includes controls for whether the worker changed industry and their job tenure on the current job, questions that were only asked in 1996. This has essentially no effect on the coefficients on previous job tenure and experience. The remaining columns of table 6.1 present separate estimates for men and women. The earnings losses of more experienced women do seem slightly less than those of more experienced men but this needs to be put into the context of the fact that the earnings profile is flatter for women than for men so that there is less to lose.

We have looked so far only at earnings losses after displacement. But it is important to remember that there are other ways in which older workers seem to suffer more after job loss: they seem to struggle to find any acceptable job at all. Estimates of probit models (not reported) for whether an individual has worked at all since job loss indicate that, controlling for other factors, a worker with 10 years of prior experience is 7% less likely to have found work afterwards. To the extent that this means that older workers are more selective from among the options available to them, the estimates of earnings losses in table 6.1 are probably an understatement of the extent of the problem facing older workers. One plausible interpretation of their plight is that their reservation wage is high relative to their earnings opportunities after displacement because it is related in part to their previous earnings (through savings or wealth effects).

This evidence suggests very strongly that, controlling for other relevant factors, more experienced workers suffer greater earnings losses on displacement. While this observation may not come as a surprise, it is not consistent with the interpretation of the returns to experience as the returns to general human capital. And, the fact that not all returns to tenure are lost also casts doubt on the interpretation of the returns to tenure as the returns to firm-specific human capital.

6.2 Sample Selection in the Cross-Sectional Earnings Profile

This section demonstrates that a considerable part of the returns to experience and job tenure observed in cross-section earnings functions is the result of the sample selection bias that arises from the fact that (as predicted by the job-shopping model) workers with higher wages are more likely to stay in their jobs. Cross-section earnings functions are usually written in such a way as to give us a relationship between average log wages, experience (a), and job tenure (t): let us denote this relationship by $w(a, t)$. However, for reasons that will become apparent, it is more convenient here to focus on average earnings as a function of the experience level when the job started (which we denote by a_0) and job tenure. Let us denote this earnings profile by $\omega(a_0, t)$. Obviously we must have $\omega(a_0, t) = w(a_0 + t, t)$ so that there is a simple one-to-one relationship between the two profiles.

The advantage of conditioning on starting experience is that those workers with a level of job tenure, t, must, in some sense, be the subset of those workers with the same level of starting experience and job tenure zero who have remained in their jobs for t periods. Of course, in a cross-section they are not literally the same workers but, if the economy was in a steady state, they would be equivalent.

If all those who started jobs at experience a_0 remained in their jobs for t years, there would be no bias in the measured increase in earnings, $[\omega(a_0, t) - \omega(a_0, 0)]$. Note that this includes both the returns to job tenure and experience. The source of the potential bias is that not all workers will survive to have job tenure of t: some of them will lose their jobs and others will move to other jobs. If these moves are random then, again, there will be no bias in the tenure profile but if the selection of workers who survive to have tenure of t is not random, then $[\omega(a_0, t) - \omega(a_0, 0)]$ will give a biased estimate of the true increase in earnings. To give an example, suppose there is no wage growth on the job but that workers with high initial wages are more likely to remain in the same job. We would then observe that $\omega(a_0, t)$ is higher than $\omega(a_0, t - 1)$ but this is entirely the result of the selection bias.

The measured return to an extra year on the job can be written as

$$\omega(a_0, t) - \omega(a_0, t - 1) = \left[\omega(a_0, t) - \omega^s(a_0, t - 1)\right]$$

$$+ \left[\omega^s(a_0, t - 1) - \omega(a_0, t - 1)\right] \quad (6.1)$$

where $\omega^s(a_0, t - 1)$ is the average log wage at starting experience a_0 and job tenure $(t - 1)$ for those workers who remain in the same job for one more year (who we call the stayers). The first term in square brackets is the wage growth for those who remain in the job. The second term in square brackets is the selection bias that arises because those who stay in the same job may not be randomly selected; we call this the stayer bias. Only the first term in square brackets can be used as an estimate of the wage growth expected for those who remain in their jobs.

With cross-section data we cannot estimate the extent of the stayer bias, but, with only rudimentary panel data one can, as the different terms in (6.1) are all readily measured. The left-hand side can be estimated using an observed cross-section and the stayer bias by comparing the lagged wages of the stayers and the non-stayers. (6.1) refers only to the one-year returns, but we can write the returns to t years of job tenure as

$$\omega(a_0, t) - \omega(a_0, 0) = \sum_{t'=0}^{t-1} [\omega(a_0, t - t') - \omega(a_0, t - t' - 1)]$$

$$= \sum_{t'=0}^{t-1} \Big[[\omega(a_0, t - t') - \omega^s(a_0, t - t' - 1)]$$

$$+ [\omega^s(a_0, t - t' - 1) - \omega(a_0, t - t' - 1)] \Big] \quad (6.2)$$

so that the cross-sectional return can be written as the cumulated wage growth for stayers and the cumulated stayer bias.

To measure the extent of the stayer bias we use the Panel Study of Income Dynamics (PSID), 1985–97, the National Longitudinal Survey of Youth (NLSY), 1980–94 for the United States and the British Household Panel Study (BHPS), 1992–98, for the United Kingdom. For the study of the evolution of wages over the life-cycle, the PSID has the big disadvantage that wage information is only collected for heads of household and their spouses. As relatively few individuals are in either category when they first enter the labor market, the sample size is small in the first years after labor market entry when earnings typically grow the fastest. The NLSY does not have this problem as it is explicitly focused on young workers: the disadvantage is that we have no observations on older workers. The BHPS does not have either of these problems as wage information is recorded for all individuals in sample households.

We could present the decomposition in (6.2) using the actual cell means observed in our data sets. But, the relatively small sample sizes mean that some experience–tenure cells are extremely small and the components of (6.2) show a lot of sampling variation. Given this, we model the various components by estimating a quartic in starting experience and job tenure with a full set of interaction terms and using the fitted values as the components in (6.2). Because of the linearity of the decomposition in (6.2) the resulting estimates are internally consistent. To estimate the cross-section profile (the left-hand side of (6.2)), we simply estimate an earnings function using current wages. To estimate the stayer bias (the final term on the right-hand side of (6.2)), we estimate an earnings func-

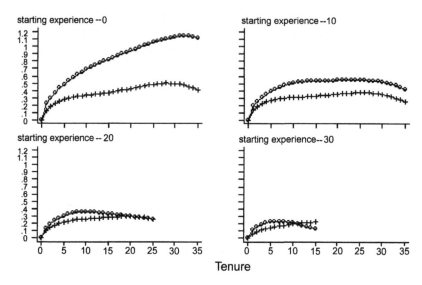

Figure 6.2 The stayer bias and the cross-sectional earnings profile: US men (PSID). O, cross-sectional earnings profile; +, cumulative stayer bias.

Notes. This figure represents the decomposition of the return to tenure of (6.2). The earnings profile is the estimated observed return to tenure in the cross-section (the left-hand side of (6.2)), and the stayer bias is the cumulative bias because those who stay are not randomly selected (the second term on the right-hand side of (6.2)).

tion for the lagged wage for all workers and for stayers, the difference between them being an estimate of the stayer bias. The wage growth for stayers must then be difference between the two.[2]

The results for the PSID are reported in figure 6.2 for years of starting experience equal to 0, 10, 20, and 30 years. The profiles all normalize the earnings of workers with zero tenure and a given level of starting experience to be zero. The measured cross-sectional returns to remaining in a job are large—for example, 50 log points for a worker with 10 years starting experience and 10 years of job tenure. But most of this is estimated to be the result of the stayer bias. The greater the starting experience, the larger the fraction of the cross-section returns that seem to be the result of the stayer bias. One might be concerned that these results are

---

[2] There is a good reason for having the wage growth for stayers as the residual. Nominal and real wages typically increase for reasons independent of the individual. In estimating wage growth for stayers, we would not want to include this aggregate wage growth. In some studies, an external measure of average wages is used to de-trend wages in the sample. This is satisfactory if one can be sure that the sample is representative of the population but quite small departures can make quite large differences given that average wage growth is not large. De-trending using within-sample information is better but still problematic and it is probably best avoided if possible (as here).

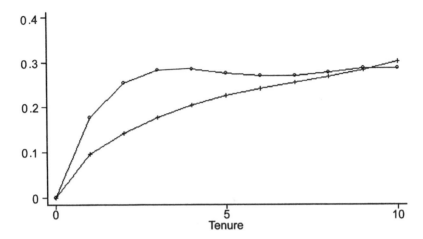

Figure 6.3 The stayer bias and the cross-sectional earnings profile: US men (NLSY). O, cross-sectional earnings profile; +, cumulative stayer bias.
Notes. This is drawn for a starting experience of zero. As for figure 6.2.

driven by the small number of observations in the PSID of individuals with low levels of experience. But the results for men with zero years of starting experience from the NLSY reported in figure 6.3 suggest a similar conclusion. Finally, figure 6.4 shows similar results for British men from

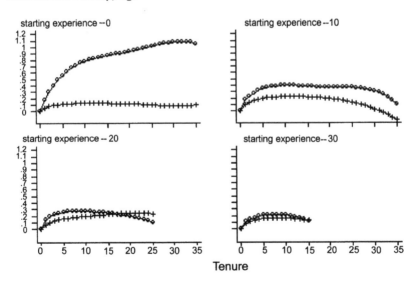

Figure 6.4 The stayer bias and the cross-sectional earnings profile: UK men (BHPS). O, cross-sectional earnings profile; +, cumulative stayer bias.
Notes. As for figure 6.2.

the BHPS although the importance of the stayer bias is much less among those starting jobs when young.

This section has shown that cross-sectional earnings functions suffer from serious bias caused by the fact that those in higher wage jobs are more likely to remain in them. Although we have shown the existence of serious problems with the traditional interpretation of earnings functions, it is not obvious that a job-shopping model can do better: this is the subject of the next section.

6.3 The Cross-Sectional Returns to Experience and Tenure in a Job-Shopping Model

This section discusses the predictions of a job-shopping model for the observed cross-sectional relationship between wages, experience, and job tenure. Because it is easy to get bogged down in the technicalities, the discussion in the main body of the chapter sticks to the intuition and all the technical material is confined to an appendix.

Individuals enter the labor market and try to work themselves into the better jobs through the process of job search. Every so often, an opportunity in the form of a job offer will arrive and the worker will take it if it is better than the current job. This process of systematically choosing better jobs means that, as workers age, we would expect to see average wages rising. However, job destruction sometimes interrupts this process and forces the worker to start again. A lifetime career then comes to resemble a game of "snakes and ladders" in which job offers represent ladders enabling workers to advance faster and job losses represent "snakes" which cause setbacks.

Now, consider a more formal model of this process. Denote job tenure by t and experience by a. In the language used in the discussion of earnings functions, this is really potential rather than actual experience but, for simplicity, we simply refer to it as experience.[3] Initially, assume that there are no "true" returns to experience and job tenure so that the only way in which wages can increase is by changing jobs: we call this the pure search model (for other discussions of this, see Burdett 1978; Manning 1998, 2000). In this case we can represent the wage-offer distribution by $F(w)$ as we have done in earlier chapters. In a later section, we consider the case where there are true returns to experience and job tenure. For simplicity, we assume that job offers arrive at a rate λ and job loss occurs at a rate δ as in the basic dynamic oligopsony model of section 2.4.

[3] One could do the analysis that follows conditioning on actual experience rather than potential although the analysis is messier. As most studies of earnings functions do not have data on actual experience, the case analyzed seems the more important in practical terms.

Three main cases are considered:

- the distribution of wages conditional on experience alone when there are no true returns to experience or job tenure (the pure search model);
- the distribution of wages conditional on experience and job tenure when there are no true returns to experience or job tenure (the pure search model);
- the distribution of wages conditional on experience and job tenure when there are true returns to experience or job tenure.

6.3.1 The Relationship Between Wages and Experience in a Pure Search Model

As we saw in figure 6.1, earnings profiles for men are typically a concave function of experience, first increasing and then decreasing. It is natural to ask whether the pure search model can explain these stylized facts. The following result summarizes Proposition 6.2, presented in more detail in the appendix. It turns out that the fraction of employment that is made up of recruits from non-employment has an important role to play in explaining the shape of the wage–experience profile.

Result 6.1. *The pure job-shopping model has the following predictions:*

1. *For low enough levels of experience, expected wages will be an increasing, concave function of experience.*

2. *A sufficient condition for expected wages to be increasing in experience is that the share of recruits from non-employment in total employment is non-increasing in experience for all lower levels of experience.*

3. *A necessary condition for expected wages to be decreasing in experience is that the share of recruits from non-employment in total employment is increasing in experience for some lower levels of experience.*

4. *A sufficient condition for expected wages to be a concave function of experience is that the share of recruits from non-employment in total employment is constant at all lower levels of experience.*

Proof. See Proof of Proposition 6.2 in Appendix 6A.

These results establish that the pure search model can go some way towards explaining the stylized facts of the earnings profile. Part 1 shows that it predicts that the earnings function must initially be an increasing, concave function of experience as we observe. The intuition for why the search model predicts this profile is that older workers tend to have worked themselves into the better jobs through the process of job search and there are diminishing returns to the search for better and better jobs. One way to understand this prediction is to think about what the profile looks like in heaven where nobody ever loses their job and everybody lives forever. Then, workers can only ever move up the job ladder so that average wages must be increasing, but all workers eventually end up in the best-paying job at which point there is no scope for increasing wages further.

But the wording of the result also makes it clear that the pure search model does not always predict that earnings will be an increasing function of experience. In particular it predicts that if, in some phase of the life-cycle, the fraction of employment recruited from non-employment rises, then we might expect to see declining average earnings. The reason is that these workers recruited from non-employment are likely to be entering employment at relatively low wages so a high fraction of these workers will tend to drag down average wages. It is interesting to test this prediction by seeing whether there is evidence for an increase in the fraction of employment previously non-employed among older workers where average earnings decline.

Figure 6.5a plots on the same graph (but using a different scale) the relationship between wages and experience and the fraction of those currently in employment who were previously in employment (previously being a month ago) for the United States. We plot the fraction previously in employment simply because this makes clearer the positive relationship between this profile and the earnings profile. This figure is not very clear as it is dominated by the rapid change in both series in the first five years after labor market entry. Figure 6.5b presents the same graph but ignoring the youngest workers (note that the scales are different from those presented in figure 6.5a). The close relationship between the two series should be clear. The earnings profile begins to turn down as the fraction of the employed previously employed falls. Figure 6.6a,b does the same exercise for British data. Again, we observe a similar picture.[4] This is consistent with a search view of the labor market as outlined in Result 6.1.

The pure search model can also explain the earnings losses suffered by more experienced displaced workers. Earnings rise with experience because workers have had longer to find a good job: involuntary displacement results

[4] Note that the fraction of those currently in employment who were previously non-employed is higher in the United Kingdom than the United States because "previously" refers to three months ago rather than a month, a result of the fact that the UK LFS is quarterly and the US CPS is monthly.

(a)

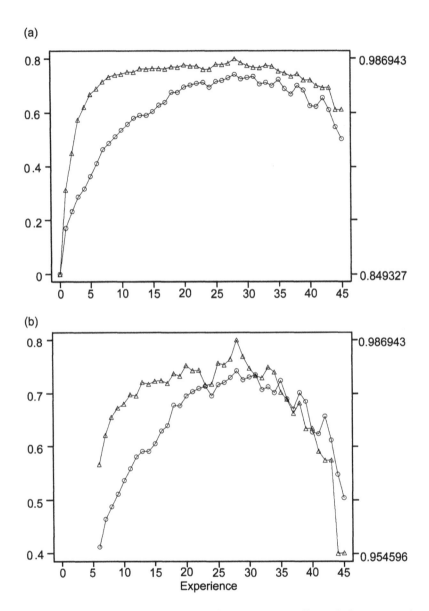

Figure 6.5 The connection between the earnings profile and the previously employed profile in the United States (CPS data). (a) All workers; (b) excluding youngest workers. ○, mean log hourly wage (left scale); △, proportion previously employed (right scale).

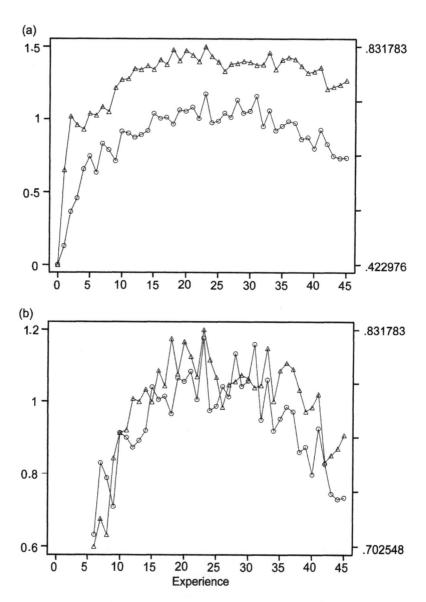

Figure 6.6 The connection between the earnings profile and the previously employed profile in the United Kingdom (LFS data). (a) All workers; (b) excluding youngest workers. O, mean log hourly wage (left scale); △, proportion previously employed (right scale).

in the loss of that job, forcing the worker to start looking for a good job again. One can think of earnings as being related to "search capital," knowledge about the location of good jobs. Unlike general human capital, some search capital is immediately destroyed on displacement. In the simple model presented here, all search capital is destroyed and the earnings of displaced workers are independent of experience. However, one might think that more experienced workers do retain some established contacts and knowledge about the labor market so that, in reality, not all search capital is destroyed immediately after displacement.

6.3.2 The Relationship Between Wages, Experience and Tenure in a Pure Search Model

Now introduce an extra conditioning variable, job tenure, into the analysis. First, consider the relationship between tenure and expected wages. The basic conclusion to remember is that the pure search model has an ambiguous prediction about the returns to job tenure. There are a number of ways of representing this ambiguity but one is summarized in the following result.

Result 6.2. *Expected wages are increasing (decreasing) in job tenure as*

$$R^u(a-t)(R^u(a-t) + \lambda) + \frac{\partial R^u(a-t)}{\partial a} > (<)0 \qquad (6.3)$$

where $R^u(a-t)$ is the fraction of recruits from non-employment in total employment at experience $(a-t)$.

Proof. See Proof of Proposition 6.3 in Appendix 6A.

Expected wages are correlated with job tenure in the pure search model for two reasons. First, a job tenure of t tells us that no better job offer than the current one has arrived in length of time t. As better job offers are less likely to arrive when the current job pays a high wage, this tends to induce a positive correlation between tenure and wages. It is this mechanism that probably lies behind the commonly expressed view that job shopping induces a positive correlation between job tenure and the wage. But, there is also another effect at work. If we also condition on the current experience of the worker, then current job tenure tells us the experience level at which the worker started the current job (which is $a-t$). If we compare two workers with the same experience but with one year's difference in tenure, the more senior worker must have started the job one year earlier in their career than the junior worker. If expected wages for workers starting jobs are increasing with experience, this effect will tend to make us predict that the senior worker had a lower starting wage than the junior worker. Result 6.2 simply gives us a condition when we can sign the net effect although the link between (6.3) and the intuition is not very clear.

One can also use (6.3) to ask the question "when does an earnings function give an unbiased estimate of the returns to tenure?" In this case the "true" returns to tenure are zero and, by inspection of (6.3), one can see that this condition is satisfied in the situation where there are never any recruits from non-employment.[5] In this case, experience is a sufficient statistic for expected wages and the two effects of job tenure exactly cancel out as emphasized in Topel (1991). But, in general, there is no reason to believe that the cross-sectional returns to tenure will be unbiased. One conclusion to be drawn is that it is the length of time in continuous employment that is a sufficient statistic for wages in this simple model: this insight is used below.

Now, consider the relationship between expected wages and experience when job tenure is also a conditioning variable. One might expect that one could reproduce something like Result 6.1 and readily provide sufficient conditions for the average wage to be an increasing function of experience. But, the introduction of tenure as an extra conditioning variable means that it is possible that, conditional on tenure, the expected wage can be declining in experience over some region even when the conditions of Result 6.1(2) are satisfied.

To understand the reason for this, suppose we observe two sets of workers with different levels of experience but with identical job tenure. We can divide each of these sets of workers into two groups:

1. those that arrived in the present job directly from another job;
2. those that arrived in the present job from non-employment.

The distribution of wages among these two groups will be different but, if we condition only on experience and tenure, the observed wage distribution will be a mixture of the two. As the wage distribution shifts up with experience (if we assume the sufficient conditions of Result 6.1(2)) the wage distribution must be higher for an older worker from group 1 than for a younger worker. In contrast the wage distribution among those from group 2 must be independent of experience as displacement is assumed to result in the loss of all search capital. In addition, the wage distribution among group 2 must be less than that among group 1. If the proportion of workers from the two groups did not vary with experience, then the fact that the wage distribution of the first group increases with experience and the wage distribution of the second group is independent of experience would mean that the distribution of the mixture of the two must be increasing with experience. But, the proportion does change and it is

[5] This is a sufficient, not necessary, condition.

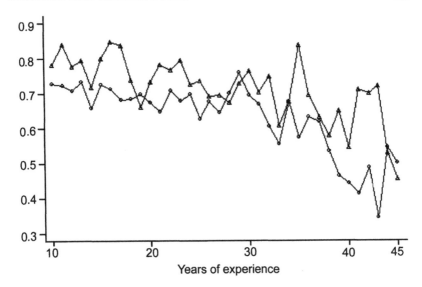

Figure 6.7 Variation in the fraction of recruits from non-employment. ○, US (PSID); △, UK (BHPS).
Notes. The left-hand scale is the fraction of recruits (i.e., those workers with tenure zero) who were in employment a year ago.

possible that this can go some way towards explaining why average earnings decline for older workers. Figure 6.7 shows, using data from the PSID for the United States and the BHPS for the United Kingdom that the fraction of mature male recruits (i.e., those with short job tenure) who were previously in employment falls with experience. When we observe an old male worker with low job tenure, it is quite unlikely that they arrived in this new job because they got a better job offer and relatively likely that they arrived in the new job after an intervening period of non-employment.

So far we have analyzed the consequences of experience and tenure for the wage distribution in a search model in which the true returns to experience and job tenure are zero. But, it is also instructive to consider the case in which the true returns are not zero.

6.3.3 The Distribution of Wages With "True" Returns to Experience and Tenure

In this case the model is modified in the following way. First, we assume that the wage offer distribution changes with experience so that the wage offer distribution at experience a can be written as $F(w - \beta_a(a))$ where

$\beta_a(a)$ is a measure of the true returns to experience.[6] We normalize $\beta_a(a)$ so that $\beta_a(0) = 0$. We also assume that log wages in a job rise at a rate β_t with tenure. The assumption that the returns to tenure are linear is restrictive but it helps to make the analysis tractable. Its advantage is that expected wage growth on two jobs is independent of the current wage and tenure so the choice between them can be made solely on the basis of which job offers the highest wage.[7]

Note that we are saying nothing about the sources of returns to experience and tenure. It may be that the traditional interpretation is correct and these are the returns to general and specific human capital. But it may be that they are the results of the wage policies of discriminating monopsonists as suggested in the previous chapter.

Understanding all the effects at work in this case is complicated and not a task to be undertaken lightly. Perhaps the only simple result is the obvious one that the addition of a true return to experience simply raises the predicted return to experience by that amount. This is unsurprising: as earnings on the job and outside offers evolve mechanically according to the function $\beta_a(a)$; there is no extra source of bias induced here.

More interesting is the return to tenure. Result 6.2 provided the condition (6.3) for the cross-sectional return to tenure to be unbiased when the true return to tenure is zero. In the appendix, it is shown that this condition being satisfied does not guarantee that the observed return to tenure is equal to the true return when there are non-zero returns to tenure (i.e., $\beta_t \neq 0$). The sign of the bias depends on the functional form of the wage offer distribution so that it is hard to form any a priori view about it. Given that the theoretical effects at work are complex, perhaps a helpful way of seeing the different effects at work is through simulation: table 6.2 presents four cases. We consider different values of the parameters β_t representing the "true" return to tenure and δ_u the rate of job loss. For convenience we assume that on-the-job and off-the-job search are equally effective, that the "true" return to experience is zero, and that the log wage offer distribution is logistic with mean zero (this will be the average log wage of a worker with zero experience). Case I is the case where there is no "true" return to tenure and no risk of job loss: Result 6.2 then applies and the return to tenure is zero in this case (read down a column). However, the apparent return to experience is sizeable (read across a row). Case II now introduces a risk of job loss (sufficient to make the

---

[6] We assume that the wage offer distribution improves mechanically with experience and does not depend on actual time in employment. This is consistent with empirical practice in which we generally do not observe "true" labor market experience. An obvious alteration to the model is to assume that the wage offer distribution only improves with time actually spent in employment: analytically this is much messier than what follows.

[7] See Topel (1986) and Mortensen (1988) for a discussion of the mobility rule for workers in the case where returns to tenure are not linear.

TABLE 6.2
Simulated Returns to Experience and Tenure

Years of job tenure	Years of experience			
	10	20	30	40
Case I. No true return to tenure ($\beta_t = 0$), no risk of job loss ($\delta_u = 0$)				
0	0.19	0.27	0.32	0.34
10		0.27	0.32	0.34
20			0.32	0.34
30				0.34
Case II. No true return to tenure ($\beta_t = 0$), risk of job loss ($\delta_u = 0.1$)				
0	0.09	0.09	0.09	0.09
10		0.24	0.24	0.24
20			0.3	0.3
30				0.33
Case III. True return to tenure ($\beta_t = 0.01$), no risk of job loss ($\delta_u = 0$)				
0	0.22	0.35	0.45	0.5
10		0.38	0.47	0.55
20			0.49	0.58
30				0.6
Case IV. True return to tenure ($\beta_t = 0.01$), risk of job loss ($\delta_u = 0.1$)				
0	0.09	0.08	0.08	0.08
10		0.32	0.32	0.32
20			0.45	0.45
30				0.56

Notes.
1. The other assumptions in these simulation are that $\lambda = 0.5$, that all workers are initially in unemployment, and that the wage offer distribution is logistic with mean zero and standard deviation of 0.2.

steady-state non-employment rate 28%). Now, the return to experience, conditional on job tenure, is essentially zero but there is a large return to job tenure. The reason is that job tenure is now a much better measure of how long a worker has been in continuous employment than experience. Case III goes back to assuming there is no job destruction but assumes the true return to tenure is 1% per year. Compared to Case I, there is now a return to job tenure in the cross-section but it is much less than the "true" return. This is an important point: search models do not always predict a higher return to tenure in the cross-section than the true tenure effect. Topel (1991: 151) was the first to make this point in the form of an example (in which there was never any unemployment so the job destruction rate was zero) but, unfortunately, he then went a bit too far and claimed that "the basic theory of search and matching implies that ... a comparison of wages for workers with different job tenures will *understate* the returns to seniority." This is not as widely true as he claimed. Another point about Case III worth noting is that the cross-sectional returns to experience are much larger than in Case I: part of the returns to tenure are "captured" in the return to experience. It is easy to understand why. Suppose we compare two workers both with zero tenure but who differ in one year of experience. The older worker could have remained in the same job in which case earnings would have grown by β_t but chose to move because a better job came along. Their earnings in this case must have grown by more than β_t. The returns to experience will then appear to be β_t while the return to tenure will actually appear to be negative. Finally, the fourth case has a true return to tenure and some risk of job loss. The returns to experience are very small while the returns to tenure are large and well above the true returns.

One use of this type of simulation is to suggest an interpretation of the negative returns to seniority often found in academic labor markets (see, e.g., Ransom 1993; Moore et al. 1998; Bratsberg et al. 2002). In academic labor markets the risk of job loss for senior faculty is plausibly thought of as low: as a result the first and third cases might be thought to be the most relevant. As we have seen, the search model there predicts that the cross-section will be an underestimate of the true return to tenure. It would be interesting to see whether other professions with similar low risks of job loss also display negative returns to job tenure.

This section and the previous one have emphasized that the search framework provides reasons for why cross-sectional returns to experience and tenure are likely to be biased. One important message is that a search approach suggests that time since last non-employed is important in determining earnings. If workers rarely leave employment then experience rather than tenure is better correlated with this variable so we would expect to see large returns to experience. But, for workers who often have spells of non-employment, job tenure might be better correlated. So, the search model tends to predict that workers with weak labor market attachment have higher returns to tenure: a human capital approach would not predict this as the incentives to invest in specific human capital are weak for these groups. We discuss this further in chapter 7 in the context of the cross-sectional returns to tenure being higher for women than men.

The two previous sections have argued that there is something wrong with the conventional human capital interpretation of earnings functions. This section has considered whether a search model can explain stylized facts about the distribution of wages conditional on experience and job tenure. We have shown that the search model has the potential to explain:

- the concavity in the experience profile of earnings;
- the decline in earnings for older workers;
- the earnings losses of more experienced displaced workers discussed in section 6.1;
- the biases in the cross-sectional returns to tenure discussed in section 6.2.

However, there are some aspects of the profile that the search model cannot explain. For example, section 6.2 pointed out that the earnings of displaced workers are positively related to previous job tenure. In addition, this section has been entirely theoretical, the theoretical predictions are often ambiguous, and theory provides little guidance for how one should try to understand the life-cycle of earnings in practice. The next section develops a more practical approach.

6.4 Empirical Approaches to the Estimation of the Life-Cycle Profile in Earnings

There is a large literature on estimating the "true" returns to tenure and experience (see Topel 1986, 1991; Abraham and Farber 1987; Altonji and Shakotko 1987; Marshall and Zarkin 1987; Altonji and Williams 1997, 1998; Teulings and Hartog 1998). The basic approach can be understood very simply.

Suppose we observe an individual in employment at experience 0 with log earnings that we normalize to zero as represented in figure 6.8a. The following year, we observe them with experience 1 but they might be in the same job or a new job (for simplicity ignore the possibility that they might not be in employment). The log earnings associated with the two possibilities are also represented in figure 6.8a. The return to experience is then estimated as the earnings growth on new jobs, that is, the distance OA and the return to tenure is estimated as the extra increase in earnings for those who remain in the same job, that is, the return to a year of tenure is estimated as AB. Of course, estimating these two returns is not as straightforward in practice as it appears in figure 6.8a as one only observes one of the two outcomes at experience 1 in figure 6.8 and one has to worry about sample selection, etc. Correcting for these problems is the main pre-occupation of the papers on estimating the returns to experience and tenure cited above.

Figure 6.8a is derived from Becker's (1993) view of the reasons for the returns to experience and job tenure in which returns to experience reflect increases in general human capital and returns to job tenure reflect increases in specific human capital. In this case, the difference (in terms of human capital) between those who remain in their job and those who

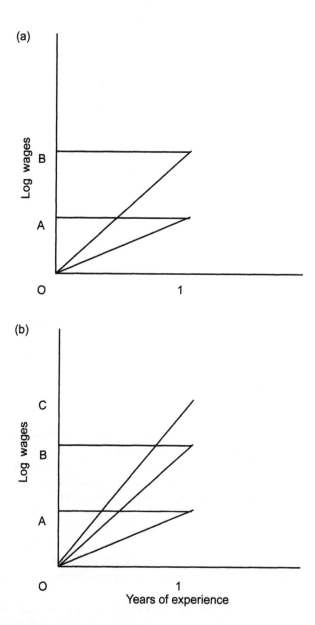

Figure 6.8 (a) The returns to experience and job tenure in the human capital model. (b) The evolution of earnings in the search model.

do not is the accumulation of one year of specific human capital (in addition to any accumulation of general human capital) so it makes sense to define the distance AB as the returns to job tenure.

However, figure 6.8a makes less sense if one uses the job-shopping model as the basis for analysis of the evolution of earnings. It then makes sense to divide those who change jobs into two groups: those who have got a better job offer and have moved voluntarily, and those who lost their initial job involuntarily and were forced to take a new job. We would expect those who move jobs voluntarily to have earnings above those who remain in their old job, and those who move involuntarily to have lower earnings. A possible picture is represented in figure 6.8b where those who change jobs voluntarily have higher earnings (OC) than those who remain in their jobs (OB), and those who lose their jobs have lower earnings (OA).

Figure 6.8b could be reduced to figure 6.8a by grouping together all those who are in new jobs: OA in figure 6.8a would then be a weighted average of OA and OC in figure 6.8b, the weight being the proportion of those in new jobs who moved involuntarily. Having reduced figure 6.8b to figure 6.8a one could then define the return to experience and job tenure in the usual way. But, there is a loss of information in doing so and it is not clear that it makes much sense. For example, an increase in the rate of job destruction would reduce the measured returns to experience and increase the measured returns to tenure, not because anything in figure 6.8b changes but because the fraction of displaced workers in those starting new jobs has changed.

If one started with figure 6.8b in mind, one could summarize it as:

1. the growth in earnings on-the-job, OB;
2. the cost of job loss, AB;
3. the return to job mobility, BC.

It makes sense to think in terms of these three components. In fact, if one asks a worker to describe how their earnings evolved over their life-cycle, it is quite likely that they would give an answer in terms of these concepts.

This result that the measured return to job tenure will be a weighted average of the returns to job mobility and the costs of job loss extends to more than the two-period model represented in figures 6.8a and 6.8b.

For example, to keep things simple assume that log wages grow on the job at the same rate, g, for everyone, that everyone faces a probability δ of losing one's job with an associated wage gain of Δ^l (that is probably negative), that everyone has a probability λ of getting a new job with an associated wage gain of Δ^m. The return to an extra year of job tenure can be written as

$$w(a,t) - w(a,t-1) = [gt + w(a-t,0)] - [g(t-1) + w(a-t-1,0)]$$

$$\times w(a-t,0) - w(a-t+1,0) + g \qquad (6.4)$$

After some algebra one can derive that, for $a > 1$, the return to an extra year of job tenure is given by

$$w(a,t) - w(a,t-1) = \lambda\Delta^m + \delta\Delta^l \qquad (6.5)$$

so that the costs of job loss and the returns to job mobility continue to be important.

There is already literature on estimating the costs of job loss (or displacement) (for surveys, see Jacobson et al. 1993a; Kletzer 1998) and the returns to job mobility or job shopping (Topel and Ward 1992). This literature co-exists with that on the returns to experience and job tenure but, as the above discussion should make clear, these concepts cannot all be independent of each other.

In the next two sections, we investigate a couple of the issues that might usefully be addressed using the framework proposed here: the return to job mobility and the declining earnings of older workers.

6.5 Estimating the Return to Job Mobility

In this section we present some estimates of the returns to job mobility using the PSID and NLSY for the United States and the BHPS for the United Kingdom. There are some papers which attempt to estimate the returns to job mobility. Topel and Ward (1992), in a sample of US young men, found an average wage gain at transition of about 10%, roughly double what the earlier studies of Mincer (1986) and Bartel and Borjas (1982) had found.

We are interested in the returns to voluntary job mobility but we do not observe directly whether job moves are voluntary or not. In all of our data sets, we define a job move as voluntary if there was no intervening period of non-employment and involuntary if there was. This classification is likely to make mistakes. Workers may have some advance warning of impending job loss but manage to find another job before they actually lose the current one (see, e.g., Jones and Kuhn 1995): we will classify these incorrectly as voluntary job moves. And some workers may arrange for a period of non-employment (a "break") between finishing an old job and starting a new one: these will be classified incorrectly as involuntary job moves. Assuming that wage growth is a motive for some job moves and that there is a cost of job loss, this inability to identify the reasons for job moves means we are likely to understate both the returns to job mobility and the costs of job loss. But, given the data available, the classification adopted here seems the best one.

Let us consider some estimates of the returns to job mobility in our data sets. Tables 6.3–6.5 show results for the PSID, NLSY, and BHPS, respectively. The first column of each table shows the coefficient on a dummy variable for whether an individual was a mover or not. The sample is workers who have been in continuous employment so all those for whom mover is zero are those who have remained in their jobs. For all our data sets, movers have significantly higher average wage growth than stayers: 5.1% in the PSID, 1.7% in the NLSY, and 4.3% in the BHPS. In these regressions, the constant is the average real wage growth for stayers: this is 2.6% in the PSID, 1.3% in the NLSY, and 2.1% in the BHPS so job mobility is estimated to double or even triple wage growth. These estimates do not control for any other characteristics. The second column introduces lagged experience and job tenure. Job tenure is lagged because it must, by definition, be zero for those who moved jobs over the year: it represents the accumulated tenure on the previous period's job. Experience is included in lagged form just for comparability. After some experimentation with higher-order polynomials, we settled on a specification with a quadratic in lagged experience and a linear term in lagged tenure. In all the data sets, this reduces the estimated gains from job mobility: to 3.9% in the PSID, 1.0% in the NLSY, and 2.4% for the BHPS. The reason is simple: those with low tenure and experience are more likely to move and these groups tend to have higher wage growth. Given that wage growth varies with tenure and experience, we might think that the gains from job mobility also vary so the third column includes interactions of mover with lagged job tenure and experience. The current returns from job mobility are declining in both experience and job tenure in all three data sets and the tenure effects are larger than the experience effects.

Why might the returns to mobility be declining in tenure? There are a number of possible explanations. The job-shopping model would suggest that, as job tenure increases, it is more likely that the worker is in one of the better jobs in which case the opportunities for wage gains from job mobility are reduced. Secondly, it may be the result of rational decision-making. If wage growth declines with job tenure (and there is some evidence of this), one of the returns to changing job is that the worker can expect faster wage growth on the new job than they would have had in the old job. A more senior worker might even be prepared to accept an instantaneous cut in wages in the expectation that future wage growth would be higher on the new

TABLE 6.3
The Returns to Job Mobility in the United States: PSID

	(1) Movers + stayers	(2) Movers + stayers	(3) Movers + stayers	(4) Movers + stayers	(5) Movers + stayers	(6) Stayers	(7) Stayers
Mover	0.051 (0.004)	0.039 (0.004)	0.073 (0.008)	0.072 (0.008)	0.080 (0.010)		
Mover × tenure $(-1)/10$			-0.068 (0.010)	-0.067 (0.013)	-0.071 (0.012)		
Mover × experience $(-1)/10$			-0.012 (0.005)	-0.024 (0.005)	-0.092 (0.006)		
Tenure $(-1)/10$		-0.0141 (0.0017)	-0.0128 (0.0018)	-0.0130 (0.0018)	-0.0121 (0.0049)	-0.0124 (0.0017)	0.0027 (0.0033)
Experience $(-1)/10$		-0.0254 (0.0043)	-0.0223 (0.0044)	-0.0227 (0.0045)		-0.0213 (0.0044)	-0.0066 (0.006)
Experience $(-1)/10$ squared		0.0039 (0.0010)	0.0034 (0.0009)	0.0038 (0.0010)		0.0033 (0.0010)	-0.0003 (0.0013)
Constant	0.026 (0.001)	0.066 (0.004)	0.062 (0.004)				
Sample selection							0.140 (0.030)
Personal characteristics	No	No	No	Yes	No	Yes	Yes
Fixed effects	No	No	No	No	Yes $(p = 1.00)$	No	Yes
Time effects	No	No	No	Yes	Yes	Yes	Yes
Number of observations	53053	53053	53053	53052	53053	48926	37555
R^2	0.003	0.007	0.008	0.013	0.010	0.007	–
Average gain to job move	0.051	0.039	0.040	0.039	0.050	0.039	0.313

Notes.
1. The dependent variable is the change in the log hourly wage.
2. The sample consists of workers who are in continuous employment from one year to the next.
3. Standard errors in parentheses.

TABLE 6.4
The Returns to Job Mobility in the United States: NLSY

	(1) Movers+ stayers	(2) Movers+ stayers	(3) Movers+ stayers	(4) Movers+ stayers	(5) Movers+ stayers	(6) Stayers	(7) Stayers	(8) Stayers
Mover	0.017 (0.006)	0.010 (0.006)	0.028 (0.010)	0.029 (0.010)	0.046 (0.014)			
Mover × tenure $(-1)/10$			−0.056 (0.043)	−0.053 (0.043)	−0.033 (0.052)			
Mover × experience $(-1)/10$			−0.030 (0.018)	−0.033 (0.018)	−0.046 (0.024)			
Tenure $(-1)/10$		−0.031 (0.014)	−0.029 (0.016)	−0.034 (0.016)	−0.050 (0.025)	−0.036 (0.014)	0.107 (0.152)	0.071 (0.039)
Experience $(-1)/10$		−0.116 (0.027)	−0.103 (0.028)	−0.054 (0.032)		−0.020 (0.033)	−0.096 (0.130)	−0.031 (0.037)
Experience $(-1)/10$ squared		0.067 (0.022)	0.064 (0.023)	0.033 (0.025)		0.004 (0.026)	0.074 (0.144)	0.017 (0.029)
Constant	0.013 (0.003)	0.052 (0.007)	0.047 (0.007)					
Sample selection							0.101 (0.129)	0.123 (0.041)
Personal characteristics	No	No	No	Yes	No	Yes	Yes	Yes
Fixed effects	No	No	No	No	Yes ($p = 1.00$)	No	No	No
Time effects	No	No	No	Yes	Yes	Yes	Yes	Yes
Number of observations	16030	16030	16030	15971	16030	11551	2336	13507
R^2	0.001	0.004	0.004	0.005	0.005	0.006	–	–
Average gain to job move	0.017	0.010	0.011	0.011	0.023	0.011	0.174	0.206

Notes.
1. As for table 6.3.

TABLE 6.5
The Returns to Job Mobility in the United Kingdom: BHPS

	(1) Movers + stayers	(2) Movers + stayers	(3) Movers + stayers	(4) Movers + stayers	(5) Movers + stayers	(6) Stayers	(7) Stayers	(8) Stayers
Mover	0.043 (0.007)	0.024 (0.007)	0.086 (0.011)	0.087 (0.016)	0.095 (0.016)			
Mover × tenure (−1)/10			−0.131 (0.017)	−0.131 (0.017)	−0.116 (0.021)			
Mover × experience (−1)/10			−0.019 (0.006)	−0.019 (0.007)	−0.025 (0.009)			
Tenure (−1)/10		−0.014 (0.003)	−0.011 (0.003)	−0.012 (0.003)	−0.027 (0.012)	−0.0111 (0.0031)	−0.0029 (0.0050)	0.0127 (0.0065)
Experience (−1)/10		−0.055 (0.006)	−0.046 (0.006)	−0.045 (0.007)		−0.048 (0.006)	−0.042 (0.009)	−0.011 (0.010)
Experience (−1)/10 squared		0.0096 (0.0015)	0.0079 (0.0015)	0.0080 (0.0015)		0.0085 (0.0015)	0.0077 (0.0018)	0.0022 (0.0021)
Constant	0.021 (0.002)	0.088 (0.006)	0.077 (0.006)					
Sample selection							0.068 (0.043)	0.250 (0.060)
Personal characteristics	No	No	No	Yes	No	Yes	Yes	Yes
Fixed effects	No	No	No	No	Yes ($p = 1.00$)	No	No	No
Time effects	No	No	No	Yes	Yes	Yes	Yes	Yes
Number of observations	17800	17800	17800	17699	17800	16032	14871	12801
R^2	0.004	0.013	0.018	0.020	0.006	0.010	–	–
Average gain to job move	0.043	0.024	0.027	0.028	0.027	0.027	0.150	0.489

Notes.
1. As for table 6.3.

job.[8] Thirdly, it may be the case that, for more senior workers, a higher proportion of job moves that we class as voluntary are, in fact, involuntary.

The fourth column introduces personal characteristics (sex, race, education, and region) and time dummies into the wage growth equations. While these variables are jointly significant, they have essentially no effect on the estimated returns to job mobility. While personal characteristics are very important in explaining differences in the level of wages, they are much less important in explaining the growth of wages among those who remain in employment. The fifth column goes further in considering whether unobserved heterogeneity can bias the returns to job mobility by introducing person-specific fixed effects. It has been argued that those with less stable work histories also tend to have lower wage growth on the job. There is some evidence for this in all of our data sets as the inclusion of fixed effects does raise the estimated return to job mobility. However, the effects are not large and, in all the data sets, one can accept the hypothesis that the person-specific fixed effects are jointly zero (the p values are reported).[9] The results here are rather different from those of Baker (1997) and Meghir and Pistaferri (2001) who emphasize the importance of growth-rate heterogeneity. Of course, this should not be taken to mean that unobserved heterogeneity is unimportant in explaining the *level* (rather than the growth) of wages and the coefficient on tenure in a cross-sectional wage equation is typically halved by the inclusion of fixed effects.

So far, all our equations have been estimated for movers and stayers together. But, a substantial part of the literature on the returns to tenure (e.g., Topel 1991) simply estimates a wage growth equation for stayers and then uses this to predict the wage growth that movers would have obtained if they had not changed jobs. The sixth column estimates a wage growth equation for stayers, then uses these estimates to predict what wage growth for the movers would have been if they had stayed and the average gain to a job move is then estimated as the gap between the actual

[8] Recognition of this point means we also have to be more careful in estimating the returns to job mobility. Suppose that a worker leaves a job with tenure t_0. Then, assuming he does not leave the new job and would not have left the old one, the gap in earnings after τ years will be given by $\Delta w_\tau = \beta_0 + [\beta_1 - \beta_2(\tau/10)](t_0/10)$ where β_0 is the coefficient on the mover dummy (0.073 in column 3 of table 6.3, β_1 is the coefficient on the mover dummy interacted with lagged tenure (-0.068 in column 3 of table 6.3), and β_2 is the coefficient on lagged tenure (-0.013 in column 3 of table 6.3). To give an example, suppose a worker leaves a job with accumulated tenure of 10 years. On starting the new job, the pay gain is estimated to be 2.5% but, five years later, the predicted pay gap from the NLSY between the new and old job is 3.7%.

[9] Note that one can no longer identify the experience effect once one has time dummies and fixed effects.

wage growth of movers and this predicted wage growth. These estimates are very similar to those obtained in earlier specifications for the simple reason that the estimated coefficients in the stayers equation are not very different from those we had obtained earlier. However, one concern with these estimates is that stayers and movers are not likely to be randomly selected so that sample selection issues arise in the interpretation of all the estimates we have discussed so far.

A simple model makes clear the potential source of the bias. Assume that, within jobs (i.e., for stayers), wage growth for individual i at date τ is given by

$$\Delta w_{i\tau}^s = \beta^s(a_{i\tau-1}, t_{i\tau-1}) + \beta_x^s x_{i\tau} + \varepsilon_{i\tau}^s \qquad (6.6)$$

and that the wage growth if they moved would be

$$\Delta w_{i\tau}^m = \beta^m(a_{i\tau-1}, t_{i\tau-1}) + \beta_x^m x_{i\tau} + \varepsilon_{i\tau}^m \qquad (6.7)$$

We also need to specify a mobility rule which tells us whether workers decide to stay or go. It is plausible to think that such a decision is based partly on the difference in wages between this job and the new job but other factors, for example, non-monetary aspects of jobs, are also likely to be relevant. So, let us define a latent index $S_{i\tau}^*$ according to

$$S_{i\tau}^* = \gamma_0[\Delta w_{i\tau}^s - \Delta w_{i\tau}^m] + \gamma_1(a_{i\tau-1}, t_{i\tau-1}) + \gamma_2 z_{i\tau} + \xi_{i\tau}^s \qquad (6.8)$$

and assume that the individual stays in the job when $S_{i\tau}^* > 0$. This mobility rule could be derived from optimizing behavior and a number of papers do this (e.g., Topel 1986; Mortensen 1988) by assuming that workers maximize a value function that depends solely on monetary rewards. However, we do not want to put this much structure on the model.

The potential source of selection bias should be apparent. If wages are important in influencing job mobility decisions, then we would expect those individuals with a larger than expected innovation to the stayers' wage growth will be more likely to stay. There is a traditional way to deal with this potential problem (Heckman 1976; Lee 1978). This involves substituting (6.6) and (6.7) into (6.8) to yield the reduced-form stayers' equation

$$S_{i\tau}^* = \gamma_0[\beta^s(a_{i\tau-1}, t_{i\tau-1}) - \beta^m(a_{i\tau-1}, t_{i\tau-1})] + \gamma_1(a_{i\tau-1}, t_{i\tau-1})$$

$$+ \gamma_0(\beta_x^s - \beta_x^m)x_{i\tau} + \gamma_2 z_{i\tau} + \gamma_0[\varepsilon_{i\tau}^s - \varepsilon_{i\tau}^m] + \xi_{i\tau}^s \qquad (6.9)$$

and then typically assuming joint normality of the errors. Let us write (6.9) in the form

$$S_{i\tau}^* = \gamma z_{i\tau}^s + \xi_{i\tau} \qquad (6.10)$$

where z^s is all the regressors from (6.9) and the variance of ξ is normalized to one. Then, as is well known, the expected wage growth for stayers, conditional on staying in the same job is given by

$$E(\Delta w^s_{i\tau} \mid S^*_{i\tau} > 0) = \beta^s(a_{i\tau-1}, t_{i\tau-1}) + \beta^s_x x_{i\tau} + \rho\sigma^s \frac{\phi(-\gamma' z^s_{i\tau})}{1 - \Phi(-\gamma' z^s_{i\tau})} \quad (6.11)$$

where σ^s is the standard deviation of ε^s and ρ is the correlation coefficient between ε^s and ξ. The last term is the sample selection correction term. If we are interested in estimating the returns to job mobility, we want to compare the wage growth of movers with the wage growth they would have achieved if they had stayed in their jobs. As we know they chose to move, this is given by

$$E(\Delta w^s_{i\tau} \mid S^*_{i\tau} < 0) = \beta^s(a_{i\tau-1}, t_{i\tau-1}) + \beta^s_x x_{i\tau} - \rho\sigma^s \frac{\phi(-\gamma' z^s_{i\tau})}{\Phi(-\gamma' z^s_{i\tau})} \quad (6.12)$$

So, our strategy is to use the standard Heckman approach to sample selection to get estimates of (6.11) and then use these estimates to estimate (6.12).

For the sample selection correction to work well, one needs variables that affect the stay–go decision but do not affect wage growth (the "z" variables in (6.9)).[10]

The BHPS and, in some years, the NLSY ask some questions about job satisfaction. For example, the BHPS asks questions about satisfaction with promotion possibilities, total pay, relations with the boss, job security, use of initiative, work itself, and hours worked while the NLSY asks questions about satisfaction with promotion possibilities, total pay, job security, ability to use and learn skills, relations with co-workers and supervisors, and the physical aspects of the job. In addition, the BHPS asks questions about whether domestic responsibilities have limited job search. We might expect some of these variables to be correlated with wage growth (e.g., satisfaction with pay, promotion possibilities, even relations with the boss) but there are some questions that we might expect to have no relationship to wage growth but do affect the appeal of the job. Our first strategy for investigating the extent of sample selection bias is to use these variables as the "z" variables. As plausibly exogenous "z" variables we used satisfaction with use of initiative, with work itself, and with hours worked for the BHPS, and satisfaction with co-workers for the NLSY. In addition, we used a question that asks whether domestic commitments have prevented job change for the BHPS. We first need to check that they are correlated with mobility. Table 6.6 presents some job

---

[10] Though an additional problem is that, if there is heterogeneity in the returns to job mobility, the use of an instrument will only give the "treatment effect on the treated."

TABLE 6.6
Job Mobility Equations

	(1) BHPS	(2) NLSY	(3) BHPS	(4) NLSY	(5) PSID
Tenure (−1)/10	0.579	3.354	0.536	2.774	0.656
	(0.038)	(0.293)	(0.041)	(0.088)	(0.025)
Experience (−1)/10	0.257	−1.014	0.056	−0.454	0.204
	(0.050)	(0.496)	(0.061)	(0.140)	(0.043)
Experience (−1)/10 squared	−0.032	1.092	0.019	0.301	−0.031
	(0.013)	(0.572)	(0.015)	(0.117)	(0.010)
Satisfaction with use of initiative	0.025				
	(0.012)				
Satisfaction with work itself	0.056				
	(0.013)				
Satisfaction with hours worked	0.047				
	(0.010)				
Satisfaction with co-workers		0.117			
		(0.054)			
Domestic constraints prevent job change	−0.206				
	(0.078)				
Log wage (−2)			0.230	0.186	0.214
			(0.042)	(0.029)	(0.025)
Personal characteristics	Yes	Yes	Yes	Yes	Yes
Time effects	Yes	Yes	Yes	Yes	Yes
Number of observations	14871	2336	12801	13509	38384
Proportion stayers	0.9	0.727	0.906	0.635	0.927

Notes.
1. The sample consists of those workers who have been in continuous employment for the past year. The dependent variable takes the value one if the individual is a stayer and zero otherwise. The estimated model is a probit. Standard errors in parentheses.
2. The sample size is much reduced for the NLSY as the detailed job satisfaction questions were only asked in 1979–82 and 1988.
3. For the NLSY, the job satisfaction variable ranges from 1 (not true at all that co-workers are friendly) to 4 (very true). For the BHPS, the job satisfaction variables range from 1 (not satisfied at all) to 7 (completely satisfied).

mobility equations. The first two columns show that, for both the BHPS and the NLSY, these variables are correlated with job mobility.

The 7th column of tables 6.4 and 6.5 then present estimates of wage growth equations for stayers with a sample selection correction term based on these mobility equations. In both cases, the coefficient on the sample selection correction term is significantly different from zero, and doing the sample selection correction makes a big difference to the estimated gain to job mobility which rises to 17 log points for the NLSY and 15 log points for the BHPS.

An alternative approach to sample selection correction is to use the lagged wage as the "z" variable in the movers equation. This is reasonable if the wage is correlated with job mobility but not with wage growth on-the-job, that is, wage growth on-the-job is a random walk with drift. Inclusion of the lagged wage in the stayers' wage growth equations (we used the specification of column 6 in tables 6.3–6.5) would not seem to support this assumption: the coefficient on the lagged wage being -0.182 (0.003) in the PSID, -0.232 (0.006) in the NLSY, and -0.193 (0.006) in the BHPS (standard errors in parentheses). But these coefficients are undoubtedly biased away from zero by the presence of measurement error in the wage. If we instrument the lagged wage using the second lag of the wage, the coefficients change to -0.029 (0.004) in the PSID, -0.038 (0.011) in the NLSY, and -0.034 (0.007) in the BHPS (standard errors in parentheses) so that the random-walk assumption does not seem such a bad assumption. So, we also experiment with the second lag of the wage as a "z" variable in the mobility equation. Columns (3)–(5) of table 6.6 indicate that the second lag is very significant in predicting job mobility.

Column (7) of table 6.3 and column (8) of tables 6.4 and 6.5 then estimate a wage equation for stayers that includes the sample selection correction term from these mobility equations: the coefficients on these terms are always significantly different from zero. The consequences for the estimated returns to job mobility are dramatic, rising to 31 log points in the PSID, 21 log points in the NLSY, and 49 log points in the BHPS. These are too large to be taken seriously as, given that the actual wage growth for movers is much more modest, they imply very negative wage growth for these workers if they had stayed with their firms. It may be that the functional form assumption is inappropriate[11] (particularly for

---

[11] Topel (1986) took a similar approach to sample selection correction, but Topel (1991) abandoned it suggesting that it was not reliable. However, his proposed "solution" was to assume there was no sample selection bias in a wage growth equation for stayers. He claimed some evidence in support of this but it was not very persuasive as wage innovations have a strong permanent component and the level of wages is strongly correlated with job mobility.

the PSID and BHPS where the share of movers in the sample is very small so that we are in the tail of the distribution), that wage growth within jobs is not a random walk, or that there is heterogeneity in the returns to job mobility and low-wage workers have potentially large gains.

From this discussion, one should conclude that there is some evidence that sample selection bias is important in estimating the returns to job mobility. But, because it is hard to find good instruments for job mobility, it is hard to get a precise estimate of the extent of the bias. But, including the job satisfaction variables does indicate that the return to job mobility may be closer to 10% than the raw figures reported in tables 6.3–6.5.

6.6 The Life-Cycle Profile of Earnings for Older Men

In this section we aim to put together the framework described in section 6.4 to understand one interesting feature of the earnings profiles seen in figure 6.1, the decline in earnings for older workers. The following proposition shows how one can decompose the change in earnings into the wage growth for continuing workers, the returns to job mobility, the costs of job loss, and one other term which we will call the leaver bias.

Proposition 6.   *If the average log wage for workers with experience a is* $w(a)$ *then*

$$w(a + 1) - w(a) = \overline{\Delta}^s(a) + \theta^m(a + 1)\overline{\Delta}^m(a) + \theta^e(a + 1)\overline{\Delta}^l(a + 1)$$

$$+ \frac{n(a + 1) - n(a)}{n(a + 1)}\overline{b}^l(a) \qquad (6.13)$$

where $\overline{\Delta}^s(a)$ *is the average log wage growth for those who stay in their jobs,* $\theta^m(a + 1)$ *is the fraction of those currently in employment who have changed jobs in the past year,* $\overline{\Delta}^m(a)$ *is the average gain from job mobility,* $\theta^e(a + 1)$ *is the fraction of those currently in employment who have come via non-employment in the past year,* $\overline{\Delta}^l(a)$ *is the average cost of job loss,* $n(a)$ *is the employment rate for experience a,* $\overline{b}^l(a)$ *is the "loser bias", the extent to which those who lose jobs are paid less than the average.*

Proof.   See Appendix 6B (where precise definitions of the different terms are also provided).

The decomposition in (6.13) may look intimidating but it says that the return to an extra year of experience can be thought of as being made up of several components:

- wage growth on-the-job, $\overline{\Delta}^s(a)$;
- the return to job mobility, $\overline{\Delta}^m(a)$, multiplied by the fraction of workers who change jobs, θ^m;
- the cost of job loss, $\overline{\Delta}^l(a)$, multiplied by the fraction of employed workers who have entered from non-employment, θ^e;
- the bias which emerges because those losing jobs are not selected at random.

Most of these terms are self-explanatory: wages can grow over the life-cycle because they grow for those in continuous employment, many workers have changed jobs and/or there is a return to job mobility or because few have lost jobs. However, the loser bias term perhaps needs a little bit more explanation. Suppose there was no on-the-job wage growth, no return to job mobility or cost of job loss, but that low-wage workers are more likely to leave employment and, once they have done so, never return to employment. Then, there will be a sample selection effect that will make wages appear to rise with experience. Trying to estimate the size of this effect is the subject of a recent paper by Blundell et al. (1999). But, it can only have an effect to the extent that the employment rate changes over time.

Let us now try to use this identity to understand the reasons why earnings decline for workers with experience in the range of 25–45 years. For this purpose, we use the PSID for the United States and the BHPS for the United Kingdom. (6.13) presents the one-year returns to an extra year of experience but we cumulate these up to present estimates of $w(a) - w(25)$. Inspection of figure 6.9a,b shows the decline in average earnings for older men that we see in the cross-section profile. However, those workers who manage to remain in their jobs actually see small gains in earnings (this is the cumulative wage growth for stayers) so that workers who manage to remain in their jobs do not experience wage declines on average at the end of their careers: this sounds plausible. Gains from job mobility are very small, partly because very few older workers change jobs and partly because the measured gains from job mobility are small for this group. The decline in earnings can be fully explained by the substantial incidence of job loss (something like 8–9% of those currently in employment have had a spell of non-employment in the last year) and the very substantial cost of job loss (measured at about 30 log points). It is the incidence and cost of job loss that accounts for the apparent decline in earnings of older men.

It should be emphasized that (6.13) is simply a decomposition that, because it is an identity, must hold true at all points in time. To move beyond the decomposition and ask questions like "if there was a higher rate of job mobility what would the profile look like?" one needs to make further assumptions, for example, that Δ^s and Δ^m are unaffected.

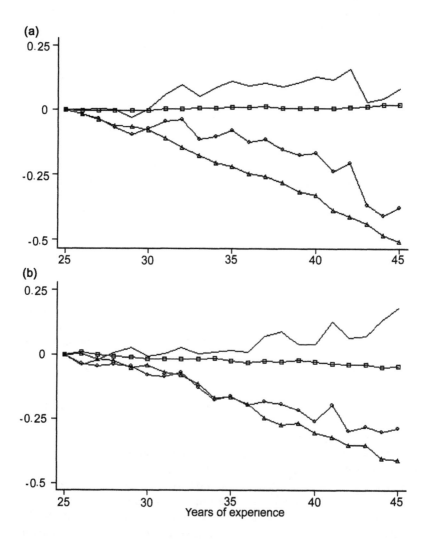

Figure 6.9 The decline in earnings for older men. (a) United States (PSID); (b) United Kingdom (BHPS). ○, change in average log wages; △, cumulative cost of job loss; □, cumulative job mobility gain; solid line, cumulative stayers wage growth.

Notes. This figure presents the decomposition of (6.13) cumulated over the last 20 years of labor market experience. The bias term of (6.13) is not presented but is very small.

6.7 Conclusions

This chapter has argued that there is something seriously wrong with the traditional interpretation of the returns to experience and job tenure in cross-sectional earnings functions. The evidence on displaced workers in section 6.1 makes it clear that not all of the returns to experience are the returns to general human capital and the evidence on the stayer bias in section 6.2 makes it clear that a large part of the apparent returns to job tenure is the result of the fact that those in high wage jobs are more likely to remain in them.

Section 6.3 then argued that a job-shopping model is a much better way to think of the way in which earnings evolve over the life-cycle. In a labor market with wage dispersion and frictions, one can think of an individual's progress through their working life as a game of snakes and ladders. If they remain in the same job their earnings will grow (although typically at a decreasing rate). But, from time to time, a "ladder" appears in the form of an opportunity to change jobs and get the wage gains that typically accrue from this mobility (although we have argued that it is difficult to estimate these gains precisely). But, there are also the snakes of job loss which typically result in sizeable earnings losses. In the early years of one's life, finding a "ladder" is more important than avoiding a "snake" (as was shown in section 6.5) but the latter is more important for older workers (as was shown in section 6.6). This representation of a working life coincides with the way that life is experienced.

Section 6.4 proposed a better way of thinking about the shape of earnings profiles: a decomposition into earnings growth within jobs, the returns to job mobility, and the costs of job loss. It was shown how the return to tenure as conventionally measured is a weighted average of the return to job mobility and the cost of job loss so compounds two very distinct concepts in a way that is unhelpful.

Our approach to understanding the profile of earnings requires panel data. But, in many situations, we have only cross-section data and this then raises the practical question of what labor economists should do when they want to estimate an earnings function. This chapter has implications not just for how labor economists should interpret earnings functions but also for how they should specify them.

There is an established "custom and practice" in the specification of earnings functions. It is not really clear whether this custom and practice is thought of as the "best specification" or the "best specification given the data available." There is perhaps a tendency to think in terms of the former when the latter would be more accurate. For example, given data on wages, experience, and tenure, most labor economists would estimate a standard earnings function with these variables as regressors. Suppose that your particular data set also had information on whether the worker was previously employed when the individual started the current job. I suspect that this variable would be very significant partly because of unobserved individual heterogeneity but also because those who were previously employed are almost certainly changing jobs because they have found a "better" job. The traditional specification of earnings functions lumps together as equivalent those who have lost their previous job involuntarily and have re-entered the labor market and those who have voluntarily changed jobs. But we have seen (and this is hardly surprising) that there are substantial differences in the labor market fortunes of the two groups. Of course, there are some benefits to having a common specification of earnings functions across data sets but there are also dangers that this leads to a "lowest common denominator" outcome. It is likely that lots of variables summarizing the working life of an individual are important predictors of earnings (for an example of this, see Light and Ureta 1995): job tenure should be just thought of as one such measure, one that is commonly available but has no particular significance attached to it. Hence, an additional message of this chapter is that labor economists should be a bit more broad-minded in both the specification and interpretation of earnings functions.

This chapter has looked at the earnings profiles for men on the grounds that the observed female cross-sectional profiles are likely to be heavily contaminated by cohort effects. The next chapter aims to redress this balance and discuss how monopsony can help us explain the differences in earnings between men and women.

Appendix 6A. Theoretical Analysis of the Returns to Experience and Job Tenure in a Search Model

The Pure Search Model

Initially, assume that there are no "true" returns to experience and job tenure so that the wage offer distribution, $F(w)$, is independent of a or t. Denote by $G(w|a)$ the fraction of workers in employment of experience a who earn less than w. Knowledge of $G(w|a)$ is sufficient to work out statistics about the wage distribution, for example, the average wage $E(w|a)$ can be written as

$$E(w|a) = \int w dG(w|a) = \int [1 - G(w|a)] dw \qquad (6.14)$$

where the second equality follows from integration by parts. Using (6.14), we have

$$\frac{\partial E(w|a)}{\partial a} = -\int \frac{\partial G(w|a)}{\partial a} dw \qquad (6.15)$$

so that $[\partial G(w|a)/\partial a] < 0$ for all w is a sufficient condition for average wages to be increasing in experience. The condition $[\partial G(w|a)/\partial a] < 0$ is simply the condition that increasing experience leads to a higher wage distribution in the sense of first-order stochastic dominance.

As earnings profiles are often concave in experience (see figure 6.1) we might also be interested in the second derivative of $E(w|a)$. Further differentiation of (6.15) leads to

$$\frac{\partial^2 E(w|a)}{\partial a^2} = -\int \frac{\partial^2 G(w|a)}{\partial a^2} dw \qquad (6.16)$$

The following proposition provides an expression for $G(w|a)$.

Proposition 6.1. *$G(w|a)$ must satisfy the following differential equation*

$$\frac{\partial G(w|a)}{\partial a} = -\lambda[1 - F(w)]G(w|a) + [F(w) - G(w|a)]R^u(a) \qquad (6.17)$$

where λ is the arrival rate of job offers and $R^u(a)$ is the flow of recruits from non-employment as a fraction of current employees.

Proof. Denote by $M(w|a)$ the number of individuals of experience a that are paid w or less. Obviously $N(a)G(w|a) = M(w|a)$ where $N(a)$ is employment of workers of experience a.

Workers leave the group of individuals paid less than w when they leave employment or they get a better job offer, that is, at a rate $[\delta + \lambda(1 - F(w))]$. Workers can only be recruited to the group of workers paid w or less from non-employment. Using the notation of Proposition 6.1 there are $N(a)R^u(a)$ recruits from non-employment of which a fraction $F(w)$ will be paid w or less. The change in $M(w|a)$ will then be the difference between inflows and outflows so will be given by

$$\frac{\partial M(w|a)}{\partial a} = -[\delta + \lambda(1 - F(w))]M(w|a) + F(w)N(a)R^u(a) \qquad (6.18)$$

Now we must have $N(a)G(w|a) = M(w|a)$ so that

$$\frac{\partial M(w|a)}{\partial a} = N(a)\frac{\partial G(w|a)}{\partial a} + G(w|a)\frac{\partial N(a)}{\partial a} \qquad (6.19)$$

and the change in employment must be given by

$$\frac{\partial N(a)}{\partial a} = -\delta N(a) + R^{u}(a)N(a) \qquad (6.20)$$

Combining (6.18)–(6.20) leads to (6.17).

The two terms in (6.17) can be readily explained. The first is the rate at which workers get jobs that pay more than a wage w. This is the rate at which workers move up the job ladder and this effect is why the wage distribution tends to increase with experience. However, some fraction of employees were previously non-employed. These workers have a distribution of wages given by $F(w)$ as they have not had any time to work themselves up the job ladder. They will tend to have a worse distribution of wages than those who have been in employment for some time.

Nothing has been said, so far, about the solution to (6.17). One cannot solve differential equations without an initial condition: in this case we need to specify $G(w|0)$. As new workers will have had no time to work themselves up the job ladder, the most natural assumption is that $G(w|0) = F(w)$ (although one might want to modify this assumption to allow for job search prior to entry into the labor market). The following proposition gives us some useful results.

Proposition 6.2

1. *For a close enough to zero, $E(w|a)$ will be an increasing, concave function of a.*

2. *A sufficient condition for $E(w|a)$ to be increasing in a is that $R^{u}(a')$ is non-increasing in a' for all $a' \leq a$.*

3. *A necessary condition for $E(w|a)$ to be decreasing in a is that $R^{u}(a')$ is increasing in a' for some $a' \leq a$.*

4. *A sufficient condition for $E(w|a)$ to be a concave function of a is that $R^{u}(a')$ is constant for all $a' \neq a$.*

Proof. 1. As the initial condition implies that $G(w|0) = F$, (6.17) then implies that $[\partial G(w|a)/\partial a] < 0$ at $a = 0$. So, for a close enough to zero, $E(w|a)$ must be increasing in a. By further differentiation of (6.17), we have

$$\frac{\partial^{2} G(w|a)}{\partial a^{2}} = -[R^{u}(a) + \lambda[1 - F(w)]]\frac{\partial G(w|a)}{\partial a}$$

$$+ [F(w) - G(w|a)]\frac{\partial R^{u}(a)}{\partial a} \qquad (6.21)$$

Using the initial condition again we have that $[\partial^2 G(w|a)/\partial a^2] > 0$ for a close enough to zero proving concavity.

2. From (6.17) we know that $[\partial G(w|a)/\partial a] < 0$ if $G(w|a) > G^*(w|a)$ where

$$G^*(w|a) = \frac{R^u(a)F(w)}{R^u(a) + \lambda[1 - F(w)]} \qquad (6.22)$$

The only way in which we can have $[\partial G(w|a)/\partial a] > 0$ is if $G(w|a) < G^*(w|a)$ for some (w, a). However, we know that $G(w|0) = F(w) > G^*(w|0)$ so this can only happen if $G(w|a)$ cuts $G^*(w|a)$ from above. As $[\partial G(w|a)/\partial a] = 0$ if $G(w|a) = G^*(w|a)$ this can only happen if $G^*(w|a)$ is increasing in a at some point. But, $G^*(w|a)$ is non-increasing in a if $R^u(a)$ is non-increasing in a. This proves part 2 of the proposition.

3. The argument of the previous section also shows that $R^u(a)$ increasing in a is necessary for expected wages to be declining in a.

4. If $R^u(a)$ is constant then (6.21) says that the earnings function will be concave if it is increasing. Part 2 of the proposition guarantees this.

The Relationship Between Wages, Experience and Tenure in a Pure Search Model

Now let us consider introducing an extra conditioning variable, job tenure, into the analysis. Denote by $G(w|a, t)$ the distribution function of wages conditional on experience and job tenure.

Proposition 6.3. *Expected wages are increasing (decreasing) in job tenure as*

$$R^u(a - t)(R^u(a - t) + \lambda) + \frac{\partial R^u(a - t)}{\partial a} > (<)0 \qquad (6.23)$$

If non-employed workers enter employment at a rate λ_u, and the non-employment rate is $u(a)$, the condition in (6.23) can be written as

$$\delta + (\lambda - \lambda_u)u(a - t) > (<)0 \qquad (6.24)$$

Proof. Denote by $m(w, t|a)$ the proportion of the population of experience a in a job paying wage w and with tenure t. What we know about these people is the following:

- they must have been recruited at experience $(a - t)$;
- they must have been recruited at this time either from non-employment or from jobs paying less than w;
- they have not lost their job or found a better paying one in the time t since then.

The number of workers of experience $(a - t)$ who are recruited into a job paying w is given by $f(w)N(a - t)[\lambda G(w \mid a - t) + R^u(a - t)]$ as a fraction $G(w|a - t)$ of workers in employment will accept a job at wage w and there is also a flow of $R^u N$ non-employed workers, all of whom will accept a job at wage w. The separation rate for these workers is $[\delta + \lambda(1 - F(w))]$ so after time t a fraction $\exp\{-[\delta + \lambda(1 - F(w))]t\}$ will remain with the firm. So, $m(w, t|a)$ is given by

$$m(w, t \mid a) = f(w) \exp\left[- [\delta + \lambda(1 - F(w))]t\right]$$

$$\times N(a - t)[\lambda G(w \mid a - t) + R^u(a - t)] \quad (6.25)$$

Now, the distribution function of wages conditional on experience and tenure is given by

$$G(w \mid a, t) = \frac{\int_{\underline{w}}^{w} m(v, t \mid a) dv}{\int_{\underline{w}}^{\bar{w}} m(v, t \mid a) dv} \quad (6.26)$$

A method for proving the impact of changes in experience and/or job tenure on expected wages is contained in the following lemma.

Lemma 6.1. *A sufficient condition for the expected wage to be increasing (decreasing) in variable x (experience or tenure) is if $d\ln(m)/dx$ is increasing (decreasing) in the wage.*

Proof. From (6.15) we have that a rise in x will raise the expected wage if we have first-order stochastic dominance (although (6.15) refers to experience, it is obvious that it can also be applied to tenure or any other conditioning variable). To work out the effect on G of x, differentiate (6.26) with respect to x (it is actually more convenient to differentiate $\ln(G)$):

$$\frac{\partial \ln G(w \mid a, t)}{\partial x} = \frac{\int_{\underline{w}}^{w} \frac{\partial m(v, t \mid a)}{\partial x} dv}{\int_{\underline{w}}^{w} m(v, t \mid a) dv} - \frac{\int_{\underline{w}}^{\bar{w}} \frac{\partial m(v, t \mid a)}{\partial x} dv}{\int_{\underline{w}}^{\bar{w}} m(v, t \mid a) dv}$$

$$= \frac{\int_{\underline{w}}^{w} \frac{\partial \ln m(v, t \mid a)}{\partial x} m(v, t \mid a) dv}{\int_{\underline{w}}^{w} m(v, t \mid a) dv} - \frac{\int_{\underline{w}}^{\bar{w}} \frac{\partial \ln m(v, t \mid a)}{\partial x} m(v, t \mid a) dv}{\int_{\underline{w}}^{\bar{w}} m(v, t \mid a) dv}$$

$$= E\left(\frac{\partial \ln m(v, t \mid a)}{\partial x} \mid v \leq w \right) - E\left(\frac{\partial \ln m(v, t \mid a)}{\partial x} \right) \quad (6.27)$$

We can sign this unambiguously if the partial derivative of $\ln(m)$ with respect to x is monotonic in w. If it is increasing in w, then $\ln(G)$ is decreasing in x which, from (6.15), means that the expected wage is increasing in x. This proves Lemma 6.1.

Now, returning to the proof of Proposition 6.3 and using Lemma 6.1, we have, by taking the logs of (6.25) and differentiating with respect to t:

$$\frac{\partial \ln m(w, t \mid a)}{\partial t} = -[\delta + \lambda(1 - F(w))] - \frac{1}{N(a - t)} \frac{\partial N(a - t)}{\partial a}$$

$$- \frac{\lambda \dfrac{\partial G(w \mid a - t)}{\partial a} + \dfrac{\partial R^u(a - t)}{\partial a}}{\lambda G(w \mid a - t) + R^u(a - t)} \tag{6.28}$$

Now, using (6.17) and (6.20), we can write this as

$$\frac{\partial \ln m(w, t \mid a)}{\partial t}$$

$$= \frac{-[R^u + \lambda(1 - F(w))](\lambda G + R^u) - \dfrac{\partial R^u}{\partial a} + \lambda^2(1 - F)G - \lambda(F - G)R^u}{\lambda G(w \mid a - t) + R^u(a - t)}$$

$$= \frac{-R^u(R^u + \lambda) - \dfrac{\partial R^u}{\partial a}}{\lambda G(w \mid a - t) + R^u(a - t)} \tag{6.29}$$

As G is increasing in w (by definition), the application of the rule in Lemma 6.1 gives (6.23) and (6.3).

To prove the second part of Proposition 6.3, note that, if non-employed workers enter employment at a rate λ_u, then we have

$$R^u(a) = \frac{\lambda_u u(a)}{1 - u(a)} \tag{6.30}$$

and

$$\frac{\partial u(a)}{\partial a} = \delta[1 - u(a)] - \lambda_u u(a) \tag{6.31}$$

Differentiating (6.30), and using (6.31) in (6.29) leads to (6.24).

The Distribution of Wages With "True" Returns to Experience and Tenure

In this case, we modify the model of the previous section in the following way. First, we assume that the wage offer distribution changes with experience so that the wage offer distribution at experience a can be written as $F(w - \beta_a(a))$ where $\beta_a(a)$ is a measure of the true returns to experience. We normalize $\beta_a(a)$ so that $\beta_a(0) = 0$. We also assume that wages in a job rise at a rate β_t with tenure. The assumption that the returns to tenure are linear is restrictive but it helps to make the analysis tractable. Its advantage is that expected wage growth on two jobs is independent of the current wage and tenure so the choice between them can be made solely on the basis of which job offers the highest wage.

As before, we are interested in the cross-section distribution of wages conditional on experience and tenure $g(w|a, t)$: this is derived in the following proposition.

Proposition 6.4

1. *The distribution of wages conditional on experience is given by*

$$[1 - u(a)]G(w \mid a) = \exp\left[- \int_0^a [\delta + \lambda(1 - F(w - \beta_a(a) - \beta_t(a - x)))]dx \right]$$

$$\times F(w - \beta_a(a) - \beta_t a)[1 - u(0)]$$

$$+ \lambda \int_0^a \exp\left[\int_s^a [\delta + \lambda(1 - F(w - \beta_a(a) - \beta_t(a - x)))]dx \right]$$

$$\times F(w - \beta_a(a) - \beta_t(a - s))u(s)ds \qquad (6.32)$$

2. *The distribution of wages conditional on experience and tenure is given by (6.26) but where $m(w, t|a)$ is now given by*

$$m(w, t|a) = \exp\left[- \int_0^t [\delta + \lambda(1 - F(w - \beta_a(a) - \beta_t(t - x)))]dx \right]$$

$$\times f(w - \beta_a(a) - \beta_t t)R \qquad (6.33)$$

where

$$R = [\lambda G(w - \beta_a(a) + \beta_a(a - t) - \beta_t t, a - t)[1 - u(a - t)] + \lambda u(a - t)]$$

3. *The expected level of wages at (a, t) given the returns to experience $\beta_a(a)$ and the return to tenure β_t, $E(w \mid a, t, \beta_a, \beta_t)$ is given by*

$$E(w \mid a, t, \beta_a, \beta_t) = E(w \mid a, t, 0, \beta_t) + \beta_a(a) \qquad (6.34)$$

so that one can, without loss of generality, restrict attention to the analysis of earnings functions in which there are no true returns to experience.

Proof

1. As before let us denote by $M(w|a)$ the number of workers of experience a with a wage less than or equal to w. One can think of this group as

being made up of workers who entered employment at different experience levels.

Consider those who were in employment at experience 0. To have wages less than w at experience a, they must have had wages at that time less than $(w - \beta_a(a) - \beta_t a)$ or else the process of wage growth would have made them end up with a wage above w at experience a. There must have been $F(w - \beta_a(a) - \beta_t a)[1 - u(0)]$ of these workers. At date x (where $a \geq x \geq 0$) their wage must have been less than $[w - \beta_a(a) + \beta_a(x) - \beta_t(a - x)]$ so that their instantaneous exit rate from the group will be $[\delta + \lambda(1 - F(w - \beta_a(a) - \beta_t(a - x)))]$. Hence, the exponential part of the first term on the right-hand side of (6.32) gives the fraction of those in employment at experience 0 with wages less than $(w - \beta_a(a) - \beta_t a)$ who are still in employment at a wage less than w at experience a.

Now consider those who last entered employment at experience s. The flow of exits from non-employment at experience s is $\lambda u(s)$. If they have a wage less than w at experience a, they must have had a wage less than $[w - \beta_a(a) + \beta_a(s) - \beta_t(a - s)]$ when they entered employment. This will have been true of a fraction $F(w - \beta_a(a) - \beta_t(a - s))$ of them. They must subsequently not have left employment for non-employment or got a wage offer which means they have a wage higher than w at experience a. At date x (where $a \geq x \geq s$) their wage must have been less than $[w - \beta_a(a) + \beta_a(x) - \beta_t(a - x)]$ so that their instantaneous exit rate from the group will be $[\delta + \lambda(1 - F(w - \beta_a(a) - \beta_t(a - x)))]$. Integrating over all the possible dates of entry to employment gives the second term in (6.32).

2. As we have done before let us denote by $m(w, t|a)$ the density of workers of experience a paid a wage w and with job tenure t. We know that these workers must have been recruited at experience $(a - t)$ at a wage equal to $[w - \beta_a(a) + \beta_a(a - t) - \beta_t t]$. These workers have come from either non-employment or from the mass of workers paid less than this wage at experience $(a - t)$. Hence, the density of recruits is given by

$$f(w - \beta_a(a) - \beta_t t)[\lambda M(w - \beta_a(a) + \beta_a(a - t) - \beta_t t|a - t) + \lambda u(a - t)]$$
(6.35)

But, of course, these recruits are only still at this wage at tenure t if they have not left the firm at a tenure $x \in [0, t]$. At tenure x their wage is given by $[w - \beta_a(a) + \beta_a(a - t + x) - \beta_t(t - x)]$. Hence, the proportion of wage offers sufficiently good to make them leave is $[1 - F(w - \beta_a(a) - \beta_t(t - x))]$. Putting this information together, we have

$$m(w, t|a) = \exp\left[-\int_0^t [\delta + \lambda[1 - F(w - \beta_a(a) - \beta_t(t - x))]]dx\right]f(w - \beta_a(a) - \beta_t t)$$

$$\times [\lambda M(w - \beta_a(a) - \beta_t t|a - t) + \lambda u(a - t)]$$
(6.36)

Changing the variable of integration in (6.36) from x to $s = (x + a - t)$ leads to (6.34).

3. A simple change of variable from w to $w - \beta_a(a)$ shows that $E(w - \beta_a(a) \mid a, t)$ is independent of $\beta_a(a)$ which gives the result in (6.34).

Let us consider in more detail the likely direction of the bias in the estimated return to tenure. From Proposition 6.3 we know that when $\beta_t = 0$ we only get an unbiased estimate of the return to tenure in the cross-section when the condition in (6.24) is satisfied. The following proposition analyzes one of these cases and shows that the return to tenure will no longer be unbiased and that the sign of the bias depends on the functional form of the wage offer distribution so that it is hard to form any a priori view about it.

Proposition 6.5. *If $u(0) = 0$ and $\delta_u = 0$, the cross-sectional estimate of the earnings function gives a biased estimate of the returns to tenure if $\beta_t > 0$. The bias is positive if*

$$-\lambda \int_0^a [1 - F(w - \beta_t s)]ds + \ln(F(w - \beta_t a)) \qquad (6.37)$$

is a convex function of w for all w and negative if it is a concave function everywhere.

Proof. Let us simplify the algebra by assuming that $\beta_a(a) = 0$. If $u(0) = 0$ and $\delta_u = 0$, no workers are ever in unemployment so that all recruits must come from employment. Using (6.36), we have

$$m(w, t \mid a) = \lambda f(w - \beta_t t) \exp\left[-\lambda \int_0^t [1 - F(w - \beta_t(t - x))]dx \right]$$

$$\times G(w - \beta_t t \mid a - t)$$

$$= \lambda f(w - \beta_t t) \exp\left[-\lambda \int_0^t [1 - F(w - \beta_t(t - x))]dx \right]$$

$$\times \exp\left[-\lambda \int_0^{a-t} [1 - F(w - \beta_t(a - x))]dx \right] F(w - \beta_t a) \quad (6.38)$$

where the equality follows from the application of (6.32) with the special assumptions made here. Changing the variable of integration to $s = (t - x)$ in the first integral and $s = (a - x)$ in the second, the final line of (6.38) can be written as

$$m(w, t \mid a) = \lambda f(w - \beta_t t) \exp\left[-\lambda \int_0^a [1 - F(w - \beta_t s)] ds \right] F(w - \beta_t a)$$

$$\equiv f(w - \beta_t t) \psi(w, a) \tag{6.39}$$

where $\psi(w, a)$ is the term involving a in (6.39). Application of (6.26) then shows that

$$E(w \mid a, t) = \frac{\int w f(w - \beta_t t) \psi(w, a) dw}{\int f(w - \beta_t t) \psi(w, a) dw} \tag{6.40}$$

Transforming the variable of integration to $v = w - \beta_t t$, we have

$$E(w \mid a, t) = \beta_t t + \frac{\int v f(v) \psi(v + \beta_t t, a) dv}{\int f(v) \psi(v + \beta_t t, a) dv} \tag{6.41}$$

Differentiating this with respect to t, we have

$$\frac{\partial E(w \mid a, t)}{\partial t}$$

$$= \beta_t + \beta_t \left[\frac{\int v f(v) \psi'(v + \beta_t t, a) dv}{\int f(v) \psi(v + \beta_t t, a) dv} - \frac{\int f(v) \psi'(v + \beta_t t, a) dv}{\int f(v) \psi(v + \beta_t t, a) dv} \frac{\int v f(v) \psi(v + \beta_t t, a) dv}{\int f(v) \psi(v + \beta_t t, a) dv} \right]$$

$$= \beta_t + \beta_t \left[E\left(v \frac{\psi'}{\psi} \right) - E(v) E\left(\frac{\psi'}{\psi} \right) \right]$$

$$= \beta_t + \beta_t \mathrm{Cov}\left(v, \frac{\psi'}{\psi} \right) \tag{6.42}$$

where the expectation is taken with respect to $(f\psi)$ and ψ' represents the derivative of $\psi(w, a)$ with respect to w. The sign of the bias then depends on the covariance term which depends on whether $\ln(\psi)$ is convex or concave in w. Using (6.39) this can be written as (6.37).

Appendix 6B

Proof of Proposition 6

Although our ultimate interest is simply the unconditional correlation between earnings and experience, we condition on job tenure in what follows because it has previously been shown to be important. One could modify the decomposition to condition on other variables thought relevant.

First, let us introduce the following (lengthy) notation:

- $w(a)$ is the average log wage for workers of experience a;
- $w(a, t)$ is the average log wage for workers of experience a and job tenure t;
- $w^s(a, t)$ is the average log wage for workers of experience a and job tenure t who stay in their jobs over the coming year;
- $w^m(a, t)$ is the average log wage for workers of experience a and job tenure t who move jobs over the coming year;
- $w^l(a, t)$ is the average log wage for workers of experience a and job tenure t who lose their jobs over the coming year;
- $w^e(a)$ is the average log wage for workers of experience a who were not in employment last year;
- $g^s(a, t)$ is the average log wage growth for workers with experience a and job tenure t who stay in their current job;
- $g^m(a, t)$ is the average log wage growth for workers with experience a and job tenure t who move from their current job;
- $n(a)$ is the number of workers of experience a;
- $n(a, t)$ is the number of workers of experience a and job tenure t;
- $n^e(a)$ is the number of workers of experience a who were not in employment last year;
- $\delta(a, t)$ is the fraction of workers of experience a and job tenure t who lose their jobs in the coming year;
- $\lambda(a, t)$ is the fraction of workers of experience a and job tenure t who change their jobs in the coming year.

To keep matters relatively simple, we will restrict attention to a steady state in which all the above are constant over time.

The following relationships must be true by definition.

The current average log wage for those of experience a and job tenure t must be equal to a weighted average of wages for stayers, movers, and job losers:

$$w(a, t) = [1 - \delta(a, t) - \lambda(a, t)]w^s(a, t) + \lambda(a, t)w^m(a, t) + \delta(a, t)w^l(a, t)$$
(6.43)

The current average log wage for those of experience a must be equal to a weighted average of the log average wage for those with experience a and different tenure levels:

$$n(a)w(a) = \sum_{t=0}^{a} n(a, t)w(a, t)$$
(6.44)

The numbers currently in employment with experience $(a + 1)$ and job tenure $(t + 1)$ must be equal to those in employment with experience a and job tenure t who have stayed in their jobs:

$$n(a + 1, t + 1) = [1 - \delta(a, t) - \lambda(a, t)]n(a, t) \qquad (6.45)$$

The numbers currently in employment with experience $(a + 1)$ must be equal to those in employment with experience a who have not lost their jobs plus entrants to employment at experience $(a + 1)$:

$$n(a + 1) = \sum_{t=0}^{a} n(a, t)[1 - \delta(a, t)] + n^e(a + 1) \qquad (6.46)$$

Total wages paid out to workers of experience $(a + 1)$ must be equal to a weighted average of the wages for stayers with experience a plus their average growth, the wages for movers with experience a plus their average growth, and the average wage for entrants to employment:

$$n(a + 1)w(a + 1) = \sum_{t=0}^{a} n(a, t)[[1 - \delta(a, t) - \lambda(a, t)][w^s(a, t) + g^s(a, t)]$$

$$+ \lambda(a, t)[w^m(a, t) + g^m(a, t)]] + n^e(a + 1)w^e(a + 1) \qquad (6.47)$$

Now let us consider how we can manipulate these identities to end up with (6.13). First use (6.43) to eliminate $w^s(a, t)$ from (6.47) which leads to

$$n(a + 1)w(a + 1)$$

$$= \sum_{t=0}^{a} n(a, t)\left[w(a, t) + g^s(a, t) + \lambda(a, t)\Delta^m(a, t) - \delta(a, t)\left[w^l(a, t) + g^s(a, t) \right] \right]$$

$$+ n^e(a + 1)w^e(a + 1) \qquad (6.48)$$

where $\Delta^m(a, t) \equiv [g^m(a, t) - g^s(a, t)]$ is an uncorrected measure of the return to job mobility for workers with experience a and job tenure t. As $n(a) = \sum_t n(a, t)$, (6.48) can be written as

$$n(a + 1)w(a + 1) = n(a)\left[w(a) + \overline{\Delta}^s(a) + \overline{\lambda}(a)\overline{\Delta}^m(a) \right] + n^e(a + 1)w^e(a + 1)$$

$$- \sum_{t=0}^{a} n(a, t)\delta(a, t)\left[w^l(a, t) + g^s(a, t) \right] \qquad (6.49)$$

where $\overline{\Delta}^s(a)$ is the average wage growth for stayers, $\overline{\lambda}(a)$ is the average job mobility rate and $\overline{\Delta}^m(a)$ is the move-weighted return to job mobility. Using (6.46), we can write (6.49) as

$$n(a + 1)w(a + 1) = n(a + 1)\left[w(a) + \overline{\Delta}^s(a)\right] + n(a)\overline{\lambda}(a)\overline{\Delta}^m(a)$$

$$+ n^e(a + 1)\left[w^e(a + 1) - w(a) - \overline{\Delta}^s(a)\right]$$

$$- \sum_{t=0}^{a} n(a, t)\delta(a, t)\left[w^l(a, t) + g^s(a, t) - w(a) - \overline{\Delta}^s(a)\right]$$

$$(6.50)$$

Now let us define the cost of job loss $\overline{\Delta}^l(a + 1)$ by

$$\overline{\Delta}^l(a + 1) = w^e(a + 1) - \frac{\displaystyle\sum_{t=0}^{a} n(a, t)\delta(a, t)\left[w^l(a, t) + g^s(a, t)\right]}{\displaystyle\sum_{t=0}^{a} n(a, t)\delta(a, t)} \qquad (6.51)$$

This definition compares the earnings of those entering employment from non-employment with an estimate of the earnings those losing their jobs the previous year could have expected if they had stayed in their jobs. If all workers were always in employment, one could compute a more disaggregated measure of the cost of job loss but we typically cannot do that for our data sets. Also, let us define the leaver bias, $b^l(a, t)$ as

$$b^l(a + 1) = w^l(a, t) - w(a, t) \qquad (6.52)$$

Then, using (6.51) and (6.52), we can write the second and third lines of (6.50) as

$$n^e(a + 1)\overline{\Delta}^l(a + 1) + \left[n^e(a + 1) - \sum_{t=0}^{a} n(a, t)\delta(a, t)\right]$$

$$\times \left[\frac{\displaystyle\sum_{t=0}^{a} n(a, t)\delta(a, t)\left(b^l(a, t) + w(a, t) + g^s(a, t) - w(a) - \overline{\Delta}^s(a)\right)}{\displaystyle\sum_{t=0}^{a} n(a, t)\delta(a, t)}\right]$$

$$(6.53)$$

The terms in square brackets consist of two sorts of leaver bias. First, the fact that leavers tend to have lower wages than movers and stayers for a given level of experience and job tenure ($b^l > 0$). Second, the distribution of tenure among leavers may differ from that in the population as a whole. But the leaver bias only has an effect to the extent that there are changes in employment. Denote the whole leaver bias by $b^l(a)$. Putting (6.53) into (6.50) leads to the expression in (6.13).

7

Gender Discrimination in Labor Markets

LABOR market discrimination is usually defined as a situation where workers who are identical in ability have different labor market outcomes. It should not come as a surprise that monopsony or oligopsony has something to say on these issues as, in such a labor market, we know that wages are determined by factors other than productivity. But, this wage dispersion is not quite what is commonly meant by discrimination, a phrase that is generally reserved for a situation where certain groups, for example, women or ethnic minorities systematically receive worse treatment from the labor market.

While the disadvantages suffered by these two groups do have some common features, there are also important differences. For example, the constraints imposed on women by the traditional allocation of domestic responsibilities are not faced by black males, while women do not face the geographical concentration (the extreme form of which is ghettoes, a model of which was presented in section 3.6) that is a feature of the economic predicament of many black workers. This chapter restricts its attention to gender discrimination not because racial discrimination is less important but because monopsony has more to say about gender discrimination.

The outline of the chapter is as follows. The next section documents the most important features of the gender pay gap in the United Kingdom and the United States and shows how these are mirrored in a gender gap in the pattern of labor market transitions, something that is in line with the predictions of a view of the labor market in which employers have some market power. Gender differences in constraints on job search and the reasons for job mobility are then discussed. It is shown that women's job mobility is more constrained by domestic responsibilities than is the case for men and that their job moves are less motivated by money. This shows up in a gender gap in the returns to job mobility. All of this evidence suggests that the wage elasticity in the supply of female labor to a firm should be lower than the male, making the female market less competitive. However, as shown in section 7.6 there is no strong evidence that the wage elasticity of separations is lower for women than for men.

An emphasis on gender differences in labor market attachment is hardly new in discussions of the gender pay gap. The human capital approach also emphasizes these factors but suggests they act to reduce the productivity of women. A direct test of the monopsony and human capital approaches would investigate the role of productivity differences in explaining wage differences: unfortunately direct data on productivity is very rare making it hard to distinguish between the two theories. However, sections 7.8 and 7.9 present two pieces of evidence to suggest that the monopsony approach may be preferable. First, the returns to job tenure appear to be higher for women than men, a finding that is argued to be readily explainable by the monopsony model but more difficult to explain using the human capital approach. Second, an analysis of the impact of the UK Equal Pay Act suggests that the gender pay gap was reduced very substantially without any adverse effect on job opportunities for women.

The chapter concludes with a brief discussion of how the existence of frictions in the labor market is likely to amplify the consequences of any prejudice among employers as proposed by Becker (1971).

7.1 The Gender Pay Gap

Women earn substantially less than men. In the United States, the raw gap in log hourly earnings in 1998–99 was about 19 log points (from the monthly CPS out-going rotation groups): in the United Kingdom, it was about 30 log points (from the LFS). In both countries, the gender pay gap has narrowed in the last 15 years and there was also a rapid narrowing in the United Kingdom from 1970 to 1975 connected with the introduction of the Equal Pay Act. The gender pay gap also has some demographic variation. It is hard to be precise about these variations in the gender pay gap because their existence and size seem to depend on the other variables included in the earnings equation.[1] But, the most consistent variations in the gender pay gap are:

- The return to potential experience (years since left full-time education) is much lower for women than men (although the returns are much closer if actual rather than potential experience is used). There is no earnings gap between men and women in the first 5 years after leaving full-time education in the United Kingdom although a small gap remains in the United States.

[1] Controls for actual experience, job tenure, industry, and occupation seem to be the crucial variables here. For example, Groshen (1991b) finds little gender pay gap exists within occupations within establishments suggesting it is the process of sorting of female workers into jobs that is important in understanding the gender pay gap. However, see Bayard et al. (1999) for rather different results.

- The returns to job tenure are, if anything, somewhat higher for women than men (see, e.g., Becker and Lindsey 1994).
- The pay gap is larger for those who are married and those who have children (the so-called "family penalty" (see Waldfogel 1998a,b)).
- The pay gap is smaller for those from ethnic minorities.

A good explanation of the gender pay gap should be able to explain not just the raw differential but also the variation in the differential. The next section considers how monopsony may explain the gender pay gap.

7.2 Monopsony and the Gender Pay Gap

There is an established "human capital" approach to explaining the gender pay gap. In a perfectly competitive labor market, differences in wages reflect differences in productivity (abstracting from compensating differentials), so the gender pay gap can only be explained by a gender productivity gap. The origin of this gender productivity gap is then identified as being women's weaker attachment to the labor market, mainly the result of the traditional allocation of domestic and child-care labor.

The original discussion of monopsony in Robinson (1933: 302–4) contains an application to the gender pay gap. But, her argument as to why monopsony might be relevant is confined to an example in which men are unionized and women are not, and the slightly enigmatic statement that "a cursory view of existing conditions seems to suggest that [this analysis of the rate of exploitation] may have some bearing upon actual cases" (Robinson 1933: 303). But, monopsony has more to offer on this subject than is apparent from Robinson's analysis. At the end of chapter 2, we emphasized how the monopsonistic approach to labor markets adds other factors to the list of possible determinants of wages, notably labor market transition rates (job offer arrival rates and job destruction rates) and the reservation wage. Even if the productivity of men and women is the same, there will be a gender pay gap if their labor market transition rates differ.

So, a natural starting point for considering how well monopsony can explain the gender pay gap is the discussion at the end of chapter 2. There we proposed a simple statistic, the proportion of recruits from non-employment, as a measure of monopsony power. We have already seen in table 2.2 how a higher fraction of female recruits come from non-employment so that this can explain the overall gender pay gap. But, can it explain the variation in it? Table 7.1 investigates this.

TABLE 7.1
Aspects of the Gender Pay Gap

	US (CPS)		UK (LFS)	
	Log Wage	Recruited from Employment	Log Wage	Recruited from Employment
Single male, children	0.014	−0.027	−0.105	0.024
	(0.004)	(0.008)	(0.008)	(0.009)
Single female, no children	−0.098	0.053	0.029	0.136
	(0.024)	(0.048)	(0.010)	(0.011)
Single female, children	−0.147	−0.031	−0.104	0.017
	(0.024)	(0.048)	(0.009)	(0.011)
Married male, no children	0.114	0.128	0.163	0.176
	(0.004)	(0.009)	(0.005)	(0.009)
Married male, children	0.129	0.111	0.189	0.156
	(0.003)	(0.008)	(0.005)	(0.009)
Married female, no children	−0.071	0.011	0.078	0.183
	(0.024)	(0.048)	(0.010)	(0.012)
Married female, children	−0.093	−0.103	−0.039	−0.015
	(0.024)	(0.046)	(0.010)	(0.013)
R^2	0.38	–	0.4	–
Number of observations	195274	65880	214184	61376

Notes.
1. The reference category is a single male without children.
2. The US regression uses data from January 1998 to June 2000. Other controls include experience (interacted with gender), region, qualifications, month of interview, and black (interacted with gender).
3. The UK regression uses data from December 1992 to November 1999. Married includes those who are living together as a couple. Other controls include experience and tenure (interacted with gender), region, qualifications, month of interview, and black (interacted with gender).
4. In the column headed "recruited from employment" the sample is all those in new jobs and the dependent variable is binary taking the value 1 if the individual was previously employed and 0 otherwise. The reported coefficients are the marginal effects. In the column headed "log wage" the reported coefficients are from an earnings function.

Table 7.1 reports the results from a standard earnings equation and a probit equation where the sample is workers in new jobs and the dependent variable is whether the worker was previously employed (as estimated in table 2.2). Recall that the simple model of chapter 2 predicts less monopsony power in labor markets where a high fraction of recruits were previously employed. The reference category is a single male without children so the estimated coefficient in a particular row is the difference in the outcome between an individual of that type and the reference category. The most striking differences in earnings in both the United States and the United Kingdom are the premium for being married for men[2] and the penalty for having children for women. For the most part, these differences in wages also show up in the fraction recruited from employment. The evidence in table 7.1 is broadly supportive of a monopsony explanation of the gender pay gap based on differences in labor market dynamics. Bowlus (1997) and Barth and Dale-Olsen (1999) take a different approach to the same idea, showing how, in the Burdett and Mortensen (1998) model, the degree of monopsony power is a function of the labor market transition rates and showing how these are systematically different for men and women.

The gender difference in labor market transition rates provides an incentive for employers to pay otherwise identical men and women different wages (for further explanation of this, see Bowlus 1997; Barth and Dale-Olsen 1999). But, it is important to realize that the differences in labor market transition rates will result in a gender pay gap even if individual employers do not discriminate against women. Women will simply find it harder to work their way up the job ladder[3] and a gender pay gap will remain even if there is fully effective equal pay legislation. Groshen (1991b) concluded that the gender pay gap disappears once one includes detailed controls for occupation and employer suggesting that this effect may be more important in current labor markets. However, Bayard et al. (1999) cast some doubt on Groshen's conclusion, finding that there are still substantial gender pay differences within occupations within particular employers. This is an important issue where further research would be welcome.

However, the analysis so far is all based on the very simple version of the Burdett–Mortensen model of chapter 2.4 and there are good reasons for wanting to delve a little deeper as that model is overly simplistic in at least two areas which might be thought to be very relevant for explaining the gender pay gap.

First, the simple Burdett–Mortensen model assumes that labor is supplied inelastically to the market as a whole. Conventional wisdom says that individual labor supply is much more elastic for women than

---

[2] How these family effects should be interpreted is a matter of some debate. One interpretation would be a causal one from marriage and/or children to earnings. Others would emphasize how these household characteristics are correlated with unobserved factors (perhaps the old standby "ability") that also correlate with earnings.

[3] Proposition 6.1 is relevant here as it shows that an increase in the fraction of recruits from non-employment results in a lower position of workers on the job ladder.

men.[4] Secondly, the simple model assumes that all job moves are motivated by money. There are good reasons for thinking that there may be important gender differences in the reasons for job mobility that may affect the average level of earnings. The next few sections pursue these issues.

7.3 The Elasticity in Labor Supply to the Firm and the Market

There are a number of ways of introducing some elasticity into the supply of labor to the market as a whole into the basic model of an oligopsonistic labor market. Two ways of doing so were introduced in chapter 3: a fixed cost of entry (the model of section 3.3) and heterogeneity in reservation wages (the model of section 3.4). There are others: for example, one could make search intensity endogenous in which case the arrival rate of job offers will depend on the expected return to search. This line is discussed in chapter 9 but it is not the main reason why labor economists think that female labor supply is more elastic. More in line with traditional thinking is to introduce some heterogeneity in reservation wages.

A model of this type has already been introduced in section 3.4 where it was assumed that there is a distribution of the value attached to leisure, b, in the population. Denote by $H(b)$ the fraction of the population with value of leisure b or less. $H(b)$ tells us about the elasticity of the labor supply curve to the market as a whole. Perhaps the easiest way to see this is to consider a simple monopsonist who would choose the wage to maximize $(p - w)H(w)$. For a single monopsonist, $H(w)$ is both the supply of labor to the individual firm and to the market as a whole.

Why should $H(w)$ be more elastic for women than men? One explanation is that there is more heterogeneity in the value attached to home time among women than men because of greater heterogeneity in domestic responsibilities. Another explanation is based on the greater prevalence of part-time work among women combined with fixed costs of going to work. Suppose there is a simple monopsonist who faces an upward-sloping supply curve of labor, $H(U)$, where U is the utility that workers obtain from employment. Assume, for simplicity, that the elasticity of this supply curve is a constant and the same for men and women: denote it by ε_{HU}. Suppose that each hour of work pays w but has disutility b and

---

[4] Indeed, some economists have argued against Joan Robinson's views on the grounds that female labor is supplied more elastically than male labor. There is something a little odd about this argument as its proponents generally believe in competitive labor markets in which there is an enormous assumed gap between the elasticity in the supply of labor to the market as a whole and to an individual firm (as that is assumed infinite). But, there is clearly an issue here that needs to be sorted out.

that there is a fixed cost C of going to work. Utility is given by $U = (w - b)e - C$ where e is hours of work. The employer will be concerned about the wage elasticity of the labor supply curve which is given by

$$\varepsilon_{Hw} = \frac{w}{H}\frac{\partial H}{\partial w} = \frac{w}{U}\frac{U}{H}\frac{\partial H}{\partial U}\frac{\partial U}{\partial w} = \frac{we}{(w - b)e - C}\varepsilon_{HU} \qquad (7.1)$$

Suppose some individuals ("women") work part-time, that is, e is low. Then, (7.1) says that the wage elasticity of the labor supply curve facing the employer will be higher because a given percentage increase in the wage leads to a higher percentage increase in the utility.

Now, consider what happens to the labor supply curve facing an employer when we introduce other firms into the market. The following proposition provides the answer using the notation introduced in chapters 2 and 3.

Proposition 7.1. *The supply of labor to an individual firm is given by*

$$N(w) = \frac{\delta\lambda H(w)}{M[\delta + \lambda(1 - F(w))]^2} \qquad (7.2)$$

Proof. See proof of Lemma 3.1.

(7.2) shows that the elasticity of the labor supply to an individual firm combines, in a neat way, both the elasticity of the labor supply to the market as a whole (measured by $H(w)$) and the effect of competition from other firms (measured by $F(w)$). Note that as the labor market becomes more competitive (λ increases), the contribution of the supply of labor to the market as a whole becomes relatively less important. In the limiting case of perfect competition, $(\lambda/\delta) \to \infty$, (7.2) says that the supply of labor to the individual employer will be infinitely elastic at the maximum wage offered in the labor market. Using (7.2) to think about reasons for a gender gap in the elasticity of labor supply to the firm, competition from other firms may be less severe in the case of women but the elasticity of supply to the market as a whole is likely to be higher. So, it is unclear, a priori, whether the elasticity in the supply of female labor to a firm is greater or less than the male elasticity.

7.4 Money and Motivation

Another way in which the previous discussion may be too simplistic is that it assumes that all job moves are motivated by money and that a wage gain of a cent is enough to guarantee a move. In reality, other factors are important, for example, the location of the job, the hours offered, etc. Altonji and Paxson (1988, 1992) use the PSID to show that workers who obtain more favorable hours when they change jobs have lower wage growth suggesting that workers are trading off pecuniary and non-pecuniary aspects of jobs. It is quite likely that these other factors loom larger in the minds of women who often have the twin burdens of domestic responsibility for children and work for money.

The UK BHPS asks some questions on whether domestic responsibilities act as a constraint on job search and mobility. The answers to these questions are tabulated in table 7.2 and show that the extent of constraints on job search and mobility is much greater for married women with children than for either men or single women. For example, only 1.4% of single men report that domestic constraints have prevented job change compared to 13.2% of married women with children.

The UK BHPS also asks individuals about their reasons for changing jobs. The answers are tabulated in table 7.3. More men than women (26.7% against 24.3%) and more single women than married women with kids (22.9% against 20.4%) report that their job move was the result of a promotion, a pecuniary factor. Similar proportions of men and women report moving for a better job, but, as table 7.4 makes clear, many more men (47.1%) than women (33.8%) report pecuniary factors as the reason the job is better. Although there remains a gap between men and women in the motivation for leaving jobs, this gap is much narrower now than it used to be. Part of the BHPS collects retrospective data on life-time employment history including a question on the reason for leaving jobs. Figure 7.1a presents the proportion of job changes that were motivated by "career" concerns by year of job change:[5] men are more likely to be driven by these concerns but the gap is much smaller than it used to be. Figure 7.1b presents a similar picture but for the fraction of job changes motivated by "domestic" concerns: again, we see the gender gap declining.

All this adds up to a picture in which women and men differ in the attributes of jobs that are most valued with men putting relatively more emphasis on money. Similar results are reported for the United States by Keith and McWilliams (1999) for the NLSY and by Sicherman (1996) who uses a firm-level data set to show that, while overall levels of job turnover are similar for men and women, the reasons for turnover are very different with women much more likely than men to leave their jobs for non-market reasons.

[5] There is a problem with identifying life-cycle and cohort effects here but a regression in which there is a control for age comes up with the same conclusions: there is a convergence in motivation between men and women.

TABLE 7.2
Domestic Constraints on Job Search: UK BHPS

	Prevented Job Search	Prevented Taking Job	Prevented Job Change	Required Job Change	Required Leaving Job	Led to Less Work Hours	Number of Observations (Approx.)
All	3.6	2.9	4.4	1.3	0.6	2.9	31704
Men	1.5	0.8	2.3	0.7	0.2	1.2	15761
Women	5.7	5.0	6.4	1.9	1.0	4.7	15943
Married men	1.6	0.8	2.7	0.8	0.2	1.4	11280
Single men	1.3	0.6	1.4	0.2	0.1	0.6	4480
Married women	6.1	7.6	6.9	2.1	1.1	7.3	11509
Single women	4.8	3.6	5.0	1.4	0.8	2.9	4434
Married men, children	2.2	1.2	4.0	1.2	0.3	2.2	5583
Married men, no children	1.0	0.4	1.4	0.5	0.2	0.5	5697
Married women, children	12.3	11.2	13.2	3.3	1.9	10.5	5084
Married women, no children	1.2	1.1	2.0	1.1	0.5	1.2	6425

Notes.
1. The question asked is whether family commitments prevented job search, taking job, etc.
2. The sample is all those in employment. The number of observations differs slightly from column to column. The source is the BHPS 1991–98.

TABLE 7.3
Reasons for Jobs Ending: UK BHPS

	Promoted	Better Job	Lost Job	Retirement/ Health	Domestic Responsibilities	Other	Number of Observations
All	27.6	37.7	16.6	1.8	0.7	19.7	9870
Men	26.7	37.5	17.5	1.6	0.1	18.5	5101
Women	24.3	37.6	17.7	1.9	1.3	20.9	4769
Married men	28.3	33.2	16.3	1.7	0.1	19.9	3427
Single men	22.5	40.3	19.8	1.6	0.1	17.8	1673
Married women	24.8	37.2	14.6	2.1	1.4	21.9	3187
Single women	22.9	38.8	18.9	1.5	1.1	19	1581
Married men, children	29.8	32.8	14.7	1.2	0.1	21.4	1764
Married men, no children	27.8	33.6	18.1	2.2	0.0	18.3	1662
Married women, children	20.4	36.3	17.7	1.9	2.8	23.5	1400
Married women, no children	28.3	34.3	14.1	2.3	0.3	20.7	1787

Notes.
1. The sample is all those who left a job for a new job with another employer. The source is the BHPS 1991–98.

TABLE 7.4
Reasons Given for Why New Job Is Better: UK BHPS

	Pecuniary Factors	Non-pecuniary Factors	Number of Observations
All	40.6	59.4	2717
Men	47.1	52.9	1389
Women	33.8	66.2	1328
Married men	47.8	54.1	892
Single men	49.4	50.6	496
Married women	30.7	69.3	892
Single women	40.0	60.0	435
Married men, children	47.2	54.8	449
Married men, no children	46.5	53.5	443
Married women, children	29.3	70.7	396
Married women, no children	31.8	68.1	496

Notes.
1. The sample is all those who left a job for a new job with another employer and reported that the reason they left the previous job was because they had obtained a better job. The source is the BHPS 1991–98.

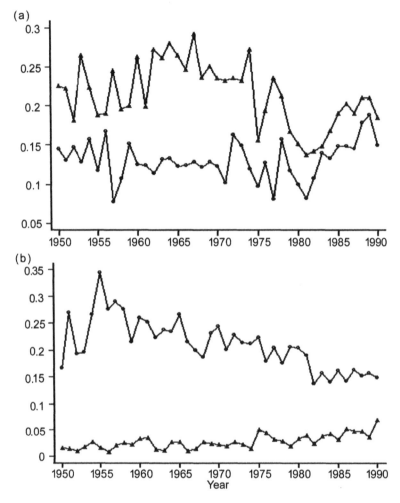

Figure 7.1   (a) The fraction of jobs ending with move to a better job. O, men; Δ, women. (b) The fraction of jobs ending because of domestic responsibilities. *Notes.* Both (a) and (b) are from the lifetime history record collected in the BHPS in 1994. (a) is the fraction of jobs ending where the reason given was "better job" while (b) presents the fraction giving "to have a baby" or "domestic responsibilities" as the reason. The year is the year in which the job ended.

Another aspect of the constraints on women is in terms of how far they can travel to work. If women are constrained by domestic responsibilities to take part-time work, then the fixed time and money costs of getting to work become relatively more important so that the worker is likely to be less prepared to travel long distances to work thus restricting the range of

TABLE 7.5
Travel-to-Work Times in Britain

	(1) All	(2) Men	(3) Women	(4) Men	(5) Women	(6) Men	(7) Women
Constant	27.11	27.21	23.20	27.00	24.33	–	–
	(0.06)	(0.16)	(0.11)	(0.16)	(0.11)		
Female	−6.12						
	(0.09)						
Married		2.62	−3.20	2.16	−2.87	1.35	−0.72
		(0.18)	(0.13)	(0.19)	(0.13)	(0.22)	(0.13)
Number of children				0.66	−1.74	0.26	−2.37
				(0.07)	(0.05)	(0.07)	(0.05)
Other controls	No	No	No	No	No	Yes	Yes
Number of observations	260504	123313	114915	123059	114797	121939	113955
R^2	0.018	0.002	0.006	0.002	0.015	0.561	0.619

Notes.
1. The dependent variable is the usual one-way home to work travel time in minutes. Sample is from the autumn UK LFS 1995–99.
2. Standard errors in parentheses.
3. Married is a 0–1 dummy variable taking the value 1 if the individual is married or living as one of a couple. Number of children is the number of dependent children under the age of 19 in the household.
4. The other controls are educational qualifications, race, county of residence, the year and month, and a quadratic in experience.

possible jobs. Table 7.5 presents some evidence on travel-to-work times from the UK LFS. On average, men take 27 minutes to get to work while women take 6 minutes less (column (1)). Married men travel more than single men (column (2)) while married women travel less (column (3)). Men with children travel more than childless men while the reverse is true for women (columns (4) and (5)). These effects survive the introduction of controls (columns (6) and (7)). This suggests that women, particularly women with domestic responsibilities, are restricted in the distance they can travel to work, one of the non-pecuniary factors that is likely to lower their earnings and make their labor market less competitive.

The bottom line from this discussion is that there are reasons to believe that female job-to-job changes are less sensitive to the wage than male and that the wage gains from job mobility are lower for women. The next two sections investigate these predictions.

7.5 Gender Differences in the Returns to Job Mobility

This section explores whether there are any significant gender differences in the returns to job mobility. The qualitative evidence presented in the previous section suggested that we would expect to see significantly lower returns from job mobility for women than for men.

Table 7.6 presents estimates of the returns to job mobility for men and women using our three panel data sets, the US PSID and NLSY, and the UK BHPS. The dependent variable is the change in log wages for workers in continuous employment. We include as controls a dummy variable for gender and a gender dummy interacted with whether the individual has changed jobs.

For each data set we present two specifications, one in which there are no controls apart from the dummy variables for gender and having moved jobs plus the interaction between them, and one in which other controls are included. For the PSID, the gender gap in the return to job mobility (the coefficient on the female mover variable) is significantly negative so that the returns to job mobility are lower for women than for men, whether controls are included or not. For the BHPS, we obtain the same result, although the gap is only significant once other controls are included in the equation. The

TABLE 7.6
Gender Differences in the Returns to Job Mobility

	PSID		NLSY		BHPS	
Mover	0.0586	0.0812	0.0120	0.0246	0.0539	0.1031
	(0.0058)	(0.0087)	(0.0080)	(0.0119)	(0.0097)	(0.0133)
Female mover	−0.0158	−0.0181	0.0125	0.0091	−0.0214	−0.0310
	(0.0083)	(0.0082)	(0.0125)	(0.0125)	(0.0134)	(0.0134)
Female	0.0051	0.0027	−0.0044	−0.0065	−0.0014	−0.0019
	(0.0023)	(0.0023)	(0.0065)	(0.0065)	(0.0041)	(0.0042)
Other controls	No	Yes	No	Yes	No	Yes
Number of observations	53053	53052	16030	15971	17800	17699
R^2	0.0030	0.0116	0.0005	0.0053	0.0025	0.0201

Notes.
1. The dependent variable is the change in log hourly wages. The sample is those workers in continuous employment from one year to the next.
2. Where included, the other controls are mover status interacted with lagged experience and job tenure, a quadratic in lagged experience, lagged job tenure, education, ethnicity, region, and year dummies.

NLSY has rather different results with no evidence of lower returns to job mobility for women.

However, there are a number of other studies which have examined gender differences in the returns to job mobility using the NLSY. Loprest (1992) reports significantly lower returns to job mobility for women at the very start of their labor market careers. Keith and McWilliams (1997) extended this analysis by disaggregating the causes of separation. They concluded that the returns to different types of job mobility were similar for men and women but that there was a gender gap in the incidence of the different types of job mobility. Women were more likely to have a family-related quit (which has a wage penalty) and less likely to have voluntary job-to-job separations. Keith and McWilliams (1999) extended this analysis to investigate the returns to job-related search finding, again, the returns to this activity were similar for men and women but women do less of it

7.6 Gender Differences in the Wage Elasticity of Separations

The previous sections have highlighted gender differences in the labor market transitions of men and women. A consistent picture in which women's job opportunities are more constrained and job decisions less motivated by money has emerged. It is well known that the separation rate is higher for women than men (although the gap is much less than it used to be) but these factors suggest that we might expect to find a gender gap in the wage elasticity of separations. This section examines this prediction.

Table 7.7 presents estimates of separation elasticities for the PSID and NLSY for the United States, and for the BHPS and LFS for the United Kingdom. These estimates are obtained using the approach of section 4.7. The reported coefficients measure the elasticity of the separation rate with respect to the wage. We show the estimated elasticities for two specifications: both without and with the controls listed at the bottom of the table.

First, consider the wage elasticity for all separations. Without controls, the male elasticity is higher than the female for three of the four data sets although the differences are small and not significantly different from zero. However, this result does not stand up to the introduction of controls: now the female elasticity is larger than the male in three of the data sets and the gap is actually more significant. We might expect female separations to non-employment to be more sensitive to the wage than male separations. Without controls, there is no evidence for this although this pattern does emerge in three of the four data sets once

TABLE 7.7
The Wage Elasticity of Separations with Respect to the Wage

Sample	Gender	No controls			Controls		
		All Separations	Separations to Other Jobs	Separations to Non-employment	All Separations	Separations to Other Jobs	Separations to Non-employment
PSID	Male	-1.005 (0.055)	-0.927 (0.054)	-1.046 (0.088)	-0.880 (0.058)	-0.889 (0.038)	-0.868 (0.085)
PSID	Female	-0.971 (0.034)	-0.744 (0.042)	-1.059 (0.039)	-1.055 (0.045)	-0.936 (0.055)	-1.101 (0.048)
NLSY	Male	-0.580 (0.042)	-0.500 (0.056)	-0.676 (0.049)	-0.554 (0.046)	-0.544 (0.062)	-0.507 (0.057)
NLSY	Female	-0.548 (0.041)	-0.415 (0.066)	-0.651 (0.043)	-0.629 (0.048)	-0.575 (0.079)	-0.678 (0.049)
BHPS	Male	-0.968 (0.058)	-0.914 (0.079)	-1.042 (0.081)	-0.742 (0.078)	-0.753 (0.107)	-0.735 (0.110)
BHPS	Female	-0.901 (0.091)	-0.886 (0.131)	-0.917 (0.118)	-0.566 (0.120)	-0.471 (0.172)	-0.677 (0.162)
LFS	Male	-0.642 (0.029)	-0.591 (0.039)	-0.726 (0.042)	-0.452 (0.042)	-0.481 (0.053)	-0.414 (0.068)
LFS	Female	-0.652 (0.036)	-0.565 (0.047)	-0.744 (0.044)	-0.540 (0.039)	-0.438 (0.057)	-0.659 (0.055)

Notes.
1. The samples are the same as those used in table 4.7.
2. All equations contain the following additional controls: education, race, marital status, children, region, a quartic in experience, and year dummies. Tenure is excluded: its inclusion lowers the estimated wage elasticities while preserving the qualitative results. See section 4.7 for a discussion of whether tenure should be included or excluded from these equations.

controls are included. Conversely, one might expect that the male elasticity is greater than the female elasticity for separations to other jobs. There is weak evidence for this although, again, the gender gap is not very large or robust.

The results presented here are consistent with other estimates of these elasticities. Viscusi (1980), using data from the PSID in 1975–76 found a wage elasticity close to -1.0 for both men and women. Other estimates can be found in Royalty (1998) where, although the specification estimated does not make it very easy to work out the implied elasticities, there does not seem to be a very striking gender gap.

One possible explanation for the finding that there is no systematic gender gap in the wage elasticity of separations is that the differences in the labor turnover behavior of men and women are now quite small. The differences in separation rates were almost certainly once higher, for example, Viscusi (1980) reports that female quit rates in US manufacturing were 80% above the male rate in 1958, but only 16% higher in 1968. However, the finding of Viscusi (1980) that there was no gender gap in wage elasticities in the mid-1970s casts some doubt on the hypothesis that female wage elasticities used to be below those of men.

Consequently, the gender differences that we have identified in previous sections do not show up strongly in these estimated elasticities. Whether this is because this approach to estimating elasticities is not very informative or because the total effect of the gender differences in constraints and motivation is small, is an issue that deserves further consideration.

7.7 Human Capital Explanations of the Gender Pay Gap

The discussion so far has paid little or no attention to well-established explanations of the gender pay gap based on human capital theory. These theories also emphasize the constraints imposed on women by the traditional division of labor within the household but model the impact on wages as being through an impact on productivity. Perhaps the simplest way to see the human capital approach at work is in the papers that make the distinction between actual and potential experience and investigate whether the gender differences in the returns to potential experience that we have already noted, can be explained in terms of a common return to actual experience, and gender differences in the level of experience (see, e.g., Light and Ureta 1995).[6] Direct data

---

[6] On the whole this literature claims some success although the search approach can also explain such findings and a substantial gender pay gap remains. And, it is typically found that any interruption in paid employment, however short, reduces earnings.

on productivity are rare so it is difficult to provide a direct test of the human capital and monopsony approaches. The study of Hellerstein et al. (1999) finds evidence that the gender pay gap across firms is much larger than the gender productivity gap suggesting that the human capital approach is not the whole story. But, in the absence of direct data on productivity, there are some differences in implications of the two theories that one might hope to exploit.

First, consider the returns to tenure. In the human capital approach, the returns to tenure are thought to represent a share of the returns to investments in firm-specific human capital. If women are more likely to leave a firm than men, we would then expect the incentives for investments in firm-specific human capital to be reduced and the observed returns to tenure to be lower for women as a given level of job tenure is likely to be associated with a lower level of firm-specific human capital. In contrast, the search model predicts a stronger correlation between tenure and wages for those groups with weak labor market attachment as tenure becomes a better measure of the time elapsed since the individual was last non-employed (see table 6.2 and the discussion surrounding it).[7] Table 7.8 reports estimates of the cross-sectional returns to tenure for women and men from the US CPS and the UK LFS. The reported returns are the estimated gap in earnings between someone with the reported years of tenure and someone just starting a job. For the United States, the female return to job tenure is noticeably *higher* than the male at all experience and tenure levels. In the United Kingdom, the gender gap in the returns to tenure is much smaller but there is not much evidence that the male return to job tenure is higher. This evidence is consistent with the monopsony approach. Such an empirical finding is not new: Becker and Lindsay (1994) report estimates from the US PSID consistent with this. They chose to explain the empirical findings using a variant of the Hashimoto (1981) model in which, although incentives to invest in firm-specific human capital are lower for women, they are predicted to receive a higher share of those returns. However, they obtain this result by assuming that women quitters are harder to identify, an arbitrary assumption that is at variance with the findings of Light and Ureta (1992).

Another approach to distinguishing between monopsony and competitive approaches to the gender pay gap is to look at predicted differences in response to policy changes. This approach is taken in the next section where we investigate the impact of UK equal pay legislation.

---

[7] Also, see Manning (1998), who compares actual returns to tenure with those predicted from a simple search model and observed labor market transition rates.

TABLE 7.8
Gender Differences in the Returns to Job Tenure

	5 years of job tenure		10 years of job tenure		20 years of job tenure	
	US CPS	UK LFS	US CPS	UK LFS	US CPS	UK LFS
10 years of potential experience						
Men	0.129	0.156				
	(0.016)	(0.005)				
Women	0.216	0.187				
	(0.016)	(0.005)				
20 years of potential experience						
Men	0.124	0.168	0.217	0.244		
	(0.018)	(0.005)	(0.020)	(0.006)		
Women	0.200	0.184	0.326	0.294		
	(0.018)	(0.005)	(0.019)	(0.006)		
30 years of potential experience						
Men	0.133	0.146	0.228	0.238	0.350	0.328
	(0.024)	(0.006)	(0.023)	(0.007)	(0.022)	(0.006)
Women	0.161	0.111	0.281	0.200	0.444	0.326
	(0.022)	(0.006)	(0.022)	(0.006)	(0.022)	(0.007)

Notes.
1. The US data come from the 1996 and 1998 Job Tenure Supplements to the CPS. The estimated returns to experience and job tenure come from a quartic in both variables with all interactions between them. Other controls included are: education, black, a year dummy, state dummies, dummies for being married, and the presence of children (and the interaction between them). Total number of observations is 19,281.
2. The UK data come from the LFS from 1992 to 1999. The estimated returns to experience and job tenure come from a quartic in both variables with all interactions between them. Other controls included are: education, black, Asian, month dummies, region dummies, dummies for being married, and the presence of children (and the interaction between them). Total number of observations is 212,478.
3. Standard errors in parentheses.

7.8 The Effect of UK Equal Pay Legislation

In the early 1970s two pieces of legislation designed to attack labor market discrimination against women were passed in the United Kingdom. The Equal Pay Act which essentially required equal pay for men and women doing similar work was passed in 1970 but did not have the force of law until the end of 1975. The 1975 Sex Discrimination Act, which came into force at the same time, made it unlawful to discriminate against women in matters relating to access to jobs. There is little doubt that the two pieces of legislation had a substantial effect on the relative earnings of women as, having been approximately constant for the period prior to the early 1970s, they then rose sharply and were roughly constant thereafter until they began to rise again in the mid-1980s.[8] This rise in women's relative wages over a short period of time is almost certainly the sharpest change in relative wages in the post-war period and it confronted employers with a change in relative wages that was largely exogenous to them. If labor markets were initially competitive with all workers, male and female, being paid their marginal products one would expect the rise in female relative earnings to be mirrored by a fall in relative employment. This prediction would be shared by other models (perhaps Becker's (1971) model of discrimination) in which the introduction of equal pay legislation would be predicted to lead to a situation in which there is an excess supply of female labor. On the other hand, if labor markets were monopsonistic the rise in women's wages might actually lead to an increase in employment. So, one can think of the experience of the Equal Pay Act as providing helpful insights into the workings of the labor market.

Unfortunately, the period of the introduction of the Equal Pay Act was largely before the availability of micro data. The best data available for investigation of its impact is industry-level data for manufacturing industries: in what follows we use data on something like 100 three-digit industries (for more detailed description of the data, see Manning 1996). From the early 1960s to the late 1960s the wages of women in manufacturing actually fell by 1.3% relative to men, but from the early 1970s to the late 1970s they rose by 21%. In terms of relative employment, female relative employment fell by an average of 7.7% in the 1960s and 2.1% in the 1970s (although the growth of other sectors of the economy meant that relative employment of women rose in the economy as a whole). That the relative employment of women fell more slowly at a time when their relative wages were rising faster is interesting but not persuasive evidence in favor of monopsony.

But, we can exploit the fact that the Equal Pay Act had a different impact on different industries. One of the reasons that the Equal Pay Act had such a quick, large effect on the relative wages of women was the prevalence of collective bargaining (overall union coverage was approximately 75%). Prior to the Equal Pay Act it was commonplace for union-negotiated contracts to have lower wages for women on the same jobs written into them (typically at the "biblical" fraction of two-thirds). Once the Equal

[8] The large impact of equal pay legislation in the United Kingdom is not mirrored in all other countries. In particular, the Equal Pay legislation of 1963 in the United States did not seem to have any very noticeable impact on women's relative pay. We will suggest explanations for this below.

Pay Act was in force, this was clearly illegal and the contractual pay rates of women and men on the same jobs had to be equal. So, we might expect the Equal Pay Act to have raised the relative wages of women more in industries where collective bargaining was more prevalent. Secondly, the Equal Pay Act contained a clause stating that the lowest pay rate for a woman on any job could not be below the lowest pay rate for a man on any job (a crude attempt to deal with the occupational segregation of men and women). So, we might expect to see a larger rise in the relative wages of women where the level of relative wages was initially low.

Both of these hypotheses seem to be confirmed by the data. The first column of table 7.9 looks at the impact on relative wage changes in the 1970s of the initial level of relative wages and the levels of female and male union coverage. High levels of female union coverage are associated with higher increases in relative wages as are lower initial levels of the relative wage. That it is plausible to ascribe these effects to the Equal Pay Act is given additional support by estimating a similar equation for relative wage changes in the 1960s reported in the second column. None of the regressors are significant and relative wages seem to have followed a random walk in this period.

However, we are more interested in the impact of the Equal Pay Act on the relative employment of women if we want to have some insight into the workings of labor markets. To keep things simple, assume that the revenue function can be written as $Y(N, X)$ where N is a composite measure of labor inputs and X is all other inputs. N is assumed to be given by

$$N = \left[AN_f^\chi + (1 - A)N_m^\chi \right]^{1/\chi} \qquad (7.3)$$

where N_f is female employment and N_m is male employment.

Assume, in the interests of generality that the labor markets for both men and women might be monopsonistic and that the labor supply curve to the firm is given by

$$W_i = B_i N_i^{\varepsilon_i}, \qquad i = f, m \qquad (7.4)$$

In the absence of equal pay legislation we assume that the firm is free to choose W_f independent of W_m. A necessary condition for profit maximization is that (N_m, N_f) (and the associated wages) are chosen to minimize labor costs subject to the constraint that the labor index is at a particular level, N, that is,

$$\min_{(W_f, W_m, N_f, N_m)} W_f N_f + W_m N_m$$

s.t. $\quad AN_f^\chi + (1 - A)N_m^\chi = N^\chi, \qquad W_i = B_i N_i^{\varepsilon_i}, \qquad i = f, m \quad (7.5)$

TABLE 7.9
The Impact of the UK Equal Pay Act

Dependent Variable	Change in Log Wage of Women Relative to Men		Change in Log of Female Employment Divided by Male Employment			
	1970s	1960s	1960s	1970s	1970s	1960s
Estimation method	OLS	OLS	OLS	OLS	IV	IV
Initial relative wage	−0.234 (0.051)	−0.038 (0.044)				
Female union coverage	0.134 (0.047)	0.001 (0.003)				
Male union coverage	−0.016 (0.039)	−0.038 (0.029)				
Change in relative wage of women			0.315 (0.344)	−0.099 (0.173)	0.234 (0.382)	0.394 (2.045)
Constant	−0.002 (0.036)	−0.004 (0.030)	−0.067 (0.012)	−0.0004 (0.035)	−0.069 (0.076)	−0.069 (0.0.29)
Number of observations	108	96	103	113	107	96
R^2	0.24	0.04	0.01	0		

Notes.
1. The data in this regression are from three-digit manufacturing industries. Data on employment come from the Census of Employment, data on hourly earnings from the October Earnings Enquiry and data on union coverage from the 1973 and 1978 New Earnings Survey. Relative earnings (employment) growth for the 1960s (1970s) refers to growth between the average level of earnings (employment) in 1965–68 (1975–78) compared to the average in the period 1960–62 (1970–72).

Simple manipulation of the first-order conditions of the solution to (7.5) allows us to derive

$$\log\left(\frac{N_f}{N_m}\right) = \frac{1}{1-\chi}\log\left(\frac{A}{1-A}\right) - \frac{1}{1-\chi}\left[\log\left(\frac{W_f}{W_m}\right) + \log\left(\frac{1+\varepsilon_f}{1+\varepsilon_m}\right)\right]$$
(7.6)

This simply says that the ratio of the marginal products must be equal to the ratio of the marginal costs of labor. It is more convenient to write (7.6) in difference terms so that we have

$$\Delta\log\left(\frac{N_f}{N_m}\right) = \frac{1}{1-\chi}\Delta\log\left(\frac{A}{1-A}\right)$$
$$- \frac{1}{1-\chi}\left[\Delta\log\left(\frac{W_f}{W_m}\right) + \Delta\log\left(\frac{1+\varepsilon_f}{1+\varepsilon_m}\right)\right] \quad (7.7)$$

Suppose that the labor market was competitive (set $\varepsilon_f = \varepsilon_m = 0$ in (7.7)). Then, controlling for relative demand shifts, we should expect to see a negative correlation between relative employment and relative wage changes. The third column of table 7.9 looks at this correlation in the 1960s. The correlation between relative employment and relative wage changes is positive although insignificantly different from zero. One plausible explanation for this is that the estimated coefficient is biased because, if the labor supply to an industry is not perfectly elastic (which is still consistent with the labor supply curve to an individual firm being perfectly elastic), there will be a positive correlation between the relative demand shocks $A/(1 - A)$ and the relative wage in (7.7).

But, the earlier analysis suggested that relative wage changes in the 1970s were driven in large part by factors other than relative demand shifts. So we might expect to see a more negative correlation between relative employment and relative wage changes in that period. The fourth column of table 7.9 provides some support for this view although the negative correlation between relative wage and relative employment changes is not significantly different from zero. However, we can do better than this. If we want to get a consistent estimate of the wage elasticity of relative demand, then we want to instrument relative wages using variables that are not correlated with the relative demand shocks. Our earlier regressions explaining relative wage changes suggested good instruments (the initial relative wage and the unionization rate) that were correlated with relative wage changes because of the Equal Pay Act. But, the IV results, reported in the fifth column, actually make the estimated elasticity positive, although not significantly different from zero (one can accept the over-identifying restrictions implied by this specification). For completeness the sixth column presents the equivalent results for the 1960s but the weakness of the instruments for that period shows up in an enormous standard error.

These results are hard to explain in the context of a competitive model of the labor market as we might hope to able to see the employment effects of such a large change in relative wages. They are more readily explained if labor markets are monopsonistic. The relevant issue is how the marginal cost of female relative to male labor is affected by the Equal Pay Act. One can interpret the requirement not to pay women differently from men as something that is similar to a minimum wage for women which we would expect to reduce the elasticity of the labor supply curve facing firms. In this case, it is possible that changes in the marginal cost of labor are negatively correlated with changes in the wage, thus explaining the result. The bottom line is that the Equal Pay Act seems to have had a substantial impact on the relative wages of women without harming their relative employment.

7.9 Prejudice and Monopsony

The discussion of discrimination so far has focused on the consequences of gender differences in attachment to the labor market. But, there are other potential sources of discrimination. Black (1995) combines the "competitive" model of discrimination of Becker (1971) with its assumption that some agents are racially prejudiced and simply refuse to hire blacks with the Albrecht and Axell (1984) model of monopsony. The consequence of the refusal of some employers to hire blacks is that the effective job offer arrival rate will be lower for blacks, making their labor market less competitive. As one would expect, and as Black (1995) shows, this is to the general disadvantage of blacks and even firms that are not prejudiced end up paying blacks lower wages than whites. Wolpin (1992) and Bowlus and Eckstein (2000) estimate structural models to assess how much of racial differences in economic outcomes can be explained in this way.

There is ample evidence that some racial prejudice remains in studies as diverse as the prices of baseball cards by Nardinelli and Simon (1990) and the performance of English soccer teams by Szymanski (2000). And audit studies where there is some attempt to match job applicants in every characteristic but race (or gender) also suggest that racial discrimination remains in many firms (for a review of the US evidence, see Altonji and Blank 1999; for a recent study, see Bertrand and Mullanaithan 2002). However, these studies are not without their critics (Heckman 1998). At best, they estimate the average level of discrimination. But, in a competitive market, the average level of discrimination is irrelevant. As Heckman (1998: 102) puts it, "the impact of market discrimination is not determined by the most discriminatory participants in the market, or even by the average level of discrimination among firms, but rather by the level of discrimination at the firms where ethnic minorities or women actually end up buying." In a frictionless competitive labor market, black workers would have no problem in escaping a wage penalty even if there was only a single non-discriminatory firm (as long as all black workers can be employed there). But, there is an important difference here between competitive labor markets and labor markets with frictions. As soon as there are frictions, the Heckman argument no longer holds: one suffers a real disadvantage as soon as any firm in the market refuses to consider you for employment (a point made by Altonji and Blank 1999). The model of Black (1995) confirms one's intuition on this point. And, any initial disadvantage may be reinforced by social networks (Montgomery 1991b). So, the fact that there are any discriminatory employers in the market is a matter of concern if labor markets are monopsonistic.

7.10 Conclusions

In this chapter we have discussed how an approach to labor markets based on the idea that employers have non-negligible market power can explain certain features of the differences in labor market outcomes for men and women. We have argued that the gender pay gap can be understood as the result of a gender gap in attachment to the labor market and the motivation for job mobility. There is no need to have recourse to differences in productivity between men and women to explain differences in outcomes. Of course, such differences may exist and it is difficult to prove their existence or otherwise. However, the fact that UK equal pay legislation led to a dramatic rise in the relative pay of women without harming their relative employment suggests that the monopsony story may contain some element of truth.

8

Employers and Wages

In a competitive labor market, wages should, after controlling for other relevant characteristics of the worker, only be related to employer and job characteristics to the extent that they affect the non-pecuniary aspects of the job. That is, the only wage variation associated with employers should be compensating wage differentials.

One of the "puzzles" of the observed structure of wages is that wages are correlated with a whole range of employer characteristics (for a survey of this, see Groshen 1991a). One might single out the following:

- industry affiliation (e.g., Krueger and Summers 1988; Gibbons and Katz 1992);
- employer size (e.g., Brown and Medoff 1989; Brown et al. 1990; Oi and Idson 1999);
- profits or profits per worker (e.g., Revenga 1992; Abowd and Lemieux 1993; Blanchflower et al. 1996; Hildreth and Oswald 1997);
- productivity (e.g., Nickell and Wadhwani 1990).

There have been attempts to explain these findings within the competitive model, the main approach taken being to argue that worker quality is observed very badly and that unobserved worker quality may be correlated with employer characteristics (for this type of argument applied to inter-industry wage differentials, see Murphy and Topel 1990). One of these correlations, the employer size–wage effect, has already been investigated in chapter 4 where it was argued that it cannot plausibly be fully explained by a competitive model or a rent-sharing model.

The second section of this chapter shows that the assumption of an upward-sloping supply of labor to the individual employer offers simple and plausible explanations of the empirical regularities listed above. We then turn to compensating wage differentials and discuss the implication of our modeling framework for differences in the non-pecuniary aspects of jobs. We also discuss the likely impact of regulation of the non-wage characteristics of jobs and finish with a discussion of the determinants of hours of work, arguing that working hours are best thought of as simply another non-wage aspect of jobs rather than as a separate topic, that of "labor supply."

8.1 Explaining the Correlations between Employer Characteristics and Wages

This section shows how an upward-sloping supply curve of labor to an individual employer can explain the empirical regularities described in the introduction to this chapter. The employer size–wage effect is, of course, nothing more than another way of saying the supply curve slopes upwards so that empirical regularity is quickly dealt with. But, what about the other correlations?

Consider employers who all face the same supply curve of labor, $N(w)$, but who differ in their revenue function. Denote the revenue function by $Y(N, A)$ where the difference in A is the source of the employer heterogeneity. Assume that $(\partial Y/\partial A) > 0$ so an increase in A is a good shock for the employer.

Obviously each employer will want to choose the level of employment (or, equivalently, the wage) to maximize profits:

$$\pi = Y(N, A) - w(N)N \tag{8.1}$$

leading to the first-order condition

$$\frac{\partial Y(N, A)}{\partial N} = w(N) + \frac{\partial w(N)}{\partial N}N = w(N)[1 + \varepsilon(N)] \tag{8.2}$$

where $w(N)$ is the inverse of the labor supply curve to the firm and $\varepsilon(N)$ is the inverse of the wage elasticity of the labor supply curve facing the firm. The notation has been chosen to make clear that the value of the elasticity might depend on the level of employment chosen.

What is the effect of an increase in A on the wage that the firm pays? The answer depends on how A affects the marginal revenue product of labor $(\partial Y/\partial N)$. If, as seems the most plausible case, an increase in A raises both the average and the marginal revenue product of labor, then an increase in A raises the left-hand side of (8.2) and the optimal wage rises. There is then a positive correlation between the level of profits and the wage paid. A simple diagram makes this clear. Figure 8.1 draws the standard picture of a monopsonistic firm. An increase in the marginal revenue product of labor (MRPL) curve from P_0 to P_1 increases the optimal wage paid from w_0 to w_1. Profitable firms have a high demand for labor and can only get extra labor by paying higher wages. Explaining the positive correlation between the level of profits and the wage paid is embarrassingly simple.

But, what about the correlation between profit per worker and the wage? We are interested in how variations in A affect $(\pi/N) = (Y/N) - w$. Obviously the fact that this depends negatively on the wage makes

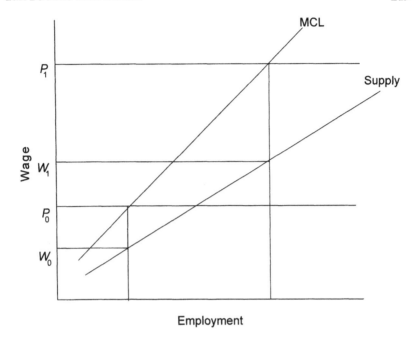

Figure 8.1 Employer heterogeneity and wages.

it harder for the model to explain a positive correlation here. If we denote the elasticity of the revenue function with respect to N by $\alpha(N, A)$, then we have

$$\frac{\pi}{N} = \frac{Y}{N} - w = \frac{1}{\alpha(N, A)} \frac{\partial Y}{\partial N} - w = w \left[\frac{1 + \varepsilon(N)}{\alpha(N, A)} - 1 \right] \qquad (8.3)$$

(8.3) makes it clear that, if both the revenue function and the labor supply function are iso-elastic, then the model predicts a positive correlation between profits per worker and wages.[1] It is possible to overturn this if the labor supply function is not iso-elastic: in particular, if ε is declining in N as then the right-hand side of (8.3) could conceivably be declining in the wage.[2]

This section has shown how monopsony can explain, rather effortlessly, the correlations between employer characteristics and wages.

---

[1] One should not claim too much here. If the labor market is competitive with $\varepsilon = 0$, then there is still a positive correlation predicted, something that many studies of the link between profits and wages ignore. The better studies (e.g., Abowd and Lemieux 1993) try to find a variable that affects A and use this as an instrument for profitability.

[2] Perhaps, rather unfortunately, the Burdett and Mortensen (1998) model does have this feature as $(p - w)N$ must be constant for different values of w. This obviously requires that profit per worker $(p - w)$ is decreasing in w. One can reconcile this with (8.3) once one notes that this model has ε as a decreasing function of N.

These correlations are often taken as evidence that the labor market is not competitive and the conclusion is often drawn that wages are above market-clearing levels. But, it is important to realize that we have derived these results in the context of a labor market model in which all workers are being paid below their marginal product. While we have argued that the empirical findings are not consistent with the competitive model, they cannot be used as evidence that wages are above market-clearing levels.

8.2 Monopsony and Compensating Wage Differentials

Non-wage aspects of jobs are important and this section investigates the implications for the structure of wages when jobs differ in their non-pecuniary attributes. The interest in this subject originates in the Wealth of Nations and has assumed considerable importance in discussions about the structure of wages that are based on competitive models. In his survey of the issue in the *Handbook of Labor Economics*, Rosen (1986: 641) wrote that the theory of equalizing differences "can make legitimate claim to be *the* fundamental (long-run) market equilibrium construct in labor economics" (his emphasis). In the competitive model, identically productive workers should receive the same level of utility so that differences in wages should exactly offset differences in the value of non-wage attributes.[3] As Rosen (1986: 641) says, the empirical importance of this result is that it can be used for "making inferences about preferences and technology from observed wage data." The idea is that a competitive labor market should ensure that $U(w, e) = U_0$ where $U(w, e)$ is the utility function, e is the non-wage aspect of the job, and U_0 is the market level of utility. If one controls for labor quality (which will affect U_0) then a regression of w on e should give an estimate of the marginal rate of substitution between e and w. However, compensating wage differentials have not proved of great value in explaining wage variation.[4] The basic problem is that it is hard to find evidence that, other things being equal, more unpleasant jobs are rewarded with higher wages. Often it seems that better-paid jobs have better working conditions.

The most common explanation for these anomalous findings is unobserved worker ability: as Rosen (1986: 671) put it "workers with greater earning capacity would 'spend' some of it on more on-the-job consumption," that is, pleasant working conditions are a normal good (for a

---

[3] Strictly speaking, this is true only for the marginal worker: if workers differ in the value they attach to non-wage attributes, then there is no single compensating wage differential.

[4] With the possible exception of the returns to education that are sometimes interpreted as a compensating wage differential.

working-out of this intuition, see Hwang et al. 1998). However, it is not clear that this is the root of the problem. For example, Brown (1980) found that, even when panel data are used to control for individual fixed effects (which we might expect to pick up a lot of unobserved ability), it is still hard to find evidence for compensating wage differentials.[5]

This section examines the implications of labor market frictions for the theory of compensating wage differentials and the application of that theory. To keep matters simple, assume all firms have the same productivity p, but that firms differ in the pleasantness of the job offered. Denote the non-pecuniary aspect of the job by e which can be thought to represent effort. Workers are assumed to dislike a high level of e. For the moment, treat e as exogenous: the next section analyzes the case where it is a choice variable for the firm. Assume that workers have a utility function $U(w,e)$ which represents their trade-off between wage income and e. It is natural to think of pleasant work conditions as being a normal good so that, presented with a trade-off between wages and work conditions, workers with higher non-wage income will choose lower wages and better work conditions. This amounts to the condition that

$$[U_{ww}U_e - U_w U_{ew}] > 0$$

In this model the labor supply to the firm will not depend solely on the wage that it offers but on the utility that it offers. Denote the labor supply to a firm that offers utility U by $N(U)$. Also, denote by $w(e,U)$ the wage that needs to be paid by a firm if it wants to offer workers utility U and has working conditions e. Obviously $w_e(e, U) > 0$ and the normality of leisure implies that $w_{eU}(e, U) > 0$ as well. Profits of a firm if it offers utility U will be given by $[p - w(e, U)]N(U)$ and U will be chosen to maximize this.

It is straightforward to show that U must be non-increasing in e so that there is less than full compensation for bad working conditions. The first-order condition for the maximization of profits is given by

$$[p - w(U, e)]N'(U) - w_U(U, e)N(U) = 0 \qquad (8.4)$$

The sign of the response of utility to e is given by the sign of the partial derivative of (8.4) with respect to e (using the second-order condition that we must be at a maximum). So we have

$$\operatorname{sgn} \frac{\partial U}{\partial e} = \operatorname{sgn}[-w_e N' - w_{Ue}N] = \operatorname{sgn}\left[-w_e - \frac{w_{Ue}(p - w)}{w_U} \right] \qquad (8.5)$$

[5] On the other hand, Duncan and Holmlund (1983) do find evidence for compensating wage differentials but that is for Sweden where the wage structure is highly regulated which just goes to prove the dictum that "the only labour markets consistent with the competitive model are regulated labour markets."

where the second equality follows from (8.4). Now $w_e > 0$, and it is simple to check that the normality condition implies that $w_{Ue} > 0$, so that (8.5) implies that high values of e are associated with lower values of U. The implication of this is that workers do not get fully compensated for bad working conditions so that measures of the value attached to working conditions that are based on the assumption of full compensation (and this is the assumption normally made) are likely to be understatements of the true value.

Although the way in which worker utility varies with U is unambiguous, this does not directly tell us about the way that w varies with e. One might expect that a higher value of e is associated with a higher value of w but the higher wage only partially compensates the worker. But, one can construct examples in which a higher e is actually associated with a lower wage.

The model presented so far suggests one reason why estimates of the value of working conditions from earnings functions are so often unsuccessful. The reason is that, in the absence of perfect competition, compensation will not be complete and could even go in the wrong direction. In labor markets with frictions, it is important to remember that even workers of identical ability will receive different levels of utility so that the problem raised here is worse than the problem of unobserved ability that is usually recognized in the competitive model. The existence of frictions can explain why Brown (1980) failed to find evidence of compensating wage differentials even when he controlled for individual fixed effects. Earnings functions alone cannot be relied upon to estimate the value of non-wage job attributes.

This raises the question as to whether there is a potentially better way to estimate the value of working conditions in labor markets with frictions. One appealing way is to consider the estimation of separation functions. As the separation rate depends on worker utility, we might write the separation function in the form $s(U(w, e), x)$ where x represents other relevant factors. The ratio of the coefficients on e and the wage then gives us an estimate of the marginal disutility of bad working conditions. This is the approach taken by Gronberg and Reed (1994) who investigate the impact of four aspects of working conditions (bad working conditions, stooping or kneeling, repetitive work, and heavy lifting). Using the standard hedonic wage equation approach, only bad working conditions have a significant impact in the expected direction. Unfortunately when the impact of these variables is investigated using data on job duration (which will be related to the separation rate), the results are not much better although the disutility of bad working conditions is now much larger as one might expect given the above framework. So, the potential advantage of this approach is not really proved by their study. van Ommeren et al. (1999) use this approach to estimate

TABLE 8.1
The Compensating Differential for Night-Shift Working in the UK LFS

	Coefficient on Log Wage	Coefficient on Night Work	Number of Observations
Earnings equation	1.00	−0.045 (0.024)	20488
Separations equation	−0.511 (0.051)	0.278 (0.196)	20464
Job-to-job separations equation	−0.525 (0.068)	0.492 (0.241)	19967

Notes.
1. The data come from the Autumn LFS for 1997–2000 inclusive. Night-working is defined as those who report that they work the night shift. Other controls are controls for a quartic in experience, gender, race, education, marital status, the presence of children, and region and month dummies.

the marginal willingness to pay for commuting, and their results are more satisfactory.

Table 8.1 provides an application of this approach to estimating the disutility associated with night-shift working using data from the LFS. Only a small minority of workers (1.5%) report that they work night shifts. The first row shows the results of estimating a standard earnings equation. The coefficient on night-working is negative (although insignificant) suggesting that there is little disutility associated with working nights. The second row uses the Gronberg–Reed approach to estimate a separations equation (as described in section 4.5). The coefficient on night-working is now positive suggesting that, given wages, those working nights are more likely to leave their jobs. However, the estimated coefficient is not significant. The third row restricts attention to job-to-job separations on the grounds that these are more likely to be initiated by the individual and, hence, better reflect their preferences. The coefficient on night-working is larger and now significant at conventional levels. Note that the ratio of the coefficient on night-working to the coefficient on wages gives an estimate of the marginal rate of substitution between earnings and night-working so that these estimates suggest there is a large disutility associated with night-working that is not apparent from a standard earnings function.

8.3 Choice of Working Conditions

So far, working conditions, e, have been assumed exogenous: this section considers the case where e is a choice variable for the firm. A firm will only choose a higher level of e if there is some improved productivity as a result so we assume that productivity is given by

$p(e)$ where $p'(e) > 0$. For simplicity, assume that this function is the same for all firms.

Start by considering what would be the optimal choice of e by workers in perfect competition where they get paid for all the output produced from their effort. They would be interested in maximizing $U(p(e), e)$ which leads to the first-order condition

$$U_w(p(e), e)p'(e) + U_e(p(e), e) = 0 \qquad (8.6)$$

Now consider what will happen in a labor market characterized by frictions. The labor supply to firms will depend on the level of utility offered which we continue to denote by $N(U)$. Firms have two instruments to alter the level of utility offered: they can vary the wage and they can vary e. A necessary condition for profit maximization is that, given the level of utility offered by the firm, w and e must maximize $p(e) - w$, that is, firms need to solve the problem

$$\max_{(w,e)} p(e) - w \qquad \text{s.t. } U(w, e) \equiv U \qquad (8.7)$$

A necessary condition for profit maximization is that

$$U_w(w, e)p'(e) + U_e(w, e) = 0 \qquad (8.8)$$

This is outwardly the same first-order condition that workers would choose in their utopia, (8.6). But, one needs to be careful in drawing the conclusion that the choice of working conditions is efficient. As workers get less than the full value of their contribution to output (w will be less than $p(e)$), effort levels will tend to be higher than they would be in the utopia. But, given the level of utility that workers are going to get, the choice of wages and effort levels is efficient.

To solve for the model, one can then derive e and w as functions of U so that profits can be written as $[p(e(U)) - w(U)]N(U)$. One can then solve for the equilibrium $N(U)$ as all firms must make the same level of profits and the lowest level of utility offered must be the reservation level. Hwang et al. (1998) work out a model of this type more explicitly for a special case where utility is of the form $U(w, e) = w - c(e)$ and where firms differ in the technology of providing e. There is no particular interest in repeating that exercise here except to quote the conclusion of Hwang et al. (1998: 839) that "estimates of workers" marginal willingness to pay derived from the conventional methodology will be biased", a conclusion also reached in the previous section when working conditions were assumed exogenous.

8.4 Mandated Benefits

In a competitive labor market there is little reason to intervene to regulate the conditions under which work is conducted. Yet, in reality, we see many such regulations of the non-wage conditions of work from health and safety regulation, to maximum hours legislation, to parental leave entitlements. All of these types of regulation can be thought of as putting an upper bound on the value of e that is allowed in employment contracts.

Consider the likely impact of such a regulation in a partial equilibrium model of a single firm. First, consider a competitive firm that must pay its workers the market level of utility, U. If it chooses working conditions e, it must pay a wage $w(e, U)$. In the absence of government regulation, e will be chosen to maximize $[p(e) - w(e, U)]$ leading to the first-order condition

$$p'(e) - w_e(e, U) = 0 \qquad (8.9)$$

which is the same condition as (8.8) written in a different way.

If the government now intervenes to put a binding upper bound on the value of e, the first effect will be to reduce the profits of the firm without making the workers any better off (which was the presumed intention of the policy). Employers will simply lower wages so that worker utility is still equal to U. In a general equilibrium context, the impact of reduced profits might be to reduce the demand for labor so that the market-clearing level of utility actually falls and workers are made worse off by the well-intentioned intervention (for further discussion, see Summers 1989). But, of course, there are no real grounds for intervention in the first place as the original level of e negotiated between firms and workers is efficient.

What happens in a labor market in which employers have some market power? We have already emphasized that, because workers get less than the full value of their output, there is a tendency for effort to be above the efficient level. This might be thought of as grounds for intervention. But, matters are not that simple because employers may respond to imposed changes in effort by changing wages.[6] Let us assume that the firm faces a supply curve of labor given by $N(U)$. (8.9) will continue to be valid as the first-order condition for the choice of e given U, but the level of utility offered is now also a choice variable for the employer. The first-order condition for the choice of U will be

$$[p(e) - w(e, U)]N'(U) - w_U(e, U)N(U) = 0 \qquad (8.10)$$

---

[6] Of course, they may be prevented from doing so by minimum wages but this is not the situation we are considering here.

Now consider the imposition of a binding upper bound on e. Obviously (8.9) will no longer be valid and the left-hand side will be positive as employers would like to choose a higher value of e. However, (8.10) will still be valid and we can use this first-order condition to work out the impact on U of a change in e. The answer is in the following proposition.

Proposition 8.1

1. *If the restriction on effort is just binding and pleasant working conditions are a normal good, then worker utility must always increase.*

2. *If a binding upper bound is imposed on e, then the sign of the effect on the employer's choice of U is given by*

$$\mathrm{sgn}\!\left(\frac{\partial U}{\partial e}\right) = \mathrm{sgn}([p'(e) - w_e(e, U)]N'(U) - w_{Ue}(e, U)N(U)) \quad (8.11)$$

Proof. See Appendix 8.

This result, as applied to hours restrictions can be found in de Meza et al. (1998). The first part is, perhaps, surprisingly strong. The intuition for it is that normality implies that, at high levels of effort, a higher increase in the wage is needed to bring about a given increase in worker utility. As higher wages are bad for profits, this acts as a disincentive to raising worker utility. Lowering worker effort can then alter the trade-off between wage costs and employment in such a way as to encourage firms to choose a higher level of utility and employment.

This result does not mean that all intervention will necessarily make workers better off. First, it is a partial equilibrium result and one cannot generalize immediately to a general equilibrium model (although for one way of doing this, see Manning 2001b). Secondly, as one lowers effort there will come a point where worker utility falls. As effort moves further away from the point the employer would choose, $[p'(e) - w_e]$ becomes more positive and this can eventually make the sign of (8.11) positive. Any intervention is likely to be a blunt instrument, laying down common restrictions on e on firms that would otherwise have chosen very different levels of e. Hence, it is likely that the impact is to improve the lot of workers in firms where the constraint just binds, but to worsen it in firms where the constraint is more serious.

Our discussion of working conditions so far has been very abstract. In the next section we study one aspect of working conditions, hours of work, in more detail.

8.5 Hours of Work

One possible interpretation of the e in the previous model is that it represents hours of work and the wage variable represents total earnings. Hours of work are normally modeled differently from other non-wage aspects of jobs but, because, given total labor earnings, hours raise output and reduce worker utility, there is no good reason for this. So, this is the natural place to discuss the implications of our framework for the modeling of labor supply.[7]

In the literature on labor supply, it is conventional to start from a framework in which the worker is faced with a single hourly wage rate and can freely choose hours: what Pencavel (1986: 26) has called the "canonical model". Let us denote the hourly wage rate by w^h. The worker will choose e to maximize $U(w^h e, e)$ where e is now hours of work. The first-order condition for utility maximization is given by

$$w^h U_w + U_e = 0 \qquad (8.12)$$

It is one of the great unsolved mysteries in labor economics why the canonical model should have received so much attention as there is no particular reason to think that workers would be on their labor supply curve even in a perfectly competitive labor market. To see this, note that perfect competition implies that $w^h = p(e)/e$ but for (8.12) to be consistent with (8.6) requires that $w^h = p'(e)$. These are only mutually consistent if $p(e) = pe$ for some constant p.[8] To give the canonical labor supply model a chance, let us assume that the technology does have this form.

A helpful way of rewriting the profit maximization problem for the firm is to imagine that the choice of the firm is hours of work e and an hourly wage w^h. The first-order condition for the maximization problem in (8.7) can then be written as

$$p - w^h + \frac{1}{U_w}\left[w^h U_w + U_e\right] = 0 \qquad (8.13)$$

Now we must have $p > w^h$ as otherwise the firm will make no profits. So, (8.13) implies that the term in square brackets must be negative. What this implies is that workers are off their supply curves and being forced to work more hours than they would choose given the single hourly wage

[7] Strictly speaking, we are going to discuss only the intensive margin of labor supply, hours of work. The extensive margin, that between employment, inactivity, and unemployment, is discussed in chapter 9.

[8] A more general result is that the canonical model only holds in a perfectly competitive equilibrium if the production function can be written as $f(Ne)$, that is, output is a function solely of total hours worked. This point was first made by Lewis (1969): see Manning (2001c) for further discussion.

rate. One implication of this is that it is not worker preferences alone that will determine hours of work: employer characteristics will also be important. The parallel here is with the earnings equation literature where, under perfect competition, wages will be unrelated to employer characteristics but, as we have seen, that is not the case when employers have some market power. A similar result is given in (8.13): if we have perfect competition then $p = w^h$ and worker preferences alone will be important in determining hours of work, but if employers have some market power this is no longer the case.

There are a number of ways in which workers might be forced off their classical labor supply curves. One approach is simply to dictate a wage–hours package, another to offer a non-linear relationship between hours and wage. In reality, both of these strategies are used.

Table 8.2 presents some evidence on the extent of over-employment. In the BHPS, individuals are asked whether, at their hourly wage, they want to work more hours, fewer hours, or continue as they are. 33% of workers want to work fewer hours as opposed to 9% who want to work more. Men are more likely than women to want fewer hours. This is supportive of the view that there is a tendency towards excessive hours (from the worker's point of view). However, it is not consistent with a literal interpretation of the result in (8.13) that *all* workers should be over-employed. One needs to explain why some workers may be under-employed and others content with their lot.

TABLE 8.2
Desired Hours: BHPS

	Work Fewer	Continue the Same	Work More	Sample Size
Percentages				
All	32.1	60.0	8.9	20630
Men	34.8	57.0	8.2	9661
Women	29.7	60.8	9.4	10969
Average hours				
All	38.2	32.9	26.4	20630
Men	41.0	38.8	35.5	9661
Women	35.3	28.0	19.5	10969

Notes.

1. The data in this table come from the BHPS for 1991–98 and tabulate the responses for those in employment to the question "Thinking about the hours you work, assuming that you would be paid the same amount per hour, would you prefer to work fewer hours, more hours or continue with the same hours." The average hours are the number of hours normally worked per week.

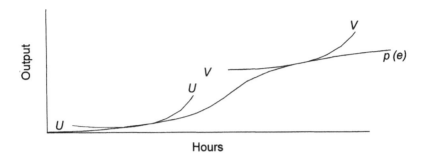

Figure 8.2   Under- and over-employment in a competitive labor market.

First, there is a tendency in many jobs for hours of work to be equalized across workers because of the technological importance of having workers "on-site" at the same time. The standard working day is the best example of this. With heterogeneity in preferences, this will inevitably result in some workers being under-employed even if, on average, workers are over-employed. Secondly, the result that individuals are at their desired hours conditional on their average hourly wage is only true in a competitive model if the production function can be written as linear in hours. If it is not, then individuals will tend to be over- or under-employed. Figure 8.2 clarifies this point. Suppose the relationship between output produced and hours is given by the $p(e)$ function. The justification for the shape is that there are "set-up" costs associated with the job so that output is initially a convex function of hours but that exhaustion means that there are eventually diminishing returns to hours. In a competitive labor market, the chosen point will be a point of tangency between an indifference curve and this production function. Workers will feel over-employed if the average wage exceeds the marginal wage and under-employed if the opposite is the case. So, someone with preferences UU who is working a small number of hours would feel over-employed while someone with preferences VV who is working a lot of hours would feel under-employed. Given the shape of the production function, there is a tendency for those employed at high hours to feel under-employed and those employed at low hours to feel under-employed. As the second half of table 8.2 shows, this is not what we see in the data. This makes no attempt to control for characteristics but the study of Stewart and Swaffield (1997) comes to the same conclusion. It is those who work long hours who are more likely to feel over-employed. So, a competitive model with a more flexible specification of the production function does not seem able to explain the data.

Table 8.2 also shows that a majority of workers are happy with the hours they are working. Stewart and Swaffield (1997) interpret these individuals as working the exact number of hours they desire. However, it may be that these responses reflect an acceptance of the labor market realities, that is, satisficing rather than optimizing. For example, individuals are also asked how satisfied they are with the pay in their job: 60% of respondents say that they are at least satisfied with their level of pay. Yet, I suspect that most of these would happily accept a pay rise.

This discussion raises the issue of how an empirical investigation of the determinants of hours of work should be conducted. There is a huge amount of existing research (summarized in Blundell and MaCurdy 1999), the vast bulk of which starts from the canonical model and assumes that workers have a free choice of hours of work and that the average hourly wage paid to them is also their marginal hourly wage (abstracting from taxes). It is a pity that quite so much attention should have been lavished on the canonical model for, as we have already discussed, there is little reason to think that a perfectly competitive labor market would have workers on their classical labor supply curves.

It is perhaps best to think of hours of work as just another non-wage attribute of jobs and, if one believes in a competitive labor market, to use the compensating wage differentials literature to estimate the marginal rate of substitution between income and hours. Suppose that individuals have preferences $U(w, e, x_f)$ where w is total earnings, e is hours of work and x_f is other characteristics affecting preferences. In a competitive labor market, workers of a given quality, x_q, will get a level of utility $U_0(x_q)$ so that the trade-off between income and hours will be given by $U(w, e, x_f) = U_0(x_q)$. A regression of log earnings on a suitable function of hours and other characteristics could then give an estimate of the marginal rate of substitution between income and hours. If w is a linear function of hours, then this reduces to the canonical case.

However, we discussed above why this conventional approach to estimating marginal willingness-to-pay is unlikely to give the correct answer if employers have some market power. In the current context, if leisure is a normal good, then those in high-paying jobs are, other things being equal, likely to be in jobs with lower hours. An earnings function will then tend to underestimate the disutility of work. As an alternative, we could use the Gronberg–Reed methodology and relate separations to earnings and hours of work.

Table 8.3 shows what happens when we do this using data from the US PSID and the UK LFS and BHPS. First, consider the results using the PSID in table 8.3a. The first row is an estimate of an earnings function for men where the dependent variable is the log of weekly earnings and the log of hours is included on the right-hand side. The estimate of 1.051 can be thought of as a crude estimate of the marginal rate of substitution

TABLE 8.3a
Labor Supply: PSID

Sample	Equation	Coefficient on Log (Weekly Earnings)	Coefficient on Log (Hours)	Coefficient on Log (Hours) (Hours < 30)	Coefficient on Log (Hours) (Hours > 30)	Number of Observations
Men	Earnings function	1.000	1.051 (0.018)			31471
Men	Separations function	−0.838 (0.062)	0.604 (0.108)			25343
Men	Job-to-job separations	−0.838 (0.062)	0.827 (0.096)			22315
Men	Earnings function	1.000		1.208 (0.036)	0.954 (0.016)	31471
Men	Separations function	−0.855 (0.060)		0.806 (0.096)	0.429 (0.172)	25343
Men	Job-to-job separations	−0.893 (0.043)		0.993 (0.176)	0.720 (0.151)	22315
Women	Earnings function	1.000	1.146 (0.009)			29295
Women	Separations function	−0.838 (0.062)	0.610 (0.081)			24319
Women	Job-to-job separations	−0.838 (0.062)	0.821 (0.138)			19864
Women	Earnings function	1.000		1.102 (0.017)	0.954 (0.016)	29295
Women	Separations function	−0.972 (0.052)		0.487 (0.091)	0.914 (0.108)	24319
Men	Job-to-job separations	−0.914 (0.066)		0.564 (0.148)	1.258 (0.156)	19864

Notes.
1. The other controls included are a quartic in experience and job tenure, education, race, marital status, the presence of children, year, and state dummies.
2. For details of how the separation equations are estimated, see section 4.5.

TABLE 8.3b
Labor Supply: LFS

Sample	Equation	Coefficient on Log (Weekly Earnings)	Coefficient on Log (Hours)	Coefficient on Log (Hours) (Hours < 30)	Coefficient on Log (Hours) (Hours > 30)	Number of Observations
Men	Earnings function	1.000	0.831 (0.009)			35731
Men	Separations function	−0.464 (0.042)	−0.012 (0.076)			30383
Men	Job-to-job separations	−0.493 (0.053)	0.152 (0.109)			29770
Men	Earnings function	1.000		1.254 (0.015)	0.497 (0.013)	35731
Men	Separations function	−0.449 (0.042)		−0.229 (0.101)	0.302 (0.126)	30383
Men	Job-to-job separations	−0.479 (0.054)		−0.082 (0.165)	0.359 (0.158)	29770
Women	Earnings function	1.000	1.048 (0.004)			37218
Women	Separations function	−0.526 (0.040)	0.049 (0.055)			31809
Women	Job-to-job separations	−0.432 (0.058)	0.230 (0.083)			30867
Women	Earnings function	1.000		1.100 (0.006)	0.841 (0.016)	37218
Women	Separations function	−0.523 (0.040)		0.018 (0.062)	0.203 (0.157)	31809
Men	Job-to-job separations	−0.437 (0.058)		0.276 (0.101)	0.871 (0.214)	30867

Notes.
1. The other controls included are a quartic in experience and job tenure, education, race, marital status, the presence of children, year, and region dummies.
2. For details of how the separation equations are estimated, see section 4.5.

TABLE 8.3c
Labor Supply: BHPS

Sample	Equation	Coefficient on Log (Weekly Earnings)	Coefficient on Log (Hours)	Coefficient on Log (Hours) (Hours < 30)	Coefficient on Log (Hours) (Hours > 30)	Number of Observations
Men	Earnings function	1.000	0.761 (0.037)			15758
Men	Separations function	−0.765 (0.078)	0.336 (0.154)			9189
Men	Job-to-job separations	−0.743 (0.107)	0.875 (0.257)			8513
Men	Earnings function	1.000		1.224 (0.062)	0.314 (0.048)	15758
Men	Separations function	−0.689 (0.078)		−0.349 (0.202)	1.070 (0.209)	9189
Men	Job-to-job separations	−0.663 (0.107)		−0.230 (0.351)	1.466 (0.265)	8513
Women	Earnings function	1.000	1.111 (0.014)			16582
Women	Separations function	−0.761 (0.066)	0.329 (0.089)			10337
Women	Job-to-job separations	−0.704 (0.100)	0.449 (0.144)			9204
Women	Earnings function	1.000		1.164 (0.019)	0.860 (0.069)	16582
Women	Separations function	−0.752 (0.066)		0.253 (0.101)	0.689 (0.243)	10337
Men	Job-to-job separations	−0.693 (0.100)		0.360 (0.164)	0.802 (0.367)	9204

Notes.
1. Data are from the BHPS 1991–98. The other controls included are a quartic in experience and job tenure, education, race, marital status, the presence of children, year, and region dummies.
2. For details of how the separation equations are estimated, see section 4.5.

between log hours and log income in the utility function.[9] However, when we estimate a separations equation using as dependent variable an indicator taking the value 1 if the individual left their job and 0 if they did not, then, as we would expect, separations are less likely if earnings are high and hours are low. However, the estimated marginal rate of substitution is lower than that implied by the earnings function at 0.721 (=0.604/0.838). However, if attention is restricted to job-to-job separations (on the grounds that these are more likely to be voluntary), the estimated marginal rate of substitution rises to 0.987. For women, in the PSID, the results are qualitatively similar. These results do not suggest that the standard earnings function approach understates the marginal rate of substitution.

For the United Kingdom, the results are rather different. Table 8.3b reports the results from the LFS and table 8.3c those from the BHPS. For men in the LFS, the coefficient on log hours in the separations equation is lower than in the PSID and often insignificant. However, this seems to be the result of a non-linearity. If a spline is estimated using 30 hours as the break point, the results suggest that higher hours do lead to higher separations when hours are high but not when hours are low. At low levels of hours, an increase in hours makes British men less likely to quit, evidence perhaps that men dislike part-time work as it is overwhelmingly "female" and undermines the perception of their "masculinity." Table 8.3c confirms the existence of this effect for the BHPS. However, as shown in some rows of table 8.3a, US men show no evidence of this effect. For women, this effect is much less marked. Separation rates seem to be increasing in hours whatever the level of hours worked. But, it remains the case that the approach to estimating the marginal rate of substitution based on separations equations does not always lead to a higher estimate of the disutility of work so here, as in the previous analysis of night-working, the Gronberg–Reed approach does not perform as one might expect.

This section has been excessively cursory to economize on space but it does suggest an alternative approach to estimating "labor supply curves" from that which is most commonly used in the literature. A more convincing analysis should pay attention to the impact of tax and welfare systems on the utility of individuals and use more general specifications of the utility function.

8.6 Conclusion

This chapter has shown how a model of the labor market in which employers have some market power can explain the correlations between

---

[9] We do not experiment here with alternative functional forms of the utility function or with adequate treatment of the tax system, the sophisticated treatment of which is the hallmark of much empirical work on labor supply (see Blundell and MaCurdy 1999).

employer characteristics and wages which have often been regarded as puzzles that need to be explained away. It has also shown how a monopsonistic perspective has important implications for how one estimates the value attached to working conditions, for the determination of hours, and for the likely impact of mandated benefits. It has argued that an alternative approach to labor supply is to regard hours of work as a "disamenity" and to estimate the marginal rate of substitution between hours and wages using the methodology proposed for other compensating wage differentials.

Appendix 8

Proof of Proposition 8.1

Write the left-hand side of (8.10) as $\pi_U(U, e)$ where the notation captures the idea that this is the first-order condition for profits with respect to utility. This must be equal to zero even with the imposition of a binding regulation on e. Hence, the way in which utility must vary with a change in e is given by

$$\pi_{UU} \frac{\partial U}{\partial e} + \pi_{Ue} = 0 \tag{8.14}$$

π_{UU} must be negative by the second-order condition for (8.10) to give us the profit-maximizing level of U. Hence, we have that $\text{sgn}(\partial U/\partial e) = \text{sgn}(\pi_{Ue})$. Differentiating (8.10) then gives us (8.11) which proves part (2). Now, if the constraint is just binding, (8.9) must be satisfied which, using (8.11) means that $\text{sgn}(\partial U/\partial e) = -\text{sgn}(w_{Ue})$ which is negative if pleasant working conditions are a normal good. This proves part (1).

Part Three ⸺⸺⸺⸺⸺⸺⸺⸺⸺⸺⸺

LABOR DEMAND AND SUPPLY

9

Unemployment, Inactivity, and Labor Supply

This chapter discusses the determinants of the level and structure of non-employment. In a frictionless, perfectly competitive labor market, workers are out of work whenever the utility they could obtain in the market is below the utility obtainable when out of it. In most discussions, however, allowance is made for some frictional component to unemployment.[1] Perhaps the most celebrated statement of this is Friedman (1968: 8)

> the natural rate of unemployment is the level ... that would be ground out by the Walrasian system of general equilibrium equations, provided there is embedded in them the actual structural characteristics of the labor and commodity markets, including market imperfections, stochastic variability in demands and supplies, the cost of gathering information about job vacancies and labor availabilities, the costs of mobility and so on.

Consequently, there is a large literature that uses a search approach to analyze unemployment (for surveys, see Mortensen 1986; Mortensen and Pissarides 1999). The consequence of this is that, as mentioned at the end of chapter 2, thinking about unemployment using search theory is much more familiar than thinking about the wage distribution using these tools. So, there is even less that is "new" in this chapter than in the preceding ones.

Using the notation of the basic Burdett and Mortensen (1998) model introduced in section 2.4, the non-employment rate of a worker with reservation wage r can be written as

$$u = \frac{\delta_u}{\delta_u + \lambda(1 - F(r))} \tag{9.1}$$

where δ_u is the rate of job destruction, λ is the rate at which job offers arrive when unemployed, $F(w)$ is the wage offer distribution, and r is the reservation wage.[2] In the basic model of section 2.4, δ_u and λ were

---

[1] As discussed in chapter 1, it is unclear how one can reconcile a belief in frictions in labor markets with a belief in a perfectly competitive method of wage determination.

[2] In the version of the model used in section 2.4, $F(r) = 0$ as all workers were assumed to have the same reservation wage and there was no point in any employer offering a wage lower than that. The specification given here is more appropriate when there is heterogeneity in reservation wages as in the version of the model discussed in section 3.5.

assumed exogenous, and the reservation wage was equal to the flow of utility obtainable when non-employed because it was assumed that on- and off-the-job searches were equally effective in generating job offers. A more adequate discussion of non-employment requires more attention to all of these parameters. The transition rates can obviously be influenced by the actions of both workers and employers. The arrival rate of job offers will be affected both by the level of search intensity of a non-employed worker and by the recruitment intensity of employers. And, the separation rate will be affected by both the quit decisions of workers and the lay-off decisions of employers. This chapter considers the workers' actions that are likely to affect the transition rates while the next chapter considers the actions of employers.

The plan is as follows. The first section of this chapter allows individuals to choose the intensity of job search and discusses the implications of this for the non-employment rate and the determinants of the reservation wage. Evidence is presented to suggest that off-the-job search is more effective than on-the-job search. The second section discusses the difference between unemployment and inactivity, a distinction commonly made in labor market statistics. As these two labor market states are distinguished primarily using a measure of search intensity (the unemployed being those who have looked for work in the recent past and the inactive those who have not), a model of endogenous search intensity can provide a meaningful theory of the difference between inactivity and unemployment. This approach is described in the second section where there is an application to the discouraged worker effect.

The third section discusses the job search intensity of the employed. This does not directly affect the non-employment rate in (9.1) but this seems the natural place to discuss it. Theory predicts that on-the-job search intensity should be negatively related to wages and empirical evidence strongly confirms this. The fourth section discusses the quit behavior of workers showing how a model with a stochastic reservation wage can readily explain the fact that quits to non-employment are negatively related to the wage.

Another aim of this chapter is to improve the understanding of the nature of unemployment in an oligopsonistic labor market. In the basic models of monopsony used so far, all firms are trying to recruit workers all the time and a match between a worker and employer only ever fails to be consummated because the wage offered is below the reservation wage of the worker. This does not seem to give an adequate description of the difficulties that many of the unemployed have in finding work. So, the fifth and sixth sections of this chapter shows how one can marry conceptions of involuntary unemployment, efficiency wages and monopsony. It turns out that this is not problematic.

9.1 Endogenizing Job Search Activity

An individual will determine the level of job search by equating marginal benefits and costs. Denote the cost to a non-employed individual of generating job offers at a rate λ by $c_u(\lambda, z)$ where z represents other relevant factors. Some of these other factors may be individual-specific (e.g., the appeal of the individual to employers) while others may be beyond their control (e.g., the state of the aggregate labor market). Similarly define $c_e(\lambda, z)$ to be the cost to an employed individual of generating job offers at a rate λ for employed workers. The cost functions for employed and non-employed individuals may differ for a number of reasons: non-employed workers have more time (an advantage) but less money (a disadvantage), or employers may discriminate against non-employed job applicants (for some UK evidence in support of this view, see Manning, 2000). The relative importance of on-the-job and off-the-job searches turns out to be of some importance and is discussed further below.

Denote by λ_u the arrival rate of job offers for an unemployed worker. A non-employed worker will choose λ_u to maximize the value of being unemployed, V^u, which will be given by

$$\delta_r V^u = \max_{\lambda_u} b + \lambda_u \int_r [V(x) - V^u] dF(x) - c_u(\lambda_u, z) \qquad (9.2)$$

where $F(x)$ is the wage offer distribution, r is the reservation wage, and $V(x)$ is the value of a job that pays wage x. The first-order condition for this maximization problem can be written as

$$\frac{\partial c_u(\lambda_u, z)}{\partial \lambda_u} = \int_r [V(x) - V^u] dF(x) \qquad (9.3)$$

The right-hand side of (9.3) is the expected gain from taking a job above the reservation wage so (9.3) says that the marginal cost of an extra job offer should be equal to the marginal expected benefit from one. The reservation wage appears in (9.3) although one should remember that this is endogenous. Some comparative statics are simple: if the level of utility obtainable when out of employment, b, rises (perhaps because of a rise in welfare benefits), then the reservation wage will rise and (9.3) says that the search intensity of the unemployed will fall (as has been claimed by Barron and Mellow 1979).[3]

---

[3] It is worth noting that a literature has also grown up surrounding the lack of robustness of this conclusion emphasizing how, in a world where the unemployed are liquidity-constrained (Hamermesh 1982; Ben-Horim and Zuckerman 1987) or leisure is locally inferior (van den Berg 1990), increased benefits may lead the unemployed to search more intensively. Blau and Robins (1990), Wadsworth (1991) and Schmitt and Wadsworth (1993) find evidence that benefit entitlement increases search effort. Of course, this may be the conse-

Now, consider the choice of search intensity by the employed. The value function for an employed worker can be written as

$$\delta_r V(w) = \max_{\lambda_e} w + \lambda_e \int_w [V(x) - V(w)] dF(x) - \delta_u (V(w) - V^u) - c_e(\lambda_e, z)$$

(9.4)

leading to the first-order condition

$$\frac{\partial c_e(\lambda_e, z)}{\partial \lambda_e} = \int_w [V(x) - V(w)] dF(x)$$

(9.5)

Denote the solution to this by $\lambda_e(w)$ as the solution will depend on the wage (this is discussed in section 9.3). The following expression for the reservation wage can be derived.

Proposition 9.1. *The reservation wage, r, is given by the solution to*

$$r + (\lambda_e(r) - \lambda_u) \int_r \frac{[1 - F(x)]dx}{\delta + \lambda_e(x)[1 - F(x)]} - c_e(\lambda_e(r), z) = b - c_u(\lambda_u, z)$$

(9.6)

Proof. See Appendix 9.

There are a number of uses to which the reservation wage of equation (9.6) can be put, but also certain potential uses of it that are a bit misleading as it is based on a partial equilibrium model in which the wage distribution is treated as fixed. Consider, for example, the argument that the payment of welfare benefits when out of work reduces work incentives and leads to a lower employment rate. At one level, (9.6) supports this prediction as an increase in unemployment insurance payments for an individual will raise the reservation wage and reduce search intensity, both effects tending to increase the non-employment rate. But, caution is needed before generalizing this conclusion to an economy-wide increase in welfare benefits. The problem is that this conclusion is based on the assumption that the distribution of wages is fixed. However, a general increase in welfare benefits is likely to affect the distribution of wages (for an example of this, see section 2.4) in which case it is not necessarily true that the non-employment rate rises. An interesting application of this idea can be found in van Vuuren et al.

---

quence of the fact that benefit receipt is often made conditional on a certain level of search intensity. It is simple to show in this case that some workers who would otherwise search less than the threshold will search at the threshold intensity and so can only increase their search intensity, while those who were initially above the threshold will reduce their intensity though not so much as to fall below the threshold.

(2000) who consider what happens when there is dispersion in unemployment benefits.

Some other features of (9.6) also deserve discussion. One special case is where the functions $c_u(\lambda, z)$ and $c_e(\lambda, z)$ are identical: in this case comparison of (9.3) and (9.5) (and using the fact that $V(r) = V^u$) shows that we will have $\lambda_e(r) = \lambda_u$ and (9.6) then implies that $r = b$. So, if on- and off-the-job searches are equally effective, the reservation wage will equal the disutility of leisure. Note that this does not mean that all employed workers will search at the same intensity as the non-employed, just that those at the reservation wage will.

Whether on- or off-the-job search is more effective is a question that economists have worried about and several substantive issues depend on the answer to this question (e.g., see the discussion about the impact of trade unions on non-union wages in chapter 12). The existing literature on the subject is not particularly satisfactory. For example, Holzer (1987) finds, using the NLSY, that the unemployed use more search methods than employed job searchers, spend more time on it, get and accept more job offers. He concludes that off-the-job is more effective than on-the-job search. In contrast, Blau and Robins (1990) find that employed job seekers are slightly more successful than unemployed job seekers in getting offered jobs. However, as only 10% of employment spells are associated with job search, and we are interested in the average rate at which employed workers change jobs, one might reasonably argue that their study suggests that off-the-job search is more effective. Both these papers have the problem that all employed job seekers are lumped together whereas (9.6) shows that one should compare unemployed job seekers with those employed at the reservation wage.[4]

Here we take a different approach to the problem using the reservation wage equation (9.6). Suppose we consider a variable, call it labor quality, q, which raises the wage offer distribution in the sense of first-order stochastic dominance. Represent the wage offer distribution by $F(w, q)$: the assumption of first-order stochastic dominance implies that $F_q(w, q) < 0$. By differentiating (9.6) it is simple to show that a rise in q will raise (reduce) the reservation wage if off-the-job search is more (less) effective than on-the-job search. However, average wages will be increasing in labor quality in both cases. This suggests testing the relative effectiveness of on-the-job and off-the-job search by investigating the impact of variables that raise labor quality on the reservation wage.

The UK British Household Panel Survey (BHPS) asks those who are looking for work but do not currently have a job about their reservation

---

[4] If those employed at higher wages search for another job less intensively, this may not be because they are at a disadvantage in job search but because the perceived returns on job search are smaller. This hypothesis is tested below.

wage. We can use this information to estimate a reservation wage equation. This equation is like a standard human capital earnings function but with the addition of variables that we think might affect b, the value of leisure. We include investment income and welfare benefit income in the previous month (converted to an hourly basis by dividing by 170). We also include a dummy variable for whether the household is in receipt of family credit, a benefit that is designed to also be received by those in work. The first column of table 9.1 presents a standard earnings function although we include the investment income and benefit variables for comparison. The findings are familiar: earnings increase with education (the omitted education category is those with a college degree), and are a concave function of experience (although flatter for women), there is a pay premium for married men, and a pay penalty for women with children. Earnings are strongly positively related to investment income (which probably reflects high past earnings) and negatively with benefit

TABLE 9.1
The Determinants of the Reservation Wage

Dependent Variable	Log Hourly Wage	Log Reservation Wage
"A" levels	−0.373 (0.010)	−0.253 (0.029)
GCSEs	−0.546 (0.010)	−0.351 (0.028)
No qualifications	−0.712 (0.012)	−0.432 (0.029)
Female	0.114 (0.047)	0.031 (0.066)
Experience	0.046 (0.001)	0.028 (0.002)
Experience squared	−0.00085 (0.00003)	−0.00049 (0.00003)
Experience × female	−0.021 (0.002)	−0.013 (0.003)
Experience squared × female	0.00032 (0.00004)	0.00024 (0.000050)
Married	0.161 (0.013)	0.141 (0.023)
Married × female	−0.139 (0.017)	−0.142 (0.030)
Children	0.027 (0.011)	−0.029 (0.024)
Children × female	−0.125 (0.015)	0.046 (0.032)
White	0.104 (0.032)	−0.049 (0.045)
White × female	−0.052 (0.045)	−0.046 (0.060)
Health problems	−0.076 (0.013)	−0.026 (0.015)
Household investment income	0.023 (0.002)	0.015 (0.007)
Household benefit income	−0.020 (0.002)	0.004 (0.002)
Family credit receipt	−0.225 (0.026)	−0.092 (0.039)
Number of observations	15393	3634
R^2	0.43	0.23

Notes.
1. The sample is drawn from the BHPS 1991–98. Regional and year dummies are also included. The omitted education category is a college degree.

receipt (which reflects the rules of benefit entitlement). The second column now estimates a reservation wage equation. What is striking is the similarity of the coefficients although, as we might expect, benefit income now has a positive impact on the reservation wage.[5] The impact of the "quality" variables, education and experience, suggests that off-the-job search is more effective than on-the-job search as we would otherwise expect measures of labor quality to have opposite impacts on the two equations. This is not to say that there are no parts of the labor market where the reverse may be true (it is probably harder to get a job as a university lecturer if one is unemployed): just that, on average, it is easier to get a job when unemployed.

9.2 Unemployment and Inactivity

The discussion so far has not made a distinction between unemployment and inactivity: there is only a distinction between employment and non-employment. Labor market statistics often divide the non-employed into two groups, the unemployed and the inactive, using a definition provided by the International Labour Organization. To be classified as unemployed rather than inactive, one must not have worked at all in the reference week or be temporarily away from a job and:

either   have looked for work in the past four weeks
and   be available to start work within two weeks
or   be waiting to start a job within two weeks

In practice the first definition is the most important: only 2% of the unemployed in the United Kingdom fail the first test but pass the second. The purpose of the definition is to distinguish those who want a job but have not got one (a cause of public policy concern) from those who do not want a job. In recent years, this clear-cut distinction has become somewhat blurred, for example, there has been a striking rise in the inactivity rates of less-educated prime-age males in the both the United States (Juhn et al. 1991) and the United Kingdom (Nickell and Bell 1995, 1996). Many of these are inactive because of reported health problems (e.g., see Autor and Duggan 2001) yet it is hard to see what epidemic has been sweeping these countries making millions of men too sick to work. If their labor market was in a healthier state, many of these would almost certainly be in employment.

Models of labor supply based on competitive models of the labor market find it hard, if not impossible, to have a meaningful distinction

---

[5] Although its impact is small; at the average level of benefit income (£1.72 per hour), the elasticity of the reservation wage with respect to benefits is 0.015.

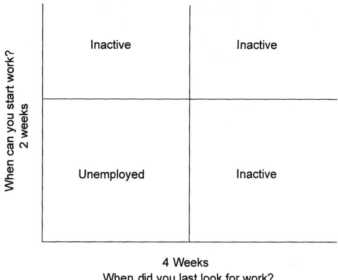

Figure 9.1 The distinction between inactivity and unemployment.

between unemployment and inactivity. The problem is that, in a friction-less labor market, workers can always get a job immediately if they want one. The process of looking for work does not really exist and anyone who is not currently working is assumed not to want a job in spite of any protestations to the contrary. There are some labor supply researchers who feel uneasy with this implication of their approach (e.g., see Blundell et al. 1987), but no entirely satisfactory way of dealing with the problem has been developed.

Search models are ideally suited to modeling the distinction between inactivity and unemployment as the process of "looking for work" is the core of the model. Labor force surveys typically ask the question "have you looked for work in the past four weeks?" and "are you available to start work within two weeks?" but imagine that the questions were "when did you last look for work?" And "when is the earliest you could start work?". One could plot the answers to these questions in figure 9.1. The unemployed will be those with answers in the bottom left-hand box: all the others will be classed as inactive. In practice, the search intensity requirement seems to be more important than the job availability requirement[6] so that modeling the distinction between unem-

---

[6] Those who are searching for work but not available to start a job within 2 weeks tend to be specific groups like those in full-time education or caring for children who have a good idea of when they will want a job in the future.

ployment and inactivity is primarily a question of modeling search intensity. This is the approach taken in Burdett and Mortensen (1978), Burdett et al. (1984), and Blundell et al. (1998) who all model a search–no search decision.

Figure 9.1 should make it clear that the discrete distinction between the unemployed and the inactive is an arbitrary classification placed on what is really a continuous underlying measure of attachment to the labor market. There is a literature, starting with Flinn and Heckman (1983), that asks whether unemployment and inactivity are distinct labor market states and tries to answer this question by examining labor market transition rates. A glance at figure 9.1 should make it clear that this is not a well-posed question: on average, the inactive are less likely to enter employment than the unemployed but, at the margin, the transition rates are likely to be identical. This view is confirmed by the studies of Jones and Riddell (1999) and Gregg and Wadsworth (1996) who find that some of the inactive are more attached to the labor market than others. It is not the mystery sometimes claimed that there are direct moves from inactivity into employment as some of the inactive have low but non-zero job search activity. One should not think of the inactive as having no attachment to the labor market, just a low attachment.

Once one recognizes that the conventional classification of the non-employed into the inactive and the unemployed is an arbitrary one, one begins to wonder whether it is a helpful distinction or the best way of classifying the non-employed into different categories. Jones and Riddell (1999) divide the inactive as conventionally measured into two groups, which they call the marginally attached and the inactive. But, one could go further in subdividing the inactive. The logical end-point of this subdivision is to say that one would like to know the full distribution of λ_u. Alternatively, one could start from the premise that, in the interest of having published statistics that are easily understood, we want to divide the non-employed into a small number (say two) of groups (which we will call the unemployed and the inactive), and ask whether the current way of doing this classification is the best, given the information available on attachment to the labor market.

One issue that has interested labor economists in the past is whether a worsening in the general state of the labor market tends to increase labor force participation (the added-worker effect) or reduce it (the discouraged worker effect). A worsening in the labor market can be thought of as saying that, for a given level of search intensity by the individual, job offers arrive at a slower rate than before so that $c_z < 0$. But, from (9.3), one can see that a lower level of z leads to a lower (higher) level of λ_u as $(\partial^2 c_u / \partial z \partial \lambda_u) > (<)0$. The sign of this cross-partial derivative is unclear a priori.

If job offers arrive more slowly than before this may either increase or reduce the marginal value of a given level of search intensity. It is possible that in bad times job offers are so hard to find that it is simply not worth trying: this is one version of the discouraged-worker effect. Or, it may be the case that, in good times, job offers arrive at a fast rate with very little effort and extra effort brings little extra reward: this is a version of the added-worker effect. The main interest in this type of exercise is whether we should think of search intensity as pro- or counter-cyclical or whether the discouraged- or added-worker effect dominates.

Figure 9.2 presents some evidence on this. Figure 9.2a plots the inactivity rate for men aged 45–60 against a measure of the state of the local labor market, the employment/population ratio for prime-aged men (those aged 25–44) for US states (excluding Alaska) for the period 1998–2000 inclusive. There is a negative relationship between the two suggesting that when the labor market is worse in a state, more older men move out of the labor force into inactivity. The regression line is also marked on the figure: the slope coefficient is -1.04 with a standard error of 0.15. Figure 9.2b plots the same relationship for UK counties over the period 1998–99 inclusive. Again, there is a negative relationship: this time the slope coefficient is -1.17 with a standard error of 0.09. This evidence suggests that when labor markets worsen, some older men reduce their search intensity so much that they exit the labor force and are no longer classified as unemployed.

But, one might wonder whether there is any evidence that search intensity also falls among those who remain in the labor force. Gregg and Wadsworth (1996), using British data from the 1980s and early 1990s suggest, rather tentatively, that, among job searchers, the number of job search methods used increases as the labor market worsens. Some further evidence on this point from the US CPS and the UK LFS is presented in table 9.2. It is obviously hard to measure search intensity: the best measure commonly available is the number of search methods used. For those who are inactive this will (except for the small group who are unavailable for work) be equal to zero, while for those who are unemployed it must be greater than zero. Table 9.2 investigates the impact of the state of the local labor market on the average number of search methods used by those in the labor force. As in figure 9.2, the state of the local labor market is measured by the prime-age (25–54) male employment/population ratio for the region in which the individual lives. The results are very similar for the United Kingdom and the United States. Most of the specifications (which include varying combinations of personal, regional, and time controls) suggest a significant positive effect of the employment/population ratio on the number of search methods used. This is consistent with the earlier conclusion that a good labor

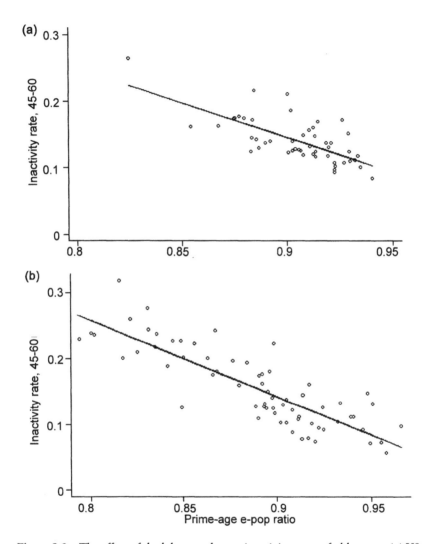

Figure 9.2   The effect of the labor market on inactivity rates of older men. (a) US states. (b) UK counties.

Notes. The US data are from the monthly CPS files for January 1998 to December 2000. Each observation is an individual state (Alaska excluded). The prime-age employment/population (e-pop) ratio is for men aged 25–44. The UK data are from the LFS November 1998 to October 1999 inclusive. Each observation is an individual county. The prime-age employment/population ratio is for men aged 25–44.

TABLE 9.2
The Impact of the Labor Market on Job Search Intensity of the Unemployed

Country	Prime-Age Employment/ Population Ratio	Personal Controls	Region Effects	Time Effects	Number of Observations
US	0.86 (0.12)	No	No	No	176160
US	0.72 (0.12)	Yes	No	No	176160
US	1.03 (0.21)	Yes	Yes	No	176160
US	0.49 (0.11)	Yes	No	Yes	176160
US	0.23 (0.20)	Yes	Yes	Yes	176160
UK	0.87 (0.44)	No	No	No	179979
UK	0.67 (0.30)	Yes	No	No	179979
UK	0.97 (0.53)	Yes	Yes	No	179979
UK	0.66 (0.30)	Yes	No	Yes	179979
UK	−0.89 (0.39)	Yes	Yes	Yes	179979

Notes.
1. The US data are from the basic monthly CPS for January 1994 to December 2000. The UK data are from the LFS for March 1992 to November 2000. The sample is those not in employment who report they have looked for work in the past four weeks.
2. The standard errors for the coefficient on the employment/population ratio are computed assuming clustering on region–time interactions.
3. The personal controls are gender, race, age, age squared, and four education dummies. The regional dummies are by state for the United States and by region for the United Kingdom. The time dummies are the month for the United States and the year for the United Kingdom.

market encourages job search. However, the inclusion of both regional and time controls makes the employment/population ratio change sign and be significant in the United Kingdom. It may be that there is little in the way of cyclical fluctuations left in the data once one has controlled for regional and time effects, but this result should induce some caution in the conclusions drawn.

9.3 The Job Search of the Employed

This section briefly discusses the determinants of job search among the employed. The employed will choose their search intensity to satisfy (9.5). A very clear prediction from this model is that search intensity should be decreasing in the wage. The intuition for this is straightforward: the higher the wage, the less the potential gain from job search as there are fewer higher wage jobs to find.

The US CPS does not regularly ask questions about job search among the employed but, in the Contingent Worker and Alternative Employment Supplement (conducted every two years starting in 1995), workers are asked whether they have looked for alternative employment in the past three months. In the UK LFS, questions are always asked about job search among the employed: whether they are currently looking for a different job and, in addition, questions on the search methods they use.

In the United States, approximately 6% of employed workers report having looked for another job in the past three months: in the United Kingdom approximately 7% say they are currently looking for another job and these report using an average of 3.3 search methods. Table 9.3 examines the determinants of these variables.

The first two columns present estimates for the United States of a model where the dependent variable is a binary variable taking the value 1 if the worker has looked for another job in the past three months. Separate estimates for men and women are presented as the equations are rather different. But, for both men and women the probability of looking for another job is negatively related to the wage as predicted by the model although the effect is stronger for men. More educated workers are more likely to be looking for another job, married women less likely. This last result gives extra support to the argument of chapter 7 that part of the gender gap is the result on constraints on women that prevent them from seeking out and exploiting job opportunities that may arise.

The third and fourth columns estimate a similar equation for the United Kingdom where the dependent variable is now whether the respondent is currently looking for another job. The results are very similar. Ceteris paribus, a higher wage is associated with a lower probability of looking for another job. Married women are again less likely to be looking for alternative employment and there is a very large effect from the presence of children on female job search. As the UK data have a longer time series, the regional employment/population ratio was also included as a regressor: however, its effect is not significant.

The final two columns look at another dependent variable to measure search intensity: the number of search methods used (this is only available for the United Kingdom). Those who reported that they were not looking for another job are assumed to have used no search methods. The same qualitative results are found as when the dependent variable was a 0/1 dummy: in particular the wage is negatively related to the number of search methods used.

This section has shown how, other things being equal, those in better-paying jobs are less likely to be looking for an alternative job. This is in line with the view that frictions in the labor market lead to the existence of wage dispersion for identical workers.

TABLE 9.3
The Determinants of On-the-Job Search

Dependent Variable	Looking for Another Job				Number of Search Methods	
	US Men	US Women	UK Men	UK Women	UK Men	UK Women
Log (wage)	−0.019	−0.016	−0.032	−0.014	−0.464	−0.273
	(0.007)	(0.007)	(0.001)	(0.001)	(0.014)	(0.021)
Married	−0.009	−0.033	0.0005	−0.0274	−0.032	−0.438
	(0.0067)	(0.006)	(0.0018)	(0.0014)	(0.029)	(0.023)
Child	−0.0084	−0.0042	−0.0034	−0.0077	−0.057	−0.162
	(0.0063)	(0.0059)	(0.0014)	(0.0013)	(0.021)	(0.025)
Black	0.003	−0.0047	0.016	0.026	0.325	0.529
	(0.008)	(0.0067)	(0.008)	(0.005)	(0.088)	(0.059)
Asian (UK only)			0.012	0.004	0.183	0.155
			(0.004)	(0.004)	(0.060)	(0.070)
Education level 1	0.080	0.041	0.052	0.040	0.743	0.632
	(0.022)	(0.017)	(0.003)	(0.003)	(0.034)	(0.041)
Education level 2	0.045	0.022	0.018	0.020	0.306	0.384
	(0.013)	(0.011)	(0.002)	(0.003)	(0.033)	(0.041)
Education level 3	0.012	0.001	0.014	0.012	0.230	0.255
	(0.010)	(0.001)	(0.002)	(0.002)	(0.035)	(0.025)
Experience/10	0.013	0.0021	0.027	0.013	0.373	0.124
	(0.010)	(0.008)	(0.002)	(0.002)	(0.031)	(0.034)

Experience/10 squared	-0.0064 (0.0025)	-0.0022 (0.0021)	-0.0076 (0.0004)	-0.0051 (0.0004)	-0.108 (0.006)	-0.070 (0.007)
Tenure/10	-0.027 (0.006)	-0.032 (0.006)	-0.068 (0.002)	-0.055 (0.003)	-1.382 (0.047)	-1.231 (0.059)
Tenure/10 squared	0.0016 (0.0009)	0.0011 (0.0004)	0.011 (0.001)	0.0087 (0.0010)	0.227 (0.015)	0.188 (0.023)
Regional employment/ population ratio			-0.036 (0.037)	-0.047 (0.037)	-0.243 (0.815)	0.586 (0.732)
Number of observations	5133	5490	167390	173858	167398	173866
Mean of dependent variable	0.062	0.057	0.076	0.065	0.26	0.22
Pseudo R^2	0.092	0.089	0.069	0.057	–	–

Notes.

1. The US data are from the Contingent Workers and Alternative Employment Supplement to the CPS in February 1997 and 1999. The UK data are from the LFS for the period March 1993 to December 2000. Education level 1 is a college degree in both countries, education level 2 is some college (US) or "A" level (UK), education level 3 is high school graduate (US) or GSCE level (UK) and the omitted education category is a high school dropout (US) or someone with no formal educational qualifications (UK). State and year dummies are also included for the United States and month, year, and region dummies are also included for the United Kingdom. For the United Kingdom, the standard errors are clustered on year–region interactions to correct the standard errors on the regional employment/population ratio: this variable is not included for the United States because of the small number of observations.

2. When the dependent variable is "looking for another job," a probit model is estimated. When the dependent variable is "number of search methods," a Poisson model is estimated.

9.4 Quits

The model of transitions from employment to non-employment used so far is extremely rudimentary as it assumes that these transitions occur at a rate that is beyond the control of workers and employers. We have already seen in section 4.5 that these transitions are often as sensitive to the wage as the job-to-job mobility rate so this model is obviously not adequate. In popular discussion, a distinction is often made between "voluntary" (what we will call quits) and "involuntary" (what we will call lay-offs) transitions to non-employment. We have already used the idea that lay-offs are involuntary when discussing the earnings losses of displaced workers in chapter 6.

But many labor economists argue that the distinction between a quit and a lay-off is not a meaningful one (see, e.g., McLaughlin 1991). A match between a worker and an employer will be dissolved when there is no surplus left, that is, the reservation wage of the worker exceeds the marginal product. When this happens, it is irrelevant whether the final wage is above the reservation wage of the worker (so there will be a lay-off) or below the marginal product (so there will be a quit). The distinction between quits and lay-offs does become meaningful if there is some form of wage rigidity. For example, Hall and Lazear (1984) considered the case where wages are fixed ex ante and not altered in response to shocks to the productivity of workers or the value of leisure. As there is evidence that such wage rigidity does exist (see chapter 5), the distinction between quits and lay-offs is a meaningful one. This section considers separations initiated by workers: the lay-off decision is considered later in section 10.6.

A natural approach to the quit decision is to assume that quits occur when the reservation wage of a worker rises above the offered wage. In chapter 5 we argued that wages are not likely to be very responsive to the reservation wage because this is plausibly the private information of the worker: this gives us the wage rigidity necessary for a theory of quits. To have an interesting model of the quit decision one obviously needs some variation in reservation wages as, for the worker to have ever started the job, their reservation wage must initially have been below the wage.

Take the model embodied in the value functions (9.2) and (9.4) and slightly modify it. First, to simplify matters, assume that job offer arrival rates are exogenous but might differ for the employed (denoted by λ_e) and the non-employed (denoted by λ_u). Secondly (and this is the crucial innovation), assume that at a rate, κ, there is a shock to the value of leisure, b, and that, when this happens, the new value of leisure has a distribution function $H(b)$. We still assume that workers face a lay-off rate δ_u that is beyond their control. The reservation wage and separation rate are then given by the following proposition.

Proposition 9.2

1. *The quit rate to non-employment is decreasing in the wage.*

2. *The reservation wage, $r(b)$, satisfies*

$$r(b) + (\lambda_e - \lambda_u) \int_{r(b)} \frac{[1 - F(x)]dx}{\delta + \lambda_e[1 - F(x)] + \kappa[1 - H(\rho(x))]}$$

$$+ \kappa \int^b \frac{H(\beta)d\beta}{\delta + \lambda_u[1 - F(r(\beta))] + \kappa} = b \qquad (9.7)$$

Proof. See Appendix 9.

The first part of the proposition is easy to understand. The higher the wage, the lower is the chance that the shock to b will result in a reservation wage above w. Hence, the quit rate will be lower as we found in table 4.7.

The second part of the proposition shows the way that the reservation wage rule needs to be modified if the reservation wage is stochastic. In fact, in the case this chapter has argued is the most plausible ($\lambda_u \geq \lambda_e$), the impact of potential change in the value of leisure is always to lower the reservation wage below what it would otherwise have been. This means that a worker who thinks that their value of b might change in the future will be prepared to take a job that someone with the same current value of b but no prospect of future change would not. For example if $\lambda_u = \lambda_e$ then, in the absence of variation in the value of leisure, the reservation wage is equal to b. But, once there is potential variation in b, the reservation wage will be less than b. The intuition is simple. The option to quit employment for non-employment is always present but the ability to get work is not. Consequently, workers will be prepared to take jobs they might not want now in the hope that b will fall in the future and they will then get utility gains from being in work.

This section has shown how one can provide a more adequate model of quits. However, a model with endogenous quits is messy to work with and we will not use it in what follows. The most important conclusion is that we would expect quits to non-employment to be negatively related to the wage as is observed in the data.

9.5 Involuntary Unemployment

Several sorts of unemployment have appeared in previous chapters. There
is unemployment caused by the fact that it takes time for an unemployed
worker to find an employer: this is frictional unemployment as conventionally understood. Secondly, if there is heterogeneity in reservation
wages (e.g., the model of section 3.4) some potentially productive
matches may not be consummated because the wage offered is below
the reservation wage of the worker. The resulting unemployment is
often described as voluntary unemployment (as it is the worker who
vetoes the match) and we will follow this terminology here.[7] Although
it is sometimes useful from the conceptual point of view to divide unemployment into these two components, one should not think of them as
being determined independently. For example, the extent of frictional
unemployment depends on the reservation wage that will be determined
by the wage offer distribution which will itself determine the extent of
voluntary unemployment.

But, the types of unemployment we have described are a poor description of unemployment as experienced by many of the unemployed. In the
models used so far, a worker could get a job offer (at some wage) from
any employer simply by approaching them. If they remain unemployed
that is only because this wage offer is below their reservation wage. But
the predicament of the unemployed is often not so much the problem of
finding a job paying an acceptable wage as a problem of employers refus-
ing to offer any employment at all. This is what is often called involuntary
unemployment. Involuntary unemployment is said to exist when unemployed workers strictly prefer employment to unemployment at prevailing wages (and identical workers are in employment at those or better
terms) but cannot obtain employment (see, e.g., the definition offered by
Taylor 1987). In a static model of a perfectly competitive labor market,
this corresponds to employment being on the labor demand curve and off
the labor supply curve. The obvious question to answer in this case is why
wages do not fall to clear the labor market. One explanation is that
institutions like minimum wages or unions prevent this wage adjustment
but many economists feel that involuntary unemployment exists even in
unfettered labor markets and there has been a considerable amount of

---

[7] This terminology does have some unfortunate connotations. For example, inefficient
voluntary unemployment is often thought of as being "caused" by excessive levels of welfare
benefits. But, in the model here it is "caused" by wages being low relative to reservation
wages and this could equally be due to wages being too low or reservation wages too high.
The traditional one-sided view of the problem is the result of implicitly using a competitive
model in which one thinks of the wage as being the marginal product independent of the
level of benefits. But, in a monopsonistic labor market, this is not the case.

research into the reasons why this might be the case, a branch of research that has been grouped together into efficiency wage theory.

At first sight, one might think that efficiency wages and monopsony are incompatible as the simplest efficiency wage model has an equilibrium on the labor demand curve but off the labor supply curve while the simplest monopsony model has an equilibrium on the labor supply curve but off the labor demand curve. However, as we shall see, one can reconcile the existence of involuntary unemployment with an upward-sloping supply curve of labor to the employer.

One immediate problem is that the usual definition of involuntary unemployment is not well suited to a labor market with frictions. The definition is typically applied in models where there are well-defined labor demand and supply curves, and there is a single wage in the market. Our first task is to suggest a definition more suited to our purposes.

Definition. *Involuntary unemployment exists whenever, given a match between an unemployed worker and a firm, the match is not consummated even though the worker wants the job at the offered terms and there are equally productive workers employed in this or identical firms at terms that the worker would also accept.*

Several parts of this deserve discussion. First, by considering involuntary unemployment to exist only when a match fails to be consummated and not the absence of a match, we avoid defining as involuntary unemployment a situation in which the worker knows there is a single high wage job in the economy but does not know where it is. The requirement that the worker wants the match on the offered terms corresponds to the fact that the worker would like to be employed at the offered contract. The condition that other equally productive workers are employed at these or better terms ensures that the worker could "reasonably" aspire to getting the job.

It should be apparent that involuntary unemployment on this definition does not exist in the basic models of the labor market we have used so far. When a match is made, the employer will always want to employ the worker if the wage is below the marginal product and the worker is prepared to do the job. The employer would not be prepared to employ the worker at a wage above his/her marginal product but no worker would be obtaining such a wage so that is not classed as involuntary unemployment.

But, as the following section shows, it is possible for monopsony and involuntary unemployment to be compatible. This is shown using the most common models of involuntary unemployment, efficiency wage models.

9.6 Efficiency Wages and Monopsony

Akerlof and Yellen (1986) describe four main types of efficiency wage models: the shirking model, the turnover model, the adverse selection model, and the fairness model. We consider each of these in turn.

9.6.1 The Shirking Model

As presented by Shapiro and Stiglitz (1984), the idea of the shirking model is that monitoring of workers is less then perfect. To ensure that workers put in an appropriate level of effort, workers who are caught shirking must be punished in some way. It is assumed that the only form of feasible wage contract is a fixed wage if employed, so that the worst punishment that can be inflicted on a worker is to be fired. But, if workers are as well off when unemployed as when employed, they will not care whether they keep or lose their jobs so that they will always shirk. So, employers must always offer workers a contract such that they are strictly better off in work (and not shirking) than out of work. But, this will mean that some unemployed workers cannot obtain employment even though they would be prepared to work for lower wages than currently employed workers. So, equilibrium is off the labor supply curve and unemployment is involuntary.[8] Now consider how these ideas can be put into the models we have used.

Assume that workers are heterogeneous in b, the utility received when non-employed and that the distribution function of b is given by $H(b)$. A worker employed in a job paying wage w and not shirking has utility $(w - e)$ while a shirking worker has utility w. Workers who do not shirk have a marginal product equal to p but workers who shirk produce nothing. Job offers arrive at a rate λ for both employed and unemployed workers (this makes the analytics simpler without losing any of the features of the model that we want to emphasize here). These assumptions imply that the reservation wage of a worker who does not shirk is $(b + e)$. Workers also exit the labor force at an exogenously given rate δ.

---

[8] It should be noted that there is a debate about whether the results of this model are a product of an arbitrary restriction in the form of employment contracts (see Carmichael 1985; Macleod and Malcomson 1989). This is essentially a debate about whether workers can be made to post bonds that are lost if their performance is inadequate. This is an issue that we have already considered when we discussed the ways in which the employer might become a discriminating monopsonist in chapter 5. The upshot of our discussion there was that, while there are reasons to think that employers will try to find ways to use more sophisticated contracts, there are also good reasons to think that their ability to eliminate all the problems is less than perfect. In this case, the insights of the simple model will still be relevant.

Assume that employers set a wage for the job and, while they can observe b, they do not attempt to fine tune their wage offers to the individual characteristics of job applicants.[9] We also follow Shapiro and Stiglitz (1984) in assuming that the only available form of labor contract is a fixed wage with shirkers being fired. Together, these two assumptions mean that employers turn away workers who they think will shirk at the going wage. We assume there is imperfect monitoring of workers; in particular that the incidence of monitoring is a Poisson process with arrival rate θ. Workers who are caught shirking are assumed to be fired.

The following proposition shows that the minimum wage at which an employer is prepared to hire a worker is strictly above their reservation wage.

Proposition 9.3. *An employer will refuse to hire some workers who want employment at the offered wage. The minimum wage, $w(b)$, that must be paid to a worker to prevent them from shirking solves*

$$w(b) = b + e + \frac{\delta + \lambda[1 - F(w(b))]}{\theta} e \qquad (9.8)$$

Proof.   See Appendix 9.

An employer will only want to employ the worker if, given b, the wage offered is above $w(b)$ as given by (9.8). As $w(b) > (b + e)$, the reservation wage of workers, (9.8) implies that the employer will sometimes be turning away workers who want the job. The gap between $w(b)$ and the reservation wage is larger if monitoring is less effective (θ is smaller), and the separation rate $[\delta + \lambda(1 - F(w(b)))]$ is larger. The intuition for the last result is that the worker is more worried about losing a job that is expected to last a long time. Using the definition provided, some workers are involuntarily unemployed as long as some identical worker (i.e., with the same b) is in employment in the economy at a wage at which this worker would also like work. This will be the case if there are any workers with the same level of b in employment in the economy. Those in employment in this model will be receiving higher wages.

[9] Some discussion of this is in order. In chapter 5 we argued that wages were not likely to depend on b because it was likely to be private information of the worker. But if this was the case in the model here, employers would be unable to tell which workers will shirk and which will not. So, we are implicitly assuming that firms set a single wage for the job, something for which we have argued in chapter 5 that there is considerable empirical evidence. One could obtain the results reported here as long as employers have some information on b which is not incorporated into the wage offer.

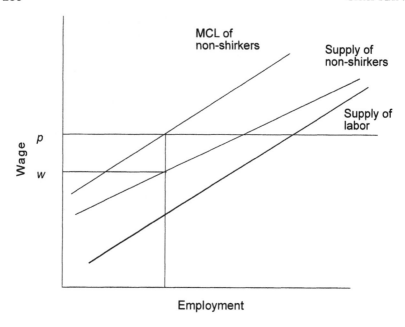

Figure 9.3 Involuntary unemployment and monopsony in the shirking model.

It is simple to provide a diagram to explain how one can reconcile this involuntary unemployment and monopsony in the shirking model. Because of labor market frictions and heterogeneous workers, the supply curve of labor to the firm is not perfectly elastic and is as drawn in figure 9.3. But, the employer knows that some of the workers who want to work in the firm will shirk so that the supply of non-shirkers lies somewhere to the left of the labor supply curve as also drawn in figure 9.3. It is the gap between the two lines that gives the existence of involuntary unemployment. The firm, like any good mono-psonist, will choose a level of employment where the marginal cost of labor derived from the supply curve of non-shirkers is equal to the marginal revenue product of labor as drawn in figure 9.3. In figure 9.3, this results in the choice of wage, w.

In this section we have shown how one can introduce the ideas of Shapiro and Stiglitz (1984) into our model of the monopsonistic labor market.[10] The result is a model in which there are both features of mono-psony and involuntary unemployment: the insights of these models are not incompatible. Let us now consider other versions of the efficiency wage model.

---

[10] See Manning (1995) for a way to do this in a general equilibrium framework.

9.6.2 The Turnover Model

In Salop (1979), the basic idea is that the labor turnover rate depends on the wage and that the presence of turnover costs then means that an employer may not be prepared to cut wages to employ workers who cannot get work. As the idea that turnover depends on the wage is central to this book, his model can be expressed simply using our existing terminology.

Assume that the firm incurs total turnover costs of $T(R)$ where R is the recruitment rate.[11] If $s(w)$ is the separation rate then employment, N, will be given by $N = (R/s)$. Assume that revenue is given by $Y(N)$. Profits in a steady state can be written as

$$\pi = Y(N) - wN - T(s(w)N) \tag{9.9}$$

The employer chooses the wage and the level of employment to maximize (9.9) subject to the constraint that

$$N \le \frac{R(w)}{s(w)} \tag{9.10}$$

where $R(w)$ is the flow of recruits to the firm. Involuntary unemployment occurs whenever the constraint in (9.10) does not bind, that is, the firm does not want to hire all the recruits attracted to the firm.

There are some cases in which involuntary unemployment cannot occur. If the production function has constant returns to scale and the costs of turnover are linear in the number of recruits, then the profit function of (9.9) will be linear in N and, assuming the employer wants to hire any workers at all, it will want to hire all the workers it can. But, if there are decreasing returns to scale or increasing marginal turnover costs, it is quite possible that the employer will not want the constraint in (9.10) to bind.[12]

However, there is something a little unsatisfactory about this as a model of involuntary unemployment. The supply of labor to the firm as written in (9.10) assumes that the employer only has a single instrument, the wage, to influence the flow of recruits to it. If, as in the generalized model of monopsony of section 2.3, the employer can also choose the

---

[11] There are other specifications of the turnover cost function that might be plausible. For example, one might assume that total turnover costs can be written as a function $T(R, N)$ where $T(\cdot)$ is homogeneous of degree one in its arguments. As $sN = R$ in equilibrium this amounts to having a turnover cost function of the form $RT(s)$ which, if s depends on w implies a per worker turnover cost that is a declining function of w.

[12] Manning (1995) shows that, in the case where $T(R)$ is a convex function of R, a minimum wage that just binds must raise employment even if there is involuntary unemployment.

level of recruitment intensity, then recruitment activity will always be set at a level at which the labor supply constraint to the firm is just binding so there will be no involuntary unemployment. However, the model of vacancies as accidents introduced in the next chapter does go some way to alleviate this problem as that assumes that the labor supply to a firm is inherently stochastic making it impossible for the employer to fine tune its labor supply in this way.

9.6.3 The Adverse Selection Model

In the adverse selection model, due to Weiss (1980), the wage paid is assumed to affect the quality of workers. Cutting wages is assumed to cause the better workers to leave as they are assumed to have better outside options. Obviously this can only happen if the employer is unable (or unwilling) to pay different wages to workers of different quality. One problem for this model is to explain why this employer cannot observe worker quality but the outside options are better so that somebody else can.

In chapter 5 we argued that the empirical evidence suggests that employers do not seem to take account of all observable worker ability in setting wages. In the extreme, they pay a single wage to all workers and turn away workers who are thought not to be of sufficient quality. The higher the wage paid, the higher will be the average quality of workers in the firm. So, this does have the critical feature of the Weiss model. And the workers who are turned away will be experiencing involuntary unemployment because the employer is reluctant to cut wages to get them into employment.

9.6.4 The Fairness Model

Underlying all of the efficiency wage models discussed above is a reluctance on the part of employers to pay different wages to different types of workers. We argued in chapter 5 that there is reason to believe that this is the case. But, why employers seem to behave in this way is unclear. Akerlof and Yellen (1990) have suggested that workers are concerned with fairness. This might be fairness among workers, so that offering workers different wages will, if seen as unfair, reduce worker effort and morale so that output falls. Or it might be fairness between worker and employer, in that cutting wages for all workers has the same effect. These ideas have been used by Akerlof to explain involuntary unemployment: as we have seen, they implicitly underlie much of the discussion that has gone before.

9.6.5 Is Involuntary Unemployment a Useful Concept?

In this section we have argued that the concept of involuntary unemployment is perfectly compatible with the idea that employers have non-negligible market power. But, it has done nothing to show that involuntary unemployment exists or is a helpful concept. Perhaps the clearest evidence that involuntary unemployment exists comes not from looking at the process by which the unemployed get jobs, but from the process by which the employed lose them. The fact that many workers are unhappy when they lose jobs is indication that employers destroy jobs when there is still some surplus remaining to workers. This then also suggests that they would be reluctant to hire some workers (e.g., those just laid off) when there is some surplus to workers, the condition needed for involuntary unemployment. A formal analysis of the determinants of job destruction in an efficiency wage model is not developed here. It would not be difficult to do: one could take the Mortensen and Pissarides (1994) matching model of job destruction (in which jobs are only destroyed when the surplus is zero) and add some part of the shirking model.

Is the distinction between voluntary and involuntary unemployment a helpful one? To illustrate the circumstances in which it might be helpful, consider a policy that provides a subsidy to the employment of a small group of individuals, for example, the long-term unemployed as targeted in the US unemployment bonus experiments (for a review, see Meyer 1995) or the UK New Deal scheme. If wage setting is individualistic, it does not matter whether the subsidy is given to the employer or the worker as the wages paid can be adjusted accordingly to ensure that the net real wage received by the worker and paid by the employer are independent of who receives the subsidy. This is the well-known result in public finance that the economic incidence of a tax or subsidy is independent of the formal incidence.

But if wage setting is not individualistic (and we have argued that this is the case), then who receives the subsidy does matter. Consider the case where there is no impact of the scheme on the wages paid by employers to workers. If unemployment is all voluntary, then giving the subsidy to the employer will do nothing to increase employment and the subsidy should be given to the worker. However, if unemployment is involuntary, then it is the action of employers not workers that is the constraint on employment, and the subsidy will be more effective if given to employers. So, the theoretical distinction between voluntary and involuntary unemployment may have some practical benefit in the presence of wage rigidities. It should be noted that Meyer (1995) finds that giving the subsidy to the worker seems more effective than giving it to the employer although there is also the suspicion that this may be because workers are reluctant to inform employers that they are eligible for the subsidy in the first place.

9.7 Conclusions

This chapter has considered the actions of workers in a labor market characterized by wage dispersion caused by the existence of frictions. The search approach to unemployment is a familiar one so this chapter has done little more than reinforce pre-existing ways of thinking about the determinants of unemployment.

This chapter has a number of substantive contributions. First, it has provided a coherent distinction between inactivity and unemployment based on the level of job search activity and provided evidence on how job search activity responds to variations in the overall state of the labor market (job search among the non-employed seems to be pro-cyclical). It has provided evidence (based on the determinants of reservation wages) that off-the-job search is more effective than on-the-job search. It has provided evidence that those in higher wage jobs are less likely to be looking for alternative employment, evidence that there is a wage dispersion in the labor market. It has suggested that quits to non-employment depend negatively on the level of wages because of the impact of shocks to the value of leisure. And, finally, the chapter has shown how one can reconcile search models of unemployment with ideas of involuntary unemployment.

This chapter has been about how the actions of workers can affect their employment opportunities. But, this is also influenced by the actions of employers: this is the subject of the next chapter.

Appendix 9

Proof of Proposition 9.1

The reservation wage, r, will satisfy $V(r) = V^u$. Evaluating (9.4) at $w = r$, and subtracting this from (9.2) leads to

$$r + (\lambda_e(r) - \lambda_u) \int_r [V(x) - V(r)]dF(x) - c_e(\lambda_e(r), z) = b - c_u(\lambda_u(r), z)$$

(9.11)

Now, differentiate (9.4) with respect to the wage to yield

$$\frac{\partial V(w)}{\partial w} = \frac{1}{\delta + \lambda_e(w)(1 - F(w))}$$

(9.12)

where $\delta = \delta_u + \delta_r$. In deriving (9.12) we have used the envelope condition for the choice of λ_e. Now integrate the term under the integral sign in (9.11) by parts to obtain

$$\int_r [V(x) - V(r)]dF(x) = \int_r \frac{\partial V(x)}{\partial x}[1 - F(x)]dx \qquad (9.13)$$

Substituting (9.12) into (9.13) and then putting it back into (9.11) yields (9.6). (9.6) uniquely defines the reservation wage as the left-hand side is strictly increasing in r.

Proof of Proposition 9.2

The value of being in a job or non-employed now depends on b so we write the value functions as $V^u(b)$ and $V(w,b)$. The decision rule for a worker with value of leisure b will, as before, be to accept any job where the wage is above the reservation wage $r(b)$ where $r(b)$ satisfies $V(r(b), b) = V^u(b)$. Let us define $\rho(w)$ to be the highest level of b consistent with being prepared to work in a firm paying a wage w, that is, we must have $r(\rho(w)) = w$. If the worker is in a job paying w and their value of b changes to be above $\rho(w)$, then they will quit. With this in mind, the value functions (9.2) and (9.4) need to be modified to

$$\delta_r V^u(b) = b + \lambda_u \int_{r(b)} [V(x, b) - V^u(b)]dF(x) + \kappa \int [V^u(\beta) - V^u(b)]dH(\beta)$$

$$(9.14)$$

and

$$\delta_r V(w, b) = w - \delta_u[V(w, b) - V^u(b)] + \lambda_e \int_w [V(x, b) - V(w, b)]dF(x)$$

$$+\kappa \int^{\rho(w)} [V(w, \beta) - V(w, b)]dH(\beta) + \kappa \int_{\rho(w)} [V^u(\beta) - V(w, b)]dH(\beta)$$

$$(9.15)$$

The reservation wage must satisfy $V(r(b), b) = V^u(b)$ which, using (9.14) and (9.15), can be written as

$$r(b) + (\lambda_e - \lambda_u) \int_{r(b)} [V(x, b) - V(r(b), b)]dF(x)$$

$$+ \kappa \int^b [V(r(b), \beta) - V^u(\beta)]dH(\beta) = b \qquad (9.16)$$

where we have used the fact that $\rho(r(b)) = b$. Integrating the integral terms in (9.16) by parts, can be written as

$$r(b) + (\lambda_e - \lambda_u) \int_{r(b)} \frac{\partial V(x, b)}{\partial x}[1 - F(x)]dx$$

$$- \kappa \int^b \left[\frac{\partial V(r(b), \beta)}{\partial \beta} - \frac{\partial V^u(\beta)}{\partial \beta} \right] H(\beta)d\beta = b \qquad (9.17)$$

Now differentiating (9.15) we have

$$[\delta + \lambda_e(1 - F(w)) + \kappa]\frac{\partial V(w, b)}{\partial w} = 1 + \kappa \int^{\rho(w)} \frac{\partial V(w, \beta)}{\partial w} dH(\beta)$$

$$\qquad (9.18)$$

Note that the solution to (9.18) will be independent of b so that we obtain

$$\frac{\partial V(w, b)}{\partial w} = \frac{1}{\delta + \lambda_e(1 - F(w)) + \kappa(1 - H(\rho(w)))} \qquad (9.19)$$

Now, differentiating (9.15) with respect to b we have

$$\delta_r \frac{\partial V(w, b)}{\partial b} = \delta_u \left(\frac{\partial V^u(b)}{\partial b} - \frac{\partial V(w, b)}{\partial b} \right) - \kappa \frac{\partial V(w, b)}{\partial b} \qquad (9.20)$$

where we have used the fact that $\partial^2 V(w, b)/\partial w \partial b = 0$ so that

$$\frac{\partial V(x, b)}{\partial b} = \frac{\partial V(w, b)}{\partial b}$$

Differentiating (9.14) with respect to b leads to

$$\delta_r \frac{\partial V^u(b)}{\partial b} = 1 - \lambda_u[1 - F(r(b))]\left(\frac{\partial V^u(b)}{\partial b} - \frac{\partial V(w, b)}{\partial b} \right) - \kappa \frac{\partial V^u(b)}{\partial b}$$

$$\qquad (9.21)$$

Combining (9.20) and (9.21) leads to

$$\frac{\partial V^u(b)}{\partial b} - \frac{\partial V(w, b)}{\partial b} = \frac{1}{\delta + \lambda_u(1 - F(r(b))) + \kappa} \qquad (9.22)$$

Substituting (9.22) and (9.19) into (9.17) leads to (9.7). This proves part 2. Part 1 is proved simply by noting that the quit rate to non-employment is given by $\kappa[1 - H(\rho(w))]$ which is decreasing in the wage.

Proof of Proposition 9.3

If a worker with utility of b when unemployed (call them a b-worker) and a firm paying wage w are matched, employment will result if the worker wants the job and the firm wants the worker. Let us consider when this will be the case. Define $V(w, b)$ to be the value for a b-worker of being employed in a wage paying w when they do not shirk. Similarly define

$V^s(w, b)$ to be the value of the job when they do shirk. Similarly define $V^u(b)$ to be the value of being a b-worker when unemployed. It will turn out that a b-worker will get employment whenever w exceeds some threshold level $w(b)$ (which is derived below).[13] $w(b)$ is the minimum wage at which a b-worker will not shirk. Then

$$\delta_r V(w, b) = w - e + \lambda \int_{\max(w, w(b))} [V(x, b) - V(w, b)] dF(x)$$

$$+ \delta_u [V^u(b) - V(w, b)] \tag{9.23}$$

$$\delta_r V^u(b) = b + \lambda \int_{w(b)} [V(x, b) - V^u(b)] dF(x) \tag{9.24}$$

$$\delta_r V^s(w, b) = w - \theta [V^s(w, b) - V^u(b)]$$

$$+ \lambda \int_{\max(w, w(b))} [V(x, b) - V(w, b)] dF(x) dF(x)$$

$$+ \delta_u [V^u(b) - V(w, b)] \tag{9.25}$$

In these equations we consider what happens if a worker is employed at a wage below $w(b)$ in order to derive the no-shirking condition although, in equilibrium, this will never happen. As

$$\frac{dV(w, b)}{dw} = \frac{1}{\delta + \lambda[1 - F(\max(w, w(b)))]}$$

$$> \frac{1}{\delta + \theta + \lambda[1 - F(\max(w, w(b)))]} = \frac{dV^s(w, b)}{dw} \tag{9.26}$$

$V(w, b) - V^s(w, b)$ is increasing in the wage so that the no-shirking condition will a be a cut-off rule of the form $w \geq w(b)$ where $V(w(b), b) = V^s(w(b), b)$. Using (9.23) and (9.25), this condition can be written as

$$V(w(b), b) = V^u(b) + \frac{e}{\theta} \tag{9.27}$$

(9.27) is an example of what is called a no-shirking condition as it says that the utility the worker gets from the job must be strictly larger than the utility available when unemployment to prevent shirking. As $\theta \to \infty$ and monitoring becomes perfect, the premium that needs to be paid to

[13] It is simple to prove that the equilibrium cut-off rule must be of this form (see (9.26)) but allowing for a general hiring rule at this stage introduces tedious additional notation which only complicates the presentation.

workers to prevent them from shirking goes to zero. However, we can provide a more convenient expression for $w(b)$.

Integrating the final term in (9.23) and (9.24) by parts, and using the first part of (9.26), we can derive

$$\delta_r V(w(b), b) = w(b) - e + \lambda \int_{w(b)} \frac{[1 - F(x)]}{\delta + \lambda[1 - F(x)]} dx$$

$$+ \delta_u [V^u(b) - V(w(b), b)] \tag{9.28}$$

$$\delta_r V^u(b) = b + \lambda [V(w(b), b) - V^u(b)][1 - F(w(b))]$$

$$+ \lambda \int_{w(b)} \frac{[1 - F(x)]}{\delta + \lambda[1 - F(x)]} dx \tag{9.29}$$

Combining (9.28) and (9.29) with (9.27) allows us to write the no-shirking condition as (9.8).

10

Vacancies and the Demand for Labor

THE previous chapter considered the role of workers' actions in influencing labor market transition rates and, hence, employment, unemployment, and inactivity rates. This chapter considers how the actions of employers affect the same variables. The main way in which firms can influence the arrival rate of job offers is by creating vacancies and spending resources in trying to fill them, and the main way in which they can influence the separation rate is by the lay-off decision.

Part of this chapter is concerned with the choice of recruitment intensity by firms. One way of thinking about this extra choice is that, for a given wage, variation in the recruitment intensity will determine employment in the firm. So, this chapter is the substitute for what in a more traditional labor economics textbook is the chapter on labor demand as that subject normally studies the amount of labor demanded by the firm for a given wage (although, in a competitive market, the firm has no control over the wage). There is an enormous amount of research that purports to provide estimates of "labor demand curves" (for a survey, see Hamermesh 1993). These labor demand curves are generally thought to estimate the relationship "marginal revenue product of labor equals the wage" so, on the face of it, they would seem to be inconsistent with a view of the labor market in which employment might be thought to be primarily supply-determined (as in the simple textbook model of monopsony) and wages are less than the marginal revenue product. But, it is simple to reconcile the apparent existence of labor demand curves with monopsony. For employers with some market power, one can write the first-order condition for employment as

$$Y'(N) = w(1 + \varepsilon) \qquad (10.1)$$

where ε is the inverse of the elasticity of the labor supply curve facing the firm. (10.1) makes it apparent that anything that changes the wage but leaves ε unchanged (i.e., iso-elastic shifts the labor supply curve) will lower employment leading to an apparent labor demand curve. But, these labor demand curves will not be a good guide to the impact of policies like the minimum wage and equal pay legislation, which are likely to change ε as well as the wage.

CHAPTER 10

There are other reasons why one might think it implausible that employment is primarily supply-determined. In the simplest models of monopsony (like the Burdett–Mortensen model of section 2.4), the matching process is modeled as one in which workers find it difficult to locate employers and get employment immediately they find a firm that pays them a wage above their reservation wage. Yet, when one thinks about the real world, finding employment often does not seem to be that easy. It is more helpful to think of the matching problem, not as a problem of finding an employer (one can simply look them up in the business pages of the phone book) but of finding vacancies. Associated with this view that it is hard to find employment, reported vacancy rates are generally very low, the number of applicants for jobs is quite large, and vacancy durations are often very short. Typically only a small proportion of firms report difficulties in hiring labor. These facts might seem to be inconsistent with the idea of a labor market that is monopsonistic and in which one thinks of employment as primarily determined by the supply of labor to the firm.

The second section of this chapter offers an interpretation of this conundrum and argues that the data on vacancy rates and durations are perfectly consistent with employers having non-negligible market power. The problem with the simplest models of monopsony is that there is no real notion of a vacancy (an unfilled job) within them. When one modifies the model to provide a well-defined notion of a vacancy, the monopsony model can explain the stylized facts about vacancy rates very well. We will argue that information on vacancy rates, etc. contains essentially no information about the extent of labor market power possessed by employers.

The basic argument can best be summarized by an analogy to oligopoly in the product market. Oligopolists want to sell more output at their price so that they have an "excess supply of output" in the same way as a monopsonist has an "excess demand for labor." But we do not expect oligopolists to produce the output they would like to sell but cannot. The absence of large stocks of unsold goods is not evidence that the product market is competitive. In the same way, monopsonists do not create jobs they would like to fill but do not expect to be able to. But, they find it difficult to exactly predict separations and recruits so that sometimes there is an unfilled job. These vacancies should be thought of as "accidents" rather than as an indicator of the general excess demand for labor.[1]

The fourth section of the chapter considers the process by which workers contact firms. In all the formal models of monopsony used so far, it

[1] The vacancy rate may be more useful as an indicator of the cyclical level of demand as, if firms do not vary wages much over the business cycle, the vacancy rate is likely to exhibit sharp swings.

has been assumed that workers contact firms at random. Burdett and Vishwanath (1988) term this random matching and consider an alternative matching technology in which the arrival rate of job applicants is proportional to the number of workers so that large firms have an intrinsic advantage over small firms in recruitment—what they term balanced matching. The conclusion will be that the empirical evidence does not suggest that random matching is particularly important.

Finally, section 10.5 presents evidence on the costs of recruitment for employers. In the generalized model of monopsony introduced in section 2.3, it was pointed out that an important question is whether employers face increasing marginal costs of recruitment with perfect competition the case where the marginal cost of recruitment is constant and "monopsony" the case where it is increasing in the level of employment. It is hard to get data on recruitment costs but some empirical evidence is presented in favor of the view that there are diseconomies of scale in recruitment.

10.1 The Interpretation of Vacancy Statistics

Perhaps the best source of information on the recruitment activities of firms are statistics on vacancies, although it should be noted that, even on this subject, there are relatively few papers. For example, only 15 out of 300 pages in the survey by Devine and Kiefer (1991) of the search approach to labor markets is concerned with the process of recruitment.

But, what studies there are seem to show a consistent picture. Studies from the United States (Holzer 1994), the United Kingdom (Beaumont 1978; Roper 1986, 1988) and the Netherlands (van Ours 1989; van Ours and Ridder 1992) all find that vacancy rates are low, that there are typically many applicants for vacancies, and that average vacancy durations are very short (particularly in comparison with the durations of spells of unemployment). Combined with the casual empiricism suggesting that workers have difficulty in finding jobs, one might conclude that firms could hire more workers at close to zero cost if they so desired and the fact that they appear to employ less workers than they could would suggest that the profit obtained from the marginal worker is zero. This picture of the labor market does not seem to be consistent with the simple monopsony model in which all firms always want more suitably qualified workers at a given wage as their marginal product exceeds the wage. Given this model, one might expect to see all employers engage in recruitment activities that are basically costless with signs outside their gates declaring "now hiring" and all firms would record permanent vacancies with public employment services.[2] This simply does not seem an accurate description of the way in which labor markets work.

But, the problem is that the notion of a vacancy is not well defined in the models used until now. For example, the definition of a vacancy in British statistics is "a job which is currently vacant, available immediately and for which the firm has taken some specific recruiting action during the past four weeks."[3] In the standard models of monopsony, when asked about the number of vacancies, employers would not be able to give a meaningful answer. They would simply shrug their shoulders and explain that they had engaged in recruitment activity in the past four weeks but that there were an unlimited number of openings for suitably qualified workers.

The problem is that there is no notion of a "job" that can be filled or vacant, and without a notion of a "job" there can be no meaningful definition of a vacancy. It has been implicitly assumed that when a suitably qualified worker arrives at a firm, the employer can instantaneously endow him/her with the capital required for the job and has an immediate market for the output he/she will produce. There are some types of employment that are like this. For example, reading the situations vacant columns of London newspapers, one will generally see advertisements for minicab drivers. If one replies to these adverts, one typically finds that one can start work as soon as one has arranged appropriate insurance and if one has a suitable four-door car. In this job, the workers themselves provide the capital so that they can be put to work straight away. In this sector, it is probably true that there is no meaningful definition of a vacancy.

But most jobs are not like that. Typically, capital must be committed in advance of a worker being recruited: this might be in the form of an investment in machines or an investment in creating a market for the output. At any moment in time, there is then a well-defined number of jobs in each firm which may or may not be filled. Let us consider a modification of our basic model of monopsony that captures this feature of the world.

To keep matters simple, consider a model of a single firm. Assume that the decision for the firm is the wage that it pays, w, and the number of jobs, J. Assume that the cost of creating J jobs is cJ. Assume that output

[2] Mackay et al. (1971) do discuss the fact that, in the United Kingdom, a few firms used to have permanent vacancies recorded at employment exchanges, a practice that died out when unemployment rose but may now be reviving as labor markets tighten.

[3] Perhaps not surprisingly, different countries have different definitions of vacancies (for details, see Roper 1986). In the United States, a 600 page book was once devoted to *The Measurement and Interpretation of Vacancies* (NBER 1966) concluding, more or less, that the task was impossible. US measures of vacancies remain one of the few economic statistics measured in inches.

produced if employment is N is pN if $N \leq J$ and pJ for $N > J$.[4] Denote the number of workers who want to work for the firm at any moment in time by $N(w)$. Then steady-state expected profits will be given by

$$\pi = (p - w)E(\min(N(w), J)) - cJ \qquad (10.2)$$

and (w, J) will be chosen to maximize (10.2).

The basic model of monopsony with its assumption of infinitesimal workers has one unfortunate implication for the analysis of vacancies. The law of large numbers implies that the labor supply to a firm is non-stochastic and is given by $N(w) = [R(w)/s(w)]$. Given w, it is then obviously optimal for the firm to set $J = N(w)$ and then to choose w to maximize

$$\pi = (p - c - w)N(w) \qquad (10.3)$$

This obviously leads back to the standard model of monopsony.

What is the vacancy rate in this case? As all firms always have total employment equal to the number of jobs, the vacancy rate is zero. And vacancy durations are also zero as all workers who leave the firm are replaced immediately with probability one. So this seems approximately consistent with the real world in which vacancy rates and durations are very low, and vacancies are hard to find. But, on the other hand, every worker who contacts a firm in this model manages to get a job as they miraculously contact the firm at the instant that another worker is leaving. In some sense the number of applicants per job is one with probability one. And, the proportion of firms who have had a vacancy in any finite period of time, however short, is also one. These predictions do not sit comfortably with our perception of the way in which labor markets actually work.

The problem lies with the assumption that every individual worker is infinitesimal in relation to the size of the firm. To avoid this problem, assume that workers are of non-negligible size in relation to every firm. J and N must now be integers rather than any non-negative number.

The model we use is the following. At any moment in time, there is a stock of workers who would be prepared to work for the firm for a wage w and who the firm would be prepared to employ if they had an available job. Individual workers leave this pool of potential workers because, for example, they get a better job elsewhere, or because their personal circumstances change and a job in the firm is no longer attractive to them. Similarly, some other workers join the pool of potential workers.

---

[4] This assumes that both idle jobs and surplus workers produce no output. In reality the consequences of vacancies are more than just lost output. One might use the approach taken in Manning (1994a) to assume that production is most efficient when $N = J$ but that extra workers always produce some output.

So, at any point in time there will be a stock A of individuals who are interested in the job: we will call these potential workers. A will be a random variable: let us denote the steady-state probability that there are A potential workers by f_A. This density function is derived below.

Suppose that a firm has a vacancy so that $N < J$. For simplicity assume that the cost of posting a vacancy is zero as this seems a reasonable approximation to the cost of putting a sign on the gate of the firm or registering a vacancy with a public employment service. Assume that all the individuals in the applicant pool who do not already have employment in the firm see the vacancy immediately and apply for the job.[5] If there are one or more applicants, the vacancy will be filled immediately. If there are no applicants, then the firm is assumed to keep up the sign for the vacancy and wait for a suitable applicant to arrive.[6] The consequences of this are that employment will be the minimum of A and J, and that expected profits will be given by

$$\pi = (p - w) \sum_{A=0}^{\infty} \min(J, A) f_A - cJ \qquad (10.4)$$

This is simply the equivalent of (10.2) and (w, J) will be chosen to maximize (10.4). To be able to make any progress, we need to say something about f_A.

To derive f_A, some assumptions about the rate at which individuals enter and leave the pool of potential workers are needed. Assume that if there are A potential workers in the pool, an extra individual joins at a rate $r_A(w, J)$. This arrival rate will depend on the wage because a higher wage makes a job in this firm more attractive, and possibly on J because this affects the level of employment which could conceivably affect recruitment rates. Similarly, assume that workers leave the pool at a rate $s_A(w, J)$. The possible dependence on w arises because the wage affects the desirability of jobs in this firm relative to other firms. The separation rate might depend on J because of differences in the effectiveness of employed and unemployed search. The simplest assumption is to assume that matching is random so that $r_A(w, J) = r(w)$ and that the rate at which people leave the pool of potential workers is independent of their status within it so that $s_A(w, J) = s(w)A$.

The problem described is analogous to well-known problems in queuing theory. One can think of A as being the stock of customers in the system at any moment in time. There are J counters dealing with the customers. If $A > J$, then there is a queue of customers and any counter

---

[5] This assumption is extreme but demonstrates that nothing depends on assuming that interested job applicants take time to see vacancies.

[6] This is essentially the stock-flow approach to matching suggested by Coles and Smith (1998), and used by Gregg and Petrongolo (1997) and Coles and Petrongolo (2002).

that becomes free will be occupied immediately. On the other hand, if $A < J$ there will be free counters. There is an enormous literature on the analysis of this sort of problem that can be drawn on to help us solve the problem (see, e.g., Gross and Harris 1974). A helpful result plus the special case of the basic model is provided in the following proposition.

Proposition 10.1. *The steady-state distribution of the number of potential workers is given by*

$$f_A = \frac{r_{A-1}r_{A-2}\dots r_0}{s_A s_{A-1}\dots s_1} f_0 \tag{10.5}$$

where f_0 is the probability that there are no potential workers. f_0 is then solved by using the fact that the sum of the density function must be equal to one.

If $r_A(w,J) = r(w)$ and $s_A(w,J) = s(w)A$, A has a steady-state Poisson distribution which is given by

$$f_A = \frac{\exp(-N(w))N(w)^A}{A!} \tag{10.6}$$

where $N(w) = r(w)/s(w)$.

Proof. See Appendix 10.

The notation $N(w)$ is used for the ratio of the flow of recruits to the separation rate as this is the supply of labor to the firm in the non-stochastic model. In the current model, it is the expected number of potential workers in the Poisson distribution (10.6). But, unlike the basic model there is some uncertainty about the actual number of potential workers: in fact, a feature of the Poisson distribution is that the variance is also given by $N(w)$.[7]

This framework reduces to the basic model of monopsony in two situations. First, if the set-up cost of a job c is zero, then there is no constraint on the number of jobs that a firm can create at no cost so it is obviously optimal to set $J = \infty$. Employment is then always the number of workers in the pool, the expected value of which is given by $N(w)$, that is, what we have used as steady-state employment in our basic models. In this case the only meaningful measure of a vacancy rate, $(J - E(N(w)))/J$, is one although, if the world was structured in this way, the concept of vacancy would probably never have occurred to anyone.

The other case in which this model reduces to the basic one is when we assume that workers are infinitesimal. Assume that each individual

---

[7] One can relax this; for example, it is well known that if there is some uncertainty about $N(w)$ then one can derive a negative binomial distribution for the number of applicants.

worker provides Δ of an efficiency unit of labor. Total employment of efficiency units of labor is then given by ΔN. We want to consider what happens as $\Delta \to 0$. As we consider this limit, we want to assume that the arrival rate of efficiency units of labor is the same so that we replace r by r/Δ. The expected number of workers is given by $N_\Delta(w) = r(w)/(s(w)\Delta)$. The expected number of efficiency units of labor in the pool is given by $E(\Delta N) = \Delta N_\Delta(w) = r(w)/s(w)$, that is, it is independent of Δ. But the variance of the number of efficiency units of labor in the pool is given by $\text{Var}(\Delta N) = \Delta^2 \text{Var}(N(w)) = \Delta^2 N_\Delta(w) = \Delta(r/s)$ which goes to zero as $\Delta \to 0$. Hence, the variance of the stock of potential workers goes to zero, that is, becomes non-stochastic. This then means it is optimal to have the firm set J equal to this level and the model then reduces to the simple model of (10.3) although vacancy rates are zero in this model.

So, for the analysis of vacancy rates to be interesting requires both that there is some set-up cost for a job and that an individual worker is non-negligible in relation to the size of the firm. Fortunately, neither of these assumptions is unreasonable.

The employer in this model wants to choose the wage, w, and the number of jobs, J, to maximize expected profits that are given by

$$\pi = (p - w)E(N) - cJ = (p - w)\sum_{A=0}^{\infty} \min(A, J)f_A - cJ \qquad (10.7)$$

This maximization problem is a bit awkward because the choice of J is restricted to the set of integers. This is rather inconvenient so we will, henceforth, approximate the Poisson distribution of (10.6) by assuming that A is normally distributed with mean $N(w)$ and variance $N(w)$, and that A can take any value. This is known to be a good approximation to the Poisson for values of $N(w)$ above 10 so that the error induced by doing this is likely to be small for firms of a reasonable size (one can verify this).

It is more convenient to model the choice variables for the firm not as (w, J) but as (w, X) where $X = [J - N(w)]/\sqrt{N(w)}$. Given that $N(w)$ is both the expected number of applicants and the variance in the number of applicants, $\Phi(X)$ is then the probability that $A \le J$ and is therefore the probability of the firm having a vacancy. The first-order conditions for (w, X) are given in the following proposition.

Proposition 10.2. *The first-order conditions for (w, X) where $X = [J - N(w)]/\sqrt{N(w)}$ can be written as*

$$\Phi(X) = \frac{p - w - c}{p - w} \qquad (10.8)$$

and

$$\frac{(p - c - w)\left[\dfrac{1}{2} + \dfrac{1}{2}\dfrac{N(w)}{E(N)}\right] - \dfrac{1}{2}c\left[\dfrac{J - E(N)}{E(N)}\right]}{w} = \varepsilon \tag{10.9}$$

where ε is the inverse of the elasticity of $N(w)$ with respect to w.

Proof. See Appendix 10.

As the left-hand side of (10.8) is the probability of a vacancy, this first-order condition can be interpreted as saying that a vacancy is more likely the lower is the wage and the lower is c relative to p. The intuition for this is straightforward. If the wage is low, profit-per-worker will be high so that the opportunity cost of having workers approaching the firm who cannot be employed because there are no jobs for them to do is high. This encourages the employers to create more jobs, raising the probability of a vacancy. And, the higher c is relative to $(p - w)$ the higher is the cost of having an unfilled job so that the employer will create few jobs.

(10.9) has some similarities to the usual first-order condition for the choice of the wage in monopsony. To see this, consider some special cases. For example, if $c = 0$, it reduces to the familiar condition $(p - w)/w = \varepsilon$. And, if the variance in labor supply goes to zero and $E(N) \to N(w)$, then $J = E(N)$, and (10.9) becomes $(p - w - c)/w = \varepsilon$. This suggests that the important ideas of monopsony still hold in this model. That is not surprising because this model still has the feature that the supply of labor to the firm is not infinitely elastic. But, a more interesting question is whether this model is consistent with the statistics on vacancies referred to earlier.

Proposition 10.3. *Some statistics on vacancy rates are as follows.*

1. *The proportion of firms with a vacancy is*

$$\text{probability of a vacancy} = \Phi(X) \tag{10.10}$$

2. *The average vacancy rate is given by*

$$\text{vacancy rate} = \frac{\sqrt{N(w)}[\phi(X) + X\Phi(X)]}{N(w) + \sqrt{N(w)}X} \tag{10.11}$$

3. *The expected number of applicants for a vacancy is*
   expected number of applicants

$$= \frac{\sqrt{N(w)}[N(w) + \sqrt{N(w)}X][\phi(X) - X(1 - \Phi(X))]}{N(w) - \sqrt{N(w)}[\phi(X) - X(1 - \Phi(X))]} \tag{10.12}$$

4. *The expected duration of a vacancy is given by*

expected vacancy duration

$$= \frac{\sqrt{N(w)}[N(w)[\phi(X) + X\Phi(X)] - \sqrt{N(w)}\Phi(X)]}{r(w)[N(w) - \sqrt{N(w)}[\phi(X) - X(1 - \Phi(X))]]} \quad (10.13)$$

Proof.   See Appendix 10.

While the equations, (10.10)–(10.13), provide the relevant information, they are not very informative. Accordingly, we present some simple
simulations in table 10.1. With the exception of the vacancy duration, all
the statistics in Proposition 10.3 depend only on $N(w)$ and X. The
vacancy duration also depends on $r = sN(w)$ so that information on the
separation rate can enable us to compute vacancy durations as well. We
normalize p to be equal to $(1 + c)$ so that the net productivity of workers
is independent of the ex ante cost of a job. We assume that the supply of
labor to the firm has a constant elasticity equal to ε_{Nw} and that $N(w)$ is

TABLE 10.1
Simulated Vacancy Statistics

Cost of a Job, c	Vacancy Rate (%)	Probability of a Vacancy	Expected Number of Applicants	Expected Vacancy Duration (Days)	Wage
A. Elasticity of labor supply facing the firm = 4					
0.2	5.6	0.5	3	62.4	0.8
0.4	3.2	0.33	4.8	34	0.803
0.6	2.2	0.24	6.1	22.9	0.805
0.8	1.7	0.19	7.1	17	0.806
B. Elasticity of labor supply facing the firm = 8					
0.2	3.6	0.35	4.5	37.5	0.89
0.4	1.9	0.21	6.7	19	0.892
0.6	1.2	0.15	8.1	12.4	0.894
0.8	0.9	0.12	9.2	9.1	0.895

Notes.
1. These simulations are based on the additional assumptions that $p = (1 + c)$, that the
annual separation rate is 25% and that the expected level of employment at the simple
monopsony wage is equal to 50. The optimal solution is found by solving the first-order
conditions in (10.8) and (10.9).
2. The vacancy rate is computed using the formula in (10.11), the probability of a vacancy
using the formula in (10.10), the expected number of applicants using the formula in
(10.12), and the expected vacancy duration using the formula in (10.13).

scaled such that, at the wage a simple monopsonist would choose, $(\varepsilon_{Nw}/(1 + \varepsilon_{Nw}))$, the size of the firm is 50. Finally, we assume that 25% of workers leave the firm in the course of the year and then use this to compute a daily flow of recruits to the firm $(=r)$.

Table 10.1 presents some statistics on vacancies and the wage chosen by the firm for different values of c, the set-up cost of a job and two values of ε_{Nw}, the elasticity of the labor supply curve facing the firm. By inspection of the final column in table 10.1, one can see that the wage chosen by the firm differs only very marginally from the optimal wage that a simple monopsonist would choose. The presence of ex ante set-up costs makes very little difference to the deviation between the marginal product and the wage.

However, these costs make an enormous difference to statistics on vacancies. If the set-up cost is low, for example, $c = 0.2$, one can see that if $\varepsilon_{Nw} = 4$, 50% of firms will have vacancies at any moment in time and 5.6% of jobs will not be filled. But if $c = 0.8$, only 19% of firms have vacancies and the vacancy rate will be 1.7%.

The extent of monopsony in the labor market does make a difference to the vacancy rate. The second half of table 10.1 presents vacancy statistics when the labor market is more competitive and $\varepsilon_{Nw} = 8$. The wage paid is now higher and, through (8.23) firms create fewer jobs. The vacancy rate if $c = 0.8$ is now only 0.9%. But, the important point is that vacancies can still be rare and vacancy durations short even in labor markets that have considerable monopsony power.

This very simple model does quite well in explaining the data. The US data used in Holzer (1994) and Holzer et al. (1991) has a vacancy rate of about 1.5%, suggesting that $c = 0.8$ if $\varepsilon_{Nw} = 4$. The model predicts that 19% of firms will have a vacancy, roughly consistent with the 12% estimated by Holzer (1994) for firms of that size. The predicted number of applicants for a job is 7, roughly consistent with the figures of 10 quoted by Holzer et al. (1991) particularly once one recognizes that the model here refers to the number of the applicants who are acceptable to the employer, while the figures in Holzer et al. (1991) also include workers who are not acceptable. And, finally the predicted vacancy duration is 17 days, compared with the 8 weeks reported in Holzer et al. (1991) (given that we have ignored the duration of the administrative procedure).

This section has shown how one can reproduce summary statistics about the incidence and duration of vacancies even in labor markets where employers have substantial market power. The reason why the observed vacancy rate has nothing to do with the extent of monopsony power is that the wage the firm pays is determined primarily by the elasticity of the expected supply of labor with respect to the wage.

Given the chosen wage, the number of jobs will be chosen to be approximately equal to the expected size of the labor pool. It will not be exactly equal: whether it is above or below $N(w)$ will depend on the job cost c. Vacancies are then "accidents," unavoidable but essentially random and conveying no useful information about the state of "labor demand" relative to "labor supply." Note, also that the fact that the majority of employers have no vacancy at a particular moment in time makes worker search for alternative jobs more difficult, contributing to the lack of competition in labor markets.

10.2 Filling Vacancies

This section investigates in more detail whether the empirical determinants of vacancies are consistent with the framework presented above. It uses data from a supplement to the 1990 UK Workplace Industrial Relations Survey (WIRS), the Employers' Manpower and Skills Practices Surveys (EMSPS). WIRS is a sample of slightly over 2000 workplaces that have more than 25 employees. It asks a wide range of questions about the personnel practices and other aspects of the workplace. The EMSPS is a supplementary survey completed by 1693 establishments designed to provide further information on recruitment, training, and turnover.

One of the questions asked in EMSPS is "how easily have you been able to fill vacancies in each occupational group in the last 12 months." Table 10.2 tabulates the responses for the nine occupational groups for which the question was asked. Employers report having most difficulty in filling vacancies in craft and skilled service occupations, and professional positions, and fewest problems in filling the least skilled manual jobs, and clerical and secretarial positions. In offering an explanation of this, we first need to offer an interpretation of the answers to the survey question. It seems most plausible to interpret the responses as being related to duration: vacancies are reported as hard-to-fill if the expected vacancy duration is long.[8]

One explanation for the occupational variation seen in table 10.2 is that employers are most likely to report problems with recruiting specialist workers because it is hard to cover for the lack of these

---

[8] If employers reported that they found it difficult to fill vacancies they were asked a subsequent question about whether this difficulty took the form of too few applicants or too low a quality. The responses were split approximately equally. This is consistent with our interpretation if one recognizes that applicants differ in quality and an employer also has a decision about a minimum acceptable quality of employee. See also Green et al. (1998) for a discussion of how this question relates to ideas of "skill shortages."

TABLE 10.2
The Difficulty of Filling Vacancies: UK EMSPS

| | How Easily Have You Been Able to Fill Vacancies in Each of the Occupational Groups in the Last 12 Months? (Percent) | | | | | |
	1 very easily	2	3	4	5 very difficult	Number of Observations
Routine, unskilled	32.2	41.9	10	11.6	4.3	768
Operative + assembly	32.9	40.9	11.8	10.6	3.7	550
Sales	20.2	33.6	18.3	24	3.9	432
Personal + protective services	24	42.2	15.1	13.7	5.1	396
Craft and skilled services	16.5	27.7	17.8	22.1	15.9	646
Clerical and secretarial	26.1	42.1	18.6	10.4	2.8	1061
Professional, associate, and technical	15.3	26.9	24	24.1	9.8	642
Professional	12.8	27.7	22.9	20.8	15.8	644
Management and administration	18.3	38.3	15.5	21.1	6.8	814

Notes.
1. All responses are weighted.

workers when there is a vacancy. Hence, forgone output is likely to be high when there is a vacancy in these jobs. On the other hand, vacancies in jobs that require general skills cause less of a problem because other workers in the firm can adjust their work patterns to mitigate the costs of the vacancy.

We might also be interested in the type of establishments that report recruitment difficulties within a given occupation. The main prediction of the monopsony model is that, other things being equal, we would expect a higher wage to be associated with fewer problems in recruitment. This is for two reasons. First, a higher wage leads to a lower level of job creation (see (10.8)) and, hence, a lower level of vacancies in higher-wage firms. Then, when vacancies do occur, there is more likely to be a suitable initial applicant and, hence, a higher chance of the vacancy being filled immediately. Second, the flow of recruits is likely to be higher so that vacancies are likely to be filled quicker even if there is no suitable initial applicant.

Table 10.3 presents some ordered probit models for the responses to the question on recruitment difficulties tabulated in table 10.2 for four occupational groups: the unskilled, operatives, the skilled, and clerical/ secretarial.[9] The first column for each occupational group shows that recruitment difficulties are less likely in high-wage firms. The second column then includes some information on the extent of the recruitment activity of the firm by including the log of employment in the relevant occupation in the establishment, the recruitment rate (defined as the number of recruits, both internal and external, as a fraction of employment in the previous year), and the fraction of recruits to that occupational group that are internal. There is strong evidence that recruitment difficulties are less in higher-wage firms. There is also strong evidence that recruitment is easier in labor markets with high unemployment rates for the unskilled and the skilled, and that recruitment difficulties are greater when the recruitment rate is higher. This last result could be because, in a steady state, the recruitment rate is the separation rate and a high separation rate indicates that a job in the establishment is not very attractive. Alternatively, it may be that a high recruitment rate places greater strains on resources within the establishment.

This section has shown that, except for specialized positions, few firms report difficulties in filling vacancies. But, as the previous section has emphasized, this implies little about the extent of monopsony in the labor market. The evidence that, within occupations, high-wage firms do have fewer recruitment difficulties is consistent with the monopsony model.

[9] Not all the groups reported in table 10.2 are included because the wage information in WIRS is not recorded for the same occupations as the recruitment information.

TABLE 10.3
The Determinants of the Difficulty in Filling Vacancies

Occupation	Routine Unskilled		Operative and Assembly		Craft and Skilled Service		Clerical and Secretarial	
	1	2	1	2	1	2	1	2
ln(hourly wage)	-0.47	-0.39	-0.68	-0.46	-1.32	-1.39	-0.31	-0.42
	(0.17)	(0.19)	(0.25)	(0.29)	(0.40)	(0.52)	(0.16)	(0.18)
ln(employment)		0.002		0.022		-0.028		0.167
		(0.051)		(0.065)		(0.104)		(0.047)
Recruitment rate		0.699		0.665		0.414		1.44
		(0.169)		(0.218)		(0.624)		(0.251)
Proportion of internal recruits		0.711		0.306		-0.286		0.632
		(0.287)		(0.254)		(0.405)		(0.158)
Proportion female	0.047	0.143	0.133	0.114	-0.804	-1.28	0.726	0.843
	(0.175)	(0.197)	(0.219)	(0.248)	(0.389)	(0.54)	(0.230)	(0.258)
Local unemployment rate	-0.166	-0.142	0.036	0.082	-0.119	-0.169	-0.020	-0.009
	(0.029)	(0.033)	(0.037)	(0.043)	(0.049)	(0.064)	(0.022)	(0.025)
Number of observations	532	421	364	302	202	142	846	710
Pseudo-R^2	0.075	0.095	0.071	0.084	0.142	0.178	0.034	0.06

Notes.
1. The dependent variable is the response to the question described in table 10.2. A higher value indicates greater difficulty in filling vacancies. The estimation method is an ordered probit.
2. The recruitment rate is the number of recruits (both internal and external) into that occupation in the previous 12 months. The proportion of internal recruits is the fraction of those recruits who came from elsewhere in the firm.
3. All observations are weighted.

10.3 The Technology of Matching: Random versus Balanced Matching

Previous discussion has assumed that workers are equally likely to contact any employer, large or small, that is, we have what Burdett and Vishwanath (1988) term random matching. They suggest the alternative of "balanced matching" where the probability of contacting an employer is proportional to employment in the firm.[10] There are plausible reasons for thinking that not all matching may be random. For example, a common search method is to ask friends and family about job openings: this method is likely to sample firms in proportion to their employment, leading to balanced matching. One might wonder why this matters but, as shown below, the relative importance of balanced and random matching is important in determining the amount of long-run monopsony power that employers possess.[11]

Consider the following simple way of combining both balanced and random matching in the same model (this draws heavily on the set-up in Mortensen and Vishwanath 1994). Assume that the flow of recruits to the firm is given by

$$R(N, w) = [\alpha + (1 - \alpha)N]R(w) \qquad (10.14)$$

If $\alpha = 1$ this reduces to the random matching model in which the flow of recruits depends only on the wage and not on employment, while if $\alpha = 1$ we have pure balanced matching and the flow of recruits is proportional

---

[10] Burdett and Vishwanath (1988) criticize the assumption of random matching on the grounds that "an unfortunate consequence of random matching is that a firm, by splitting itself in two, can increase its number of potential employees ... and, thus, possibly increase its profits." (p. 1050). One must be careful about accepting this criticism of random matching as its validity depends on what exactly a firm is thought to be. One should probably think of firms as being located in some space, their position defined by their geographical location and by the type of jobs that they offer. Although we have set up the model as being one in which all firms are attractive to all workers, one could easily modify the model to an isomorphic one in which only a certain proportion of workers are interested in working for a particular firm whatever the wage. In this case, a firm cannot simply divide itself and double the number of applicants. It would need to locate elsewhere in the product space. In our basic model where we assumed that the number of firms is fixed, we effectively assumed that it is infinitely costly to set up a new firm: in this case, one cannot even conceive of a firm dividing itself. That is obviously too extreme but, in the free entry model of section 3.1, firms in equilibrium are simply making a level of profits equal to the set-up cost. In this case, the firm cannot divide itself without also doubling its fixed costs so that total profit will be unchanged.

[11] Note that the discussion here is about whether large employers have an intrinsic advantage over small firms in recruitment. This is not the same as the question of whether large firms choose to spend more resources on recruitment: the model of section 3.2 discussed this issue.

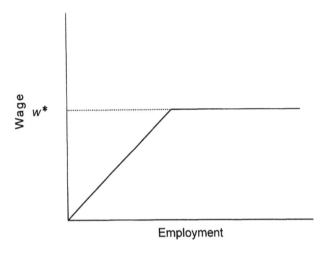

Figure 10.1 The long-run supply of labor to the firm with balanced and random matching.

to employment. Hence, α can be thought of as a measure of the relative importance of random matching. In a steady state, we must have $s(w)N = R(N, w)$ which, using (10.14) can be written as

$$s(w)N = [\alpha + (1 - \alpha)N]R(w) \qquad (10.15)$$

If all matching is random $(\alpha = 1)$, this leads to the familiar upward-sloping labor supply curve. However, if all matching is balanced $(\alpha = 0)$, matters are very different. If the wage is such that $s(w) > R(w)$ then the firm will, in the long-run, see its employment decline to zero. Alternatively if the wage is such that $s(w) < R(w)$ employment can (if the firm so wishes) grow without limit. What this means is that the long-run supply of labor to the firm is perfectly elastic at the wage where $s(w) = R(w)$, that is, the labor supply curve to an individual firm is effectively the competitive one.

For the intermediate case where $0 < \alpha < 1$ the labor supply curve will resemble that drawn in Figure 10.1 where w^* solves $s(w^*) = (1 - \alpha)R(w^*)$.[12] It can readily be seen that the labor supply curve to an individual firm has a monopsonistic part and a competitive part. The lower is α, the more important is the competitive part of the labor supply schedule.

The conclusion that labor markets will be less monopsonistic the more important is balanced matching in the recruitment process can be found in the general equilibrium models analyzed by Burdett and Vishwanath

---

[12] Note that there may be no wage at which this equality can be satisfied.

(1988) and Mortensen and Vishwanath (1994). Both of these papers show that equilibrium is the perfectly competitive equilibrium if there is only balanced matching.

Given that the extent of monopsony in labor markets is related to the importance of balanced matching, the next section considers some empirical evidence on the matter.

10.4 Empirical Evidence on Random and Balanced Matching

To investigate the importance of balanced matching, one might think of taking a direct approach and investigating whether the flow of recruits is higher in larger firms, that is, to try to estimate (10.14) directly. However, this is not likely to be a fruitful approach as there is a serious problem of reverse causality in the estimation of (10.14) as employment will be higher in firms with a high level of recruits. To work, this approach would need to use as an instrument a variable that affects the separation rate (as this affects employment) but does not affect the flow of recruits directly: it is hard to imagine what such a variable might be.

Instead of using the absolute flow of recruits to estimate the importance of balanced matching, one could use the relative flow of recruits through random and balanced methods. We have

$$\text{probability of recruit through balanced matching} = \frac{\dfrac{1-\alpha}{\alpha}N}{1+\dfrac{1-\alpha}{\alpha}N}$$

$$(10.16)$$

so that how this probability varies with N can be thought to give some estimate of α. If we could identify which recruits came from balanced matching and which from random, it would be a simple matter to determine the relative importance of balanced matching. Of course, the relevant data are not available but we do have information on the search methods used by job-seekers and those recruited into jobs. Some search methods are more plausibly thought of as leading to random matching and some to balanced matching. For example, large firms have little advantage over small firms in the use of the public employment service while large firms have an advantage in the use of existing workers to inform their friends and relatives of job opportunities (this is the motivation for balanced matching given in Mortensen and Vishwanath 1994). Of course, there is likely to be some element of guesswork in deciding whether a particular search method is associated with random or

TABLE 10.4
Number of Search Methods

Number of Search Methods	US (CPS)	UK (LFS)	
	Unemployed (%)	Unemployed (%)	Employed (%)
1	33.2	7.3	16.5
2	53.9	9.5	19.1
3	8.2	14	18.6
4	3.1	16.2	18.7
5	1.6	17.8	14.4
6	0	17.9	8.4
7	–	11.5	3.3
>8	–	5.8	1
Mean (standard deviation)	1.86 (0.81)	4.58 (1.96)	3.39 (1.74)
Number of observations	47169	60416	59104

Notes.
1. Data from the CPS are from the period 1/97–12/98 and from the LFS for 12/96–11/98.

balanced matching but we can test our guesses by seeing whether large firms recruit more frequently through balanced methods.

The US CPS asks unemployed job-seekers to list up to six search methods that they have used in the previous four weeks. The UK LFS allows the unemployed to list up to eleven methods[13] and also asks the same question of employed job-seekers. In addition, they are asked to name their most important search method. Table 10.4 starts to analyze these answers by tabulating the number of search methods recorded on average. In the United States, the average number of search methods reported by the unemployed is 1.9 while it is 4.6 in the United Kingdom. Employed job-seekers in the United Kingdom report using rather fewer search methods—the mean is 3.4. There are a number of possible explanations for why the unemployed in the United Kingdom report more search methods than those in the United States. One is that they are given the option to list more. Although no-one takes the opportunity to list the maximum allowed, there is a considerable amount of overlap in some of the methods listed which may lead to multiple recording of what is essentially the same activity. For example, the UK LFS lists separately "answer advertisements in newspapers," "study situations vacant in newspapers," and "wait for the results of an application."

[13] Actually 14, if the three search methods specific to those seeking self-employment are included.

TABLE 10.5
Methods of Looking for Work

	US (CPS) method mentioned	UK (LFS) method mentioned		UK (LFS) Most Important Method	
	Unemployed	Unemployed	Employed	Unemployed	Employed
Contacted public employment service or other public body	22.4	74.9	23	28.7	6.6
Applied directly to employers	64	56.9	43.1	2.9	7.4
Placed or answered advertisements	14.3	64.4	53.9	9.9	13.4
Sent out resumes/applications	40	49.3	44.5	8.8	2.3
Looked at advertisements	19.6	91.2	87.2	35.3	49.6
Contacted friends/ relatives/unions	14.9	66.5	47.1	2.9	9.1
Private employment agency	5.6	23.9	23.9	10.3	7
Other	4	8.9	9.3	1.2	2.3
Number of observations	47169	60416	59104	60100	58650

Notes.
1. Data from the CPS are from the period 1/97–12/98 and from the LFS for 12/96–11/98.
2. The classification of search methods is different in the two countries and some re-classification has been done.

Table 10.5 summarizes the data on the search methods mentioned. The listing of search methods is not exactly the same in the two countries and this table reflects some judgments as to the equivalence of particular answers. As job-seekers in the United Kingdom report using more methods than those in the United States it is dangerous to compare the US and UK numbers too literally. But several factors stand out. First, use of the public employment service (PES) is much more widespread in the United Kingdom than the United States. There is little surprise here as the US PES has a reputation for attracting only low-quality workers and jobs. The same is true of the United Kingdom (note that the employed are much less likely to use the PES than the unemployed) but to a lesser extent.[14] But the unemployed in the United Kingdom also seem more likely to use private employment agencies and friends and/or relatives. In contrast, direct approaches to employers seem to be more prevalent in the United States. The final two columns examine the most important search methods as reported by UK job-seekers. Newspapers are the most important search method for both the unemployed and the employed although the PES is also important for the unemployed.

Which search methods should be classified as balanced matching and which as random? As the PES is free to employers, large firms are likely to have no advantage over small firms in its use. One might think the same is true of the use of private employment agencies and newspaper advertisements as the cost of using these is the same for small and large firms (although there may be cost advantages to large firms if they can advertise multiple vacancies). For these search methods, it is natural to assume that, for a given intensity of recruitment, the flow of job applicants will depend only on the wage and not on employer size, that is, we have random matching.

On the other hand, it is plausible to believe that large employers have an advantage over small employers when recruitment is through the friends and relatives of its current workforce as it is plausible to believe that the number of recruits forthcoming through this method will be increasing with the size of the firm.

For direct approach by workers to employers, it is unclear whether it is better to model this matching process as random or balanced. It depends on whether the search of workers is completely random or directed in some way and, if directed, the method of sampling used. It seems plausible to think that workers are more likely to approach the local sweet factory about work than the local sweet shop so that workers disproportionately approach larger employers: in this case, balanced matching would be more important than random matching.

---

[14] There is probably a vicious circle here. The lower the quality of jobs available through the PES, the less likely are "good" workers to use it, which then discourages firms from trying to fill good jobs through it.

TABLE 10.6
How Workers Get Jobs: UK LFS

	Total	Number of Employees				
		1–10	11–19	20–24	25–49	50+
Replying to a job ad	26.8	24.0	26.3	28.4	28.5	28.0
Public employment service	11.6	11.8	13.3	13.7	11.9	10.7
Private employment agency	8.3	3.7	4.3	5.6	7.5	12.5
Hearing from employee	28.7	33.0	30.9	28.1	28.8	25.5
Direct application	13.4	11.7	13.9	14.3	13.3	14.3
Other	11.2	15.7	11.2	9.9	9.9	9.0
Number of observations	66693	18320	7103	3360	8275	29635

Notes.
1. These data are the responses to the question of how current job was obtained asked in the UK LFS of those with less than three months of job tenure. Data come from the period 12/92–11/97. Public employment service includes the responses "jobcentre", "careers office" and "jobclub" (the last two categories are small).

The UK LFS also has information on the method by which new employees were recruited. Table 10.6 tabulates this information against employer size. As can be seen from the first column, "heard through employee" is the largest single category accounting for the method that 28% of new employees used to find their job. We might expect the importance of this method to give an advantage to large firms in recruitment. However, as the subsequent columns show, the proportion of hires through this method is actually smaller in large firms which is not what we would expect from (10.16) if balanced matching was important.

Of course, it is possible that these results come from a failure to control adequately for other factors. So, table 10.7 estimates a multinomial logit model for the method of recruitment. The omitted category is the "heard through employee." But, controlling for other factors does not make very much difference. New recruits in large firms are more likely to have been recruited through channels other than "word-of-mouth" for every method except "other." These differences are highly significant.

This section has argued that large firms do not seem to have a relative advantage over small firms in the use of recruitment methods which we would, a priori, have expected. In particular, they do not seem more likely to recruit workers through word-of-mouth. Why might this be the case? One plausible explanation is that large firms know their workers less well and are less likely to trust workers recommended to them. For example, some large shops refuse to recruit relatives or friends of existing workers for fear that they will find it easier to collude in shop-lifting. So, while the

TABLE 10.7
Determinants of Methods of Obtaining Job

	Replying to Job Ad	Public Employment Service	Private Employment Agency	Direct Application	Other
Log (workplace size)	0.111	0.025	0.495	0.148	-0.141
	(0.011)	(0.014)	(0.020)	(0.013)	(0.014)
Female	0.559	-0.069	0.190	0.156	-0.039
	(0.028)	(0.034)	(0.042)	(0.032)	(0.035)
Black	-0.142	0.000	-0.181	-0.017	-0.065
	(0.072)	(0.091)	(0.101)	(0.086)	(0.094)
Experience/10	0.070	-0.639	-0.084	-0.194	0.049
	(0.033)	(0.004)	(0.053)	(0.040)	(0.042)
(Experience/10) squared	-0.017	0.106	0.003	0.029	0.022
	(0.008)	(0.010)	(0.013)	(0.010)	(0.010)
Degree	0.703	-0.364	0.675	0.363	0.613
	(0.075)	(0.100)	(0.116)	(0.087)	(0.091)
A-Level	0.198	-0.044	0.205	0.144	0.006
	(0.074)	(0.094)	(0.117)	(0.086)	(0.091)
O-Level	0.049	0.170	0.099	-0.052	-0.083
	(0.072)	(0.089)	(0.113)	(0.083)	(0.087)
No qualification	-0.482	0.061	-0.903	-0.130	-0.442
	(0.077)	(0.094)	(0.132)	(0.088)	(0.093)
Number of observations	41972				
Pseudo-R^2	0.038				

Notes.
1. The estimated model is a multinomial logit where the omitted category is "heard through employee." The data used are as described in table 10.6.

flow of applicants through balanced matching may be larger in the large firms, the average quality may be lower.

10.5 Estimating the Labor Cost Function

Section 2.3 introduced the concept of the "labor cost function" as a way of thinking in more general terms about monopsony. Recall that the labor cost function, $C(w, N)$ is defined as the cost per worker of keeping employment at N if the employer pays a wage w. The most important elements of the labor cost function are likely to be recruitment and training costs. As this chapter is (at least in part) about the recruitment process, this seems the natural place to discuss empirical evidence on the form of the labor cost function. As discussed in chapter 2, the critical issue is whether there are diseconomies of scale in recruitment. This hypothesis is difficult to test as data on recruitment and training costs are hard to come by: for this reason we use a survey conducted by the UK Institute for Personnel Development (IPD) each year from 1997 to 1999. These surveys were the latest in a series of postal surveys of personnel professionals in the private and public sectors: there were 2016 respondents in our sample period. The survey asks questions about the number of staff that have left and been recruited over the previous year for ten broad occupational groups and on recruitment difficulties, redundancy, and, importantly from our point of view, the costs of labor turnover. The main weaknesses of these data are that the sample is non-representative, there is no information on wages, and only rudimentary information on workplace characteristics.

Respondents were asked to estimate the cost of turnover per individual employee: the answers were banded and are summarized in the first seven rows of table 10.8. Using mid-points of the bands, we get the estimates reported in the row of table 10.8 labeled "average turnover cost". From this, it might seem that turnover costs are much higher for the more skilled occupations. However, the labor cost function is defined as the cost per employee, not per recruit so that these estimates have to be multiplied by the turnover rate to get an amortized cost per employee. This reduces the differences in the turnover costs because turnover rates are higher for less-skilled workers. One also needs to evaluate these costs relative to weekly earnings. The penultimate row of table 10.8 shows weekly earnings from the LFS for comparable broad occupational groups. Turnover costs as a fraction of total labor costs are then presented in the final line. There no longer seems to be any particular relationship between turnover costs and skill levels so turnover costs would seem to be as important at the bottom end of the skills distribution as at the top.

TABLE 10.8
The Size of Turnover Costs: UK IPD Data

Turnover cost (£)	Managerial	Professional	Technical	Clerical	Sales	Personal	Craft and Skilled	Operatives	Unskilled
<750	6.0	3.7	6.0	23.9	15.3	31.7	35.5	63.1	44.8
750–1500	11.0	8.7	15.9	33.6	15.8	33.6	32.2	24.5	19.1
1500–3000	22.7	24.2	32.6	29.8	26.8	20.8	22.6	9.3	22.4
3000–5000	27.8	28.6	22.7	8.8	19.1	9.1	6.5	1.6	7.7
5000–7500	15.1	17.9	13.3	2.6	12.4	1.5	1.9	0.4	3.3
7500–10000	9.2	9.7	5.7	1.0	6.3	2.2	0.7	0.5	1.0
>10000	8.2	7.0	3.7	0.3	4.3	1.1	0.5	0.5	1.7
Average turnover cost	4749	4823	3736	1783	3574	1777	1528	1170	937
Turnover rate (% per year)	15.6	23.4	19.0	26.2	26.6	28.4	23.7	28.3	34.2
Turnover rate × turnover cost (£ per week)	15.2	20.6	14.1	10.1	17.7	7.4	7.5	6.5	6.3
Average weekly earnings	482	449	353	208	158	169	294	262	
Turnover cost as fraction of total cost	3.1	4.6	4.0	4.8	11.2	4.4	2.6	2.4	2.4

Suppose that the cost of a given level of recruits can be written as the following iso-elastic function of the wage, recruitment, and employment:

$$\ln C(w, R, N) \equiv \beta_0 - \beta_w \ln(w) + \beta_R \ln(R) - \beta_N \ln(N) \qquad (10.17)$$

Both the level of recruitment and employment are included to allow for the possibility (amongst others) that it is the ratio of recruitment to employment that determines the costs of recruitment. We would like to be able to estimate this function but, unfortunately, the IPD data has no information on wages. However, we can still obtain some insight into the marginal costs of recruitment. Assume that the separation rate can be written as $\ln(s) = s - \gamma \ln(w)$. Then, as $sN = R$, the labor cost function can be written as the following function of w and N:

$$\ln C(w, N) \equiv \beta_0 + \beta_R s - (\beta_w + \beta_R \gamma) \ln(w) + (\beta_R - \beta_N) \ln(N) \quad (10.18)$$

so that it is $\beta \equiv \beta_R - \beta_N$ that determines whether there are diseconomies of scale in recruitment. The wage will be chosen to satisfy (2.12); the first-order condition for this can be written as

$$\ln(w) = \frac{(\beta_0 + \beta_R s) + \ln(\beta_w + \beta_R \gamma) + \beta \ln(N)}{1 + \beta_w + \beta_R \gamma} \qquad (10.19)$$

Substituting into (10.18) leads to

$$\ln C \equiv \frac{\beta_0 + \beta_R s + \beta \ln(N)}{1 + \beta_w + \gamma \beta_R} - \frac{\beta_w + \gamma \beta_R}{1 + \beta_w + \gamma \beta_R} \ln(\beta_w + \gamma \beta_R) \quad (10.20)$$

(10.20) expresses the labor cost function in terms of N alone. Note, that the coefficient on N is not the β in which we are interested but $\beta/(1 + \beta_w + \gamma \beta_R)$ so the coefficient is biased towards zero. But one can still look to see whether there is evidence that $\beta > 0$.

In estimating (10.20) there is an endogeneity problem associated with the fact that unobserved differences in turnover costs that are in the error in our equation are likely to be negatively correlated with the level of employment. It is not clear that much can be done about this with the limited data available in the IPD data set except to notice that this will tend to bias our coefficients towards zero so that a finding that $\beta > 0$ remains convincing evidence against the hypothesis that $\beta = 0$.

Table 10.9 presents some estimates of the labor cost function of (10.20) using the IPD data. In the first row, all the observations are pooled together and job, sector, and year controls are included, and an interval regression is estimated as the dependent variable is banded. The coefficient on the log of employment is 0.060 and is significantly different from zero. This is evidence that $\beta > 0$ and the labor cost function is increasing in employment. The next row estimates the model by OLS using midpoints of the turnover cost bands as measures of the turnover costs: this

TABLE 10.9
The Costs of Recruitment: UK IPD Data

Sample	Estimation Method	Coefficient on Ln(Employment)	Firm Controls	Sector Controls	Job Controls	Number of Observations	R^2
All	Interval regression	0.060 (0.008)	No	Yes	Yes	4761	
All	OLS	0.059 (0.009)	No	Yes	Yes	4761	0.40
All	OLS	0.023 (0.008)	Yes	No	Yes	4819	0.61

Notes.
1. The dependent variable is for the log of the recruitment cost per worker. All regressions pool the responses for 1997–99. Sector dummies, job dummies (where appropriate), and year dummies are included. The classification of sectors differs in the two years so dummies for each sector-year combination are included. Regressions are weighted using the level of employment. All standard errors are hetero-scedastic consistent.

makes little difference to the estimated coefficient. The third row estimates a more demanding model where individual firm dummies are included. The coefficient drops (as we might expect from the likely increase in the importance of measurement error) but still remains significantly different from zero so that recruitment costs are significantly higher within firms in occupations where there is a high level of employment.

These results do suggest the presence of diseconomies of scale in recruitment but the quality of the data means that caution should be exercised in interpreting these results.

10.6 Lay-Offs

So far this chapter has discussed the decisions of employers on hiring and recruitment activities. But, this is only a partial picture of the employer policies that influence the level of employment in a firm: the other side of the coin is the decision to lay off existing workers.

The simple models we have worked with do not have an interesting model of lay-offs: we have simply assumed an exogenously given job destruction rate. An interesting theory of lay-offs requires some variation in productivity over time so that a worker who is profitably employed now need not be profitably employed in the future. There are a number of models of this type in the matching literature, starting with Mortensen and Pissarides (1994) who endeavor to explain the empirical regularities identified by Davis et al. (1996). One could readily develop similar models for wage-posting firms.

There are a number of implications from such models. First, if it is costly and/or difficult to hire workers, one will not fire workers immediately their productivity falls below their wage. The reason is that there will be some probability that their productivity will increase in the future. The result will be something like labor hoarding, where employment fluctuations are smoothed.

Second, lay-offs in the Mortensen–Pissarides model are voluntary: they only occur when there is no surplus left in the match. But, in reality, most lay-offs seem to be involuntary. There are a number of ways of generating this. As discussed in the previous chapter, lay-offs will typically be involuntary if some type of efficiency wage effect is at work: just as employers will not want to hire workers at their reservation wage, they will want to fire them before their wage is that low. Some type of wage rigidity can help to explain why lay-offs are involuntary. Employers undoubtedly have more market power over existing workers than new potential recruits. If an employer gets a reputation for cutting wages (for reasons that may be hard to justify to workers), this may hinder their ability to recruit workers. Lay-offs are different from wage cuts in that the former hurt both employers and workers, whereas the latter benefit employers. Hence, there are good reasons to think that lay-offs will be primarily involuntary.

10.7 Conclusions

This chapter discusses the process by which firms recruit workers. This takes the place of the labor demand curve in more traditional labor economics. A theoretical framework is provided for interpreting vacancy statistics based on it being costly to create jobs and the supply of labor to a firm being stochastic. We have argued that this framework can easily explain the stylized facts about vacancies (that vacancy rates and vacancy durations are typically very low) and these facts are perfectly compatible with employers having non-negligible market power. The channels by which employers recruit workers has been discussed; we found that there is little evidence that large employers have an advantage over small employers because of the importance of personal contacts in the recruitment process. Finally, some evidence on recruitment and training costs has been presented to suggest that employers do face increasing marginal costs of recruitment as is required for employers to have market power.

Appendix 10

Proof of Proposition 10.1

The easiest way to see the validity of (10.5) is to consider the steady state of a process in which f_A might change over time. So, let us denote by $f_A(\tau)$ the probability of A potential workers at time τ and by $f_A(\tau + \Delta)$ the probability a short time Δ later. We must have

$$f_A(\tau + \Delta) = [1 - r_A\Delta - s_A\Delta]f_A(\tau) + s_{A+1}\Delta f_{A+1}(\tau) + r_{A-1}\Delta f_{A-1}(\tau)$$
$$(10.21)$$

(10.21) says that the probability of having A potential workers at $(\tau + \Delta)$ is the probability of A workers at τ multiplied by the probability that no-one has left or arrived plus the probability there were $(A + 1)$ workers at τ and one has left plus the probability there were $(A - 1)$ workers at τ and one has arrived. In a steady-state, we must have $f_A(\tau + \Delta) = f_A(\tau)$ in which case (10.21) becomes

$$(r_A + s_A)f_A = s_{A+1}f_{A+1} + r_{A-1}f_{A-1} \qquad (10.22)$$

which can be thought of as saying that separations equal recruits. One can readily verify that $f_{A+1} = (r_A f_A)/s_{A+1}$ implies (10.22) and repeated substitution leads to (10.5).

If $r_A(w, K) = r(w)$ and $s_A(w, J) = s(w)A$, substitution into (10.5) confirms that (10.6) is the solution.

Proof of Proposition 10.2

The expected level of employment $E(N)$ is given by

$$E(N) = \int \min[A, J]f(A)dA = \int^J Af(A)dA + J\int_J f(A)dA \qquad (10.23)$$

Using the fact that $A \sim N(N(w), N(w))$, the definition of X as $X = [J - N(w)]/\sqrt{N(w)}$ and well-known results on means of truncated normal distributions (see Maddala 1983), (10.23) can be written as

$$E(N) = N(w) - \sqrt{N(w)}[\phi(X) - X(1 - \Phi(X))] \qquad (10.24)$$

where $\phi(\cdot)$ is the density function for the standard normal distribution. Hence, profits in (10.7) can be written as

$$\pi = (p - c - w)N(w) - \sqrt{N(w)}[(p - w)[\phi(X) - X(1 - \Phi(X))] + cX]$$
$$(10.25)$$

Taking the first-order condition of (10.25) with respect to X, and using the fact that for the standard normal $\phi'(X) = -X\phi(X)$, leads to (10.8). Taking the first-order condition with respect to the wage leads to

$$(p - c - w)N'(w) - N(w)$$

$$- \frac{1}{2}\frac{N'(w)}{\sqrt{N(w)}}[(p - w)[\phi(X) - X(1 - \Phi(X))] + cX]$$

$$+ \sqrt{N(w)}[\phi(X) - X(1 - \Phi(X))] \qquad (10.26)$$

which, using (10.24) to eliminate $[\phi(X) - X(1 - \Phi(X))]$ can be written as

$$(p - c - w)N'(w) - N(w) - \frac{1}{2}\frac{N'(w)}{\sqrt{N(w)}}\left[(p - w)\frac{N(w) - E(N)}{\sqrt{N(w)}} + cX\right]$$

$$+ [N(w) - E(N)]$$

$$(10.27)$$

which, using the definition of X and after some re-arrangement, can be written as (10.9).

Proof of Proposition 10.3

1. The probability of a vacancy is the probability that $A \leq J$ which is given by $\Phi(X)$, that is, (10.10).

2. The vacancy rate measured as a fraction of total jobs is $(J - E(N))/J$. Expected employment $E(N)$ is given by (10.24) and $J = N(w) + X\sqrt{N(w)}$ so that this can be written as (10.11).

3. One might also be interested in the expected number of applicants that are received when a vacancy occurs. Suppose, prior to the vacancy occurring, there were A in the pool. Then, given that one of these must have left the firm, the initial number of applicants must be given by $\max(A - J, 0)$. But the expected number of applicants is not simply $E(\max(A - J, 0)$ as vacancies are more likely to occur when employment is larger. Denote by $f^v(A)$ the probability of being in state A given that a vacancy is just about to occur. Then, given our assumption about the processes generating arrivals and separations, we must have the following relationship between $f^v(A)$ and $f(A)$:

$$f^v(A) = \frac{s\min(A, J)f(A)}{s\int \min(a, J)f(a)da} = \frac{\min(A, J)f(A)}{E(N)} \qquad (10.28)$$

The expected number of initial applicants is then given by

$$\text{expected number of applicants} = \frac{\int \max(A - J, 0)\min(A, J)f(A)dA}{E(N)}$$

$$= \frac{J\int_J (A - J)f(A)dA}{E(N)}$$

$$(10.29)$$

which, using the standard features of the expectation of a truncated standard normal and the definition of J is (10.12).

4. Assume, without loss of generality that vacancies are filled in on a first in, first out principle so that outstanding vacancies must be filled before any new vacancy. Suppose that a vacancy occurs when the initial

state was A so that this vacancy will only be filled when $(J - A)$ workers have arrived. With the assumption of a Poisson arrival process of rate r the expected time of arrival of $(J - A)$ workers is given by $(J - A)/r$. Hence, the expected vacancy duration is given by

$$\text{expected vacancy duration} = \frac{1}{r} \int \max(J - A, 0) f^v(A) dA$$

$$= \frac{\int^J (J - A) A f(A)}{r E(N)} dA \tag{10.30}$$

where the second equality follows from (10.28). Converting to X this can be written as

$$\int^J (J - A) A f(A) dA = \sqrt{N(w)} \int^X (X - x) \Big[N(w) + x \sqrt{N(w)} \Big] \phi(x) dx \tag{10.31}$$

which leads to (10.13).

11

Human Capital and Training

THIS chapter discusses the economics of human capital acquisition and training. There is a well-established, competitive market approach to this subject perhaps best represented by Becker's classic book *Human Capital* (Becker 1993). Becker's book is justly famous for its distinction between general human capital (skills that are perfectly transferable between employers) and specific human capital (skills of use to only one employer). Becker argued that workers will bear the cost of investment in general human capital as competition among employers will ensure that the wage is always equal to the marginal product so that workers will appropriate all the returns to investment. On the other hand, employers should bear the cost of investment in specific human capital as they reap the gains from this investment.[1] Furthermore, he argued that there is no reason why a competitive market (which should include a well-functioning capital market) should not provide the efficient level of training so that there is little or no case for government intervention.

Although Becker's approach dominates economic thinking about training, it is not without its problems. In particular, employers often seem to pay for the acquisition of general skills by their workers, something that should not happen in Becker's world. While it is always possible to argue that the skills being given to workers are specific, there remains a strong suspicion that this is not really true. Related to this, it seems hard to find evidence that, other things being equal, workers offered general training for which they do not pay directly are paid less than those who are not.

This chapter discusses the way in which Becker's analysis needs to be modified if employers have some market power over their workers. It discusses whether the level of investment in human capital is efficient in such a market, who will be trained, and what the consequences will be. Introducing frictions in the labor market introduces certain ambiguities in Becker's celebrated definition of general and specific human capital that were recognized by Becker himself. The reason is that frictions in the labor market make it costly (in terms of time and/or money) for a worker

[1] The conclusion about specific investments is often modified to say that both the returns to and the costs of specific investments should be shared between worker and employer in order to deter quits. As, discussed in chapter 5, this conclusion implicitly relies on the assumption that the labor market is monopsonistic.

to move from one firm to another so that the productivity of a worker is always strictly above what it is in their next best alternative. Becker (1993: 50) states that, "in extreme types of monopsony ... all training, no matter what its nature would be specific to the firm." Using this argument, the classification of a particular skill as general or specific is determined not just by technological factors but also by the nature of the labor market. Although Becker hints that monopsony in the labor market simply affects the way one classifies skills as general or specific, and hence has implications about who should pay for training but no necessary implications for the efficiency of the market for human capital acquisition, he provides no formal analysis and this chapter demonstrates that this is not generally the case.

Hence, one is left with the choice between accepting Becker's definition of the generality of skills as determined by market structure as well as technology but dropping his conclusion that the market for training will always be efficient, or to base the classification of skills as general or specific solely on technology and accept that Becker's analysis only applies to competitive markets. The latter seems the better course of action as it preserves more of Becker's contribution. So, this chapter follows Stevens (1994) in assuming that general training raises the productivity of the worker by the same amount in all similar firms (even if it is costly to find them)—Stevens (1994) terms this transferable training—and specific training only affects the productivity in this firm.

Three types of skill acquisition are discussed in this chapter. The first section considers the incentives for workers to engage in general pre-market training (that should be thought of as full-time education before entry to the labor market). The second section then considers the provision of general training within firms and the third section the provision of specific training. The presumption is that there will be under-investment in training, the intuition for which is that part of the returns to general skills will accrue to future employers who cannot be internalized in the decision-making. The chapter concludes with a discussion of the empirical literature on training.

11.1 Acquiring Education

This section considers the decision to invest in human capital outside of firms: this can be thought of as a decision about how much education to acquire.

Assume there are only two types of labor, unskilled and skilled. Assume that the marginal product of the skilled (denoted by p_1) is above that of the unskilled (denoted by p_0). Further, assume that, for technological reasons, training can only be undertaken outside firms and that each unskilled worker can be transformed into a skilled worker at a one-off cost of c. Assume that training takes no time (think of it as a costly injection) but this could be relaxed very simply and nothing of importance depends on it.

In a perfectly competitive market, the wages received by both types of worker will be their respective marginal products. As workers receive all the returns from their investment, their decision to invest (or not) will be the efficient one.

In an oligopsonistic labor market, the differences in productivity will be reflected in differences in the wage offer distribution facing skilled and unskilled workers but the wages offered will be below the marginal products. Denote the unskilled wage offer distribution by $w_0(F)$ and the skilled wage offer distribution by $w_1(F)$ where F is the position in the wage-offer distribution. This section considers only a partial equilibrium model so will treat these wage offer distributions as given: it is a simple matter to embed the model that follows into a general equilibrium framework.

On the matching side, make a familiar set of assumptions. Workers die at a rate δ_r to be replaced by workers who initially enter unemployment and are unskilled. Employed workers also leave employment for unemployment at an exogenous rate δ_u. All workers, both skilled and unskilled, both employed and unemployed, are assumed to receive job offers at a rate λ. Note that these assumptions imply that the employment rates for skilled and unskilled workers are identical: a plausible extension would be to modify the assumptions so that the educated are more likely to be in employment—the implication of doing this is discussed later.

Denote the value of being an unemployed unskilled worker by V_0^u and of an unemployed skilled worker by V_1^u. Workers will train if $[V_1^u - V_0^u] > c$. We are interested in how this condition differs in a monopsonistic labor market from what we would have in a competitive market. The value functions for unskilled and skilled workers can be written as

$$\delta_r V_i(F) = w_i(F) - \delta_u[V_i(F) - V_i^u] + \lambda \int_F^1 [V_i(f) - V_i(F)] df \quad (11.1)$$

$$\delta_r V_i^u = b + \lambda \int_0^1 [V_i(f) - V_i^u] df \quad (11.2)$$

where $V_i(F)$ is the value of being an employed worker of type i at position F in the wage distribution. A very useful result is the following.

Proposition 11.1. *The value of being unemployed can be written as*

$$\delta_r V_i^u = \frac{\delta b + \lambda E(w_i)}{\delta + \lambda} \tag{11.3}$$

Proof. See Appendix 11.

(11.3) says that the value of a job is a weighted average of the utility obtainable when out of work and the average wage when in work, the weight on the average wage being the employment rate. Using (11.3) one can provide a simple analysis of the incentives to acquire education. In a competitive labor market we would have $E(w_i) = p_i$ so that individuals will acquire skills if

$$\frac{1}{\delta_r} \frac{\lambda}{\delta + \lambda} [p_1 - p_0] > c \tag{11.4}$$

This is, of course, the efficient condition. There is a simple intuition for it. Being skilled only offers a return if the individual is employed so the difference in productivities is multiplied by the employment rate $\lambda/(\delta + \lambda)$ and also by the expected lifetime $1/\delta_r$.

In a monopsonistic labor market the condition for investment in skills becomes

$$\frac{1}{\delta_r} \frac{\lambda}{\delta + \lambda} [E(w_1) - E(w_0)] > c \tag{11.5}$$

This is more (less) restrictive than the efficiency condition if $[E(w_1) - E(w_0)] < (>)[p_1 - p_0]$, that is, if the difference in expected wages is less (greater) than the difference in productivities.

The relationship between the gap in wages and the gap in productivity is something that will recur later in the chapter. It also occurs in other papers on training in imperfect labor markets, notably Acemoglu and Pischke (1999a) who investigate the consequences of "wage compression" where the gap in wages is less than the gap in productivities.

They present a number of arguments for why wage compression might exist and argue that one should think of it as the "normal" case. Not all of their arguments are about monopsony but the presence of monopsony might also expect one to think that wage compression is the most likely outcome. For example, in the general equilibrium version of this model considered in chapter 2, expected wages are given by (2.26). Or, using the simplest monopsony model, we have that wages are proportional to productivity (see (2.3)) so that, if the rate of exploitation is the same for skilled and unskilled workers, the wage gap is less than the productivity gap. So, there is reason for believing that wage compression is the "normal" case, the consequence of which is that there is too little investment in human capital in a monopsonistic labor market. There is under-investment in the above model because workers get paid less than their marginal product when in work and the gap between wage and marginal product rises with the level of productivity

However, there are some grounds for caution in drawing this conclusion. The analysis above has been based on the assumption that the markets for skilled and unskilled labor are equally monopsonistic. There is no particular reason to believe this is the case. For example, table 2.2 showed that the fraction of recruits from non-employment is lower for better-educated workers. Hence, we might expect the labor market for educated labor to be less monopsonistic than that for the less-educated. This is not really surprising: there is more profit to be had from exploiting more skilled workers, so more firms will enter that segment of the labor market which can be expected to drive up skilled wages. But, it does mean that wages for the skilled may be closer to marginal product than for the unskilled in which case it is possible that wage compression does not exist and there is over-investment in the acquisition of skills as workers try to move into segments of the labor market where they are less exploited.

In a monopsonistic labor market the under-investment problem may not be as serious as this section has suggested because it is possible that firms have some incentive to pay for the training of unskilled workers for the simple reason that they can make profits on these workers without them leaving immediately. As much training is carried out within firms, we now turn to an analysis of this case.

11.2 Employer-Provided General Training

This section discusses the implications of monopsony for the provision by employers of general training. In Becker's analysis, employers will only provide such training if workers fully compensate them for it and, provided this condition is satisfied, it will be provided at the efficient level. These predictions are not in line with most empirical evidence which finds that employers often bear a substantial part of the of cost of general training (e.g., Acemoglu and Pischke 1999b cite estimates of the substantial costs of apprentices to German firms). A small literature has grown up to explain these findings, for example, see Katz and Ziderman (1990), Stevens (1994), Acemoglu and Pischke (1998), and Autor (2001) among others. All of these papers essentially assume some mechanism by which employers have some ex post monopsony power over their employees so that employers can extract some part of the return to general training.

As in the previous section, assume that there are only two types of worker, skilled and unskilled. It costs c to convert an unskilled worker into a skilled one. Assume that this training can be provided while in employment.[2]

In modeling the provision of training, an important first decision is about the form of contracts that can be offered by employers. Suppose that the employer can only offer an unskilled wage and a skilled wage. In this case, training a worker appears to cost the employer the full amount c as the worker does not appear to pay anything towards it. But, as has been pointed out many times before, this conclusion is not right as the provision of training will make the firm a more attractive employer to unskilled workers and hence allow the employer to reduce the unskilled wage while continuing to attract as many unskilled workers as before. An alternative contract is one in which the employer, as before, pays an unskilled and a skilled wage but can, when it trains unskilled workers, charge them directly for the privilege. The amount that can be charged to workers is the gain to them from becoming skilled. One might think that introducing this extra degree of freedom in the contract that can be offered by an employer would enable it to increase profits. But, the following proposition shows that this extra degree of freedom is worth nothing to the employer.

Proposition 11.2. *The employer makes exactly the same level of profit whether or not it can directly charge workers for being trained. If the unskilled wage in the contract where workers do not pay a direct cost is $\tilde{w}_0$, and the unskilled wage when they do pay a direct cost is w_0, then the relationship between the two is given by*

$$\tilde{w}_0 = w_0 - \chi(V_1 - V_0) \tag{11.6}$$

where χ is the rate at which workers are trained, V_0 and V_1 are the values of being unskilled and skilled in the firm which are given by

$$\delta_r V_1 = w_1 - \delta_u[V_1 - V_1^u] + \lambda \int_{w_1} [V(w_1) - V_1] dF_1(w_1) \tag{11.7}$$

and

$$\delta_r V_0 = w_0 - \delta_u[V_0 - V_0^u] + \lambda \int_{w_0} [V(w_0) - V_0] dF_0(w_0) \tag{11.8}$$

Proof.   See Appendix 11.

---

[2] There is an issue here as to whether the employer is the only possible provider of general training or whether workers can, if they so desire, obtain the training themselves from another provider. One way of thinking about this issue is whether employers should be thought of as having market power in the provision of training.

The fact that employers do not gain from charging workers directly for their training perhaps explains why this institution is rarely observed. However, from the conceptual point of view, it is much easier to assume that there is a direct charge. The reason is that it is then only the unskilled wage that affects the value of the job to the unskilled and that the share of the costs of training borne by the worker is clearly $V_1 - V_0$. So, the analysis proceeds on the assumption that this is the case. But, if one wanted to convert the theoretical variables to the observed, it would probably be better to assume that the unskilled wage is the $\tilde{w}_0$ given by (11.6) as direct payments by workers for training are not commonly observed. It is worth noting that this equivalence result does depend on there being no restriction on wages: if, for example, there is lower bound to unskilled wages (e.g., because of capital market constraints on workers or minimum wages) then the equivalence result may fail and a different analysis would be needed.[3]

Assume the employer has a revenue function $Y(N_0, N_1)$ where N_0 is unskilled employment and N_1 is skilled employment. Denote by p_0 the marginal product of unskilled labor and by p_1 the marginal product of skilled labor. If T is the level of training, then the employer's level of profits will be given by

$$\pi = Y(N_0, N_1) - w_1 N_1 - w_0 N_0 - [c - (V_1 - V_0)]T \qquad (11.9)$$

where the value functions are given by (11.7) and (11.8). The levels of skilled and unskilled employment will depend on the wages paid and the level of training intensity according to the equations

$$s_0(w_0)N_0 = R_0(w_0) - T \qquad (11.10)$$

and

$$s_1(w_1)N_1 = R_1(w_1) + T \qquad (11.11)$$

where s and R are the separation and recruitment rates which, in a monopsonistic labor market, will depend on the wage paid.

Using (11.10) and (11.11) to eliminate employment levels from (11.9), one can write profits as

$$\pi = Y\left(\frac{R_1(w_1) + T}{s_1(w_1)}, \frac{R_0(w_0) - T}{s_0(w_0)}\right) - w_1 \frac{R_1(w_1) + T}{s_1(w_1)}$$

$$- w_0 \frac{R_0(w_0) - T}{s_0(w_0)} - [c - (V_1 - V_0)]T \qquad (11.12)$$

and the employer maximization problem is to choose (w_0, w_1, T) to maximize this.

---

[3] There is a parellel here to the discussion of the discriminating monopsonist in chapter 5.

The following proposition contains the first-order conditions for profit maximization.

Proposition 11.3. *The first-order condition for profit maximization for the unskilled wage can be written as*

$$w_0 = \frac{\varepsilon_0^R - \varepsilon_0^s(1 - \theta_0)}{1 + \varepsilon_0^R - \varepsilon_0^s(1 - \theta_0)} p_0 \qquad (11.13)$$

where ε_0^R is the elasticity of unskilled recruits with respect to the wage, ε_0^s is the elasticity of the unskilled separation rate with respect to the wage, and θ_0 is the ratio of the flow trainees to the flow of unskilled recruits

$$\theta_0 = \frac{T}{R_0} \qquad (11.14)$$

For the skilled workers' wage, the first-order condition can be written as

$$w_1 = \frac{\varepsilon_1^R - \varepsilon_1^s(1 + \theta_1)}{1 + \varepsilon_1^R - \varepsilon_1^s(1 + \theta_1)} p_1 \qquad (11.15)$$

where the elasticities are those applicable to the recruitment and separation of skilled workers and θ_1 is the ratio of skilled workers recruited internally through training to those recruited externally, that is,

$$\theta_1 = \frac{T}{R_1} = \theta_0 \frac{R_0}{R_1} \qquad (11.16)$$

The first-order condition for the level of training can be written as

$$\left[\frac{p_1 - w_1}{s_1} + V_1 \right] - \left[\frac{p_0 - w_0}{s_0} + V_0 \right] - c = 0 \qquad (11.17)$$

Proof. See Appendix 11.

First, consider the intuition for the expressions for the wages in (11.13) and (11.15). As is usual, the relationship between wages and productivity is determined by the wage elasticities of the recruitment and separation rates. But, in addition, the training intensity of the firm affects wages (as measured by θ_i).

The unskilled wage is declining in the fraction of the unskilled trained as the employer becomes less concerned with deterring separations among this group as the fraction of them exiting to being skilled workers rises. On the other hand, the skilled wage is increasing in the fraction that are recruited through training. The intuition here is that a high skilled wage can, in part, be recouped through the payment for training extracted from the unskilled and this effect becomes more important, the larger this group is in relation to skilled workers recruited from outside the firm.

Note also that (11.13) and (11.15) imply that, even if the recruitment and separation elasticities for skilled and unskilled workers are the same, the rate of exploitation will be higher for the unskilled than for the skilled as long as there is any training. Hence, there is reason to think that the labor market for the less-skilled is more monopsonistic as discussed at the end of the previous section.

Turning to the first-order condition for training, (11.17), there is a very simple intuition. $[(p_i - w_i)/s_i] + V_i$ is the sum of the returns to employer and worker of having skill level i. So, (11.17) says that workers will be trained if the returns to employer and worker from doing so exceeds the costs. Note, that because workers can be charged for the training (either explicitly or implicitly, depending on the contract), returns to all parties within the firm are internalized in the training decision. But, as discussed below, this does not mean the training decision is efficient as future employers of the worker may also benefit from training and their interests are not represented in the first-order condition.[4]

Becker's analysis is readily understood using Proposition 11.2. If the labor market is perfectly competitive, then the recruitment and separation elasticities are infinite: (11.13) and (11.15) then imply that wages will be equal to marginal products. Given this, (11.17) then says that it is only the workers who will reap any returns from the investment and they will invest if the return exceeds the cost. If all other employers also pay a wage equal to the marginal product then it is simple to show that the investment decision is the efficient one.

The case of a perfectly competitive market is simple but the general case of a monopsonistic labor market is more difficult because it is so messy. The wage elasticities of recruitment and separations may differ by skill, the separation rates may differ. To simplify matters, let us start by assuming that, within each employer, the separation rates for unskilled and skilled workers are the same: one might think of this as the case where employers choose the same position in the skilled and unskilled workers' wage distribution. In this case, the crucial question is whether or not there is wage compression, that is, how the wage differential $(w_1 - w_0)$ compares with the productivity differential $(p_1 - p_0)$ as the following proposition shows.

---

[4] Note this is different from the assumption made in Acemoglu and Pischke (1999b) that workers cannot be made to contribute towards the cost of their training.

Proposition 11.4

1. If $(p_1 - p_0) > (w_1 - w_0)$ in this employer then employers will bear part of the cost of general training.

2. If $(p_1 - p_0) > (w_1 - w_0)$ in all employers then there will be under-investment in training.

Proof. The proof of this is very simple and will not be relegated to the appendix. If the separation rates of unskilled and skilled workers are identical within each firm, then re-arrangement of (11.17) shows that we must have $c > (V_1 - V_0)$ if $(p_1 - p_0) > (w_1 - w_0)$ so that not all the cost of training can be recouped from workers. Hence, employers must be bearing part of the cost of the general training that is done.

If $(p_1 - p_0) > (w_1 - w_0)$ in all firms, then this implies that the profits of all potential future employers of a worker are increased when the worker is trained. As these potential future employers are not internalized in the training decision, there must then be under-investment.

This proposition can be interpreted as simply a confirmation of Becker's intuition that the costs of training will be paid for by those who reap the returns. The difference from his analysis is that employers in a monopsonistic labor market can expect to get some of the returns even from general training.

One of the implications of the second part of the proposition is that the extent of monopsony in the labor market is likely to affect the extent of under-investment. As explained above, a perfectly competitive labor market is (in the absence of capital market imperfections) likely to deliver an efficient level of training as no potential future employers of a worker can expect to make any profits on them. At the other extreme, a very monopsonistic labor market[5] may also deliver training close to the efficient level as there are few future employers to make profits out of the worker. This point is made at greater length in Stevens (1994).

The weakness of Proposition 11.4 is that it does nothing to prove that $(p_1 - p_0) > (w_1 - w_0)$. As discussed in the previous section, one might expect that this is the "normal" case for a number of reasons. First, inspection of (11.13) and (11.14) shows that, if elasticities are the same, then we might expect skilled and unskilled wages to be a similar fraction of productivities. However, as discussed above, skilled wages will be a higher fraction of productivity than unskilled wages. One could also point to the few

---

[5] One should include implicit or explicit agreements among employers not to poach skilled workers from each other as a very monopsonistic market arrangement: such agreements are often said to help to foster employer-provided training.

studies that attempt to estimate both the productivity and wage impacts of training as evidence in favor of wage compression. Barron et al. (1997, chapter 6), using US data, find much larger effects of training on productivity than wages although the effects on productivity are so large that one might not want to examine them too closely.

Are there any testable predictions about the types of employers where training will take place? The theory predicts, unsurprisingly, that training is more likely where the benefits are larger and the costs smaller. The benefits are likely to be larger where the current employer and worker are better able to internalize the returns from training. Hence, one might expect the returns to training to be higher in employers that are further up the wage distribution. To see how this is possible, suppose that the employer chooses a skilled and unskilled wage at the same point in the distribution: denote this by F. Further, assume that the separation rate only depends on F. Then, the left-hand side of (11.17), the benefits from training, $\Omega(F)$, can be written as

$$\Omega(F) = \frac{\Delta p(F) - \Delta w(F)}{s(F)} + \Delta V(F) \qquad (11.18)$$

where $\Delta x = (x_1 - x_0)$. Differentiating (11.18) with respect to F leads to

$$\Omega'(F) = \frac{\Delta p'(F) - \Delta w'(F)}{s(F)} + \Delta V'(F) - \frac{s'(F)}{s(F)} [\Delta p(F) - \Delta w(F)]$$

$$= \frac{\Delta p'(F)}{s(F)} - \frac{s'(F)}{s(F)} [\Delta p(F) - \Delta w(F)] \qquad (11.19)$$

If there is wage compression so that $(p_1 - p_0) > (w_1 - w_0)$, the second term in (11.19) is positive suggesting that the incentives to train are higher in "better" firms. The first term is also likely to be positive, for example, if the better firms have a higher marginal product for everyone, it seems unlikely that the gap in productivities is smaller. Hence, the monopsony model has the prediction that we would expect to see more training in employers who are further up the wage distribution, essentially because a higher fraction of the returns will be internalized within firms. There are some concerns about the robustness of this conclusion. Firms higher up the wage distribution will have lower separation rates and, if training is primarily concerned with induction of new employees, may be associated with less training for this reason.

The fact that higher-wage employers may have a bigger incentive to train has the potential to explain the empirical anomaly that it is very hard, if not impossible, to find evidence of the competitive prediction that firms that offer training should pay their unskilled workers a lower wage (a compensating wage differential). Many researchers have tried to look for this relationship but most reach the same conclusion as Barron et al. (1997: 3) that "there is little evidence that training substantially reduces the starting wage." If those firms offering training are further up the unskilled worker wage distribution then there is no reason for this prediction to be true.[6]

11.3 On-the-Job Specific Training

This section considers the provision of specific training by employers. Becker's analysis suggested that workers should capture a smaller portion of the returns to specific as opposed to general training and that employers should bear some of the cost. As we shall see, this prediction does not necessarily hold up in a monopsonistic labor market.

One can use a modified version of the set-up of the previous section to discuss the provision of specific training. The first modification is that the employer cannot recruit any skilled workers from other employers: hence $R_1 = 0$. Secondly, as specific skills have no value elsewhere in the labor market, it is reasonable to assume that the separation rates and value functions of skilled and unskilled workers will depend only on the wage paid in this employer. Hence, if the employer pays their skilled workers a higher wage than the unskilled, the separation rate of skilled workers will be lower than that of the unskilled.

With these modifications, the first-order conditions in Proposition 11.3 can be used to discuss the optimal policy. First, consider the optimal skilled wage. As there are no skilled recruits, (11.16) says that we will have $\theta_1 = \infty$. (11.15) then says that the optimal policy is to set $w_1 = p_1$, that is, the employer should pay skilled workers their marginal product. As the optimal policy for the case of general skills is to pay a wage less than the marginal product, this implies that workers capture a larger share of the returns within the employer. This is in striking contrast to Becker's conclusion that workers should get a larger share of the returns to general training.

Where does this result come from? The explanation lies in the fact that the employer cannot recruit any workers with specific skills from outside the firm. If workers with general skills are paid their marginal products, then the employer is forgoing potential profits from externally recruited workers. In contrast, paying a high wage to internally trained skilled workers is not so costly to the employer as it can be clawed back in the form of a lower unskilled wage.

One must be a little cautious here. The discussion of wage discrimination in chapter 5 concluded that employers would like to use upward-

---

[6] This argument is identical to the one discussed in chapter 8 about why one often fails to find evidence of compensating wage differentials.

sloping wage–tenure profiles to extract more rents from workers. In the model of training presented here, there is a correlation between skill and job tenure because those who have been in the firm longer are more likely to have received specific training. So, the high wage returns to workers with specific skills may be an indirect way of achieving an upward-sloping wage–tenure profile when we have not explicitly allowed for it in the analysis. In this case, it may be that allowing for upward-sloping wage–tenure profiles would overturn the result described above. On the other hand, it was argued in chapter 5 that employers generally have a shortage of tools they can use in their attempt to be discriminating monopsonists so it may well be that they use every mechanism (direct or indirect) at their disposal including that of generously rewarding employees with firm-specific skills.

Perhaps it is safest to conclude that it is not so obvious in a monopsonistic labor market that workers pay for or get a larger share of the returns of general training than for specific training.

11.4 Empirical Analyses of Training

There is a large empirical literature on training. Among the questions that this literature seeks to answer are:

- To what extent is training general or specific?
- Who pays the direct costs of training?
- Who receives training?
- What is the impact of training on current wages?
- What is the impact of training on future wages?
- What is the impact of training on labor turnover?
- What is the impact of training on productivity?

However, the literature on many of these empirical correlations is confusing because there are too many endogenous variables and not enough exogenous ones, and because measures of training are often very vague. For example, wages and training receipt are almost certainly determined simultaneously (as in the models described above) and, while a number of papers attempt to use instrumental variables to deal with this problem, good instruments are rarely available.

There are also many papers in the empirical literature that look for evidence in support of the predictions of Becker's analysis. The prediction that the market will provide the efficient level of training is not really testable so attention focuses on predictions about the different allocations of costs and returns to general and specific training. But, distinguishing between general and specific training is not very easy and it is relatively easy to explain away anomalous results as the consequence of problems with the data.

Bearing this in mind, the following discussion briefly summarizes the main empirical findings in this area and attempts to point out where monopsony can help to explain empirical findings that the human capital model cannot. But, the bottom line is that the empirical results are sufficiently confusing that it is often hard to present a very clear conclusion and one cannot really use these results to provide a clear distinction between the human capital and monopsony perspective. There is one very important exception to this negative conclusion: monopsony can explain why employers often seem to pay for general training, a major anomaly from the perspective of Becker's analysis.

11.4.1 Is Training General or Specific?

It is difficult to assess whether training is primarily general or specific and there are a number of methods used in the literature. First, some surveys contain questions which seek direct answers about the generality of skills acquired in training: for example, Loewenstein and Spletzer (1999) report that in the 1993 NLSY, 63% of workers reported that all or almost all of the skills learned were useful in doing the same kind of work for another employer while, at the opposite extreme, only 11% of workers said that less than half of the skills acquired were useful to other employers. They also reported similar findings from the 1992 EOPP survey. This evidence strongly suggests that on-the-job training is primarily general.

But, most studies do not have such direct questions on the content of training, and other empirical studies that attempt to distinguish between general and specific training use either information on the place where training takes place (on the grounds that training in the workplace is more likely to be specific and training at an external educational institution is almost certain to be general) or on who pays for it (relying on Becker's conclusion that employer-paid training is more likely to be specific). Lynch (1992) and Royalty (1996) are examples of papers that use the former approach while Loewenstein and Spletzer (1998) and Veum (1997) use both. It seems plausible to believe there is some useful content in these distinctions but these measures are less than perfect.

11.4.2 Who Pays the Direct Costs of Training?

The consensus here is that, with the exception of training undertaken by individuals at their own initiative, employers pay most of the monetary costs of training. For example, Loewenstein and Spletzer (1998) report, using the NLSY, that employers pay for 96% of formal company training,

91% of seminars at work, 82% of seminars outside work, but only 42% of training at colleges (e.g., business schools or vocational institutes).

As earlier discussions have made clear, this does not mean that employers are paying the cost of training as it may be that workers indirectly bear the costs by accepting lower wages (and one should also not ignore the time cost of training which may be explicitly borne by workers). But, this empirical finding does help to focus attention on trainee wages in the attempt to see whether workers are paying for their training.

11.4.3 Who receives training?

The human capital approach to training suggests that it is benefits relative to costs that determine the receipt of training. These factors are also important in monopsony but one would also add the importance of the extent of competition in the labor market and the position of employers in the wage distribution. As these are the distinctive contributions of monopsony, the following discussion concentrates on the evidence about their impact.

A number of commentators have argued that the institutional structure of the German labor market makes it less likely that workers trained within the firm will leave to work for other employers (see, e.g., Soskice 1994, or the evidence presented in Harhoff and Kane 1997). Furthermore, it is argued that this accounts for the more extensive apprenticeship system in Germany. Crucial to this argument is the idea that industry-level bargaining in Germany means that there is little wage variation across employers so that those who have completed apprenticeships have little incentive to move. Furthermore, as Acemoglu and Pischke (1998) argue, those who do leave the employer where they have been trained may also be sending a signal that they are low quality. They present evidence that those who change employers have lower wages than those who stay but that this is not true for those who change employers because of an intervening period of military service (which can be taken to signal nothing about worker quality).

In addition, it is sometimes argued that collective employer organizations have much more power over those employers who are seen to be poaching workers from other employers in Germany than elsewhere. As a result of all these factors, it is argued that German employers are often prepared to spend large amounts of money to equip their workers with general skills.

Looking for evidence that those employers who are further up the wage distribution do more training is more difficult because of a number of complicating factors. First, there is strong evidence (see, e.g., Altonji and Spletzer 1991, for the United States and Blundell et al. 1996, for the

United Kingdom) that the more able tend to receive more training. However, there are a number of areas where there is evidence consistent with these predictions.

First, for German apprenticeships it does appear to be the case that large firms both spend more on training and retain more of their apprentices which is consistent with this prediction (see Euwals and Winkelmann 2001).

The literature on the impact of unions on training may also be informative. Trade unions may have an impact on training through a number of routes. First, if they reduce the wage gap between unskilled and skilled workers, this reduction in wage compression would be expected to increase the incentives for employers to provide training (Acemoglu and Pischke 1999b make this argument). But even if unions simply raise wages for all workers of an employer then we would expect there to be an increase in training as this move up the wage distribution will reduce the quit rate to other employers and lead to a greater internalization of the returns to training. The US evidence is very mixed with some studies reporting negative impacts of unions on training and some positive. However, the UK evidence is very clear: Green et al. (1999) show that trade unions are associated with an increased probability of receiving training.

11.4.4 The Impact of Training on Current Wages

If workers rarely pay the direct costs of general training, then the competitive model predicts that trainees should receive lower wages. Many studies have looked for evidence of this and it is a fair conclusion to say that little if no evidence for this can be found (see, e.g., Lynch 1992; Barron et al. 1997; Loewenstein and Spletzer 1998). This is an empirical puzzle for the competitive model.

The conventional explanation is that, as the receipt of on-the-job training is positively correlated with measures of human capital (like formal education) and measures of ability (e.g., the aptitude tests used by Altonji and Spletzer 1991), it is quite likely that it is correlated with unobserved ability which, in turn, is positively correlated with wages.

The monopsony model suggests an alternative explanation. As discussed above, we would expect training to be higher in high-wage employers because more of the returns will be internalized. This induces a positive correlation between wages and training. However, the competitive mechanism is still at work: (11.6) shows that, if workers do not pay directly for training, a higher training intensity will be associated with lower wages. This means that the prediction for the empirical correlation is unclear.

11.4.5 The Impact of Training on Future Wages

Most (although not all) studies have found that training is associated with increased wage growth. In fact, given the amount of training typically received, the implicit returns to training are often very large compared to the estimated returns to a year of formal education. That training is associated with increased wage growth is in line with the predictions of both the competitive and monopsony models. The two models do differ in terms of their predictions about the returns to general and specific human capital: the competitive model predicts that the returns to general human capital should be larger than the returns to specific human capital while the monopsony model (with some provisos) predicts that the opposite is possible.

The empirical evidence here is mixed. Loewenstein and Spletzer (1999) probably have the best data for distinguishing between general and specific training and do not find evidence of different returns to different types of training. Other studies have more difficulty in distinguishing the type of training but, again, the results are very mixed. Lynch (1992), using earlier data from the NLSY, reports that weeks of off-the-job training and apprenticeships are associated with higher wage growth than weeks of on-the-job training. However, the estimates of Loewenstein and Spletzer (1998) using later data from the NLSY are less clear-cut with the differences in the rate of the return to on- and off-the-job training probably not being significantly different from each other (although one should note that they use incidence as their measure of training not weeks). They do, however, report higher rates of return to off-the-job training with previous employers: this is consistent with the monopsony view as workers may only capture the returns to general training when they change jobs. For the United Kingdom, Blundell et al. (1996) report higher (but probably not significantly higher for men) wage growth for off- than on-the-job training in the current job.

These studies do not provide strong support for Becker's predictions and could potentially be explained using the monopsony model. Given the difficulties, it would be too strong to claim these empirical results as positive evidence in support of a monopsonistic perspective.

11.4.6 The Impact of Training on Labor Turnover

A number of papers have investigated the effect of training on labor turnover. As in other areas of research into training, interpretation of correlations is likely to be difficult. For example, Royalty (1996) argues that training is more likely when turnover is lower and looks for evidence of this, but other papers look at the impact of training receipt on turnover. Loewenstein and Spletzer (1999) do not find significant differences for the impact of general and specific training on job mobility. Veum (1997), using NLSY data, finds that company-financed training has no significant effect on labor turnover while self-financed training increases labor mobility. For the United Kingdom, Dearden et al. (1997) found that employer-funded training tended to reduce mobility while, in line with Veum (1995), self-funded training tends to increase mobility. Again, it is not clear that the other correlations shed much light on whether the human capital or monopsony model is the better model of training.

11.4.7 The Impact of Training on Productivity

A number of papers have investigated the link between training and productivity although it is obviously difficult to measure the latter. The consensus seems to be that there are large effects on productivity, larger than the effects of wages. Allied to the conclusion that most training is general, this does suggest that employers are getting some of the returns to general training. It is then unsurprising that they pay for it.

11.5 Conclusion

Monopsony power in the labor market leads to significant changes in the conventional wisdom about education and training that is based on Becker's analysis. Perhaps the most important conclusion is that there should be a presumption that there is under-investment in training (particularly general training) as part of the returns to training will be obtained by future employers of workers who are not internalized in the training decision. So, while Becker did discuss how his analysis should be modified if labor markets were not competitive, he gives the impression (without providing a formal analysis) that the provision of training can be efficient whatever the extent of competition in the labor market. But, that conclusion is not really true.

Another important conclusion is that monopsony can help to understand certain empirical anomalies in research on training. First, it is not surprising that we observe many employers paying for their workers to receive general training as their monopsony power means they can expect to reap part (although not all) of the returns. And, it is not surprising that empirical studies fail to find that, ceteris paribus, those workers currently receiving training have lower wages as those employers further up the wage distribution have a greater incentive to train their workers.

Some of Becker's conclusions also need to be modified. For example, monopsony predicts that, in some circumstances, workers will receive a greater part of the returns (and be asked, directly or indirectly, to pay a greater share of the costs) to specific as compared to general training. The reason is that paying workers with general skills high wages has the disadvantage of forgoing rents on externally recruited workers, rents that cannot be clawed back by paying those workers lower wages when they were unskilled. One must be cautious here: this conclusion is sensitive to the assumption about the range of employment contracts at the disposal of the employer and the empirical evidence on the prediction is not clear-cut.

Hence, monopsony does offer a distinctive and more realistic view about the allocation of the returns to and incentives for training in labor markets, and deserves to be used more widely in this context.

Appendix 11

Proof of Proposition 11.1

By differentiating (11.1), we have

$$\frac{\partial V_i(F)}{\partial F} = \frac{w'_i(F)}{\delta + \lambda[1 - F]} \tag{11.20}$$

Integrating the final integral in (11.2) by parts, this equation can be written as

$$\delta_r V_i^u = b + \lambda[V_i(0) - V_i^u] + \lambda \int_0^1 \frac{(1 - f)w'_i(f)df}{\delta + \lambda(1 - f)} \tag{11.21}$$

Now, from (11.2) and (11.1), we have

$$V_i(0) - V_i^u = \frac{w_i(0) - b}{\delta + \lambda} \tag{11.22}$$

And, using (11.22) and the result from (2.20), integrating the last term in (11.21) by parts, we have

$$\delta_r V_i^u = \frac{\delta b}{\delta + \lambda} + \int_0^1 N(f)w(f)df \tag{11.23}$$

which, using the fact that the employment rate is equal to $\lambda/(\delta + \lambda)$, can be written as (11.3).

Proof of Proposition 11.2

To see the equivalence of the two contracts, consider the following more formal analysis. First, consider the case in which workers are not charged directly for their training. Suppose that the employer trains unskilled workers at a rate χ. Then the value of being an unskilled worker in the firm, V_0, can be written as

$$\delta_r V_0 = \tilde{w}_0 - \delta_u[V_0 - V_0^u] + \chi(V_1 - V_0) + \lambda \int_{V_0}^1 [V - V_0]dF_0(V)$$

(11.24)

where $F_0(V)$ is the distribution of values on offer to the unskilled in the external labor market and V_1 is the value of being a skilled worker in the firm. Similarly for skilled workers, we have

$$\delta_r V_1 = \tilde{w}_1 - \delta_u[V_1 - V_1^u] + \lambda \int_{V_1}^1 [V - V_1]dF_1(V)$$

(11.25)

Now, profits can be written as

$$\tilde{\pi} = (p_1 - \tilde{w}_1)N_1 + (p_0 - \tilde{w}_0)N_0 - cT$$

(11.26)

where N_0 and N_1 are the employment of unskilled and skilled workers, respectively, and T is the level of training. Employment levels will be given by

$$s_0(V_0)N_0 = R_0(V_0) - T$$

(11.27)

and

$$s_1(V_1)N_1 = R_1(V_1) + T$$

(11.28)

where s and R are the separation and recruitment rates. Finally, we have the equation

$$\chi = \frac{T}{N_0}$$

(11.29)

for the training intensity.

This is quite a lot of equations but inspection of (11.24) should make it clear that an increase in the training intensity, χ, allows the employer to cut the unskilled wage while still maintaining the value of an unskilled worker in the firm. In this sense, workers do bear part of the cost of training. But, quite how much is not immediately obvious from the above equations.

Now, imagine that the employer moves from the contract in which workers are not charged directly for training to one in which they are. The amount that can be charged to workers is the gain to them from becoming skilled which is given by $V_1 - V_0$. Further, imagine that, in making this change, the employer does not want to alter the value of being an unskilled or skilled worker in the firm. As unskilled workers no longer have a capital gain on becoming skilled, (11.24) implies that the wage that is now paid to unskilled workers, w_0, must be given by

$$w_0 = \tilde{w}_0 + \chi(V_1 - V_0) \qquad (11.30)$$

while the skilled wage must be unchanged. With this change and with the fact that it now costs employers $c - (V_1 - V_0)$ whenever workers are trained, employers will make the following level of profits in the new contract:

$$\pi = (p_1 - w_1)N_1 + (p_0 - w_0)N_0 - [c - (V_1 - V_0)]T$$

$$= (p_1 - \tilde{w}_1)N_1 + (p_0 - \tilde{w}_0)N_0 - \chi(V_1 - V_0)N_0 - [c - (V_1 - V_0)]T$$

$$= \tilde{\pi}$$

$$(11.31)$$

where the last inequality follows from the use of (11.29). (11.31) says that the employer will make exactly the same level of profit.

(11.6) comes directly from (11.30), and (11.7) and (11.8) from (11.24) and (11.25) with the modification that unskilled workers make no capital gain when trained when they are charged directly.

Proof of Proposition 11.3

By differentiating (11.12) with respect to w_0 we obtain the first-order condition

$$(p_0 - w_0)\frac{\partial N_0}{\partial w_0} - N_0 - \frac{\partial V_0}{\partial w_0}T = 0 \qquad (11.32)$$

Now, from (11.7), $(\partial V_i/\partial w_i) = 1/s_i(w_i)$ so that, using (11.10), (11.32) can be re-arranged to give

$$(p_0 - w_0)s_0\frac{\partial N_0}{\partial w_0} = R_0 \qquad (11.33)$$

Now, by differentiating (11.10), we have

$$s_0\frac{\partial N_0}{\partial w_0} = \frac{\partial R_0}{\partial w_0} - \frac{\partial s_0}{\partial w_0}\frac{R_0 - T}{s_0} \qquad (11.34)$$

Using (11.34) in (11.33) leads to (11.13).

For skilled workers, by differentiating (11.12) with respect to w_1 we obtain the first-order condition

$$(p_1 - w_1)\frac{\partial N_1}{\partial w_1} - N_1 + \frac{\partial V_1}{\partial w_1}T = 0 \qquad (11.35)$$

Now, from (11.7), $(\partial V_i / \partial w_i) = 1/s_i(w_i)$ so that, using (11.11), (11.35) can be re-arranged to give

$$(p_1 - w_1)s_1 \frac{\partial N_1}{\partial w_1} = R_1 \tag{11.36}$$

Now, by differentiating (11.11), we have

$$s_1 \frac{\partial N_1}{\partial w_1} = \frac{\partial R_1}{\partial w_1} - \frac{\partial s_1}{\partial w_1} \frac{R_1 + T}{s_1} \tag{11.37}$$

Using (11.37) in (11.36) leads to (11.15).

The first-order condition for training, (11.17) follows straightforwardly from differentiation of (11.12) with respect to T.

Part Four _____

WAGE-SETTING INSTITUTIONS AND CONCLUSIONS

12

The Minimum Wage and Trade Unions

PREVIOUS chapters have assumed that employers can freely choose wages. Of course, the choice of the wage will be influenced by what is happening in the rest of the labor market but there are no external constraints on the wage that can be chosen. However, there are often restrictions on the wages that employers can pay and this chapter is about two of these constraints: the minimum wage and trade unions.

The textbook competitive analyses of minimum wages and trade unions are very similar, if not identical. Both institutions are seen as raising wages above the market-clearing level, reducing employment in the affected sectors. But, in oligopsonistic labor markets, minimum wages and trade unions are unlikely to have the same effect. If labor markets have substantial wage dispersion (and both theory and evidence suggest that they do), then minimum wages are likely to "push" the wage distribution from below as, by definition, they directly affect the lowest wages in the market while (in a given labor market) trade unions are likely to "pull" the wage distribution from the top as the existence of a union wage premium strongly suggests that they are the highest wage firms. Hence, the analysis of the two institutions is likely to be rather different.

This chapter discusses the two main issues that have concerned economists:

- what is the impact of minimum wages/trade unions on the distribution of wages?
- what is the impact of minimum wages/trade unions on employment?

The plan of the chapter is as follows. The next two sections consider the impact of minimum wages on the distribution of wages and the following section, the impact on employment. The third and fourth sections then consider the impact of trade unions on wages and employment.

12.1 The Minimum Wage and the Distribution of Wages: Spikes and Spillovers

The most noticeable impact of the minimum wage on the distribution of wages is the existence of a "spike" in the wage distribution at the legislated minimum. Of course, the height of the spike depends on the level at which the minimum wage is set but it is generally there. For example, in September 1997 the United States raised the federal minimum wage from $4.75 an hour to $5.15. The percentage of hourly paid workers (in the CPS monthly outgoing rotation group) reporting an hourly wage of *exactly* $4.75 went from 1.3% in August 1997 to 0.2% in September. The percentage paid exactly $5.15 was 0.3% in August rising to 1.9% in September. The minimum wage is not the only wage at which we observe spikes: they are also observed at "round" numbers but it is the spike that is probably most amenable to economic explanation.

The existence of a spike is sometimes regarded as something of a "puzzle" both for competitive and monopsony models of the labor market. But, this is not the case for either model. In the competitive model, the "puzzle" arises because labor economists often have in mind a model in which the marginal product of a worker is exogenously given. If this were the case, then a minimum wage would simply truncate the wage distribution at the minimum as all those previously paid below it would lose their jobs. There would be truncation, but there would be no spike. This model is a simple one and convenient to work with, but there is no particular reason to believe it to be true and plausible generalizations can readily explain the existence of a spike.

For example, suppose that marginal revenue product depends on the level of employment either because of decreasing returns in production or because falling employment in a sector may cause the price of the product produced to rise. Then, if the aggregate labor market consists of a number of distinct segments (perhaps differentiated by skill), a fraction of segments will have a wage equal to the minimum and this will be the cause of the spike. Alternatively, if there are non-pecuniary aspects to jobs (call them effort), then one would expect employers to raise effort in response to a minimum wage and the result again will be a spike (although it is probably fair to say that no evidence for these off-setting effects has ever been produced). This argument for the spike might also be thought to apply in the monopsony model.[1]

For the monopsony model, the source of the "puzzle" of the spike is the simple general equilibrium model of oligopsony described in section 2.4, the model of Burdett and Mortensen (1998). For reasons discussed in that section, the equilibrium wage distribution can have no mass points

---

[1] It is sometimes argued that the minimum wage is fatally flawed because it does not control these non-wage benefits and, as a result, minimum wage workers will actually be made worse off by the minimum wage as their employers are forced to offer an inefficient wage–effort combination. But, as Proposition 8.1 in section 8.4 showed, we would expect workers in a monopsonistic labor market to be made better off by a binding minimum wage even if employers can freely vary non-wage aspects of the job. This is consistent with the evidence found in Holzer et al. (1991).

because it would then pay employers to deviate by paying an infinitesimally higher wage. This result applies equally to the free market equilibrium and to the model with a binding minimum wage. In this model, a minimum wage affects the wage distribution by raising and compressing wages but there is no spike. Van den Berg (1999) makes this a virtue of the model arguing that there are labor markets in which there is no spike yet the minimum wage does have an impact on the wage distribution. However, it seems likely that the situations in which a binding minimum wage has no apparent spike are either the result of using earnings measures with substantial measurement error or institutional set-ups in which wages are marked up on the minimum wage, for example, by unions. Evidence for the first of these effects can be seen in the United Kingdom. The traditional way in which hourly earnings are measured is to divide weekly earnings by weekly hours. No, or a very small spike is apparent using this data: for example, the fraction of hourly paid workers in the UK Labour Force Survey (LFS) reporting being paid exactly the national minimum wage of £3.60 per hour from April to December 1999 was 1.4%. But, in Spring 1999 a direct hourly wage question was introduced and this does shows a much larger spike: the same sample of workers shows a spike of 9.4% using this measure.

The Burdett–Mortensen model of monopsony is unable to explain the spike because, as discussed in section 2.4, there is a discontinuity in the labor supply function facing each firm at every wage that is paid by a mass of firms. But real world labor supply curves are unlikely to exhibit such discontinuities (e.g., because of heterogeneity in the evaluation of non-wage attributes of jobs or mobility costs) and, if the labor supply curve is continuous, one can readily explain the spike at the minimum wage. To see this, suppose that the labor supply curve facing a firm is $N(w)$ where w is the wage paid: assume this to be a continuous function of w. Then, an employer will want to solve the maximization problem:

$$\max_{w} (p - w)N(w) \qquad \text{s.t.} \qquad w \geq w_{\mathrm{m}} \qquad (12.1)$$

where w_{m} is the minimum wage. If there is heterogeneity in p across firms, the constraint will be binding for low values of p and the result will be a spike in the wage distribution.

Hence, one should not be surprised by, or particularly interested in, the existence of a spike in the wage distribution at the minimum wage except in so far as it gives some indication of how much "bite" the minimum wage actually has. But, while the spike is the most striking evidence of the impact of a minimum wage on the wage distribution, it may be that the minimum wage also has an effect on wages further up the wage distribution: what are known as spillovers.

Providing a theoretical model in which there are spillovers is not difficult. The Burdett–Mortensen model predicts that a binding minimum
wage affects wages at every point in the wage distribution although the
effect is weaker as one moves up the percentiles.[2] But, this theoretical
model does not make it very clear why we might expect spillovers.

From the simple model in (12.1) it is not immediately obvious why
spillovers would exist. A simple-minded approach to the analysis of
(12.1) would conclude that the only effect of the minimum wage on the
wage chosen by an employer will be if it is a binding constraint but that an
employer who pays strictly above the minimum will be unaffected by
changes in it, that is, there will be no spillovers. Another way to put
this is to say that there can only be spillovers to the extent that the
minimum wage affects the productivity of workers (p) or the labor supply
curve $N(w)$.

An effect on productivity is most likely to occur if there are changes in
employment as a result of the minimum wage that affect the output of the
product and hence, through an industry demand curve, the price. Such an
effect is likely to be similar at all points in the wage distribution: the
evidence presented below is very much against this.

So, the most likely route for spillovers is through the labor supply curve
to an employer. Why might $N(w)$ depend on the minimum wage?
Consider an employer who initially pays just above what is going to be
the minimum wage. When a minimum wage is introduced, the gap
narrows between this employer's wage and the wages paid by lower-
wage employers. As a result it is less likely that workers in those employers will come to work for this one if they get a job offer and more likely
that this firm's workers leave to go to work in those firms (although they
will still be taking a wage cut, it is smaller than before). Hence, the labor
supply to this employer is likely to fall. As one moves up the wage distribution, the impact of what happens in minimum wage employers is likely
to have less and less impact on an employer. Hence, the minimum wage
will reduce labor supply to employers who pay above the minimum wage
but proportionately more in low wage employers. In mathematical terms
this can be written as

$$\frac{\partial^2 \log N(w, w_\mathrm{m})}{\partial \log w_\mathrm{m} \partial \log w} > 0 \qquad (12.2)$$

[2] It is possible to construct theoretical models in which the minimum wage can reduce
wages at some percentiles. Fershtman and Fishman (1994) present a model in which the
search intensity of workers is endogenous. As the minimum wage rises, the wage distribution
becomes compressed and the incentives for on-the-job search are reduced. But it is this on-
the-job search which determines the intensity of competition among employers for workers
so that wages at the top of the distribution may be reduced.

This implies that an increase in the minimum wage increases the elasticity of the labor supply curve facing an employer: this, through the usual mechanism in monopsony, leads them to choose higher wages. But, it is likely that this change in the elasticity is smaller in higher-wage firms as they are less influenced by the minimum wage so this effect declines as wages increase. Hence, there will be spillover effects that decline as one moves up the wage distribution.

There are other reasons why the minimum wage may affect the supply of labor to firms who pay above the minimum wage. The minimum wage is likely to affect incentives for job search. Those in low-wage jobs are likely to have less incentive to look for alternative jobs than before as the wage gap between this job and their current one is reduced (see (9.5)). For those out of work, there are likely to be two effects at work. First, higher wages in work increase the incentives to seek work. Secondly, the minimum wage may affect the arrival rate of job offers: this will again have an effect on search intensity.

How large are spillover effects in practice? The evidence on this is surprisingly small. Perhaps that is primarily because the consensus view is that the minimum wage has little effect on the wage distribution in the United States. But, a small number of papers (diNardo et al. 1996; Lee 1999; Teulings 2000) have challenged this view arguing that the minimum wage has a more substantial impact on the wage distribution than previously thought.

Both Lee (1999) and Teulings (2000) estimate the spillover effect although it is not the main focus of their papers. The approach in Teulings (2000) is based on a competitive model of the labor market in which technology is assumed to have the realistic but messy feature of a "decreasing in distance elasticity of substitution" between workers with different skill levels. Lee (1999) takes a less structural approach and this is the one we use here. He assumes that, in the absence of the minimum wage, the log wage at position F in the wage distribution is given by $w^*(F)$: call this the latent wage distribution. With the introduction of a minimum wage, w_m, the actual wage distribution, $w(F)$, will differ from the latent wage distribution. For example, if there are no spillover effects and the minimum wage is fully enforced, then the wage distribution will be given by

$$w(F) = w^*(F) + \max(w_m - w^*(F), 0) \qquad (12.3)$$

Lee (1999) generalizes this and proposes the following model that allows for spillover effects:

$$w(F) = w^*(F) + \frac{w_m - w^*(F)}{1 - \exp[-\beta(w_m - w^*(F))]} \qquad (12.4)$$

where $\beta > 0$ is a parameter which measures the size of the spillover effect. If $\beta = \infty$, the model of (12.4) reduces to that of (12.3) so that an increase in β is a reduction in the spillover effect. The spillover effect, $s(F)$, can be written as

$$s(F) = \frac{w_{\mathrm{m}} - w^*(F)}{1 - \exp[-\beta(w_{\mathrm{m}} - w^*(F))]} - \max(w_{\mathrm{m}} - w^*(F), 0) \qquad (12.5)$$

that is, it is the difference between the total effect $[w(F) - w^*(F)]$ and the direct effect as measured by the final term in (12.3). Inspection of (12.5) shows that the spillover effects in the Lee model depend only on the gap between the minimum wage and the latent wage and the single parameter β. There are several implications of the particular model of spillovers in (12.5). The spillover effects are largest for those just affected by the minimum wage (i.e., those for whom $w_{\mathrm{m}} = w^*(F)$) and, for these workers, the increase in log wages is equal to $(1/\beta)$. Secondly, the spillover effects decline as one moves away from these wages, the rate of decline also being determined by β.

In a more general model of spillovers, one might think of estimating:

- the wage at which the spillover effect is greatest;
- the maximum spillover effect;
- how wide are the spillover effects;

that is, a three parameter model instead of the single parameter model estimated by Lee (1999). However, as shown below, the Lee model does surprisingly well in estimating the spillover effects for the US aggregate wage distribution.

To estimate the model, one has to make some assumption about the latent wage distribution $w^*(F)$. We make the simple assumption that the latent log wage distribution is normal, that is,

$$w^*(F) = w_{\mathrm{med}} + \sigma \Phi^{-1}(F) \qquad (12.6)$$

where w_{med} is the log of the median wage and $\Phi^{-1}(F)$ is the inverse of the standard normal distribution function.

Table 12.1 presents some estimates of the Lee model estimated by non-linear least squares on US data from 1979 to 2000 inclusive. The model in (12.4) is fitted to all percentiles below the median where each observation is a percentile of the log hourly wage distribution in a particular state in a particular "year." Because the minimum wage is not always raised on January 1, Lee's practice of defining "year" loosely as a period of approximately a year in which the minimum wage is constant is followed here: details of the observations affected by this are given in the notes to the table. Some percentiles are below the federal minimum wage: these were simply excluded from the analysis.

TABLE 12.1
Spillover Effects of Minimum Wages on the US Wage Distribution

	Sample Period	β	σ
1	1979–2000	8.88 (0.05)	0.623 (0.001)
2	1979–84	9.44 (0.07)	0.645 (0.001)
3	1985–90	8.67 (0.10)	0.632 (0.001)
4	1990–94	8.31 (0.09)	0.625 (0.001)
5	1995–2000	6.60 (0.07)	0.633 (0.002)

Notes.
1. These are the results of the model of (12.4) and (12.6) being fitted by non-linear least squares to observations on percentile–state–year combinations. Only observations below the median are used. The sample size for the entire period is 55,200 and the $R^2 = 0.99$.
2. The maximum of the federal and state minimum wage is used. As the minimum wage is not always changed on January 1, the following deviations from calendar years were used for years in which the federal minimum was not changed at the beginning of the year: 1989 includes January–March 1990; 1990 includes January–March 1991; 1997 includes October–December 1996; and 1998 includes September–December 1997. In addition, the following state changes override other changes: for California 1987 includes until June 1988, there are "extra" years for October 1996 to February 1997 and October 1997 to February 1998; for Connecticut 1988 and 1989 include October–December 1987 and 1988, respectively, and 1990 includes January–March 1991; for Delaware 1995 includes January–March 1996, and 1998 includes September–December 1997 and January–April 1999; for Hawaii 1990 and 1991 include January–March 1991 and 1992, respectively; for Massachusetts 1987 and 1988 include July–December 1986 and 1987, respectively; for New Jersey, 1991 includes January–March 1992; for Rhode Island the years 1985–88, 1992–95, and 1999 include January–June of the following year, 1989 includes January–April 1990, 1990 includes January–March 1991, 1995 includes January–August 1996, and 1998 includes January–June 1999; for Vermont the years 1985–88 include January–June of the following year, 1989 and 1990 include January–March of the following year, and 1998 and 2000 include October–December of the preceding year; for Washington, 1990 includes January–March 1991, 1998 includes September–December 1997, and 2000 includes December 1999; for Wisconsin, 1988 includes January–June 1989, 1989 includes January–March 1990.

The first row of table 12.1 pools all the observations for the entire 22-year period. The underlying standard deviation of log wages is estimated to be 0.6 and the spillover parameter β is 8.8 which implies that the maximum size of the spillover effect is 0.11 log points.

Given the large literature on rising inequality in the United States, one might be concerned about assuming the underlying variance of wages is constant. The next four rows estimate the model for different sub-samples. As was the conclusion in Lee's paper, there is no evidence here of rising underlying wage inequality: rather, all of the observed variation in wage inequality at the bottom end of the wage distribution can be accounted for by variations in the level of the minimum wage (see

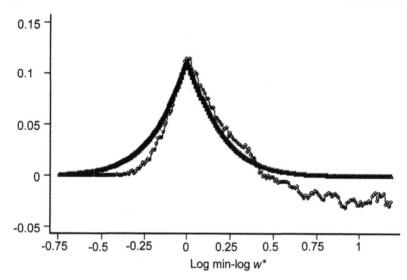

Figure 12.1 Actual and predicted spillover effects of the minimum wage. O, actual spillover; △, predicted spillover.

the next section for further discussion of this). Ironically, there seems to be more evidence of a trend in the spillover effect than in the underlying wage inequality.

To give some idea of how well the model fits the data, figure 12.1 plots the actual and predicted spillover effects against the gap between the minimum wage and the latent wage. (12.5) makes it clear that the predicted spillover effect depends only on this gap and this formula is used to compute the prediction. The actual spillover effect for each observation, s_a, is measured by

$$s_a = w - \max(w_m, w^*) \qquad (12.7)$$

that is, the difference between the actual wage and the predicted direct effect. This actual spillover effect is then averaged over values of the gap between the minimum wage and the latent wage. Note that both the actual and predicted spillover effects are estimated conditional on the value of σ reported in table 12.1.

As can be seen from figure 12.1, the model does a good job in explaining the data. The spillover does peak where the minimum equals the latent wage and decays on either side of this. There are some ways in which the model could probably be changed to fit the data even better. There is some evidence that the spillover effect for those whose latent wage is just below the minimum is over-estimated and also, perhaps, that the wages of those further up the wage distribution actually decline. But,

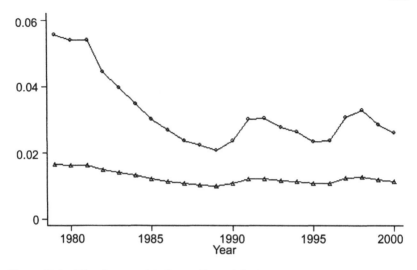

Figure 12.2 The direct and indirect effect of the US minimum wage on average wages. ○, direct effect; △, spillover effect.
Note: These use the parameter estimates from row 1 of table 12.1. The left-hand axis is the percentage increase in the average wage.

the actual deviation between predicted and observed is relatively small and these nuances are left for development elsewhere.

How big are the spillover effects? One way of getting some idea of this is to compare the implied direct and spillover effect on total mean log wages for the US economy. As this varies with the level of the minimum wage, a time series is plotted in figure 12.2. The direct impact varies a lot over time with the level of the minimum wage, being high at the beginning of the sample period and then declining through the 1980s only to increase slightly in the 1990s. In contrast, the estimated spillover effect is relatively constant implying that it raises wages by about 1.7%.

Figure 12.2 provides estimates of the impact of the minimum wage on the average level of wages. But, one might also be interested in the impact on the distribution of wages. The conventional wisdom is that the US minimum wage has a rather small impact on the overall wage distribution but, as the following section makes clear, one can make a strong case that the minimum wage is far more important than that.

12.2 The Minimum Wage and Changes in US Wage Inequality

There is an enormous literature on the evolution of US wage inequality over the past three decades (for a recent survey, see Katz and Autor 1999).

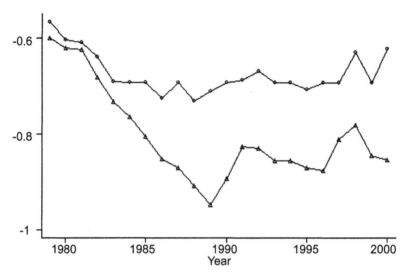

Figure 12.3 The evolution of US wage inequality and the minimum wage, 1979–2000. O, log 10–50 differential; △, log Kaitz index.
Notes. Data are from the CPS monthly outgoing rotation groups. The log Kaitz index is computed as the log of the federal minimum divided by the median wage.

The consensus view is that the increase in wage inequality is the result of technological progress that is biased in favor of skilled workers and that the increase in the supply of skilled workers has failed to match the increase in demand. The purpose of this section is to argue that the evidence for a strong underlying rise in wage inequality at the bottom (but not the top) end of the distribution is much weaker than might be thought given this literature and that what changes there have been can be ascribed in large part to changes in the minimum wage.

First, start with the trends in wage inequality in the United States that are so often discussed. As the minimum wage only affects the bottom end of the wage distribution, we do not consider what has been happening above the median. Figure 12.3 plots the log 10–50 wage differential from the CPS monthly outgoing rotation groups against the log of the ratio of the federal minimum wage to the median wage, the log of the Kaitz index. The most striking episode is the dramatic fall in the log 10–50 differential in the 1980s. But, it is important to realize that this trend has not continued in the 1990s: wage inequality at the bottom end has been in slight decline. This broadly mirrors changes in the Kaitz index. The Kaitz index fell dramatically in the 1980s as the federal minimum was constant in nominal terms; since then the general trend has been upwards although this trend comprises a few large changes between which the real value of the minimum wage is eroded by inflation. Figure 12.3 suggests there may be some link between the minimum wage and the evolution of wage inequality in the bottom half of the US wage distribution. However, the apparent close correlation between the two series in figure 12.3 may be the result of the presence of the median wage in both series so better evidence is needed.

To try to allay some of these fears, table 12.2 presents some regressions. From the CPS monthly outgoing rotation groups we constructed percentiles of the wage distribution by month for each state for the period January 1979 to December 2000. We are interested in how changes in log wages at different percentiles respond to changes in the minimum wage. Of course, the minimum wage is fixed in nominal terms but we would like some real measure of the impact of the minimum wage: consequently we measure the impact of the minimum wage as the log of the Kaitz index for the whole economy. The regressions take the form

$$\Delta \log(w_F)_{st} = \beta [\Delta \log(w_{\min})_{st} - \Delta \log(w_{50})_t]$$

$$+ \text{ state dummies} + \text{year dummies} + \text{month dummies}$$

$$(12.8)$$

where $\Delta \log(w_F)_{st}$ is the monthly change in the log wage at the Fth percentile in state s at time t (which is monthly). To avoid the problems caused by the monthly sampling variation in the median wage, the change in the Kaitz index is instrumented by the change in the minimum wage. These regressions are similar in spirit although different in detail from those in Lee (1999) who used annual data and whose sample ended in 1989. It should be emphasized that estimating equations of the form of (12.8) is quite a tough test for the impact of the minimum wage: we are looking for extra wage growth in months where the minimum wage changes.

The results from this equation are presented in Panel A in table 12.2. The first row shows a significant impact of the change in the minimum wage on the 10th percentile with an elasticity of 0.146, a smaller effect on the 25th percentile that is on the margins of statistical significance and insignificant (although negative) effects on other percentiles. How much of the changes in wage inequality can be explained using this simple regression? The answer, for the bottom end of the wage distribution is more than everything that actually occurred. Figure 12.4 plots the year effects from the regression in (12.8) for the 25th, 50th, 75th, and 90th percentiles relative to the 10th percentile. These can be thought of as giving an estimate of the evolution of wage inequality if the minimum wage had been continuously adjusted to keep the Kaitz index constant. The fall in the underlying log 50–10 wage differential says that there is an

TABLE 12.2
The Impact of the Minimum Wage on the US Wage Distribution

	(1) 10th Percentile	(2) 25th Percentile	(3) 50th Percentile	(4) 75th Percentile	(5) 90th Percentile
A.					
Change in log Kaitz index	0.146	0.074	−0.060	−0.051	−0.106
	(0.045)	(0.051)	(0.048)	(0.052)	(0.061)
Observations	13110	13110	13110	13110	13110
R^2			0.12	0.06	0.07
B.					
Change in log Kaitz index	0.330	0.241	0.107	0.000	0.110
	(0.100)	(0.115)	(0.110)	(0.116)	(0.137)
Change in log Kaitz index × wage rank	−0.408	−0.372	−0.370	−0.113	−0.481
	(0.190)	(0.218)	(0.208)	(0.221)	(0.260)
Observations	13110	13110	13110	13110	13110
R^2	0.10	0.09	0.08	0.05	0.05

Notes.
1. The individual observations are from state–month cells for the period 1979–2000 inclusive. Year, month, and state dummies are also included but are not reported. The change in the log of the Kaitz index is instrumented by the change in the log of the minimum wage, and the change in the log of the Kaitz index times the wage rank is instrumented by the change in the log of the minimum wage times the wage rank.
2. Standard errors are in parentheses.

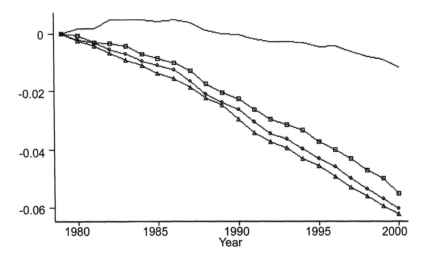

Figure 12.4 The underlying trends in US wage inequality, 1979–2000. O, under-lying change in log 50–10; △, underlying change in log 25–10; □, underlying change in log 75–10; solid line, underlying change in log 90–10. *Notes.* The under-lying change in measures of wage inequality represented in this graph come from the year dummies estimated from the models in the top half of table 12.2.

underlying trend in the economy towards reduction in this measure of wage inequality. As one can see, the results are the same for all the measures of wage inequality except the log 90–10 which is predicted to have been approximately constant.

One can go further in demonstrating the importance of the minimum wage. We would expect the impact of the minimum wage to be larger on those groups with lower wages, for example, we would expect the effect to be stronger in low-wage than high-wage states. The regressions in Panel B of table 12.2 investigate this by including as an extra regressor in (12.8), the average wage in the state in 1989 (measured on a scale from 0 to 1 where 0 is the lowest-wage state and 1 the highest) interacted with the change in the Kaitz index. We would expect this to have a negative sign as the minimum wage will have less impact in high-wage states. This is, indeed, what we find.

This section has argued that changes in the minimum wage have had a demonstrable and large effect on US wage inequality which is too often neglected. These points have been made before (diNardo et al. 1996; Lee 1999; Teulings 2000) and the evidence presented here adds to that presented in those papers—that the evolution of the minimum wage is of first-order importance in understanding trends in equality in the bottom half of the US wage distribution.

This section has shown how the minimum wage affects the wage distribution. The next section considers the impact on employment, an issue that has generated enormous controversy.

12.3 The Minimum Wage and Employment

Perhaps the most controversial aspect of the economics of the minimum wage is its effect on employment. The competitive model has the unambiguous prediction that employment should fall if a binding minimum wages is introduced or raised. There is an enormous empirical literature that seeks to provide estimates of the employment effect and there is little point in reviewing all the studies here (for a relatively recent review, see Brown 1999). Prior to the early 1990s, something of a consensus had been established about the impact of minimum wages on employment in the United States, namely that, while the minimum wage had no effect on the employment of adults (because it was set so low), it did have a modest but significantly negative effect on the employment rate of teenagers. This view was powerfully challenged by Card and Krueger (1995) who, in a series of studies, concluded that there was no evidence of a negative employment effect from the minimum wage. Perhaps their most celebrated study (Card and Krueger 1994) was the comparison of employment changes in fast food restaurants in New Jersey and eastern Pennsylvania when New Jersey raised its minimum wage above the federal minimum in April 1992. The debate about these claims was, at times, acrimonious primarily because the 1990s was a time in which the raising of the minimum wage was an active political issue. It has rumbled on for the best part of a decade: see Card and Krueger (2000) and Neumark and Wascher (2000) for the latest installments in the debate about the New Jersey study (with Card and Krueger coming off better).

Many labor economists have had problems in even conceiving of the possibility that the minimum wage does not destroy jobs, even likening (apparently with a straight face) the Card–Krueger and other similar findings to a reversal of the laws of gravity. But, if labor markets are monopsonistic, one should not really be surprised by or skeptical of such findings as it is well-known that minimum wages do not necessarily reduce employment under monopsony. Indeed, textbooks often only discuss monopsony in the context of this "contrary" prediction about the impact of the minimum wage.

In the textbook model of a single monopsonist, the relationship between employment and the minimum wage looks something like that drawn in figure 12.5. Employment is maximized by choosing a minimum

Figure 12.5   The relationship between employment and the minimum wage: the single monopsonist.

Notes. The vertical axis is the change in log employment from the free market level. The log minimum wage is measured as a deviation from the free market log wage. The parameters used are an elasticity of the labor supply curve facing the employer of five and an elasticity of the marginal revenue product curve of one.

wage that is the market-clearing level which, if the elasticity of the labor supply curve facing the employer is $(1/\varepsilon)$ and the elasticity of the marginal revenue product of labor curve is $(1/\eta)$, implies a rise of $\varepsilon \ln(1 + \varepsilon)/(\varepsilon + \eta)$ in the log wage with an associated log employment gain of $\ln(1 + \varepsilon)/(\varepsilon + \eta)$. In this textbook model of monopsony there is always some appropriately chosen minimum wage that can raise employment and the scope for minimum wages to do this is determined by the monopsony power of employers (as measured by the elasticity of the labor supply curve facing them). But, these conclusions are based on a partial equilibrium model of a single monopsonist and it is important to consider the extent to which they remain true in a general equilibrium model as the minimum wage is never a policy that affects a single employer.

There are two important distinctions between partial equilibrium models of monopsony and general equilibrium models of oligopsony. First, in general equilibrium, there is an important distinction between the elasticity of labor supply to the market as a whole and to individual employers. While the gap between the marginal product and the wage is determined by the elasticity of the labor supply curve facing an individual employer, any aggregate employment effect will be determined by the elasticity of the labor supply curve to the labor market as a whole. There is no reason why these should be the same but it is exactly that assumption that is made by the model of a single monopsonist.

Secondly, it is important to take account of heterogeneity. There is no doubt that the minimum wage is a blunt instrument, applied across whole labor markets on employers who would otherwise choose very different wages. This means that it is almost certainly the case that the minimum wage will have different effects on employment in different employers and any measure of the impact on aggregate employment must take account of this heterogeneity.

To consider these issues, we will use a model based on that used by Dickens et al. (1999) and similar to that used in the discussion of the employer size–wage effect in section 4.1. Assume firm i has a log marginal revenue product of labor curve given by

$$\mathrm{mrpl}_i = a_i - \eta n_i \tag{12.9}$$

where n is log employment and a is a shock to the MRPL that reflects demand or productivity shocks. If the labor market is perfectly competitive then the elasticity of the labor demand curve would be $(1/\eta)$.

Turning to the labor supply curve to the firm, we will use a very simple model. Analogous to the Dixit and Stiglitz (1977) model of imperfectly competitive product demand curves, assume that the share of total employment, N, going to employer i, N_i, is given by its wage, W_i, relative to an average wage index W and an employer-specific shock, B_i,[3] according to the following function:

$$\frac{N_i}{N} = \left(\frac{W_i}{B_i W}\right)^{1/\varepsilon} \tag{12.10}$$

Also, assume that the labor supply to the whole market, is given by the following function:

$$N = N_0 W^\phi \tag{12.11}$$

so that an increase in the average wage encourages more workers to enter the labor market. Combining (12.10) and (12.11), taking logs, and denoting logs of variables by lower case, we can write the labor supply curve facing the individual employer as

$$w_i = (1 - \varepsilon\phi)w + \varepsilon(n_i - n_0) + b_i \tag{12.12}$$

---

[3] B_i is a firm specific labor supply shock that could represent differences in the nonpecuniary attractiveness of work in different firms. An alternative, more general interpretation, is that it represents differences in the wages paid in different firms necessary to prevent shirking or differences in the bargaining power of workers in different firms. It is the existence of this shock that ensures that the model generates a distribution of wages even if the labor market is perfectly competitive.

If the labor market is perfectly competitive then $\varepsilon = 0$ but if $\varepsilon > 0$ the market is, to some extent, monopsonistic. Note that the impact of the average wage on the labor supply curve to an individual employer is ambiguous in sign as there are two effects. On the one hand, a higher average wage means any individual employer needs to pay a higher wage to get the same fraction of employment as before. On the other hand, a higher average wage means that the overall supply of labor to the market increases which has the opposite effect. Note that in the model of (12.12) the only route for the minimum wage to affect the labor supply curve to individual employers is through the average wage and the effect will be the same for all employers.[4]

For future use, let us rewrite (12.12) by subsuming n_0 into b_i and writing the coefficient on the average wage as θ. (12.12) then becomes

$$w_i = \theta w + \varepsilon n_i + b_i \qquad (12.13)$$

To keep the mathematics simple, assume w is the average log wage across firms.

First, consider the equilibrium when there are no minimum wages. Each firm chooses the level of employment where the log MRPL equals the log marginal cost of labor which, from (12.13) is given by

$$\text{mcl}_i = \ln(1 + \varepsilon) + w_i = \ln(1 + \varepsilon) + \theta w + \varepsilon n_i + b_i \qquad (12.14)$$

Equating (12.14) and (12.9) gives employment in firm i as

$$n_i = \frac{-\theta w - \ln(1 + \varepsilon) + a_i - b_i}{\eta + \varepsilon} \equiv n(w, a_i, b_i) \qquad (12.15)$$

and from (12.13) the wage is

$$w_i = \frac{\eta \theta w - \varepsilon \ln(1 + \varepsilon) + \varepsilon a_i + \eta b_i}{\eta + \varepsilon} \qquad (12.16)$$

(12.15) and (12.16) are easy to understand. Revenue shocks, a, have a positive effect on employment while supply shocks, b, have a negative effect. In contrast, both a and b are positively related to wages although, as we would expect, a only has an effect to the extent that the labor market is not perfectly competitive (where $\varepsilon > 0$)—these are the correlations between wages and employer characteristics described in chapter 8. For future use, define v_i by

$$v_i = \frac{\varepsilon a_i + \eta b_i}{\eta + \varepsilon} \qquad (12.17)$$

---

[4] This goes against the evidence on spillovers presented in the previous section: one could make the elasticity depend on the minimum wage but this would complicate the model without altering the basic points that will be made.

If a_i and b_i are jointly normally distributed (the most convenient assumption for what follows), then will have a normal distribution v_i. For future use denote the variance of v_i by σ_w where the notation reflects the fact that, from (12.16), this will be the variance of log wages in the absence of the minimum wage.

One can then solve the model by taking expectations of (12.16) and using the assumption that $E(w_i) = w$. Normalize so that $E(a_i) = E(b_i) = 0$: this means that in a competitive equilibrium w and n will be zero. So all the derived equilibrium expressions for w and n derived below should be thought of as log deviations from the competitive equilibrium. The free market equilibrium level of wages is given by

$$w = \frac{-\varepsilon \ln(1 + \varepsilon)}{\varepsilon + \eta(1 - \theta)} = \frac{-\ln(1 + \varepsilon)}{1 + \phi\eta} \qquad (12.18)$$

and the equilibrium level of employment across firms is

$$n = -\frac{(1 - \theta)\ln(1 + \varepsilon)}{\varepsilon + \eta(1 - \theta)} = -\phi w \qquad (12.19)$$

Both the free market level of wages and employment are below the perfectly competitive level (both expressions are negative): this is what we would expect from the textbook treatment of a single monopsonist. But, modeling interactions between firms does provide some insights that the model of a single monopsonist does not. Note that wages are always below the competitive level with the extent of the deviation depending on ε, the inverse of the elasticity of the labor supply curve to the individual employer. But, as (12.19) shows, the employment effect can be written as the wage effect multiplied by the *aggregate* labor supply elasticity. So, if aggregate labor supply is inelastic, wages will be below the competitive level but employment will not.

Now consider what happens if a minimum wage of w_m is introduced. A firm can be in one of three qualitatively distinct regimes. To understand the three regimes consider the special case where all firms face the same labor supply curve that, in the presence of a minimum wage, might be given by something like SS in figure 12.6 but they differ in the position of their MRPL curves.

In the first, which we will call the unconstrained regime, the MRPL intersects the MCL at a wage above the minimum: employment will then be on the supply curve. A firm with MRPL1 in figure 12.6 will be in the unconstrained regime. As the MRPL curve is lowered, there eventually comes a point where the wage the firm would want to pay is the minimum wage. For slightly lower MRPL curves, the firm is constrained to pay the minimum but employment will still be determined by the supply curve. Refer to these as supply-constrained firms: such a firm could be repre-

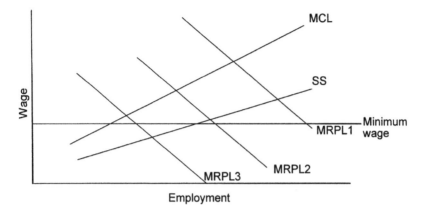

Figure 12.6 The three regimes for the impact of the minimum wage.

Notes. A firm with MRPL1 will be in the unconstrained regime as it will choose to pay a wage above the minimum as MCL and MRPL1 intersect at a level of employment requiring a wage above the minimum. A firm with MRPL2 will be in the supply constrained regime as it will choose to pay the minimum wage but employment will be on the supply curve. A firm with MRPL3 will be in the demand constrained regime as it will choose to pay the minimum wage but employment will be on the MRPL curve.

sented by MRPL2 in figure 12.6. But if the MRPL curve is lowered further still, there comes a point where the marginal revenue product of the labor supply forthcoming at the minimum wage is less than the minimum wage. These firms will be constrained to pay the minimum but employment will be at the point where the MRPL equals the minimum. Refer to these firms as demand-constrained: such a firm could be represented by MRPL3 in figure 12.6. It should be obvious from this discussion that both the supply- and demand-constrained firms actually pay the minimum wage so that there will be a mass of firms paying the minimum.

Now consider the mathematics. A firm in the unconstrained regime pays a wage above the minimum and the employment and wage rates of (12.15) and (12.16) continue to be relevant. Note that if $\theta \neq 0$, the change in w caused by the minimum wage will mean that the set of firms initially paying above w_m will not be the same as the ones now paying above w_m and that although the unconstrained firms pay above the minimum they are still affected by it (from (12.15) $n(w, a_i, b_i)$ is affected by the average level of wages). A firm will be in this regime if the desired wage as given by (12.16) is above w_m, that is, if

$$v_i \equiv \frac{\varepsilon a_i + \eta b_i}{\varepsilon + \eta} \geq w_m - \frac{\eta \theta w - \varepsilon \ln(1 + \varepsilon)}{\varepsilon + \eta} \equiv v^* \qquad (12.20)$$

For a firm with v_i slightly below the right-hand side of (12.20), it is optimal to pay w_m and accept all workers forthcoming at this wage: these are the supply-constrained firms described earlier. Employment in these firms can be found by substituting $w_i = w_m$ in (12.13). One can write this as

$$n_i = \frac{w_m - \theta w - b_i}{\varepsilon} = n(w, a_i, b_i) + \frac{1}{\varepsilon}\left(w_m - \frac{\eta\theta w - \varepsilon\ln(1 + \varepsilon)}{\varepsilon + \eta} - v_i\right)$$

$$= n(w, a_i, b_i) + \frac{1}{\varepsilon}(v^* - v_i)$$

(12.21)

where $n(w, a_i, b_i)$ is defined in (12.15). (12.21) has a simple interpretation. It says that one can think of employment in these firms as being determined by what employment would be in the absence of the minimum wage ($n(w, a, b)$) plus a measure of how much the minimum wage raises the wage in this firm above what it would otherwise be (this is $v^* - v_i$) multiplied by ($1/\varepsilon$) which is the elasticity of employment with respect to the wage along the supply curve. Employment in these firms will be higher with the minimum wage than without.

But if the MRPL curve is sufficiently low then the firm will be in a situation where it is not profitable for the firm to employ all the workers forthcoming at w_m: these are the demand-constrained firms. They pay the minimum wage and choose employment so that $\mathrm{mrpl}_i = w_m$. Using (12.9) and (12.13), a firm will be in this regime if

$$-\frac{\eta}{\varepsilon}(w_m - \theta w - b_i) + a_i < w_m \quad\Rightarrow$$

(12.22)

$$v_i < w_m - \frac{\theta\eta w}{\varepsilon + \eta} \equiv v_1^* = v^* - \frac{\varepsilon\ln(1 + \varepsilon)}{\varepsilon + \eta}$$

After some re-arrangement, one can derive the following expression for employment in these firms:

$$n_i = -\frac{1}{\eta}(w_m - a_i) = n(w, a_i, b_i) + \frac{\ln(1 + \varepsilon)}{\varepsilon + \eta} - \frac{1}{\eta}(v_1^* - v_i) \quad (12.23)$$

(12.23) has a simple interpretation as well. It says that employment will be what it would be in the absence of the minimum wage minus a measure of the bite of the minimum wage (this is given by the term $v_1{}^* - v_i$) times the elasticity of employment with respect to the wage along the MRPL curve. Note that the second term in the final expression is the standard monopsony formula for the maximal gain in employment: this implies that firms at the edge of this region will have higher employment than in the free market.

Now, analyze the effect of a rise in the minimum wage on the market as a whole. There is no closed-form analytical solution but Appendix 12A provides the requisite mathematics. Here, we concentrate on some simulations that give a flavor of the predictions of the model. The effect of the minimum wage on employment is a function of a relatively small number of parameters: the elasticity of the labor supply curve facing a firm, $(1/\varepsilon)$, the elasticity of the MRPL curve, $(1/\eta)$, the underlying variance in the distribution of wages, σ_w, and the size of the spillover effect, θ (which also embodies the elasticity of the supply of labor to the market as a whole).

First, consider what the model implies about the relationship between the minimum wage and employment. As a base case, assume that the sensitivity of wages to employer size is given by $\varepsilon = 0.2$ so that the wage elasticity of the labor supply curve to the employer is 5. For the elasticity of the labor demand curve assume that $\eta = 1$. Finally, assume that the spillover effect is $\theta = 0.25$. For these parameter values, figure 12.7a plots the deviation in employment from the free market level as a function of the spike for a number of different values of the underlying standard deviation of log wages. For small standard deviations, the impact on employment is minuscule for all values of the spike below 10%. However, as the standard deviation rises, the employment losses become larger. The intuition is that the downside risk to employment in the worst affected firms is larger than the up-side potential in the firms where the employment impact is positive (think of labeling the horizontal axis in figure 12.4 as the difference between the minimum wage and the free market wage and then averaging across the horizontal axis to get an "average" effect on employment) so that a wider spread of outcomes leads to lower employment. If there is little dispersion in wages one can "fine-tune" the minimum wage to what is desirable for the small range of wages, whereas high underlying wage dispersion implies that a minimum wage that is good for employment in some firms will have undesirable effects for others. One implication of this is that it may be desirable to have different minimum wages for different groups of workers as, within specific groups, the variance in wages will be smaller and the minimum wage will be less of a blunt instrument.

Figure 12.7b is similar but now varies the extent of monopsony power in the hands of individual employers, ε, while fixing the standard deviation of wages in the absence of minimum wages at $\sigma_w = 0.4$. Unsurprisingly, the impact of the minimum wage is more beneficial when employers have more monopsony power. Finally, Figure 12.7c varies the spillover effect. As this rises, the minimum wages does more harm. In contrast to the textbook monopsony model, an increase in the minimum wage *always* reduces employment when $\theta = 1$ whatever the amount of monopsony power possessed by individual employers. In this case,

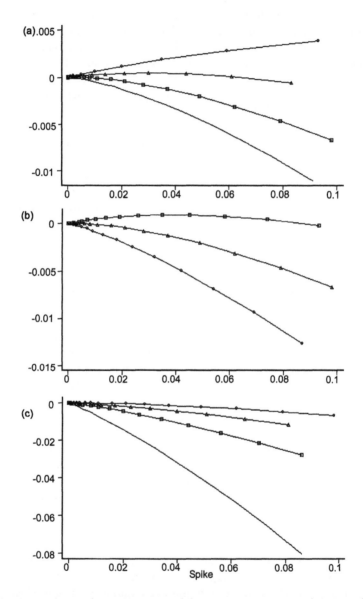

Figure 12.7 The employment impact of the minimum wage as a function of the spike. (a) The effect of varying the standard deviation of wages. O, $\sigma_w = 0.2$; $\triangle$, $\sigma_w = 0.3$; $\square$, $\sigma_w = 0.4$; solid line, $\sigma_w = 0.5$. (b) The effect of varying the degree of monopsony power. O, $\varepsilon = 0.1$; $\triangle$, $\varepsilon = 0.2$; $\square$, $\varepsilon = 0.3$. (c) The effect of varying the degree of spillovers. O, $\theta = 0.25$; $\triangle$, $\theta = 0.5$; $\square$, $\theta = 0.75$; solid line, $\theta = 1$.

labor supply to the individual employer depends only on relative wages (see (12.13)) and the supply of labor to the market as a whole is completely inelastic so that a minimum wage cannot raise total employment and can only crowd out employment in demand-constrained firms.

This discussion should have made it clear that, in contrast to textbook models of single monopsonists, a low enough level of the minimum wage does not necessarily raise employment in an oligopsonistic labor market. For what they are worth (and they are a very poor substitute for empirical research), the simulations suggest that there may be a relatively wide range of minimum wages over which the impact on employment is likely to be small but that the potential down-side from excessively high minimum wages exceeds the potential up-side for a well-chosen one. However, a well-chosen minimum wage is not beyond the reach of good policy. The impact of minimum wages on employment should primarily be an empirical issue and the results of these empirical studies should be used to inform policy.

12.4 Models of Trade Unions

The textbook analysis of trade unions primarily consists of two models (for a survey, see Booth 1995). In the labor demand curve model (sometimes also called the "right-to-manage" model), unions negotiate wages with employers but employers then unilaterally choose employment given this wage. The outcome is on the labor demand curve and, the higher the union-negotiated wage, the lower employment will be. This model lies behind the common argument that unions destroy jobs.

But, an outcome on the labor demand curve is not (as long as unions care about employment at all) efficient from the perspective of unions and employers. Both agents can be made better off by some other wage–employment deal. The assumption that wages and employment are negotiated jointly and the outcome is efficient is the efficient bargain model of McDonald and Solow (1981). In contrast to the labor demand curve model, it is now possible (it depends on union preferences) that an increase in union bargaining power leads to a rise in both wages and employment—although Layard and Nickell (1990) make the point that this conclusion often does not stand up in general equilibrium.

In both of these models, labor supply to the employer is not seen as an issue: the implicit assumption is that as soon the union wage goes above the prevailing market wage, there is a potentially infinite supply of workers wanting a job in the firm. The first change to the analysis of trade unions that needs to be made when one assumes the labor market is monopsonistic is that this is not necessarily the case: labor supply may still be a constraint even for union-negotiated wages.

Start with the simplest monopsony model in which the labor supply depends only on the wage paid by the employer, $N(w)$. In the absence of a union, the wage will be chosen to maximize profits $[Y(N) - wN]$ subject to this labor supply curve. If the employer is unionized, it is clear that the wage will rise but, in the first instance employment will still be on the labor supply curve. Note that there is no meaningful distinction here between the labor demand and efficient bargain models: given the nego-tiated wage, both union and employer will be happy to accept the higher labor supply to the firm. In this situation, the wage paid by the employer and employment will be positively correlated.

But, if the union negotiates a much higher wage, then the firm will enter a region where the marginal product of labor at the labor supply to the firm is less than the wage. This is a situation where the conventional analysis applies and, if the labor demand curve model is the appropriate one, then employment will begin to fall as the wage increases.

This analysis is based on the simplest monopsony model where labor supply can only be influenced by the wage paid. But, as emphasized in the overview of monopsony models in chapter 2, there are other ways in which labor supply can be influenced, for example, through the level of recruitment activity. Recognizing this might be thought to overturn the results above. For example, as wages rise and profits fall, one might think that the incentive for employers to recruit workers also falls and that this effect might dominate the direct effect on labor supply. However, the analysis of the generalized model of monopsony in section 2.3 showed that this is not necessarily the case: if there are increasing marginal costs of recruitment, employment may increase as the employer is forced to pay higher wages.

Recognizing the use of recruitment intensity as an additional instrument for influencing labor supply drives a distinction between the labor demand and efficient bargain models. One might think that it is very difficult (and relatively rare) for unions to influence recruitment intensity so that the labor demand curve model is more appropriate (in the sense of employers having unilateral control over recruitment intensity) but unions may be able to influence this by restrictions on the organization of work within the workplace (what is sometime called "feather-bedding").

This analysis of the impact of trade unions on employment should be recognized as being exactly the same as the analysis of the impact of the minimum wage. As the wage rises, employment first rises and then falls depending on whether labor supply or labor demand is the main constraint on employment. Perhaps consistent with this view is the empirical finding (see the estimates in table 4.4) that the correlation between wages and employer size is weaker in the union than the non-union sector.

The discussion above has assumed that collective bargaining is decentralized, between an individual employer and its workers. This is the most common institutional set-up in the United States and the United Kingdom but not in many continental European countries. There collective bargaining is often at a more aggregate level: region and/or industry in many countries and even almost at the level of the whole economy in some (although the caricature of the whole economy's wages being determined in a single bargain was always some distance from reality). This type of system is often loosely described as "corporatist" although the exact meaning of the term is the subject of a debate that is best avoided in the current context.

The comparison of "corporatist" and "competitive" systems of wage determination is the subject of an extremely interesting book by Teulings and Hartog (1998). Their preferred model of the labor market is "rent-sharing" although most if not all of their conclusions would also apply if the "free" market is monopsonistic. Perhaps the most important consequence of "corporatist" wage-setting is that it reduces equilibrium wage dispersion because it attempts to mimic a competitive market and set a single wage for the whole market. Teulings and Hartog present evidence that wage dispersion is indeed lower in corporatist countries. There is little surprise in that but, more crucially, they show that this is not because the returns to skill are particularly low but because returns to variables like industry affiliation, employer size, job tenure, and gender are markedly lower in corporatist countries. They (like this book) argue that a large part of these elements of wage dispersion are the result of labor market frictions. They conclude that corporatist institutions may lead to a structure of wages that more closely resembles the ideal of a perfectly competitive market than the "free" market.

One might expect that corporatist institutions affect not just the dispersion in wages but also the level. To the extent that centralized unions are more powerful, one might expect that this will lead to higher wages. But, there are arguments that more centralized bargaining internalizes certain externalities and that this tends to lead to lower wages. This argument was first put forward by Calmfors and Driffill (1988). The monopsony model adds another possible externality to the list: when, in a decentralized system, an employer and its union negotiate a higher wage and the labor supply to a firm increases, part of this increase in labor supply is at the expense of other firms, that is, part of the private gains are the losses of other employers and unions in the economy. In contrast, a more centralized system would recognize that any increase in employment from raising wages can only come from non-employment. Hence, there are arguments that more centralized systems of collective bargaining may lead not only to a more desirable structure of wages but also a more appropriate level. It is hard to evaluate these arguments without reference to macro-economic evidence that has many other confounding factors and, in any case, it seems slightly naive to imagine that the United States or the United Kingdom could introduce significantly greater centralization in collective bargaining. But, it is a real issue in some continental European countries.[5]

There is much theory about the impact of trade unions on employment but surprisingly little microeconometric evidence. There are a few papers that attempt to distinguish between the labor demand curve and efficient bargain models (e.g., Brown and Ashenfelter 1986; MaCurdy and Pencavel 1986) and a few papers that relate employment growth to union status (e.g., for the United States, Leonard 1992; for the United Kingdom, Blanchflower et al. 1991; Machin and Wadhwani 1991). But it is hard to find empirical papers that attempt to answer the fundamental question "what is the effect of trade unions on the level of employment?" Perhaps the main reason for this is that there are very good reasons to believe that union status is endogenous so a convincing study of the impact on employment needs a good instrument.

A recent paper by diNardo and Lee (2001) exploits the fact that, in the United States, union recognition is usually only achieved after a representation election so that there is a big difference in union status between plants in which unions get 50.1% of the votes (and gain representation) and those in which they get 49.9% and fail to get representation. However, the ex ante characteristics of these plants are likely to be very similar. Using this version of the "regression discontinuity" approach, they conclude that unions have no effect on plant closure rates and their spot estimates on the impact on employment are positive though with large standard errors. These findings are obviously hard to reconcile with the competitive view of unions but are easily consistent with the monopsony view. Undoubtedly, this is an area where more empirical research is needed.

12.5 Trade Unions and Wages

The discussion of the previous section suggests that trade unions raise wages. No surprises there, but one might be interested in whether the monopsony model has any distinctive predictions about where trade

---

[5] Teulings and Hartog (1998) also argue that corporatist institutions are more effective at introducing aggregate wage flexibility in response to shocks: their argument is interesting but rather far from the main subject here.

unions are more likely to make wage gains as, at least since the pioneering work of Lewis (1963), it has been recognized that the union wage mark-up varies across the economy. The economic theory of the trade union suggests that it is union preferences, union bargaining power, and the elasticity of the labor demand curve that determines the union wage mark-up. To this list, monopsony would also add the elasticity of the labor supply curve to the employer. But, it is not clear that this adds much to our understanding of the determinants of the union wage mark-up. Appendix 12B develops a simple model of the union wage mark-up and suggests that, although theory is ambiguous, it may be more likely that the mark-up will be higher in more monopsonistic labor markets. The intuition is simply that the wages set by very powerful unions will be independent of the extent of monopsony power in the labor market as labor supply will not be a binding constraint on these firms, but the wages of non-union firms will be lower the more monopsonistic is the labor market.

More interesting than the impact of monopsony on the union mark-up perhaps is the impact of union wages on wages in the non-union sector. Lewis (1963) set out the mechanisms that are widely presumed to be the ones at work. First, if union wages affect employment, then this will affect the demand for non-union labor if they are in the same product market and are substitutes or complements in production. One would expect this effect to work through the product market so it would depend on the extent of unionization in the product market. Second, if labor is displaced from the union sector, then this is presumed to increase the supply of non-union labor, driving down wages there. This effect is most likely to work through the local labor market so one might think that a measure of the local unionization rate would be appropriate for measuring this.

However, although the empirical evidence is mixed (see the original discussion in Lewis 1963, 1986; Kahn 1980; Freeman and Medoff 1981; Neumark and Wachter 1995 inter alia), it is certainly not the case that all the empirical evidence suggests that a higher rate of unionization in the local labor market depresses non-union wages. Indeed, many studies tend to reach the opposite conclusion. Following Lewis (1963), this is most commonly "explained" by the "threat effect", the idea that the greater the extent of unionization in the labor market, the higher the probability of being unionized and the greater the wage that non-union employers will be prepared to pay to avoid that possibility.

However, monopsony suggests another possibility. Non-union employers will be competing for labor with other employers including those who are unionized. The greater the extent of unionization, the higher wages are likely to be in the local labor market. What effect will that have on the wages that non-union employers are prepared to pay? One way to answer this question is to consider what the impact on the supply of labor is likely to be. From the analysis of the determinants of reservation wages in chapter 9 (see (9.6)), one can see that a shift in the wage offer distribution will raise (reduce) the reservation wage if off-the-job search is more (less) effective than on-the-job search. The empirical evidence presented in table 9.1 strongly suggested that reservation wages will rise. In this case, non-union employers will be forced by the greater extent of unionization to raise wages to obtain the same labor supply as before. Hence, we would expect to see evidence of a positive spillover from unionization onto non-union wages. This effect can be thought of as a variant of the Harris–Todaro "wait" model of unemployment (for a discussion of this effect in the current context, see Borjas 2000: 420–21): if off-the-job search is more effective, then one has a better chance of getting one of the high-wage union jobs if one is unemployed so one's reservation wage rises.

Some empirical evidence on this is presented in table 12.3. The data set is a panel of 110 US cities from 1990 to 2000 inclusive; this is similar to the data used by Neumark and Wachter (1995) for an earlier period. The dependent variable is the log of average non-union private-sector wages. We assume the labor market is segmented by gender and by education (to maintain sample sizes we use only two education groups—those with and without more than a high-school diploma). Other controls included are the usual controls in earnings functions (gender, race, experience, and qualification) plus city and year dummies. As well as the unionization rate in the particular city–year–gender–education cell, we also include the employment/population ratio and the proportion of private-sector workers.

The results for all the segments pooled is presented in the first column of table 12.3. There is a significant positive effect of union density on non-union wages. The second and third columns then restrict attention to low and high education groups, respectively: while there is a positive effect for both groups, it is much larger for the low-education group. These results are in line with those of Neumark and Wachter (1995) for an earlier period. They are consistent with the traditional "threat effect" interpretation as well as the "wage competition effect" suggested above.

One way to try to distinguish between these two hypotheses is to see whether the impact of union density on non-union wages is larger where the threat effect might be presumed to be larger. One way of measuring the size of the threat effect is to use union density in the industry as workers in some industries are much easier to organize than others. The fourth column of table 12.3 uses as the dependent variable the average log non-union private-sector wage in industries where unionization is

TABLE 12.3
The Impact of Unionization on Non-Union Private-Sector Wages (expressed as Log Non-union Wage): Evidence from US Cities, 1990–2000

Sample	(1) All	(2) Low Education	(3) High Education	(4) Low Education Industry Union Density <5%	(5) Low Education Industry Union Density <10%	(6) Low Education Industry Union Density <20%	(7) Low Education Industry Union Density >20%	(8) Low Education Eating and Drinking Places
Union density	0.097	0.194	0.077	0.189	0.156	0.182	0.224	0.246
	(0.024)	(0.034)	(0.040)	(0.050)	(0.043)	(0.037)	(0.058)	(0.084)
Observations	5101	2463	2638	2462	2463	2463	2461	2389
R^2	0.97	0.91	0.95	0.79	0.84	0.88	0.70	0.55

Notes.
1. The individual observations are city–year–gender–education combinations where education is split into two groups: high and low. The sample is restricted to those cities with at least 10 years of observations and an average number of observations of 50 to ensure that the unionization rate does not contain too much measurement error.
2. Other controls included in the equation are the average values by cell of gender, a quadratic in experience (interacted with gender), black (interacted with gender), education, year dummies (plus a separate trend for female wages), city dummies, the male employment/population ratio, and the percentage of private sector workers in the city in the year.
3. Standard errors are clustered on city–year interaction.

below 5%. The fifth, sixth, and seventh columns then use the average for those industries where unionization is below 10%, below 20%, and above 20%, respectively. Although the wage-raising effect of unionization does seem to be largest in the high-density industries, the differences are relatively small and do not seem to be monotonic as there is a very large effect in industries where one might expect the chances of unionization to be minimal. To reinforce this point, the final column of table 12.3 presents estimates for workers in eating and drinking places where unionization is very small (2%). There is a very large positive effect of the city unionization rate on wages.

These results do suggest a positive effect of union density on non-union wages even in industries where the threat of unionization might reasonably be presumed to be minimal. However, one should be somewhat cautious in interpreting these results, particularly as it is not clear where the variation in the union density variable comes from once one has removed city and year effects: we lack a good instrument or "natural experiment" to provide reassurance on this point. But, at the very least, the "wage competition" effect should be considered to be potentially important.

12.6 Conclusions

This chapter has analyzed the likely impact of minimum wages and trade unions in labor markets where employers have market power. That both minimum wages and trade unions raise wages for workers directly affected is no big surprise. More interesting is the impact on employment and on the wages of those who are not directly affected.

The empirical literature on the employment effect of the minimum wage is enormous and no attempt has been made here to survey or contribute to it. The chapter simply provides an analytical framework for thinking about the likely effects, a framework that is important because the partial and general equilibrium effects of minimum wages on employment may be very different in monopsonistic labor markets. In contrast, the empirical literature on the impact of unions on employment is extremely small, probably because of the difficulty in treating union status as exogenous or finding good instruments for it.

The impact of minimum wages and trade unions on the wages of those not directly affected are rather different. For the minimum wage, one is looking at the impact on the wages of those paid more than the minimum and the empirical evidence for the United States suggests these effects are quite large, so large that all of the variation in wage inequality in the bottom half of the US wage distribution can be explained by variation in the federal minimum wage. In contrast, for trade unions, the impact is on those receiving lower wages than in the union sector. The evidence presented here suggests that there are positive spillover effects of union on non-union wages, in line with the predictions of the monopsony model.

Appendix 12A

The Impact of the Minimum Wage

The following proposition outlines the relationship between the minimum wage, average wages, and employment.

Proposition 12.1

1. The relationship between w and w_m can be written as

$$w = w_m + \sigma_w \phi\left(\frac{v^*}{\sigma_w}\right) - \left[1 - \Phi\left(\frac{v^*}{\sigma_w}\right)\right]v^* \qquad (12.24)$$

where v^* is given by (12.20).

2. The fraction of firms paying the minimum wage, the "spike," is given by

$$\Phi^* = \Phi\left(\frac{v^*}{\sigma_w}\right) \qquad (12.25)$$

3. The derivative of w with respect to w_m can be written as

$$\frac{\partial w}{\partial w_m} = \frac{\Phi^*}{1 - \dfrac{\eta\theta(1 - \Phi^*)}{\varepsilon + \eta}} \qquad (12.26)$$

4. The level of employment is given by

$$n = \frac{-\theta w - \ln(1 + \varepsilon)}{\varepsilon + \eta} + \frac{1}{\varepsilon}[(\Phi^* - \Phi_1^*)v^* + \sigma_w(\phi^* - \phi_1^*)]$$

$$+ \Phi_1^* \frac{\ln(1 + \varepsilon)}{\varepsilon + \eta} - \frac{1}{\eta}(\Phi_1^* v_1^* + \sigma_w \phi_1^*) \qquad (12.27)$$

5. *The derivative of employment with respect to w_m can be written as*

$$\frac{\partial n}{\partial w_m} = \frac{-\theta}{\varepsilon + \eta} \frac{\partial w}{\partial w_m} \left(1 - \Phi_1^* + \frac{\eta}{\varepsilon}(\Phi^* - \Phi_1^*)\right)$$

$$+ \left(\frac{1}{\varepsilon}(\Phi^* - \Phi_1^*) - \frac{1}{\eta}\Phi_1^*\right) \tag{12.28}$$

Proof. The cut-off value of v_i between the unconstrained and supply constrained regimes is v^* as defined in (12.20). For unconstrained firms we have that the wage is given by (12.16) which, using (12.20), can be written as $w_i = w_m + v_i - v^*$ while constrained firms pay the minimum wage. This immediately gives (12.25) as the fraction of firms that pay the minimum wage. For the average wage, using (12.16) and (12.17) we have

$$w = E(w_i) = \left[1 - \Phi\left(\frac{v^*}{\sigma_w}\right)\right] E[w_m + v_i - v^* | v_i \geq v^*] + \Phi\left(\frac{v^*}{\sigma_w}\right) w_m \tag{12.29}$$

Using this in (12.29), we can derive

$$w = w_m + (1 - \Phi^*)[E(v_i | v_i \geq v^*) - v^*] \tag{12.30}$$

Using well-known results on the means of truncated normals (see, e.g., Maddala 1983) leads to (12.24). Differentiating (12.24) with respect to the minimum wage leads to

$$\frac{\partial w}{\partial w_m} = 1 + \left[\frac{\partial v^*}{\partial w_m} + \frac{\partial v^*}{\partial w} \frac{\partial w}{\partial w_m}\right] \left[\phi^{*\prime} + \frac{v^*}{\sigma_w}\phi^* - (1 - \Phi^*)\right] \tag{12.31}$$

Now, for the normal distribution $z\phi'(z) = -\phi(z)$. And, from (12.20), we have that

$$\frac{\partial v^*}{\partial w_m} = 1$$

and

$$\frac{\partial v^*}{\partial w} = -\frac{\eta\theta}{\varepsilon + \eta}$$

Using these facts in (12.31) leads to (12.26).

Employment will be an average of employment in the three regimes so using (12.15), (12.21) and (12.23), we have

$$n(w_m) = E(n_i) = E\big(n(w, a_i, b_i)\big) + \frac{1}{\varepsilon}(\Phi^* - \Phi_1^*)E(v^* - v_i|v_1^* \leq v_i \leq v^*)$$

$$+ \frac{1}{\eta}\Phi_1^* \frac{\ln(1 + \varepsilon)}{\varepsilon + \eta} - \frac{1}{\eta}\Phi_1^* E(v_1^* - v_i|v_i \leq v_1^*) \qquad (12.32)$$

where Φ_1^* is the fraction of employers in the demand-constrained regime. Using results about expectations of truncated normal variables leads to (12.27). Differentiation of (12.27) with respect to the minimum wage leads to

$$\frac{\partial n}{\partial w_m} = -\frac{\theta}{\varepsilon + \eta}\frac{\partial w}{\partial w_m} + \left(\frac{\partial v^*}{\partial w_m} + \frac{\partial v^*}{\partial w}\frac{\partial w}{\partial w_m}\right)$$

$$\times \left[\frac{1}{\varepsilon}\left([\Phi^* - \Phi_1^*] + \frac{v^*}{\sigma_w}(\phi^* - \phi_1^*) + \phi^{*\prime} - \phi_1^{*\prime}\right)\right.$$

$$\left. + \frac{\phi_1^*}{\sigma_w}\frac{\ln(1 + \varepsilon)}{\varepsilon + \eta} - \frac{1}{\eta}\left(\Phi_1^* + \frac{\phi_1^* v_1^*}{\sigma_w} + \phi_1^{*\prime}\right)\right]$$

After some re-arrangement, this leads to (12.28).

Discussion of Proposition 12.1

Proposition 12.1(3) shows that the effect of the minimum wage on the average wage must be positive (as long as $\theta > 0$) and less than one so that the ratio of the minimum to the average must rise as the minimum rises. If $\theta = 0$ (so there are no spillover effects), then the effect is simply Φ^* which is the fraction of firms who pay the minimum. Not surprisingly the effect is larger as the spillover effect θ increases.

Proposition 12.1(5) is surprisingly easy to understand. Consider the final term in (12.28). This says that the effect of the minimum wage on employment can be written as the proportion of firms who are supply-constrained times the elasticity of employment with respect to the wage along the supply curve minus the proportion of firms who are demand-constrained times the elasticity of employment with respect to the wage along the demand curve. If $\theta = 0$, these are the only effects but if $\theta > 0$, the rise in the general wage level reduces employment in all firms: this is the first term in (12.28).

Appendix 12B

The Union Wage Mark-Up in a Monopsony Model

A model of the union wage mark-up requires an assumption about union preferences and about the bargaining solution. Assume that union utility, V, is given by

$$\log V = \gamma \log N + \log(w - r) \tag{12.33}$$

where N is employment, w is the wage, and r is the reservation wage. (12.33) is a fairly standard specification, assuming that unions care about both employment and the surplus of wages above the reservation wage with γ giving the weight attached to employment.

Assume that wages are chosen to maximize the asymmetric Nash bargain

$$\rho \log V + \log \Pi \tag{12.34}$$

where $0 \le \rho \le \infty$ is a measure of union bargaining power. Assume that there are constant returns to scale so that profits can be written as

$$\log \Pi = \log(p - w) + \log N \tag{12.35}$$

where p is productivity. The assumption that there is constant returns to scale means that we are never going to be in the region where labor demand is the binding constraint: this helps to make the analysis simpler but is obviously not general.

Finally, we need to specify the labor supply curve facing the employer. Assume that we have

$$\log N = \log N_0 + \varepsilon \log(w - r) \tag{12.36}$$

Combining (12.33)–(12.36), we can write the Nash bargain of (12.34) as

$$[(1 + \rho\gamma)\varepsilon + \rho] \log(w - r) + \log(p - w) + (1 + \rho\gamma) \log N_0 \tag{12.37}$$

Taking first-order conditions of (12.37) with respect to the wage leads to the following expression for the negotiated wage:

$$w = \frac{\mu p + r}{\mu + 1} \tag{12.38}$$

where

$$\mu \equiv [(1 + \rho\gamma)\varepsilon + \rho] \tag{12.39}$$

(12.38) says that the negotiated wage will be a weighted average of marginal product and the reservation wage. The weight on the marginal product will be higher, the higher is union power (as measured by ρ) and the more competitive is the labor market (measured by ε).

But, we are interested in the impact of extent of monopsony in the labor market on the union wage mark-up. Because the mark-up is measured in the effect on log wages, this amounts to being interested in the sign of $\partial^2 \log w / \partial\varepsilon\partial\rho$. This can be written as

$$\frac{\partial^2 \log w}{\partial\varepsilon\partial\rho} = \frac{\partial^2 \log w}{\partial\mu^2} \frac{\partial\mu}{\partial\varepsilon} \frac{\partial\mu}{\partial\rho} + \frac{\partial \log w}{\partial\mu} \frac{\partial^2 \mu}{\partial\varepsilon\partial\rho} \qquad (12.40)$$

Using (12.38) and (12.39), this can be written as

$$\frac{\partial^2 \log w}{\partial\varepsilon\partial\rho} = \frac{k-1}{(1+\mu)^2(1+\mu k)^2}\left\{(1-\mu^2 k)\gamma - [(1+\mu k) + k(1+\mu)]\right\} \qquad (12.41)$$

where $k \equiv (p/r) \geq 1$.

The sign of (12.41) is ambiguous but is perhaps "more likely" to be negative implying that the union wage mark-up is larger in more monopsonistic labor markets. For the final term in (12.41) to be positive requires that

$$\gamma \geq \frac{(1+\mu k) + k(1+\mu)}{1-\mu^2 k} > 1 \qquad (12.42)$$

so that unions have to attach more weight to employment in their utility function than wages.

13

Monopsony and the Big Picture

THE basic idea behind this book is that employers have non-negligible market power over their workers and that our understanding of labor markets would be markedly improved by an explicit recognition of this fact. In many parts of labor economics, a trend in this direction is already visible so this book has brought together existing strands of research as much as it has proposed new ones.

But, there is still some way to go before this is the conventional approach. Labor economists need to realize that, when considering the actions and decisions of a single employer, one needs to use the textbook model of monopsony rather than that of perfect competition to think about their likely behavior. One should not get too hung up on the prefix "mono': no employer exists in isolation and if one is interested in thinking about the behavior of the labor market as a whole, it is important to analyze interactions between employers and one should think in terms of a model of oligopsony or "monopsonistic competition."

13.1 The Sources of Monopsony Power

It is frictions, broadly defined, that give employers monopsony power in the labor market. The most important sources of these frictions are:

- ignorance among workers about labor market opportunities;
- individual heterogeneity in preferences over jobs;
- mobility costs.

The view that employers have some market power can hardly be controversial: it is undoubtedly true that a wage cut of a cent does not cause all existing workers to instantaneously leave the employer. But, skeptics might more legitimately wonder whether the extent of monopsony power in the labor market is large enough to justify a heavy book on the subject.

There are two ways to address these doubts. First, one can try to provide direct evidence on the extent of monopsony power. This means trying to obtain estimates of the elasticity of the labor supply curve facing individual employers. As discussed at length in chapter 4, this simple aim is not so easy to achieve in a credible way. The estimates we have that are based on the most persuasive methodology (Staiger et al. 1999; Falch 2001) show the elasticity to be very low. But, there is scope for a lot more work here.

The second way of providing evidence on the extent of monopsony power is more indirect: to provide evidence on the predictions of monopsony and to emphasize how monopsony can provide a much better explanation of a wide range of labor market phenomena. The bulk of this book has tried to do exactly that. The market power of employers is large enough to explain, among other things, why:

- there is substantial wage dispersion in the labor market (chapter 2);
- there is an employer size wage effect (chapter 4);
- separation rates are lower for high-wage workers (chapter 4);
- employers pay higher wages to more senior workers even if productivity is no higher (chapter 5);
- more experienced displaced workers suffer larger earnings losses (chapter 6);
- part of the cross-sectional returns to job tenure is spurious (chapter 6);
- part of the gender pay gap exists (chapter 7);
- equal pay legislation does not harm the employment of women (chapter 7);
- "good" employers pay more (chapter 8);
- it is hard to find evidence of compensating wage differentials (chapter 8);
- lower-wage workers are more likely to be looking for another job (chapter 9);
- low-wage employers find it harder to fill vacancies (chapter 10);
- employers are prepared to pay for the general training of their workers (chapter 11);
- it is so hard to find evidence of job losses associated with the minimum wage (chapter 12);
- non-union employers pay higher wages in more unionized labor markets (chapter 12).

But, it is important to retain a sense of perspective on what monopsony can and cannot explain.

13.2 A Sense of Perspective

There are parts of labor economics where the conventional wisdom needs to be replaced by a new vision based on the perspective that employers have some market power over their workers. A good example would be thinking about the returns to job tenure discussed in chapter 6. But a "global search and replace" attitude is not what is needed in most of the subject. In most parts of labor economics, the perspective of monopsony does not overwrite existing labor economics: rather it adds to it. To give a very simple example, suppose that one is trying to understand the determinants of the wage of a particular type of worker. A competitive analysis would focus on the demand curve (drawn as DD in figure 13.1) which is the marginal revenue product of labor curve and the supply curve (drawn as SS); this supply curve is the supply to the market as a whole (the elasticity of supply to an individual employer must be infinite). The level of wages is then determined by demand relative to supply. An increase in demand will raise wages, an increase in supply will reduce it.

The monopsony approach does not deny the importance of these factors or of these comparative statics. Instead, it adds another factor to the analysis: the elasticity of the labor supply curve facing the individual employer. This elasticity determines the "gap" between the supply curve and the marginal cost of labor to the employer, marked as MCL in figure 13.1. The lower is this elasticity, the lower will wages be for given demand and supply curves. One can understand this very straightforwardly if one thinks of the equation:

$$w = \frac{1}{1+\varepsilon} MPL \tag{13.1}$$

where ε is the inverse of the wage elasticity of the labor supply curve to the individual employer. It is the addition of ε that is the contribution of focusing on employer market power.

How important is the value-added of monopsony depends on the issue one is considering. If one wants to understand the gap in wages between a chief executive and the person who cleans their office then, although there are arguments in favor of the view that the labor market for cleaners is

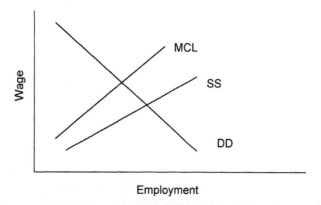

Figure 13.1   Demand and supply curves.

more monopsonistic than that for chief executives (e.g., a much higher fraction of cleaners is likely to be recruited directly from non-employment), this is not the first-order effect. Demand and supply factors are almost certainly the more important components of the explanation: it is the difference in the *MPL* part of (13.1) that is more important than the difference in the ε part in explaining the difference in wages.

But, one should not be carried away by this particular example to imagine that monopsony power is so small as to be ignorable. The frontier of labor economics is not concerned with answering easy questions like "why are chief executives paid more than cleaners?" It is about trying to answer trickier questions about the causes of changes in wage inequality, the impact of minimum wages. And, here, the impact of monopsony is of a size that labor economists cannot ignore. Few estimates of the elasticity of the labor supply curve to an individual employer exceed 5 and (13.1) then implies that wages will be 17% below marginal products, a similar order of magnitude to the union wage mark-up, the change in the log 50–10 wage differential in the United States from 1970 to 1990, and to estimates of how much minimum wages raise the earnings of the low-paid.

Virtually all of the book has been about how a market power perspective can help to explain cross-sectional regularities in labor markets. But, even if one concedes that it is helpful in that regard, one might doubt whether it is so important in explaining changes in the labor market. For example, consider the example of the chief executive and their cleaner introduced above and suppose we observe and want to explain a widening of the wage gap between them (as has occurred in the United States and the United Kingdom in the past two decades). One might explain this as the result of changes in demand relative to supply or as changes in the extent of monopsony power. It is quite likely that the former strikes most economists as the much more plausible explanation but, on closer examination, this is not so obvious.

In section 12.2, it was argued that it is the evolution of the US minimum wage that can explain essentially all of the variation in wage inequality in the bottom half of the US wage distribution in the period 1980–2000. There is no need for recourse to the currently fashionable view that it is an increase in the demand for skills out-stripping the increase in the supply of skills that is responsible. But, what has this conclusion got to do with monopsony in labor markets?

On its own, this view that the minimum wage has been the most important factor in explaining the evolution of wage inequality in the bottom half of the US wage distribution over the past 20 years need have nothing to do with monopsony in the labor market. One could believe that labor markets are perfectly competitive and still think the minimum wage is important. The answer comes when we look at employment rates.

If one believes that labor markets are perfectly competitive, then, as the minimum wage declined in importance in the 1980s, one would expect to see rises in employment rates among those whom it affected as they were priced back into work. And, in the 1990s when the minimum wage was slightly raised, one could expect to see the employment of these groups falling. But, this is not what is observed. For example, Juhn et al. (1991) document how the employment rates of less-skilled workers fell in the 1980s (when their wages were falling fastest) and Murphy and Topel (1997) show that the employment rates stabilized in the late 1980s/ early 1990s when the minimum wage was being raised. Indeed, it was exactly the observation that relative wages and employment of the least-skilled were moving in the same direction in the 1980s that led to the diagnosis of a relative demand shift as the underlying cause of the trends in employment and wages (see, e.g., the analysis in Katz and Murphy 1992). But, if the minimum wage is the cause of the changes in wage inequality in the bottom half of the distribution, then one can no longer use a perfectly competitive model to explain the changes in employment rates. In contrast, monopsony has no problem explaining the facts as there is no reason why the decline in the minimum wage in the 1980s should not have reduced the employment rates of the least-skilled.

So, the view that the labor market is fundamentally monopsonistic is necessary for understanding a "big issue"—the evolution of US wage inequality in the past two decades. Ignoring the existence of employer market power leads to incorrect conclusions on the driving force behind changes in wage inequality.

13.3 Monopsony and Labor Market Policy

One of the reasons that many labor economists feel uneasy about the use of the word "monopsony" is that it has emotive connotations that employers "exploit" workers. In the technical sense of the word, "exploitation" used by Hicks (1932) and Pigou (1924), this is true: wages are likely to be below the marginal product of labor. But, the policy conclusion that would most commonly be drawn from this fact—that wages should be raised—is not necessarily justified.

This book has been almost entirely about the positive, not the normative aspects of monopsony. This is for a good reason (described in more detail in chapter 3): one cannot draw conclusions about the merits or demerits of certain types of policy that are robust to reasonable variations in the underlying model of the labor market. The analysis of the minimum wage in chapters 3 and 12 should have made this clear: for example, the existence of monopsony power is not sufficient for the minimum wage to be a desirable policy once one moves away from the textbook model of a simple monopsonist.

This does not mean that the book has no conclusions about labor market policy. But, the main conclusion is that one should be open-minded about the impact of policy and rely on good quality empirical research on policy before reaching any strong conclusions. The reason for this is that a monopsonistic view of the labor market does make one less inclined to a rush to judgment based on theoretical arguments. Time and again, we have seen examples where the impact of policy differs from what would be expected in a competitive labor market. The analysis of the minimum wage, trade unions, restrictions on employment contracts, equal pay legislation, and even welfare benefits may differ significantly from the conventional wisdom.

Many, if not most, labor economists have no need of the advice to be open-minded and to judge policy interventions on the basis of empirical research alone. The trend in recent years has been towards a more empirical approach and that is to be welcomed and encouraged. If this book has one thing to contribute in this area, it is to weaken still further the grip that the predictions of the competitive model has on the further recesses of the mind of some labor economists.

This instruction to be open-minded also applies to the analysis of those economies where a model of monopsony or oligopsony may not be the best way to represent the labor market. The empirical work in this book has been entirely American and British for a bad reason and a good reason. The bad reason is that it is the data with which I am most familiar but the good reason is that these are labor markets in which trade unions are weak and minimum wages and other forms of government intervention are fairly small. If one wants to look at economies that approximate "free" markets, these seem the best two to examine. However, in many continental European countries, union coverage approaches 100% and no half-decent analysis of these labor markets can ignore this fact. The analysis presented here needs, at the very least, modification. But, this does not mean this book is irrelevant as the policy debate in many of these countries is whether one should reduce regulation and "free" the labor market. Many authoritative commentators argue that European labor markets vitally need "de-regulation." When one explores the source of this recommendation one finds that it often comes from the view that the "free" labor market is well approximated by the perfectly competitive model, a view this book has challenged. If the "free" labor market is monopsonistic, this makes the alternative to European-style labor markets look less attractive and this is a factor that needs to be in the minds of European labor economists and policy-makers.

13.4 Future Directions

This book has argued that our understanding of labor markets is mark-edly improved by an explicit recognition of the fact that employers have some market power in the determination of wages. This claim has been made using an analysis of many of the main topics of labor economics.

Inevitably there are topics that have been omitted where the approach could usefully be applied and other topics that have been discussed which could have been investigated in more detail than is permitted in a book of this length. For example, it is likely that the literature on the assimilation of immigrants might benefit from the job search perspective which sees part of the wage growth achieved over a working life as being the result the accumulation of "search capital" rather than "human capital."

One should also recognize that there are areas where the monopsony model does not appear such a great improvement on the competitive model. I hope that I have been relatively open about where the monop-sony model does not perform as well as one might hope. For example, in the analysis of compensating differentials discussed in chapter 8, monop-sony offers a plausible reason for why it is often hard to find evidence of compensating differentials in cross-sectional earnings functions but the alternative approach based on estimating separations rates (while intui-tively plausible) does not give a conspicuous improvement in perfor-mance.

Perhaps the most glaring omission is a good estimate of the elasticity of the labor supply curve facing an individual employer. It is this elasticity that ultimately determines the extent of monopsony power an employer has. This book has bemoaned the fact that the literature on the labor supply curve to individual employers is a huge hole in labor economics. But, while it attempts to answer this question by looking at estimates of the employer size–wage effect, or the elasticity of separations with respect to the wage, or whether there are increasing marginal costs of recruit-ment, one cannot help but feel that these analyses are far from perfect. The problem here is the need for good experiments: an exogenous increase in the wage paid by a single firm in the labor market. Such experiments are hard to find in the area of public policy where changes almost always affect more than a single employer. There are perhaps only two studies that even come close: Staiger et al. (1999) and Falch (2001) both concluded that labor supply to an individual employer is very inelastic. But we have little idea of how robust this conclusion is to other labor markets.

13.5 Conclusions

This book opened with a thought experiment: what happens if employers cut wages by a small amount? If one is tempted to doubt the relevance of believing that employers have some market power over their workers, just remember that the alternative is to believe that the workers leave so fast that the door does not stop revolving. It is just so much more plausible and reasonable to think that employers do have meaningful discretion over the wages they choose to pay. Labor economists will find that the labor market is so much less puzzling once they recognize that fact and, hopefully, they will be able to sleep more easily in their beds as a result.[1]

---

[1] Though anyone who has got far enough to read this sentence may have a lot of trouble in getting to sleep in any circumstance.

Data Sets Appendix _____

A CONSIDERABLE number of data sets are used in this book and there would be needless duplication if the way in which the data was constructed was discussed each time a data set was used.

The way in which the key variables in the main data sets were constructed is described here. All "do-files" used to run jobs are available on request and, where licensing agreements allow, copies of the data sets used are also available.

United States

The Current Population Survey

The CPS has a rolling panel structure in which sample individuals are interviewed monthly for four months, then retired for four months and then interviewed monthly for a further four months. Details about the CPS can be found at http://www.bls.census.gov/cps/cpsmain.htm. The NBER also has very useful information at http://www.nber.org/data/cps_index.html.

EDUCATIONAL ATTAINMENT

Those with completed education less than 12th grade or no diploma (PEEDUCA ≤ 38) are classed as high-school drop-outs, those with high school diploma or equivalent (PEEDUCA = 39) as high-school graduates, those with some college but less than a bachelor's degree (40 ≤ PEEDUCA ≤ 42) are classed as some college, and those with a bachelor's degree or higher (43 ≤ PEEDUCA) as college graduates.

EXPERIENCE

Experience (really potential experience) is computed as age minus 17 if PEEDUCA ≤ 36, age minus 18 if 37 ≤ PEEDUCA ≤ 39, age minus 19 if PEEDUCA = 40, age minus 20 if PEEDUCA = 41 or 42, age minus 22 if PEEDUCA = 43, and age minus 24 if PEEDUCA > 43. Experience is set to zero for all those still in full-time education.

WAGES

Earnings information is only recorded for those in the outgoing rotation groups (MIS = 4 or MIS = 8). For those who are paid by the hour, the reported straight-time hourly wage in PTERNHLY is used. For those who are not paid by the hour, the hourly wage is computed as weekly earnings, PTERNWA, divided by weekly hours, PEERNHRO. Those with hourly earnings below $1 and above $100 per hour are dropped.

ETHNICITY

An individual is coded as black if they answer "black" in the question PERACE. In addition, individuals are classed as Hispanic if they are recorded in PRORIGIN as being of Hispanic descent.

MARITAL STATUS

Marital status is derived from the variable PEMARITL. Those who record that they are currently married but with an absent spouse are treated as married.

CHILDREN

The number of dependent children in the household is computed by counting the number of individuals aged less than 18 in the household and the age of the youngest child is computed as the youngest of these individuals.

ECONOMIC ACTIVITY

This is derived from the variable PEMLR. Job changers are identified from the question PUIODP1.

The Panel Study of Income Dynamics

The PSID is a longitudinal survey of a representative sample of US individuals and their families. It started in 1968 and information was collected annually until 1997. More information can be found at http://www.isr.umich.edu/src/psid/.

EDUCATIONAL ATTAINMENT

For each individual, the maximum level of years of completed education reported is used as the basic measure of educational attainment. This is then converted to four dummy variables corresponding to:

high-school drop-out	11 or fewer years of education completed
high-school graduate	12 years of education completed
high-school graduate	13–15 years of education completed
college graduate	16+ years of education completed.

EXPERIENCE

This is computed as age minus years of completed education minus 6. Those for whom experience is negative are dropped from the sample.

JOB TENURE

First, each job observed at an interview date is labeled as a new job (NEWJOB = 1) or an old job (as compared to the previous interview date) (NEWJOB = 0). A number of rules are followed:

- if the respondent was not in employment at the previous interview, the current job is a new job;
- if the respondent was in employment at the previous interview, the current job is a new job if the recorded start date for the job is before the date of previous interview.

This leaves open the elapsed job tenure of the job held at the first wave for which the individual is observed. The recorded start date for the job is used to measure this.

Job tenure is now computed as follows. If NEWJOB = 0, tenure is previous tenure plus 1. If NEWJOB = 1, tenure is set to zero. This procedure leads to missing values for job tenure for all waves where NEWJOB is missing at some previous point in that job spell. The procedure ensures that measures of job tenure are internally consistent as recommended by Brown and Light (1992).

For those in new jobs, we are also interested in whether they have been in continuous employment or whether they have had a spell of non-employment. Individuals are recorded as having had a spell of non-employment if either of the following conditions is satisfied:

- if the respondent was not in employment at the previous interview;
- a period of non-employment (either unemployment or inactivity) lasting longer than a week is recorded between the two interview dates.

WAGES

The PSID only asks about wages for heads of household and their spouse. On the main job, workers are asked whether they are salaried, paid by the hour or some form of performance-related pay (commission, tips or other). The sample is restricted to those who report being salaried or just paid by the hour. In 1994, this is about 85% of those responding to the question. The main excluded group (about 12%) are the "other" pay system for whom it is hard to work out an hourly wage.

The salaried workers are asked to report their salary and the pay period to which it refers. Assuming they work 40 hours per week (there is no more precise information on hours worked), this is then converted to an hourly wage. The hourly paid workers are asked about their hourly wage for their regular work time.

ETHNICITY

Individuals are divided into one of two groups: white or non-white.

MARTIAL STATUS AND CHILDREN

The individual is recorded as married if a spouse is recorded as living at the same address. The presence of dependent children comes from a direct question.

WEIGHTS

Only the core sample is used and the individual weights are used for this sample.

The National Longitudinal Study of Youth, 1979

The NLSY79 is a nationally representative sample of 12,686 young US men and women who were 14–22 years old when they were first surveyed in 1979. These individuals were interviewed annually through 1994 and are currently being interviewed on a biennial basis. More information can be found at http://www.bls.gov/nls/nlsy79.htm.

EDUCATIONAL ATTAINMENT

For each individual, the maximum level of years of completed education reported at any interview before they are recorded as having left education is used as the basic measure of educational attainment. This is then converted to four dummy variables corresponding to:

high-school drop-out	11 or fewer years of education completed
high-school graduate	12 years of education completed
high-school graduate	13–15 years of education completed
college graduate	16+ years of education completed.

EXPERIENCE

The year in which the individual left full-time education is recorded as the latest year in which the respondent reported currently attending or being enrolled in school. In the first year after this, experience is given the value zero and then augments by one each year.

CURRENT JOB

Individuals are asked whether they are in employment in the week of interview. If they are in more than one job, one of them is identified as the CPS job (the one in which they worked the most hours). The details of this job are recorded for wages.

EMPLOYMENT RECORD

From the work history file a series of derived variables recording number of weeks between interviews in employment, unemployment out of the labor force, in military service or unaccounted for. From this we define those as being in continuous employment if all weeks are in employment or the military.

JOB TENURE

First, each job observed at an interview date is labeled as a new job (NEWJOB = 1) or an old job (as compared to the previous interview date) (NEWJOB = 0). A number of rules are followed:

- if the respondent was not in employment at the previous interview, the current job is a new job;
- if the respondent was in employment at the previous interview, the current job is a new job if any break in employment is recorded or the number of employers since the last interview is bigger than one.

Job tenure is now computed as follows. If NEWJOB = 0, tenure is previous tenure plus 1. If NEWJOB = 1, tenure is set to zero. This procedure leads to missing values for job tenure for all waves where NEWJOB is missing at some previous point in that job spell.

WAGES

The hourly wage on the CPS job is used. Those with hourly wages less than a dollar or more than 100 dollars are excluded.

ETHNICITY

Individuals are divided into one of two groups: white or non-white.

MARTIAL STATUS AND CHILDREN

The individual is recorded as married if a spouse is recorded as being present or that they currently live with a partner. The presence and age of own children in the household comes from a direct question.

United Kingdom

The Labour Force Survey

The LFS is the UK equivalent of the CPS. Since the inception of the quarterly panel in 1992, individuals are interviewed for five successive quarters. More information can be found at http://www.data-archive. ac.uk/findingData/lfsAbstract.asp.

EXPERIENCE

Experience (really potential experience) is computed as age minus age last left full-time education. Data on age left full-time education come from the variable EDAGE.

EDUCATIONAL ATTAINMENT

The LFS classification of educational attainment has been changed twice since the introduction of the quarterly survey in the Spring of 1992. Currently, the relevant variable is HIQUAL: prior to Spring 1996 it was HIQUAP. HIQUAL currently has 40 different levels of educational attainment: these are combined into four categories as follows:

college degree	$1 \leq \text{HIQUAP} \leq 12$
"A" level or equivalent	$13 \leq \text{HIQUAP} \leq 24$
GCSE or equivalent	$25 \leq \text{HIQUAP} \leq 37$
no formal education qualification	$\text{HIQUAP} = 38 \text{ or } 40.$

Those with $\text{HIQUAP} = 39$ (other educational qualification) are coded as missing as no indication of the level is given.

JOB TENURE

The LFS asks questions about the year the individual started work for the current employer (CONMPY) and, where this is less than 8 years ago, the month (CONMON). Tenure is then computed as the difference in months between the date of interview and the starting month. Where CONMON is not recorded it is assumed to be July.

WAGES

Earnings information is only recorded from Winter 1992 and then only for those in wave 5 (i.e., about to leave the sample) until Spring 1997 when earnings information is also collected for those in wave 1. Gross weekly pay in main job is recorded in GRSSWK. This converted to an hourly wage by dividing by the sum of total usual hours worked in main job (BUSHR) and usual hours of paid overtime (POTHR). Those with hourly wages below £1/hour or above £100/hour were excluded from the sample.

ETHNICITY

The LFS records information on twelve ethnic groups. For analysis, we combine these into three categories:

white	white, other-other, and other-mixed ethnic group (the last two groups being very small)
black	black-Caribbean, black-African, black-other (non-mixed), and black-mixed
Asian	Indian, Pakistani, Bangladeshi, Chinese, and other-Asian (non-mixed).

MARITAL STATUS

Marital status is derived from the variables MARSTT and LIVTOG. Those who record either that they are married and living with spouse or that they are living together as a couple are recorded as married: all others are regarded as non-married.

CHILDREN

The number of dependent children in the household is taken from HDPCH19 and the age of the youngest child comes from AYHL19.

ECONOMIC ACTIVITY

This is derived from the variable INECACA.

The British Household Panel Study

The BHPS is approximately the British equivalent to the PSID. It started in 1991 with some 5500 households and 10,300 individuals drawn from 250 different areas of Great Britain and has subsequently followed these individuals and others who may have ended up in a household with them.

More details can be found at http://www.iser.essex.ac.uk/bhps/index.php.

EXPERIENCE

Experience (really potential experience) is computed as age minus age last left full-time education. There are two sources of information on age last left full-time education. First, there are direct questions (SCEND and FEEND) about the age at which the respondent last left full-time education. Second, individuals may record that their current economic activity (JBSTAT) is full-time education. If this is the case, we record the last age at which this is reported as age left full-time education. We then use the maximum of these two measures as our composite measure of age left full-time education. Experience is constructed so that it augments by one year each wave by taking the lowest level of experience observed as the base.

EDUCATIONAL ATTAINMENT

The BHPS defines twelve levels of highest educational qualification (QFEDHI). These are then combined into four categories:

college education or equivalent	higher degree, first degree, teaching qualification and nursing qualification
"A" level or equivalent (left school at 18)	other higher qualification, "A" levels, apprenticeship
GCSE or equivalent (left school at 16)	"O" levels, commercial qualification, CSEs, other qualification
no qualification	no qualification.

JOB TENURE

The BHPS has the complication that the basic information on job tenure relates to the length of the spell in a single job, and not with a single employer, so that, for example, a promotion within a firm sets the tenure clock back to zero. For comparability with other data sets, it is helpful to have a measure of tenure with a single employer. This is computed in the following way.

First, each job observed at an interview date is labeled as a new job (NEWJOB = 1) or an old job (as compared to the previous interview date) (NEWJOB = 0). A number of rules are followed:

- if the respondent was not in employment at the previous interview, the current job is a new job;
- if the respondent was in full-time education at the previous interview, the current job is a new job;
- if the respondent was in employment at the previous interview, the current job is a new job if the job history file records a change in employer between the two interview dates.

This label fails to exist when there was no interview in the preceding wave or the job history information is missing from the current wave. For wave 1, we use information on the job held at September 1, 1990, to ascertain whether it is new or not.

This leaves open the elapsed job tenure of the job held at September 1, 1990. Information from the life history files are used to derive this.

Job tenure is now computed as follows. If NEWJOB = 0, tenure is previous tenure plus 1. If NEWJOB = 1, tenure is set to zero.

This procedure leads to missing values for job tenure for all waves where NEWJOB is missing at some previous point in that job spell. And, it leads to missing values wherever it is impossible to assign job tenure to the job held at September 1, 1990. The procedure does lead to an under-estimate of average job tenure but we are solely interested in being able to condition on it.

We are also interested in employment status before starting a new job. For all new jobs, we try to use the job history file (where available) to work out employment status in the spell immediately preceding starting to work for the current employer. For those workers with zero experience, we automatically assume that they were previously in non-employment.

WAGES

Hourly earnings are computed by taking usual monthly gross pay in the current job (PAYGU), dividing by number of hours per week usually worked (JBHRS + JBOT) and then multiplying by (30/7). Those observations for whom PAYGU was imputed or a proxy response are removed from the sample. Those for whom the computed hourly wage was less than £1 per hour or greater than £100 per hour were removed from the sample. In contrast to the PSID, the BHPS records earnings information for all household members in employment.

ETHNICITY

The BHPS records information on ten ethnic groups in RACE. For analysis, we combine these into three categories:

white	white and other ethnic group (the latter group being very small)
black	black-Caribbean, black-African, and black-other
Asian	Indian, Pakistani, Bangladeshi, and Chinese.

MARITAL STATUS AND CHILDREN

Marital status is taken from the variables MASTAT. Those recorded as married or living as a couple are classed as married. The number of children is the number of children in the household (NKIDS).

Bibliography

Abowd, John, M., and Thomas Lemieux. 1993. "The Effects of Product Market Competition on Collective Bargaining Agreements: The Case of Foreign Competition in Canada." *Quarterly Journal of Economics* 108(4): 983–1014.

Abraham, Katherine G., and Henry S. Farber. 1987. "Job Duration, Seniority, and Earnings." *American Economic Review* 77(3): 278–97.

Acemoglu, Daron. 1998. "Why Do New Technologies Complement Skills? Directed Technical Change and Wage Inequality." *Quarterly Journal of Economics* 113(4): 1055–89.

Acemoglu, Daron, and Jorn-Steffen Pischke. 1998. "Why Do Firms Train? Theory and Evidence." *Quarterly Journal of Economics.* 113(1): 79–119.

———. 1999a. "Beyond Becker: Training in Imperfect Labour Markets." *Economic Journal* 109(453): 112–42.

———. 1999b. "The Structure of Wages and Investment in General Training." *Journal of Political Economy* 107(3): 539–72.

Acemoglu, Daron, and Robert Shimer. 2000. "Wage and Technology Dispersion." *Review of Economic Studies* 67(October): 585–607.

Addison, John T., and W. Stanley Siebert. 1979. *The Market for Labor: an Analytical Treatment.* Santa Monica, CA: Goodyear.

Akerlof, George A., and Janet L. Yellen. 1986. "Efficiency Wage Models of the Labor Market." In *Efficiency Wage Models Of The Labor Market*, ed. George A. Akerlof and Janet L. Yellen, 1–21. Cambridge: Cambridge University Press.

———. 1990. "The Fair Wage-Effort Hypothesis and Unemployment." *Quarterly Journal of Economics* 105(2): 255–83.

Akerlof, George A., and Lawrence F. Katz. 1989. "Workers' Trust Funds and the Logic of Wage Profiles." *Quarterly Journal of Economics* 104(3): 525–36.

Albrecht, James W., and Bo Axell. 1984. "An Equilibrium Model of Search Unemployment." *Journal of Political Economy* 92(5): 824–40.

Albrecht, James W., and Boyan Jovanovic. 1986. "The Efficiency of Search under Competition and Monopsony." *Journal of Political Economy* 94(6): 1246–57.

Altonji, Joseph G., and Christina H. Paxson. 1988. "Labor Supply Preferences, Hours Constraints, and Hours-Wage Trade-Offs." *Journal of Labor Economics* 6(2): 254–76.

———. 1992. "Labor Supply, Hours Constraints, and Job Mobility." *Journal of Human Resources* 27(2): 256–78.

Altonji, Joseph G., and James R. Spletzer. 1991. "Worker Characteristics, Job Characteristics, and the Receipt of On-the-Job Training." *Industrial and Labor Relations Review* 45(1): 58–79.

Altonji, Joseph G., and Nicolas Williams. 1997. "Do Wages Rise With Job Seniority? A Reassessment." *NBER Working Paper* No. 6010.

Altonji, Joseph, G., and Rebecca M. Blank. 1999. "Race and Gender in the Labor Market." In *Handbook of Labor Economics*, vol. 3C, ed. Orley Ashenfelter and David Card, 3143–259. Amsterdam: North-Holland.

Altonji, Joseph G., and Robert A. Shakotko. 1987. "Do Wages Rise with Job Seniority?" *Review of Economic Studies* 54(3): 437–59.

————. 1998. "The Effects of Labor Market Experience, Job Seniority, and Job Mobility on Wage Growth." In *Research in Labor Economics*, vol. 17, ed. Solomon W. Polachek, 233–76. Stamford, CT: JAI Press.

Ashenfelter, Orley, and David Card (eds). 1999. *Handbook of Labor Economics*, vol. 3. Amsterdam: North-Holland.

Ashenfelter, Orley, and Richard Layard (eds). 1986. *Handbook of Labor Economics*, vols. 1 and 2. Amsterdam: North-Holland.

Autor, David H. 2001. "Why Do Temporary Help Firms Provide Free General Skills Training?" *Quarterly Journal of Economics* 116(4): 1409–48.

Autor, David H., and Mark G. Duggan. 2001. "The Rise in Disability Insurance and the Decline in Unemployment." *NBER Working Paper* No. 8336.

Baker, Michael. 1997. "Growth Rate Heterogeneity and the Covariance Structure of Life-Cycle Earnings." *Journal of Labor Economics* 15(2): 338–75.

Barron, John M., Mark C. Berger, and Dan A. Black. 1997. *On-The-Job Training*. Kalamazoo, MI: W. E. Upjohn Institute for Employment Research.

Bartel, Ann, and George J. Borjas. 1982. "Wage Growth and Job Turnover: An Empirical Analysis." In *Studies in Labor Markets*, ed. Sherwin Rosen. Chicago, IL: The University of Chicago Press.

Barth, Erling, and Harald Dale-Olsen. 1999. "Monopsonistic Discrimination and the Gender Wage Gap." *NBER Working Paper* No. 7197.

Bayard, Kimberly, Judith Hellerstein, David Neumark, and Kenneth Troske. 1999. "New Evidence on Sex Segregation and Sex Differences in Wages from Matched Employee-Employer Data." *NBER Working Paper* No. 7003.

Bayard, Kimberly, and Kenneth R. Troske. 1999. "Examining the Employer-Size Wage Premium in the Manufacturing, Retail Trade, and Service Industries Using Employer-Employee Matched Data." *American Economic Review* 89(2): 99–103.

Beaumont, Phillip B. 1978. "The Duration of Registered Vacancies: An Exploratory Exercise." *Scottish Journal of Political Economy* 25(1): 75–87.

Beck, Paul, William M. Boal, and Michael Ransom. 1998. "Empirical Tests of Labor Monopsony: Missouri School Teachers." Unpublished Paper, Brigham Young University.

Becker, Elizabeth, and M. Lindsay Cotton. 1994. "Sex Differences in Tenure Profiles: Effects of Shared Firm-Specific Investment." *Journal of Labor Economics* 12(1): 98–118.

Becker, Gary S. 1971. *The Economics of Discrimination*, 2nd edition. Chicago, IL: The University of Chicago Press.

————. 1993. *Human Capital: a Theoretical and Empirical Analysis, with Special Reference to Education*, 3rd edition. Chicago, IL: The University of Chicago Press.

Bellante, Don, and Mark Jackson. 1979. *Labor Economics: Choice in Labor Markets*. New York: McGraw-Hill.

Ben-Horim, Moshe, and Dror Zuckerman. 1987. "The Effect of Unemployment Insurance on Unemployment Duration." *Journal of Labor Economics* 5(3): 386–90.

Ben-Porath, Yoram. 1967. "The Production of Human Capital and the Life Cycle of Earnings." *Journal of Political Economy* 75(4, Part 1): 352–65.

Bertrand, Marianne, and Sendhil Mullanaithan. 2002. "Are Emily and Brendan More Employable than Lakisha and Jamal? A Field Experiment on Labor Market Discrimination." Unpublished Paper, Graduate School of Business, University of Chicago.

Bewley, Truman F. 1999. *Why Wages Don't Fall During A Recession*. Cambridge, MA: Harvard University Press.

Bhaskar, V., and Ted To, 1999. "Minimum Wages for Ronald McDonald Monopsonies: A Theory of Monopsonistic Competition." *Economic Journal* 109(455): 190–203.

Black, Dan A. 1995. "Discrimination in an Equilibrium Search Model." *Journal of Labor Economics* 13(2): 309–33.

Blanchflower, David, G., Andrew J. Oswald, and Peter Sanfey, 1996. "Wages, Profits, and Rent-Sharing." *Quarterly Journal of Economics* 111(1): 227–51.

Blanchflower, David G., Neil Millward, and Andrew J. Oswald. 1991. "Unionism and Employment Behaviour." *Economic Journal* 101(407): 815–34.

Blau, David M., and Philip K. Robins. 1990. "Job Search Outcomes for the Employed and Unemployed." *Journal of Political Economy* 98(3): 637–55.

Bloom, Gordon F., and Herbert R. Northrup. 1981. *Economics of Labor Relations*, 9th edition. Homewood, IL: R. D. Irwin.

Blundell, Richard, Howard Reed, and Thomas Stoker. 1999. "Interpreting movements in aggregate wages: the role of labour market participation." *Institute for Fiscal Studies Working Paper* No. 99/13.

Blundell, Richard, John Ham, and Costas Meghir. 1987. "Unemployment and Female Labour Supply." *Economic Journal* 97(Suppl.): 44–64.

————. 1998. "Unemployment, Discouraged Workers and Female Labour Supply." *Research in Economics* 52: 103–31.

Blundell, Richard, Lorraine Dearden, and Costas Meghir. 1996. *The Determinants and Effects of Work-Related Training in Britain* 93. London: Institute for Fiscal Studies.

Blundell, Richard, and Thomas E. MaCurdy, 1999. "Labor Supply: A Review of Alternative Approaches." In *Handbook of Labor Economics*, vol. 3C, ed. Orley Ashenfelter and David Card, 1559–695. Amsterdam: North-Holland.

Boal, William M. 1995. "Testing for Employer Monopsony in Turn-of-the-Century Coal Mining." *Rand Journal of Economics* 26(3): 519–36.

Boal, William, M., and Michael R. Ransom. 1997. "Monopsony in the Labor Market." *Journal of Economic Literature* 35(1): 86–112.

Bontemps, Christian, Jean-Marc Robin, and Gerard J. van den Berg. 1999. "An Empirical Equilibrium Job Search Model with Search on the Job and Heterogeneous Workers and Firms." *International Economic Review* 40(4): 1039–74.

————. 2000. "Equilibrium Search with Continuous Productivity Dispersion: Theory and Nonparametric Estimation." *International Economic Review* 41(2): 305–58.

Booth, Alison L. 1995. *The Economics of the Trade Union*. Cambridge, UK: Cambridge University Press.

Borjas, George J. 2000. *Labor Economics*. New York: McGraw Hill.

————. 1999. "The Economic Analysis of Immigration." In *Handbook of Labor Economics*, vol. 3C, ed. Orley Ashenfelter and David Card, 1697–1760. Amsterdam: North-Holland.

Bowlus, Audra J. 1997. "A Search Interpretation of Male-Female Wage Differentials." *Journal of Labor Economics* 15(4): 625–57.

Bowlus, Audra J., Nicholas M. Kiefer, and George R. Neumann. 1995. "Estimation of Equilibrium Wage Distributions with Heterogeneity." *Journal of Applied Econometrics* 10(Suppl.): S119–S131.

Bowlus, Audra J., and Zvi Eckstein, 2000. "Discrimination and Skill Differences in an Equilibrium Search Model." Unpublished Paper, Tel Aviv University, May.

Bratsberg, Bernt, James F. Ragan, and John T. Warren. 2002. "Negative Returns to Seniority – New Evidence in Academic Markets." *Industrial and Labor Relations Review* in press.

Bresnahan, Timothy F. 1989. "Empirical Studies of Industries with Market Power." In *Handbook of Industrial Organization*, ed. Richard Schmalensee and Robert D. Willig, 1011–57. Amsterdam: North-Holland.

Bronfenbrenner, Martin. 1956. "Potential Monopsony in Labor Markets." *Industrial and Labor Relations Review* 9(4): 577–88.

Brown, Charles. 1980. "Equalizing Differences in the Labor Market." *Quarterly Journal of Economics* 94(1); 113–34.

————. 1999. "Minimum Wages, Employment, and the Distribution of Income." In *Handbook of Labor Economics*, vol. 3, ed. Orley Ashenfelter and David Card, 2101–163. Amsterdam: North-Holland.

Brown, Charles, James Hamilton, and James Medoff. 1990. *Employers Large and Small.* Cambridge, MA: Harvard University Press.

Brown, Charles, and James Medoff. 1989. "The Employer Size-Wage Effect." *Journal of Political Economy* 97(5): 1027–59.

Brown, E. Henry Phelps. 1962. *The Economics of Labor.* New Haven, CT: Yale University Press.

Brown, James N. 1989. "Why Do Wages Increase with Tenure? On-the-Job Training and Life-Cycle Wage Growth Observed within Firms." *American Economic Review* 79(5): 971–91.

Brown, James N., and Audrey Light. 1992. "Interpreting Panel Data on Job Tenure." *Journal of Labor Economics* 10(3): 219–57.

Brown, James, N., and Orley Ashenfelter. 1986. "Testing the Efficiency of Employment Contracts." *Journal of Political Economy* 94(3, Part 2): S40–S87.

Bunting, Robert L. 1962. *Employer Concentration in Local Labor Markets.* Chapel Hill, NC: University of North Carolina Press.

Burdett, Kenneth. 1978. "A Theory of Employee Job Search and Quit Rates." *American Economic Review* 68(1): 212–20.

Burdett, Kenneth, and Dale T. Mortensen. 1978. "Labor Supply Under Uncertainty." In *Research in Labor Economics*, ed. Ronald G. Ehrenberg. Greenwich, CT: JAI Press.

————. 1998. "Wage Differentials, Employer Size, and Unemployment." *International Economic Review* 39(2): 257–73.

Burdett, Kenneth, and Kenneth L. Judd. 1983. "Equilibrium Price Dispersion." *Econometrica* 51(4): 955–69.

Burdett, Kenneth, and Melvyn Coles. 2001. "Wage-Tenure Contracts and Equilibrium Search." Unpublished Paper, University of Essex, March.

Burdett, Kenneth, Nicholas M. Kiefer, Dale T. Mortensen, and George Neumann. 1984. "Earnings, Unemployment, and the Allocation of Time over Time." *Review of Economic Studies* 51(4): 559–78.

Burdett, Kenneth, Shouyong Shi, and Randall Wright. 2001. "Pricing and Matching with Frictions." *Journal of Political Economy* 109(5): 1060–1085.

Burdett, Kenneth, and Tara Vishwanath. 1988. "Balanced Matching and Labor Market Equilibrium." *Journal of Political Economy* 96(5): 1048–65.

Burgess, Simon M. 1993. "A Model of Competition between Unemployed and Employed Job Searchers: An Application to the Unemployment Outflow Rate In Britain." *Economic Journal* 103(420): 1190–204.

Butters, Gerard R. 1977. "Equilibrium Distributions of Sales and Advertising Prices." *Review of Economic Studies* 44(3): 465–91.

Calmfors, Lars, and John Driffill. 1988. "Bargaining Structure, Corporatism and Macroeconomic Performance." *Economic Policy* 6.

Card, David E., and Alan B. Krueger. 1994. "Minimum Wages and Employment: A Case Study of the Fast-Food Industry in New Jersey and Pennsylvania." *American Economic Review* 84(4): 772–93.

————. 1995. *Myth and Measurement: The New Economics of the Minimum Wage.* Princeton, NJ: Princeton University Press.

————. 2000. "Minimum Wages and Employment: A Case Study of the Fast-Food Industry in New Jersey and Pennsylvania: Reply" *American Economic Review* 90(5): 1397–420.

Carmichael, Lorne. 1985. "Can Unemployment Be Involuntary? Comment." *American Economic Review* 75(5): 1213–14.

Cartter, A.M., and F.R. Marshall. 1972. *Labor Economics: Wages, Employment, and Trade Unionism,* revised edition. Homewood, IL: R. D. Irwin.

Coles, Melvyn G., and Barbara Petrongolo. 2002. "A Test Between Unemployment Theories Using Matching Data." *CEPR Discussion Paper* No. 3241.

Coles, Melvyn G., and Eric Smith. 1998. "Marketplaces and Matching" *International Economic Review* 39(1): 239–54.

Cox, G. 1995. *Priced into Poverty: an Analysis of Pay Rates in Former Wages Council Industries.* Manchester: Low Pay Network.

Davis, Steven J., John C. Haltiwanger, and Scott Schuh. 1996. *Job Creation and Destruction.* Cambridge, MA: MIT Press.

Dearden, Lorraine, Stephen Machin, Howard Reed, and David Wilkinson. 1997. *Labour Turnover and Work-Related Training.* London: Institute of Fiscal Studies.

de Meza, David, Robin A. Naylor, and Gareth D. Myles. 1998. "Monopsony, Labour Supply, Minimum Wages and Hours Restrictions." Unpublished Paper, University of Warwick.

Devine, Theresa J., and Nicholas M. Kiefer, 1991. *Empirical Labor Economics: The Search Approach.* Oxford: Oxford University Press.

Diamond, Peter A. 1971. "A Model of Price Adjustment." *Journal of Economic Theory* 3(2): 156–68.

————. 1981. "Mobility Costs, Frictional Unemployment, and Efficiency." *Journal of Political Economy* 89(4): 798–812.

————. 1982. "Aggregate Demand Management in Search Equilibrium." *Journal of Political Economy* 90(5): 881–94.

Dickens, Richard, Stephen Machin, and Alan Manning. 1999. "The Effects of Minimum Wages on Employment: Theory and Evidence from Britain." *Journal of Labor Economics* 17(1): 1–22.

DiNardo, John, and David S. Lee. 2001. "The Impact of Unionization on Establishment Closure: A Regression Discontinuity Analysis of Representation elections." *University of California Berkeley, Center for Labor Economics Working Paper* No. 38.

DiNardo John, Nicole M. Fortin, and Thomas Lemieux, 1996. "Labor Market Institutions and the Distribution of Wages 1973–1992: A Semiparametric Approach" *Econometrica* 64(5): 1001–44.

Dixit, Avinash K., and Joseph E. Stiglitz. 1977. "Monopolistic Competition and Optimum Product Diversity." *American Economic Review* 67(3): 297–308.

Duncan, Greg J., and Bertil Holmlund. 1983. "Was Adam Smith Right after All? Another Test of the Theory of Compensating Wage Differentials." *Journal of Labor Economics* 1(4): 366–79.

Dunlop, John. 1957. "The Tasks of Contemporary Wage Theory." In *New Concepts in Wage Determination*, ed. George Taylor and Frank Pierson. New York: McGraw-Hill.

Eckstein, Zvi, and Kenneth I. Wolpin. 1990. "Estimating a Market Equilibrium Search Model from Panel Data on Individuals." *Econometrica* 58(4): 783–808.

Edgeworth, Francis Ysidro. 1932. *Mathematical Psychics : an Essay on the Application of Mathematics to the Moral Sciences.* London: London School of Economics and Political Science.

Ehrenberg, Ronald G., and Smith S. Smith. 2000. *Modern Labor Economics: Theory and Public Policy*, 7th edition. Reading, MA: Addison Wesley.

Ellingsen, Tore, and Asa Rosen. 2002. "Fixed or Flexible? Wage Setting in Search Equilibrium." *Economica* in press.

Elliot, Robert E. 1991. *Labour Economics: a Comparative Text.* New York: McGraw-Hill.

Euwals, Rob, and Rainer Winkelmann. 2001. "Why Do Firms Train? Empirical Evidence on the First Labour Market Outcomes of Graduated Apprentices." *CEPR Discussion Paper* No. 2880.

Evans, David S., and Linda S. Leighton. 1995. "Retrospective Bias in the Displaced Worker Surveys." *Journal of Human Resources* 30(2): 386–96.

Falch, Torberg. 2001. "Estimating the elasticity of labor supply utilizing a quasi-natural experiment." *Norwegian University of Science and Technology, Trondheim, Working Paper*, October.

Fallick, Bruce C., and Charles A. Fleischman. 2001. "The Importance of Employer-to-Employer Flows in the U.S. Labor Market." *Federal Reserve Board Working Paper*, April.

Fallon, Peter, and Donald Verry. 1988. *The Economics of Labour Markets.* Deddington: Philip Allan.

Farber, Henry S. 1994."The Analysis of Inter-firm Worker Mobility." *Journal of Labor Economics* 12(4): 554–93.

————. 1997. "The Changing Face of Job Loss in the United States, 1981–1995." *Brookings Papers on Economic Activity Microeconomics* 55–128.

Fearn, Robert M. 1981. *Labor Economics: the Emerging Synthesis.* Cambridge, MA: Winthrop Publishers.

Fershtman, Chaim, and Arthur Fishman. 1994. "The 'Perverse' Effects of Wage and Price Controls in Search Markets." *European Economic Review* 38(5): 1099–112.

Filer, Randall K., Daniel S. Hamermesh, and Albert E. Rees. 1996. *The Economics of Work and Pay*, 6th edition. New York: Harper-Collins.

Fleisher, Belton M., and Thomas J. Kniesner. 1980. *Labour Economics: Theory, Evidence and Policy*, 1st edition. Englewood Cliffs, NJ: Prentice Hall.

Fleisher, Belton M., and Thomas J. Kniesner. 1984. *Labour Economics: Theory, Evidence and Policy*, 3rd edition. Englewood Cliffs, NJ: Prentice Hall.

Flinn, Christopher J., and James J. Heckman. 1983. "Are Unemployment and Out of the Labor Force Behaviorally Distinct Labor Force States?" *Journal of Labor Economics* 1(1): 28–42.

Freeman, Richard B. 1979. *Labor Economics*, 2nd edition. Englewood Cliffs, NJ: Prentice Hall.

Freeman, Richard B., and James L. Medoff. 1981. "The Impact of the Percentage Organized on Union and Non-union Wages." *Review of Economics and Statistics* 63(4): 561–72.

————. 1984. *What Do Unions Do?* New York: Basic Books.

Friedman, Milton. 1968. "The Role of Monetary Policy." *American Economic Review* 58(1): 1–17.

Gibbons, Robert, and Lawrence F. Katz. 1992. "Does Unmeasured Ability Explain Inter-industry Wage Differentials?" *Review of Economic Studies* 59(3): 515–35.

Goldberger, Arthur S. 1984. "Reverse Regression and Salary Discrimination." *Journal of Human Resources* 19(3): 293–318.

Green, Francis, Stephen Machin, and Alan Manning. 1996. "The Employer Size-Wage Effect: Can Dynamic Monopsony Provide an Explanation?" *Oxford Economic Papers* 48(3): 433–55.

Green, Francis, Stephen Machin, and David Wilkinson. 1998. "The Meaning and Determinants of Skills Shortages." *Oxford Bulletin of Economics and Statistics* 60(2): 165–87.

————. 1999. "Trade Unions and Training Practices in British Workplaces." *Industrial and Labor Relations Review* 52(2): 179–95.

Gregg, Paul, and Barbara Petrongolo. 1997. "Random or Non-Random Matching? Implications for the Use of the UV Curve as a Measure of Matching Effectiveness." *London School of Economics, Centre for Economic Performance Discussion Paper* No. 348.

Gregg, Paul, and Jonathan Wadsworth. 1996. "How Effective Are State Employment Agencies? Jobcentre Use and Job Matching in Britain." *Oxford Bulletin of Economics and Statistics* 58(3): 443–67.

Griliches, Zvi. 1977. "Estimating the Returns to Schooling: Some Econometric Problems" *Econometrica* 45(1): 1–22.

Gronberg, Thomas J., and Walter R. Reed. 1994. "Estimating Workers' Marginal

Willingness to Pay for Job Attributes Using Duration Data." *Journal of Human Resources* 29(3): 911–31.

Groshen, Erica L. 1991a. "Sources of Intra-industry Wage Dispersion: How Much Do Employers Matter?." *Quarterly Journal of Economics* 106(3): 869–84.

———. 1991b. "The Structure of the Female/Male Wage Differential: Is It Who You Are, What You Do, or Where You Work?" *Journal of Human Resources* 26(3): 457–72.

Gross, Donald, and Carl M. Harris, 1974. *Fundamentals of Queueing Theory.* New York: John Wiley.

Gunderson, Morley, and W. Craig Riddell. 1988. *Labour Market Economics: Theory, Evidence and Policy in Canada*, 2nd edition. McGraw-Hill Ryerson: Toronto.

Hall, Robert E., and Edward P. Lazear. 1984. "The Excess Sensitivity of Layoffs and Quits to Demand" *Journal of Labor Economics* 2(2): 233–57.

Hamermesh, Daniel S. 1982. "The Interaction between Research and Policy: The Case of Unemployment Insurance." *American Economic Review* 72(2): 237–41.

———. 1993. *Labor Demand.* Princeton, NJ: Princeton University Press.

Harhoff, Dieter, and Thomas J. Kane. 1997. "Is the German Apprenticeship System a Panacea for the U.S. Labor Market?" *Journal of Population Economics* 10(2): 171–96.

Hashimoto, Masanori. 1981. "Firm-Specific Human Capital as a Shared Investment." *American Economic Review* 71(3): 475–82.

Heckman, James J. 1976. "The Common Structure of Statistical Models of Truncation, Sample Selection and Limited Dependent Variables and a Simple Estimator for such Models." *Annals of Economic and Social Measurement* 5: 475–92.

———. 1998. "Detecting Discrimination." *Journal of Economic Perspectives* 12(2): 101–16.

Hellerstein, Judith K., David Neumark, and Kenneth R. Troske. 1999. "Wages, Productivity, and Worker Characteristics: Evidence from Plant-Level Production Functions and Wage Equations." *Journal of Labor Economics* 17(3): 409–46.

Hicks, John R. 1932. *The Theory of Wages.* London: Macmillan.

Hildreth, Andrew K. G., and Andrew J. Oswald. 1997. "Rent-Sharing and Wages: Evidence from Company and Establishment Panels." *Journal of Labor Economics* 15(2): 318–37.

Hoffman, Saul D. 1986. *Labour Market Economics.* Englewood Cliffs, NJ: Prentice Hall.

Holzer, Harry J. 1987. "Job Search by Employed and Unemployed Youth." *Industrial and Labor Relations Review* 40(4): 601–11.

———. 1994. "Job Vacancy Rates in the Firm: An Empirical Analysis." *Economica* 61(241): 17–36.

Holzer, Harry J., Lawrence F. Katz, and Alan B. Krueger. 1991. "Job Queues and Wages." *Quarterly Journal of Economics* 106(3): 739–68.

Hosios, Arthur J. 1990. "On the Efficiency of Matching and Related Models of Search and Unemployment." *Review of Economic Studies* 57(2): 279–98.

Hunter, Larry C., and Charles Mulvey. 1981. *Economics of Wages and Labour*, 2nd edition. London: Macmillan.

Hwang, Hae-shin, Dale T. Mortensen, and Walter R. Reed. 1998. "Hedonic Wages and Labor Market Search." *Journal of Labor Economics* 16(4): 815–47.

Ioannides, Yannis M., and Christopher A. Pissarides. 1985. "Monopsony and the Lifetime Relation between Wages and Productivity." *Journal of Labor Economics* 3(1, Part 1): 91–100.

Jacobson, Louis S., Robert J. LaLonde, and Daniel S. Sullivan. 1993a, *The Costs of Worker Dislocation*. Kalamazoo, MI: W. E. Upjohn Institute for Employment Research.

―――. 1993b. "Earnings Losses of Displaced Workers." *American Economic Review* 83(4): 685–709.

Jackson, Susan E., and Randall S. Schuler. 2000. *Managing Human Resources: A Partnership Perspective*, 7th edition. Cincinnati, OH: South-Western College Publishing.

Jones, Stephen R. G., and Peter Kuhn. 1995. "Mandatory Notice and Unemployment." *Journal of Labor Economics* 13(4): 599–622.

Jones, Stephen R. G., and W. Craig Riddell. 1999. "The Measurement of Unemployment: An Empirical Approach." *Econometrica* 67(1): 147–61.

Juhn, Chinhui, Kevin M. Murphy, and Robert H. Topel. 1991. "Why Has the Natural Rate of Unemployment Increased over Time?" *Brookings Papers on Economic Activity* 2: 75–126.

Kahn, Lawrence M. 1980. "Union Spillover Effects on Organized Labor Markets." *Journal of Human Resources* 15(1): 87–98.

Katz, Eliakim, and Adrian Ziderman. 1990. "Investment in General Training: The Role of Information and Labour Mobility." *Economic Journal* 100(403): 1147–58.

Katz, Lawrence F., and David H. Autor. 1999. "Changes in the Wage Structure and Earnings Inequality." In *Handbook of Labor Economics*, vol. 3A, ed. Orley Ashenfelter and David Card, 1463–555. Amsterdam: North-Holland.

Kaufman, Bruce E. 1988. *How Labor Markets Work*. Lexington, MA: Lexington Books.

―――. 1991. *The Economics of Labor Markets*, 3rd edition. Chicago, IL: Dryden Press.

Keith, Kirsten, and Abigail McWilliams. 1997. "Job Mobility and Gender-Based Wage Growth Differentials." *Economic Inquiry* 35(2): 320–33.

―――. 1999. "The Returns to Mobility and Job Search by Gender." *Industrial and Labor Relations Review* 52(3): 460–77.

Kiefer, Nicholas M., and George R. Neumann. 1993. "Wage Dispersion with Homogeneity: The Empirical Equilibrium Search Model." In *Panel Data and Labour Market Dynamics*, ed. Henning Bunzel, Peter Jensen, and Niels Westergard-Nielsen, 57–74. Amsterdam: North-Holland.

Kletzer, Lori G. 1989. "Returns to Seniority after Permanent Job Loss" *American Economic Review* 79(3): 536–43.

―――. 1998. "Job Displacement." *Journal of Economic Perspectives,* 12(1): 115–36.

Koning, Pierre, Gerard J. van den Berg, and Geert Ridder. 2000. "Semi-nonparametric Estimation of an Equilibrium Search Model." *Oxford Bulletin of Economics and Statistics* 62(3): 327–56.

Kreps, Juanita M. 1980. *Contemporary Labor Economics and Labor Relations: Issues, Analysis and Policies*, 2nd edition. Belmont, CA: Wadsworth.

Kreps, Juanita M., Philip Martin, Richard Perlman, and Gerald Somers. 1980. *Contemporary Labor Economics and Labor Relations*. Belmont, CA: Wadsworth.

Krueger, Alan B. 1988. "The Determinants of Queues for Federal Jobs." *Industrial and Labor Relations Review* 42: 567–81.

Krueger, Alan B., and Lawrence H. Summers. 1988. "Efficiency Wages and the Inter-industry Wage Structure." *Econometrica* 56(2): 259–93.

Lancaster, Tony. 1990. *The Econometric Analysis of Transition Data*. Cambridge: Cambridge University Press.

Lang, Kevin. 1991. "Persistent Wage Dispersion and Involuntary Unemployment." *Quarterly Journal of Economics* 106(1): 181–202.

Layard, Richard, and Steven Nickell, 1990. "Is Unemployment Lower if Unions Bargain over Employment?." *Quarterly Journal of Economics* 105(3): 773–87.

Lazear, Edward P. 1979. "Why Is There Mandatory Retirement?" *Journal of Political Economy* 87(6): 1261–84.

Lee, David, S. 1999. "Wage Inequality in the United States during the 1980s: Rising Dispersion or Falling Minimum Wage?" *Quarterly Journal of Economics* 114(3): 977–1023.

Lee, Lung-Fei. 1978. "Unionism and Wage Rates: a Simultaneous Equations Model with Qualitative and Limited Dependent Variables." *International Economic Review* 19(2): 415–33.

Lemieux, Thomas. 1998. "Estimating the Effects of Unions on Wage Inequality in a Panel Data Model with Comparative Advantage and Non-random Selection." *Journal of Labor Economics* 16(2): 261–91.

Leonard, Jonathan S. 1992. "Unions and Employment Growth." In *Labor Market Institutions and the Future Role of Unions*, ed. Morris F. Kleiner, 80–94. Oxford: Blackwell.

Lester, Richard A. 1946. "Wage Diversity and its Theoretical Implications." *The Review of Economic Statistics* 28(3): 152–9.

———. 1948. *Company Wage Policies: A Survey of Patterns and Experience*. Princeton, NJ: Princeton University Press.

———. 1952. "A Range Theory of Wage Differentials." *Industrial and Labor Relations Review* 5(4): 483–500.

———. 1964. *Economics of Labor*, 2nd edition. New York: Macmillan.

Lewis, H. Gregg. 1963. *Unionism and Relative Wages in the United States: an Empirical Inquiry*. Chicago, IL: The University of Chicago Press.

———. 1969. "Employer Interests in Employee Hours of Work." Unpublished Paper.

———. 1986. *Union Relative Wage Effects: a Survey*. Chicago, IL: The University of Chicago Press.

Lewis, Michael. 1989. *Liar's Poker*. London: Coronet Books.

Light, Audrey, and Manuelita Ureta. 1990. "Gender Differences in Wages and Job Turnover among Continuously Employed Workers." *American Economic Review* 80(2): 293–7.

————. 1992. "Panel Estimates of Male and Female Job Turnover Behavior: Can Female Nonquitters Be Identified?" *Journal of Labor Economics* 10(2): 156–81.

————. 1995. "Early-Career Work Experience and Gender Wage Differentials." *Journal of Labor Economics* 13(1): 121–54.

Loprest, Pamela J. 1992. "Gender Differences in Wage Growth and Job Mobility." *American Economic Review* 82(2): 526–32.

Loewenstein, Mark A., and James R. Spletzer. 1998. "Dividing the Costs and Returns to General Training." *Journal of Labor Economics* 16(1): 142–71.

————. 1999. "General and Specific Training: Evidence and Implications." *Journal of Human Resources* 34(4): 710–33.

Lucas, Robert E., and Edward C. Prescott. 1974. "Equilibrium Search and Unemployment." *Journal of Economic Theory* 7(2): 188–209.

Lynch, Lisa M. 1992. "Private-Sector Training and the Earnings of Young Workers." *American Economic Review* 82(1): 299–312.

Machin, Stephen J., and Alan Manning. 1997. "Can Supply Create Its Own Demand? Implications for Rising Skill Differentials." *European Economic Review* 41(3–5): 507–16.

————. 2002. "The Structure of Wages in What Should Be a Competitive Labour Market." *London School of Economics, Centre for Economic Performance Discussion Paper No. 532.*

Machin, Stephen J., Alan Manning, and Steven Woodland. 1993. "Are Workers Paid their Marginal Product? Evidence from a Low Wage Labour Market." *London School of Economics, Centre for Economic Performance Discussion Paper No. 158.*

Machin, Stephen J., and Sushil Wadhwani. 1991. "The Effects of Unions on Organisational Change and Employment." *Economic Journal* 101(407): 835–54.

MacKay, Donald Iain, D. Boddy, I. Brack, J. A. Diack and N. Jones. 1971. *Labour Markets under Different Employment Conditions.* London: Allen and Unwin.

MacLeod, W. Bentley, and James M. Malcomson. 1989. "Implicit Contracts, Incentive Compatibility, and Involuntary Unemployment." *Econometrica* 57(2): 447–80.

McConnell, Campbell R., and Stanley L. Brue. 1986. *Contemporary Labor Economics,* 1st edition. New York: McGraw-Hill.

MaCurdy, Thomas E., and John H. Pencavel. 1986. "Testing between Competing Models of Wage and Employment Determination in Unionized Markets." *Journal of Political Economy* 94(3, Part 2): S3–S39.

Maddala, G. S. 1983. *Limited-dependent and Qualitative Variables in Econometrics.* Cambridge: Cambridge University Press.

Manning, Alan. 1994a. "How Robust Is the Microeconomic Theory of the Trade Union?" *Journal of Labor Economics* 12(3): 430–59.

————. 1994b. "Labour Markets with Company Wage Policies." *London School of Economics, Centre for Economic Performance Discussion Paper* No. 214.

————. 1995. "How Do We Know That Real Wages Are Too High?" *Quarterly Journal of Economics* 110(4): 1111–25.

————. 1996. "The Equal Pay Act as an Experiment to Test Theories of the Labour Market." *Economica* 63(250): 191–212.

————. 1998. "Mighty Good Thing: The Returns to Tenure." *London School of Economics, Centre for Economic Performance Discussion Paper* No. 383.

————. 2000a. "Movin' On Up: Interpreting the Earnings-Experience Profile." *Bulletin of Economic Research* 52(4): 261–87.

————. 2000b. "Pretty Vacant: Recruitment in Low-Wage Labour Markets." *Oxford Bulletin of Economics and Statistics* 62(Supplement): 747–70.

————. 2001a. "A Generalised Model of Monopsony." *London School of Economics, Centre for Economic Performance Discussion Paper* No. 499.

————. 2001b. "Monopsony and the Efficiency of Labour Market Interventions." *London School of Economics, Centre for Economic Performance Discussion Paper* No. 514.

————. 2001c. "Labour Supply, Search and Taxes." *Journal of Public Economics* 80(3): 409–34.

Marshall, Alfred. 1920. *Principles of Economics: an Introductory Volume*, 8th edition. London: Macmillan.

Marshall, F. Ray, Vernon M. Briggs Jr., and Allan G. King. 1984. *Labor Economics: Wages, Employment, Trade Unionism and Public Policy*, 5th edition. Homewood, IL: R. D. Irwin.

Marshall, Robert C., and Gary A. Zarkin. 1987. "The Effect of Job Tenure on Wage Offers." *Journal of Labor Economics* 5(3): 301–24.

McDonald, Ian M., and Robert M. Solow. 1981. "Wage Bargaining and Employment." *American Economic Review* 71(5): 896–908.

Medoff, James L., and Katherine G. Abraham. 1980. "Experience, Performance, and Earnings." *Quarterly Journal of Economics* 95(4): 703–36.

————. 1981. "Are Those Paid More Really More Productive? The Case of Experience." *Journal of Human Resources* 16(2): 186–216.

Meghir, Costas, and Luigi Pistaferri. 2001. "Income Variance Dynamics And Heterogeneity." *Institute for Fiscal Studies Working Paper* W01/07.

Mellow, Wesley. 1982. "Employer Size and Wages." *Review of Economics and Statistics* 64(3): 495–501.

Meyer, Bruce D. 1995. "Lessons from the U.S. Unemployment Insurance Experiments." *Journal of Economic Literature* 33(1): 91–131.

Mincer, Jacob. 1962. "On-the-Job Training: Costs, Returns and Some Implications." *Journal of Political Economy* 70(5, Part 2): 50–79.

————. 1974. *Schooling, Experience and Earnings*. New York: NBER.

————. 1986. "Wage Changes in Job Changes." In *Research in Labor Economics*, vol. 8, ed. Ronald G. Ehrenberg, 171–97. Greenwich, CT: JAI Press.

Moen, Espen R. 1997. "Competitive Search Equilibrium." *Journal of Political Economy* 105(2): 385–411.

Montgomery, James D. 1991a. "Equilibrium Wage Dispersion and Inter-industry Wage Differentials." *Quarterly Journal of Economics* 106(1): 163–79.

————. 1991b. "Social Networks and Labor-Market Outcomes: Toward an Economic Analysis." *American Economic Review* 81(5): 1407–18.

Moore, William, J., Robert J. Newman, and Geoffrey K. Turnbull. 1998. "Do Academic Salaries Decline with Seniority?" *Journal of Labor Economics* 16(2): 352–66.

Mortensen, Dale T. 1986. "Job Search and Labor Market Analysis." In *Handbook of Labor Economics*, vol. 2, ed. Orley Ashenfelter and Richard Layard, 849–919. Amsterdam: North-Holland.

———. 1988. "Wages, Separations, and Job Tenure: On-the-Job Specific Training or Matching?" *Journal of Labor Economics* 6(4): 445–71.

———. 1998. "Equilibrium Unemployment with Wage Posting: Burdett-Mortensen Meet Pissarides." Unpublished Paper, Northwestern University, September.

———. 2002, *Wage Dispersion: Why Are Similar Workers Paid Differently?* Cambridge, MA: MIT Press.

Mortensen, Dale T., and Christopher A. Pissarides. 1994. "Job Creation and Job Destruction in the Theory of Unemployment." *Review of Economic Studies* 61(3): 397–415.

———. 1999. "New Developments in Models of Search in the Labor Market." In *Handbook of Labor Economics*, vol. 3B, ed. Orley Ashenfelter and David Card, 2567–627. Amsterdam: North-Holland.

Mortensen, Dale T., and Tara Vishwanath. 1994. "Personal Contacts and Earnings: It Is Who You Know!" *Labour Economics* 1(2): 187–201.

Murphy, Kevin M., and Finis Welch. 1990. "Empirical Age-Earnings Profiles." *Journal of Labor Economics* 8(2): 202–29.

Murphy, Kevin M., and Robert H. Topel. 1990. "Efficiency Wages Reconsidered: Theory and Evidence." In *Advances in the Theory and Measurement of Unemployment*, ed. Yoram Weiss and Gideon Fishelson, 204–40. New York: St. Martin's Press.

———. 1997. "Unemployment and Nonemployment." *American Economic Review* 87(2): 295–300.

Nardinelli, Clark, and Curtis Simon. 1990. "Customer Racial Discrimination in the Market for Memorabilia: The Case of Baseball." *Quarterly Journal of Economics* 105(3): 575–95.

NBER. 1966. *The Measurement and Interpretation of Job Vacancies: a Conference Report*. Cambridge, MA: NBER.

Neal, Derek A. 1995. "Industry-Specific Human Capital: Evidence from Displaced Workers." *Journal of Labor Economics* 13(4): 653–77.

———. 1998. "The Link between Ability and Specialization: An Explanation for Observed Correlations between Wages and Mobility Rates." *Journal of Human Resources* 33(1): 173–200.

Neal, Derek A., and William R. Johnson. 1996. "The Role of Pre-market Factors in Black-White Wage Differences." *Journal of Political Economy* 104(5): 869–95.

Nelson, Phillip. 1973. "The Elasticity of Labor Supply to the Individual Firm." *Econometrica* 41(5): 853–66.

Neumark, David, and Michael L. Wachter. 1995. "Union Effects on Nonunion Wages: Evidence from Panel Data on Industries and Cities." *Industrial and Labor Relations Review* 49(1): 20–38.

Neumark, David, and William Wascher. 2000. "Minimum Wages and Employment: A Case Study of the Fast-Food Industry in New Jersey and Pennsylvania: Comment." *American Economic Review* 90(5): 1362–296.

Nickell, Steven J., and Brian Bell. 1996. "Changes in the Distribution of Wages and Unemployment in OECD Countries." *American Economic Review* 86(2): 302–8.

Nickell, Steven J., and Sushil B. Wadhwani. 1990. "Insider Forces and Wage Determination." *Economic Journal* 100(401): 496–509.

Oi, Walter Y., and Todd L. Idson. 1999. "Firm Size and Wages." In *Handbook of Labor Economics*, vol. 3B, ed. Orley Ashenfelter and David Card, 2165–214. Amsterdam: North-Holland.

Parsons, Donald O. 1972. "Specific Human Capital: An Application to Quit Rates and Layoff Rates." *Journal of Political Economy* 80(6): 1120–43.

———. 1973. "Quit Rates Over Time: A Search and Information Approach." *American Economic Review* 63(3): 390–401.

Petrongolo, Barbara, and Christopher A. Pissarides. 2001. "Looking into the Black Box: A Survey of the Matching Function." *Journal of Economic Literature* 39(2): 390–431.

Pencavel, John H. 1972. "Wages, Specific Training, and Labor Turnover in U.S. Manufacturing Industries." *International Economic Review* 13(1): 53–64.

———. 1986. "Labor Supply of Men: a Survey." In *Handbook of Labor Economics*, vol. 1, ed. Orley Ashenfelter and Richard Layard. Amsterdam: North-Holland.

Peters, Michael. 1991. "Ex Ante Price Offers in Matching Games Non-steady States." *Econometrica* 59(5): 1425–54.

Pigou, Arthur C. 1924. *The Economics of Welfare*, 2nd edition. London: Macmillan.

Pissarides, Christopher A. 1985. "Short-run Equilibrium Dynamics of Unemployment Vacancies, and Real Wages." *American Economic Review* 75(4): 676–90.

Polachek, Solomon W., and Walter S. Siebert. 1992. *The Economics of Earnings*. Cambridge: Cambridge University Press.

Postel-Vinay, Fabien, and Jean-Marc Robin. 2002. "Wage Dispersion with Worker and Employer Heterogeneity." *Econometrica* in press.

Ransom, Michael R. 1993. "Seniority and Monopsony in the Academic Labor Market." *American Economic Review* 83(1): 221–33.

Rees, Albert. 1993. "The Role of Fairness in Wage Determination." *Journal of Labor Economics* 11(1, Part 1): 243–52.

Reinganum, Jennifer F. 1979. "A Simple Model of Equilibrium Price Dispersion." *Journal of Political Economy* 87(4): 851–58.

Revenga, Ana L. 1992. "Exporting Jobs? The Impact of Import Competition on Employment and Wages in U.S. Manufacturing." *Quarterly Journal of Economics* 107(1): 255–84.

Reynolds, Lloyd G. 1946a. "The Supply of Labor to the Firm." *Quarterly Journal of Economics* 60(3): 390–411.

———. 1946b. "Wage Differences in Local Labor Markets." *American Economic Review* 36(3): 366–75.

———. 1951. *The Structure of Labor Markets: Wages and Labor Mobility in Theory and Practice*. New York: Harper and Brothers.

Reynolds, Lloyd G., Stanley H. Masters, and Colletta H. Moser. 1991. *Labor Economics and Labor Relations*, 10th edition. Englewood Cliffs, NJ: Prentice Hall.

Robinson, Joan. 1933. *The Economics of Imperfect Competititon.* London: Macmillan.

Roper, Stephen. 1986. "The Economics of Job Vacancies." *London School of Economics, Centre for Labour Economics Discussion Paper* No. 252.

————. 1988. "Recruitment Methods and Vacancy Duration." *Scottish Journal of Political Economy* 35(1): 51–64.

Rosen, Sherwin. "The Theory of Equalizing Differences." In *Handbook of Labor Economics*, vol. 1, ed. Orley Ashenfelter and Richard Layard, 641–92. Amsterdam: North-Holland.

Rothschild, Michael. 1973. "Models of Market Organization with Imperfect Information: A Survey." *Journal of Political Economy* 81(6): 1283–308.

Royalty, Anne Beeson. 1996. "The Effects of Job Turnover on the Training of Men and Women." *Industrial and Labor Relations Review* 49(3): 506–21.

————. 1998. "Job-to-Job and Job-to-Nonemployment Turnover by Gender and Education Level." *Journal of Labor Economics* 16(2): 392–443.

Rubinstein, Ariel. 1982. "Perfect Equilibrium in a Bargaining Model." *Econometrica* 50(1): 97–109.

Salop, Joanne, and Steven C. Salop. 1976. "Self-Selection and Turnover in the Labor Market." *Quarterly Journal of Economics* 90(4): 619–27.

Salop, Steven, C. 1979. "A Model of the Natural Rate of Unemployment." *American Economic Review* 69(1): 117–25.

Salop, Steven C., and Joseph E. Stiglitz. 1977. "Bargains and Ripoffs: A Model of Monopolistically Competitive Price Dispersion." *Review of Economic Studies* 44(3): 493–510.

Sapsford, David, and Zafiris Tzannatos. 1993. *The Economics of the Labour Market.* London: Macmillan.

Schmitt, John, and Jonathan Wadsworth. 1993. "Job Search Activity and Changing Unemployment Benefit Entitlement: Pseudo-Panel Estimates for Britain." *London School of Economics, Centre for Economic Performance Discussion Paper* No. 148.

Shapiro, Carl, and Joseph E. Stiglitz. 1984. "Equilibrium Unemployment as a Worker Discipline Device." *American Economic Review* 74(3): 433–44.

Sicherman, Nachum. 1996. "Gender Differences in Departures from a Large Firm." *Industrial and Labor Relations Review* 49(3): 484–505.

Slichter, Sumner H. 1950. "Notes on the Structure of Wages." *Review of Economic Statistics* 32(1): 80–91.

Smith, Adam. 1970. *The Wealth of Nations.* London: Harmondsworth Penguin.

Solow, Robert M. 1990. *The Labor Market as a Social Institution.* Oxford: Blackwell.

Soskice, David. 1994. "Reconciling Markets and Institutions: The German Apprenticeship System." In *Training and the Private Sector: International Comparisons*, ed. Lisa M. Lynch, 25–60. Chicago, IL: The University of Chicago Press.

Staiger, Douglas, Joanne Spetz, and Ciaran Phibbs. 1999. "Is There Monpsony in the Labor Market? Evidence from a Natural Experiment." *NBER Working Paper* No. 7258.

Stevens, Margaret. 1994. "A Theoretical Model of On-the-Job Training with Imperfect Competition." *Oxford Economic Papers* 46(4): 537–62.

————. 1998. "Wage-Tenure Contracts in a Frictional Labour Market: Strategies for Recruitment and Retention." Unpublished Paper, Oxford University.

Stewart, Mark B., and Joanna K. Swaffield. 1997. "Constraints on the Desired Hours of Work of British Men." *Economic Journal* 107(441): 520–35.

Stigler, George J. 1961. "The Economics of Information." *The Journal of Political Economy* 69(3): 213–25.

————. 1962. "Information in the Labor Market." *The Journal of Political Economy* 70(5): 94–105.

Sullivan, Daniel. 1989. "Monopsony Power in the Market for Nurses." *Journal of Law and Economics* 32(2, Part 2): S135–S178.

Summers, Lawrence H. 1989. "Some Simple Economics of Mandated Benefits." *American Economic Review* 79(2): 177–83.

Szymanski, Stefan. 2000. "A Market Test for Discrimination in the English Professional Soccer Leagues." *Journal of Political Economy* 108(3): 590–603.

Taylor, John B. 1987. "Involuntary Unemployment." In *The New Palgrave*, ed. J. Eatwell, M. Milgate, and P. Newman. London: Macmillan.

Teulings, Coen N. 2000. "Aggregation Bias in Elasticities of Substitution and the Minimum Wage Paradox." *International Economic Review* 41(2): 359–98.

Teulings, Coen, and Joop Hartog. 1998. *Corporatism or Competition? Labour Contracts, Institutions and Wage Structures in International Comparison.* Cambridge: Cambridge University Press.

Tobin, James. 1972. "Inflation and Unemployment." *American Economic Review* 62(1/2): 1–18.

Topel, Robert H. 1986. "Job Mobility, Search, and Earnings Growth: A Reinterpretation of Human Capital Earnings Functions." In *Research in Labor Economics*, vol. 8, ed. Ronald G. Ehrenberg, 199–233. Greenwich, CT: JAI Press.

————. 1991. "Specific Capital, Mobility, and Wages: Wages Rise with Job Seniority." *Journal of Political Economy* 99(1): 145–76.

Topel, Robert H., and Michael P. Ward. 1992. "Job Mobility and the Careers of Young Men." *Quarterly Journal of Economics* 107(2): 439–79.

van den Berg, Gerard J. 1990. "Search Behaviour, Transitions to Nonparticipation and the Duration of Unemployment." *Economic Journal* 100(402): 842–65.

————. 1999. "Empirical Inference with Equilibrium Search Models of the Labor Market." *Economic Journal* 109: 283–306.

van den Berg, Gerard J., and Geert Ridder. 1998. "An Empirical Equilibrium Search Model of the Labor Market." *Econometrica* 66(5): 1183–221.

Van Ommeren, Jos, Gerard van den Berg, and Cees Gorter. 1999. "Estimating the Marginal Willingness to Pay for Commuting." Unpublished Paper, Free University of Amsterdam.

Van Ours, Jan C. 1989. "Durations of Dutch Job Vacancies." *De Economist* 137(3): 309–27.

Van Ours, Jan C., and Geert Ridder. 1992. "Vacancies and the Recruitment of New Employees" *Journal of Labor Economics* 10(2): 138–55.

van Vuuren, Aico, Gerard J. van den Berg, and Geert Ridder. 2000. "Measuring the Equilibrium Effects of Unemployment Benefits Dispersion." *Journal of Applied Econometrics* 15(6): 547–74.

Veum, Jonathan R. 1995. "Sources of Training and Their Impact on Wages." *Industrial and Labor Relations Review* 48(4): 812–26.

———. 1997. "Training and Job Mobility among Young Workers in the United States." *Journal of Population Economics* 10(2): 219–33.

Viscusi, W. Kip. 1980. "Sex Differences in Worker Quitting." *Review of Economics and Statistics* 62(3): 388–98.

Wadsworth, Jonathan. 1991. "Unemployment Benefits and Search Effort in the UK Labour Market." *Economica* 58(229): 17–34.

Waldfogel, Jane. 1998a. "The Family Gap for Young Women in the United States and Britain: Can Maternity Leave Make a Difference?" *Journal of Labor Economics* 16(3): 505–45.

———. 1998b. "Understanding the 'Family Gap' in Pay for Women with Children." *Journal of Economic Perspectives* 12(1): 137–56.

Walker, E. Ronald. 1943. *From Economic Theory to Policy.* Chicago, IL: The University of Chicago Press.

Webb, Sidney, and Beatrice Webb. 1897. *Industrial Democracy.* London: Longmans Green and Co.

Weiss, Andrew W. 1980. "Job Queues and Layoffs in Labor Markets with Flexible Wages." *Journal of Political Economy* 88(3): 526–38.

———. 1984. "Determinants of Quit Behavior." *Journal of Labor Economics* 2(3): 371–87.

———. 1990. *Efficiency Wages: Models of Unemployment, Layoffs, and Wage Dispersion.* Princeton, NJ: Princeton University Press.

Weiss, Andrew W., and Henry J. Landau. 1984. "Wages, Hiring Standards, and Firm Size." *Journal of Labor Economics* 2(4): 477–99.

Wolpin, Kenneth I. 1992. "The Determinants of Black-White Differences in Early Employment Careers: Search, Layoffs, Quits and Endogenous Wage Growth." *Journal of Political Economy* 100(3): 535–60.

Index

Milton Keynes UK
Ingram Content Group UK Ltd.
UKHW020058300924
448990UK00004B/59